SACROSANCTUM OECUMENICUM CONCILIUM
VATICANUM SECUNDUM

DECRETUM
DE OECUMENISMO

TYPIS POLYGLOTTIS VATICANIS

THE THIRD SESSION

Xavier Rynne

�֍

THE
THIRD
SESSION

�֍

THE DEBATES AND DECREES OF
VATICAN COUNCIL II
SEPTEMBER 14 TO NOVEMBER 21, 1964

New York
Farrar, Straus & Giroux

The authors are grateful to the editors of *The New Yorker,* in whose pages some of the material in this book first appeared in somewhat different form.

TO THE MEMORY OF
CARDINAL ALBERT MEYER
ARCHBISHOP OF CHICAGO
1903–1965

Contents

✠

List of Illustrations

✠

Preface

✠

ON APRIL 9, 1965, as this volume was going to press, Cardinal Albert Meyer, Archbishop of Chicago, died. We dedicate *The Third Session* to his memory. His death, as Cardinal Cushing has said, "deprives the church in America of one who, from many points of view, was the greatest churchman of our times." In calling him a "great priest, brilliant scholar, and devoted shepherd," Cardinal Spellman said that "the church universal grieves at his untimely passing." Cardinal Meyer's role at all the sessions of Vatican Council II was an important one, both as a member of the Council Presidency and as a leading American prelate, but his role at the Third Session (as you will learn in the pages that follow) was crucial. His intellectual attainments, his scholarship—especially in Biblical studies—his fine character, and his unfailing courtesy and tact made a deep impression on all the Council Fathers. Cardinal Meyer's work for a declaration on religious liberty, and his concern that such a declaration be proclaimed by the Council before it adjourns (a text on this subject failed

to come to a vote at the Third Session) should inspire the
Council Fathers, and the American bishops especially, to see
that the job is successfully completed by the final session in
tribute to his memory. *Requiescat in pace.*

*   *   *

In this third volume in a series, it would seem to be unnecessary for the authors to explain exactly what they are up
to. From the beginning, it has been our intention to tell what
has happened at each of the sessions of Vatican Council II.
Not to tell what we thought *ought* to have happened, but
what actually did happen. This attempt at recording the
most important religious event of the century we called, in
the first book, an "essay in theological journalism." Perhaps
due to the fact that the expectations aroused by the First
Session were somewhat disappointed during the Second
Session, a few reviews of *The Second Session* implied that we
were at fault for not having a better story to tell. However,
we are reporting history as it is happening, not inventing it.
Of course a point of view affects our reporting, but until the
events of Vatican Council II can be seen in the perspective
of later years, when much more complete documentation is
available, this is inevitable. We believe our point of view has
been consistent from the start, and find reassurance and
consolation in the knowledge that, although our first book
was not believed in some quarters and denounced in others,
no one now seriously questions its accuracy.

Though the Pentecostal nature of the Council has become
more obvious than ever with the passing of each year, there
are Catholics who deplore and resist the renewal and reform
of the Church. They believe this to be a *break with* "tradition," by which they usually mean the practices of the nineteenth, eighteenth, and seventeenth centuries, when in reality
the changes represent a *return to* the traditions of earlier
centuries. As we state in the first chapter, "No matter how
much obstructionism there is, it is no longer possible for the
Church to turn back the clock of renewal and reform. It can

be impeded, and stalled, and perhaps even stopped momentarily, but a return to pre-Conciliar and pre-Johannine thinking is no longer possible for the Church."

* * *

We feel we should report that an English review of *The Second Session* has accepted Dr. Robert McAfee Brown's theory of the identity of Xavier Rynne. G. P. Gooch wrote in *Contemporary Review* (November 1964) that Xavier Rynne "is only a *nom de plume,* for the author is Phyllis McGentey (*sic*), who had already received much praise for a similar venture on the First Session. Let us hope that in due course she will favour us with another masterly record of the Third Session. . ." When the publishers showed this and the original article by Dr. Brown to the well-known poet and writer, Phyllis McGinley, she replied: "I should like to help you refute the notion I wrote [the Xavier Rynne books]. The only trouble is that I, too, have been doing some textual cryptography and have come up with the following logical conclusion:

"1. I believe implicitly in Robert McAfee Brown.

"2. Robert McAfee Brown has proved I am Xavier Rynne.

"3. Therefore: I believe I am Xavier Rynne."

XAVIER RYNNE

THE THIRD SESSION

I

The Opening of the Third Session; Chapters VII and VIII of "The Church"; the Pastoral Office of Bishops

THE THIRD SESSION, it can be accurately said, accomplished more work than any other session of Vatican Council II. For one thing, it covered more ground than the previous sessions, since the Fathers took up fourteen conciliar texts, as compared with five at the First Session and three at the Second. For another, it promulgated three decrees, the most important of which was the Constitution on the Church, with its crucial Chapter III on collegiality. This Constitution in Pope Paul's words may come to be considered the crowning achievement that "distinguishes this solemn and historic synod in the memory of future ages." The other promulgated decrees were those on Ecumenism and the Eastern Churches. When this record of achievement is compared with that of the First Session (no documents promulgated) and the Second Session (two documents promulgated), the latest session must be ranked high in terms of performance.

Why, then, in view of its obvious accomplishments, does the feeling prevail that the Third Session was nevertheless the most disappointing of all? Why was it possible for the world press to describe the bishops attending the closing ceremony as "stony-faced" and "unresponsive"? Why did so many Fathers leave Rome in a state of sadness and bewilderment? Why did the phrase *"magno cum dolore"*—the opening words of an urgent petition to the Pope at a moment of crisis (see page 65)—become a kind of catchword for the whole session? Why did a session that began with such promise end in such gloom?

The answer would seem to hinge on one thing—the character of Pope Paul. In contrast to the spirit of joyous expectancy that pervaded the world when Pope John XXIII announced the Council and brought its initial session to a successful close, the hopes of men seem to have been dampened by the more timorous and cautious Pauline spirit. If the character of Pope Paul has been called enigmatic and contradictory, it may be due to the fact that he has taken apparently conflicting positions on crucial matters at important junctures. For example, in his opening address at this session the Pope called upon the bishops to pass the Constitution on the Church and define the collegiality of the bishops, described by him as "the weightiest and most delicate" problem before the Council. Yet in his encyclical, *Ecclesiam suam,* issued shortly before the start of the session, he warned: "We reserve to ourselves the choice of the proper moment and manner of expressing our judgment, most happy if we can present it in perfect accord with that of the Council Fathers." Observers at the time were struck by the mysterious Olympian tone and icy aloofness that seemed to be evident in this remark, coming at the end of a long passage expressing confidence in the work of the Council. In the same encyclical, speaking of dialogue with the separated brethren, he recommended observance of the wise precept, "Let us stress what we have in common rather than what divides us," but then proceeded to accentuate the differences by stressing the prerogatives of the papacy in uncompromising terms. He incidentally accused the separated brethren of wishing the Catholic Church to be "without the Pope," an opinion that many of them regard as a strange travesty of their real views. The same contrast was noticeable in his remarks opening the Chair of Unity Octave in January, 1965. After commending the movement of prayer on behalf of Christian unity that has been going on for many years, he suddenly warned against "a temptation that sometimes works its way easily into good souls"—namely, a desire to "hide, weaken, change, deny if need be those teachings of the Catholic Church which are not acceptable today by the separated brethren." In analyzing the Pope's penchant for qualifying almost every statement he makes, *The Economist* of London pointed out the disconcerting fact that "but" is a key Pauline word, and characterized him as "The Pope of Buts."

Though well intentioned, Paul's methods are unfortunate in that they produce an impression of negativity, as well as a feeling that he is not wholeheartedly in favor of the positive steps taken. At the Third Session, after the doctrine of collegiality was defined by the Council and overwhelmingly approved, as the Pope had asked, the bishops were obliged to accept without discussion a hair-splitting Explanatory Note at his bidding. It was another, and regrettable, example of "Yes, but."

No evidence has come to light of any fundamental disagreement between the Pope and the majority of the bishops over the ultimate goals of the Council, but the Third Session's final week, inevitably dubbed "Black Week" because of the wave of disappointing events climaxing its closing days, furnished abundant proof that there *are* differences over methods. Aside from the difficulties caused by the Pope's apparent

4	THE THIRD SESSION

contradictions, there is found to be a certain amount of tension arising from the structural instability of the Catholic system, divinely ordained, with bishops *and* Pope sharing supreme authority in the Church. Medieval theorists used the argument that a body with two heads would be a monstrosity to exalt the Pope's role at the expense of the bishops. Vatican Council II has now re-established the rights of the episcopal college, without resolving the delicate problem of the balanced relationship between the college and its head. According to Cardinal Alfrink, the close of this session was marked, not by a "collision of the Pope with the rest of the college of bishops nor a collision between the Pope and the majority of the bishops," but by a "meeting or possibly a collision of two views of the Church"—i.e., the monarchical and the collegial.

Professor H. A. Oberman, of the Harvard Divinity School, has used geometric figures to describe what appears to be a confrontation between these two different conceptions of supreme power in the Church. Figure one is that of two concentric circles around a single point—the inner circle standing for the Pope, the outer circle for the Pope *with* the bishops. Figure two is an ellipse with two points or centers which do not coincide—one standing for the Pope acting alone, the other for the Pope acting *with* the bishops. Figure one could be said to portray the ideal of collegiality as envisioned by its most ardent supporters, implying a constant harmony and identification of thought and action between Pope and bishops. This is the image of collegiality that the bishops thought they would get in the Constitution on the Church. Figure two reports what they actually received—an image of unresolved, and at times conflicting, dual headship—the image underlined by the Explanatory Note with its concern for asserting, at all costs, the Pope's independence of action, which the bishops have never questioned.

The final days of the Third Session were also proof that the period of a Johannine honeymoon between Pope and bishops was over, and that relations must soon be put on a more stable, business-like basis. A foreboding of tension, foreseen only as a remote possibility earlier, suddenly became a harsh reality even before final approval had been given to collegiality. Apart from the doctrinal innuendos of the Explanatory Note, nothing was probably so irritating to the bishops as the inconsiderate way in which they were presented at the last minute—without any opportunity for debate—with an official papal interpretation of the doctrine they were to vote. The alternative was the risk of killing the all-important document on the Church, and possibly causing a breakup of the Council itself if they voted no. They were again put in a similar position a few days later over the nineteen last-minute changes in the decree on Ecumenism. No wonder, therefore, if they felt humiliated—as one bishop put it later, "We were treated like children"—or that there was a distinct impression that the spirit, if not the letter, of conciliar freedom had somehow been infringed.

Among the more level-headed voices heard in explanation of the events of "Black Week" was that of the Dutch Bishop Bekkers of 's Hertogenbusch, who called for "a Council that will never end" because of the need for enlightening "people from completely Catholic countries [who are] afraid of full religious freedom, ecumenism, and freedom within the Church." The bishop put his finger on a sore point when he deplored "the methods sometimes used by the minority within the Council," and asked for a program to "insure the success of Vatican II," including the reform of the Curia, the establishment of an episcopal "Senate," and overhauling of canon law, freedom within the Church, and Catholic respect for "the spirit of veracity and sincerity," in addition to some form of continued existence for the Council itself. Together with the goal of ecumenism, described by Cardinal Heenan in a recent statement as now "part of the normal outlook of intelligent Christians everywhere," these points remain the ultimate goal of Pope John's *aggiornamento*.

It is no news that the goals not only of the Council, but the whole program of *aggiornamento,* continue to be fiercely opposed by a small, well-knit group known conveniently as "the minority," nor that the campaign they are waging occasionally erupts onto the surface. What the Third Session has revealed more clearly than ever before, however, are the lengths to which Pope Paul is willing to go to soothe the feelings and assuage the doubts of this powerfully placed group of resisters who, it is commonly believed, have no intention of accepting what they regard as virtual apostasy. Their attitude may be summed up by what a professor of moral theology once told his students: "This is the doctrine on marriage which I have always taught; the Church has allowed me to teach it; therefore the Church is committed to this teaching and cannot repudiate it." Persuasion through argument seems powerless against such rigorism and irrationalism.

While numerically small, as repeated test-votes have shown, the minority makes up for lack of numbers by astuteness, cohesion, and the influence it can bring to bear through members well-placed in Rome. Far from having abandoned its intransigent attitude, as might be assumed from the apparent collapse of opposition to collegiality (and other measures it could no longer effectively oppose), it has merely shifted tactics. Efforts are currently being concentrated on preventing any important concessions in the expected papal Motu Proprio on mixed marriages; postponing as long as possible the announced reform of the Curia, and above all the establishment of the proposed episcopal "Senate"; confusing the channels of authority in such a way that, when these two great aims become a reality, the Curia will still be left in a position to veto any unwanted measures; defending to the last ditch the entrenched position of the Congregation in charge of seminaries; buttonholing bishops in support of Thomism and scholasticism, two time-honored props of the existing system; scuttling the Declaration on Religious Liberty altogether, but if this proves impossible, then watering it down so that it will amount to little more than a reflection of the curial view on "toleration"; hindering the work of those conciliar commissions on which they are particularly well represented, e.g. the missions and religious orders; holding off as long as possible with any concrete measures designed to further "intercommunion" with other Churches allowed by the decrees on Ecumenism and the Eastern Churches, from fear that once fraternal accord has become a reality the clock can never be turned back. They do not seem to realize that, at this point, no matter how much obstructionism there is, it is no longer possible for the Church to turn back the clock of renewal and reform. It can be impeded, and stalled, and perhaps even stopped momentarily, but a return to preconciliar and pre-Johannine thinking is no longer possible for the Church. What is perplexing and alarming is not that the Pope should feel he must conciliate the small group of officials whom he daily sees, but that he should be willing to risk making the mistake of Pius IX in 1870, in reverse, by appearing to sacrifice the majority to the minority.

The Third Session opened on September 14, 1964, with Pope Paul being carried into St. Peter's on his portable throne, surrounded by the papal court, but a happy Pauline touch was evident as soon as he reached the altar. There, dismounting from his throne, he immediately joined twenty-four waiting prelates, all vested in red, with whom he intended to concelebrate the mass, as if to anticipate, symbolically, the doctrine of episcopal collegiality, not yet proclaimed by the Council. The altar, which stands directly above the tomb or shrine of St. Peter beneath Bernini's splendid canopy, had been enlarged to a rectangular shape, and was decorated with a severely simple white cloth and six low candles. Attended only by his two masters of ceremony, the 80-year-old Archbishop Dante, secretary of the Congregation of Rites, and Monsignor Capoferri, the Pope began the prayers at the foot of the altar in a resolute but peculiarly clouded voice. The basilica choir rendered the introductory motet in the plainest Gregorian chant, in striking contrast to its ordinarily pompous polyphony, while the full congregation recited the Gloria, the Credo, the Sanctus and the Agnus Dei in alternate verses. At the offertory, the *orationes super populum,* or special prayers for the people in litany form, were re-introduced after centuries of omission, and during the canon of the mass, all the concelebrating prelates said the prayers out loud including the words of consecration over the bread and wine. Communion was received by the participating concelebrants, each of whom took a piece of one of three large hosts used for the occasion, and a spoonful of wine from the common chalice; then the sacrament was distributed to the people. While sharp liturgical eyes criticized some of the details as not in accord with the most advanced liturgical thinking, the impression on the assembled prelates and the laity was decisive. Only three members of the Curia—Cardinal Tisserant, the dean of the Sacred College of Cardinals; Cardinal Larraona, and Archbishop Felici, Secretary General of the Council—were among the concelebrants, the rest being residential bishops, including Cardinal Lercaro of Bologna, Archbishops Krol of Philadelphia and Shehan of Baltimore, and two heads of religious orders.

Pope Paul's address was a discourse of single purpose. He declared the convocation of the Council a free and spontaneous act on Pope John's part, which he Paul had immediately supported. Recognizing that a primary conciliar objective was to complete the Church's teaching on the governing power of the bishops, he said that, with the aid of the Holy Spirit, the Fathers were to "determine the prerogatives of the bishops, describe the relations between our apostolic Roman see and this episcopate, and demonstrate how, in the diverse expressions typical of the east and the west, the idea of the constitution of the Church is still homogeneous. [The Council] should teach both Catholics and our separated brethren the true nature of this hierarchy of which the Holy Spirit has instituted the members as bishops to pasture the Church of God with an indisputable and valid authority."

Paul referred to the need for the papal office to insure the unity guaranteed to the Church by the presence of Christ, and indicated by Christ's selection of Peter as the head of the apostles. He stated that he had no choice but to continue in this function, and that it was not a domination but a service (*diakonia*). In having to place certain restrictions on the exercise of episcopal power, to make doctrinal decisions, and clarify positions, the Pope was only acting for the good of the whole Church; actually it was his wish to strengthen the position of the bishops, delegating both authority and faculties to local pastors. Paul had words of encouragement for the religious and the laity who form the diverse members of Christ's body. He greeted the Catholic lay auditors and the non-Catholic observer-delegates, thanking them for the time and effort which they were devoting to help demonstrate the ecumenical character of the Council, and he expressed his confident hope that in the mystery of Providence, evident in the calling of the Council, the true reconstitution of the full Church of Christ would not be far off. Of exceptional significance were his emotionally charged exhortation at the end of his speech to the various "Churches" still separated from Catholic communion, and his explicit recognition of the ecumenical principle of "pluralism in practice." "Our thoughts go out to the world about us," he concluded, "with its own interests, with its indifference too, perhaps even its hostility."

Conciliar business began the following morning, Tuesday, September 15, 1964, with a series of instructions read, first by Cardinal Tisserant as senior member of the board of Council Presidents, by Cardinal Agagianian as senior of the Council Moderators, and by Archbishop Felici as Secretary General of the Council. Among the modifications in conciliar procedure was an explicit acknowledgment that the Moderators would henceforth have control of both the lists of speakers and the course of the debates, thus clarifying their authority with respect to that of the Secretary General and the board of Presidents. Once cloture was voted, the signatures of seventy bishops were required to enable a speaker to make a final intervention. All, including the cardinals, would have to hand in summaries of their speeches five days before the topic was due to be discussed.

It was immediately apparent that under pressure from the Coordinating Commission, in accordance with a plan agreed upon during the intersessional period, a positive attempt would be made to accelerate the proceedings, and all three speakers indicated the hope that, despite the work load, this session might prove to be the final one of the Council. Speaking "like an English headmaster"—the phrase was used by Douglas Woodruff writing in the London *Tablet*—Cardinal Tisserant cautioned the Fathers about observing great prudence in discussing conciliar business outside the Council hall, particularly matters that were still under the secrecy of the commissions. Archbishop Felici read out a set of rules binding on the *periti*—they must only give opinions when requested to do so by conciliar commissions; they must not grant interviews; and they must be circumspect in what they wrote and divulged about conciliar activities. These were considered offensive by most of these hard-working priests and monsignori, particularly when the archbishop added a threat to deprive *periti* of their privileges if they engaged in lobbying or in the distribution of literature intended to influence the thinking of the bishops. Though couched in humorous terms, Archbishop Felici's warning to the bishops to remain in their seats during the voting periods, and his announcement that the two coffee bars would only open at 11 A.M., instead of 10 A.M. as in previous years, caused some audible groans. Questioned the following day as to the Secretary General's authority for these restrictions, one of the Moderators said that he had overstepped his mandate; but no

attempt was made to correct the generally unfavorable impression they had made. Throughout the session it was apparent that the Secretary General had the interests of the
minority at heart.

This attitude was caught by the correspondent of the
Italian daily *Il Messaggero,* Carlo Lazoli, who wrote: "These
limitations on the *periti* and Fathers can hardly be considered
impartial. They doubtless favor the wing of the assembly
which is interested in reducing to a minimum the expression
of opinion and the problems being discussed."

The actual debate was begun with a consideration of Chapter VII of the schema on the Church, concerning the eschatological aspects of the Christian vocation. Cardinal Ruffini led
off with an attack on the significance of the scriptural passages
quoted, and maintained that there was a lack of order in the
discussion of the last things of human existence, namely
death, judgment, heaven or hell. Purgatory was hardly mentioned, he complained, and the condemnation of those dying
in the state of mortal sin was passed over in silence. He was
for rejecting the text outright. On the other hand, Cardinal
Urbani of Venice in his only intervention in the Third Session, proclaimed that any major change in the chapter would
destroy the harmony of the text which organically embodies
dogmatic, apologetic, pastoral and ecumenical aspects of the
subject. Cardinals Santos of the Philippines and Rugambwa
of Tanganyika agreed, but the Latin rite Patriarch of Jerusalem, Alberto Gori, called for an express mention of the doctrine on hell, and Archbishop Nicodemo of Bari, Italy, likewise demanded an explicit mention of eternal damnation for
unrepentant sinners. It was Archbishop Hermaniuk, the
Ukrainian metropolitan of Winnipeg, who pointed out that
the true significance of the Chapter was to give the church a
sense of expectancy, of vigilance, of preparation for death
which was right around the corner for everybody, and of the
end of time which stares the modern world in the face. The
debate was continued until 12:30 instead of 12 noon, the

extra half hour added to the conciliar time allowing four more Fathers to speak each day.

With the opening of the second general congregation on Wednesday, it was obvious that a pattern and rhythm had been established for the session and that the tempo would be fast. A schedule listing the order in which the various documents would come up for debate was announced; it included the Pastoral Office of Bishops, the Declarations on Religious Liberty and the Jews, the schemas on Divine Revelation and the Apostolate of the Laity, the propositions on the Priesthood, the Missions, Seminaries, and Religious Orders, and finally the schema on the Church in the Modern World—Schema 13. Those wishing to speak on the subjects of Religious Liberty and the Jews were told to hand in the summaries of their speeches by Friday. A vote was taken on the schedule for voting the first six chapters of *De Ecclesia*, the amended text of which was now distributed.

In concluding the debate on eschatology, Cardinal Suenens attacked the present system of canonizations in the Church, complaining that under the present Rome-controlled official processes, religious orders accounted for 85 per cent of canonized saints and 13 European countries monopolized 90 per cent. The procedures were too complicated, financially burdensome, and so far, discriminatory to the laity. The last speaker in this debate was Bishop D'Agostino, of Vallo di Lucania, Italy, who made a final pitch to remind modern man of the existence of hell.

The debate on the place of Mary in the economy of salvation, which constitutes Chapter VIII of *De Ecclesia*, was introduced by Archbishop Roy of Quebec and immediately found Cardinal Ruffini on his feet with a mild remonstrance calling for a clearer text, making it obvious to non-Catholics that in speaking of Mary's part in man's salvation the Church was in no way detracting from the dignity of Jesus Christ. Thirteen other Fathers spoke, but before the morning's end Bishops Charue of Namur, Belgium, took the microphone to present the *relatio* on Chapter I of the schema *De Ecclesia*, which the Fathers proceeded to vote on (2114 *placet*, 11 *non placet*, 63 *placet iuxta modum*, and 1 null vote). Thursday, Chapter II of *De Ecclesia* concerned with the People of God was voted in four parts during continuation of the debate on Mary. *Non Placet* votes came only to 30, 12, 48 and 67, but despite reiterated warnings from the Secretary General, each round always produced a series of null votes. This continued until the third week when, with unfeigned relief, Archbishop Felici was able to announce that at least one round of voting had taken place without a single invalid vote.

Despite the pleasure felt over the rapid pace at which the Council was proceeding, there was an uneasy feeling that the desire to make the Third Session the final one could bode no good. The minority were known to be as resolutely opposed to the aims of the Council as ever, and in urging the authorities to bring the Council to an end with much of its work left unfinished or perhaps only half-finished, their ultimate purpose was to allow the Curia to return everything to normal as if there had been no *aggiornamento* at all. The announcement that summaries of the speeches to be made on Religious Liberty and the Jews would have to be submitted in only two days was regarded as particularly outrageous and ominous. This impression was reinforced by the tone of the speeches of the minority when the next item of business was taken up.

On September 18 the revised schema on the Pastoral Office of Bishops was distributed in the council hall, after Secretary General Felici had announced that the administrative section of his office had provided accident insurance coverage for all the members of the Council. While a number of missionary bishops who drove ancient vehicles were pleased that their dioceses might benefit from their sudden demise on the traffic-snarled streets of Rome, the more cynically-minded bishops remembered the squabble that had accompanied the discussion of this schema when it was presented at the Second Session under the provoking title, "The Relations between the Hierarchy and the Roman Curia." They presumed that Felici's office was taking no chances on any violent reactions this time. The same morning the whole of Chapter II of *De Ecclesia* was submitted to a vote resulting in 1615 *placet,* 553 *placet iuxta modum,* 19 *non placet* and 3 invalid votes, and the Secretary General announced that while it had been approved by a substantial majority, the commission would pay careful attention to the *modi* or suggested amendments. This chapter, dealing with the Church as the People of God, was actually the heart of the Council's break-away from a scholastic approach to the theology of the Church. It described the mystery of the Church in biblical terms adapted to the existentialist world in which the Church now finds itself.

The *relatio* on the Pastoral Office of Bishops was read by Archbishop Veuillot, Coadjutor Archbishop of Paris, after Cardinal Marella delivered a brief introduction in which he explained the history of the revision since the last session. The archbishop declared that the principles motivating the present document had been taken from the theological explanation of the episcopal office as contained in Chapter II of the schema on the Church, and the validity of the collegial principle was assumed. Since it dealt with the bishop's office or *munus,* this term was defined as a duty or service or ministry, of teaching, sanctifying and feeding the flock of Christ. A new article had been added asserting the essential freedom of the bishop in the exercise of his office, particularly with respect to the civil authorities in so-called Catholic countries as well as in Communist-dominated states, in each of which influence was commonly brought to bear by way of controlling the nomination of bishops and the exercise of their authority.

Cardinal Richard, of Bordeaux, France, while praising the excellent directives given in the document, felt that too many details were left to the decision of post-conciliar commissions and suggested that a number of these be spelled out as already belonging to bishops, such as full freedom in the appointment of pastors, the responsibilities of national conferences of bishops, and jurisdiction in cases of appeals between dioceses. He felt something further should be said about super-parochial or inter-parochial activities in a diocese. Cardinal Browne, followed immediately by Bishop Carli, attacked the basic presupposition of the document by challenging the doctrine of collegiality. The bishop claimed that the doctrine was objectionable on "historical, juridical, dogmatic, liturgical and other grounds." He did not hesitate to state unabashedly: "If this text is approved, we expose ourselves to the accusation of using two standards—we will have adopted a policy of extreme caution in dealing with the Virgin Mary, and a policy of broad liberality in our treatment of the bishops."

Bishop Rupp of Monaco complained that after a show of grandeur in its initial parts, the document backed down to a mumble when it came to discuss the reorganization of dioceses. In praising its pastoral directives, he felt it failed in not realizing that no diocese is made up of a static or stabilized population; that as migration is characteristic of modern man, some consideration should be given to this aspect of the pastoral problem on both the local, national, and international levels. Bishop Pildain y Zapiáin, of the Canary Islands, expressed his desire for an absolute break with governmental interference in ecclesiastical affairs.

The remaining speakers touched on the relations between religious orders and diocesan administration, which the schema attempts to coordinate and reconcile, while preserving the right of religious orders to exemption from episcopal control so far as the internal affairs of their various houses are concerned. Archbishop Fares, of Catanzaro e Squillace, Italy, called for a warning to bishops to protect their flocks from error, while Archbishop Lucey got in a plug for the Confraternity of Christian Doctrine as the most effective instrument in catechetical instruction, and Bishop Drzecnik, of

Yugoslavia, called for a section on pastoral sociology and the setting up of a special diocesan commission in each diocese to promote study of this problem. It was Bishop Kaiser, of Peru, who introduced a practical collegial note, however, by suggesting a remedy for the unequal distribution of the clergy, in accordance with the Lord's injunction that a man should give away his tunic even if he had only two.

Continuing the discussion of the schema, Cardinal Léger, of Montreal, made a distinct contribution to the pastoral atmosphere of the Council by mentioning the specific reasons for the reorganization of the episcopal office in the contemporary world. Bishops must learn to know the mind of modern *homo technicus*, whose attitude toward religion was highly critical, he said. Modern man thinks of obedience in different terms from his predecessors. We must adapt our teaching to those who are to receive it, by being humble and not becoming involved in affairs which do not concern us, particularly in the secular field. There must be closer bonds between the bishop and his clergy and between the bishop and the faithful. The schema should say something about the desired simplification of episcopal titles, honors, dress, etc. in a spirit of poverty. His intervention was greeted with applause.

Bishop Compagnone, of Anagni, Italy, and Archbishop Agnelo Rossi, of Ribeirão Prêto, Brazil, both spoke about the relations between bishops and religious orders, but from slightly different angles, the latter being of the conviction that all agreements must be carefully written out, so that there would be fewer disputes between religious superiors and bishops. Bishop Staverman, apostolic prefect in Indonesia, brought up the delicate subject of fallen priests and suggested that there ought to be a more reasonable and less rigoristic attitude toward them. The solution need not be the same everywhere. The principle of decentralization could be applied here. For example, some of them should certainly be allowed to marry.

Bishop Guyot of Coutances, Bishop Renard of Versailles,

Archbishop Urtasun of Avignon, Bishop Sauvage of Annecy, and Bishop Maziers, auxiliary of Lyons, all spoke on some aspect of the theme that there should be closer relations between bishops and their priests. Archbishop Guerry of Cambrai felt that the usual role of the bishop as "doctor" or teacher was too conventional. The times have changed, he said. While teaching did not cease to be a primary episcopal function, bishops were now also called upon to be abreast of social, economic, demographic and other matters, including war and peace. Pope Pius XII had led the way in promoting this new type of pastoral emphasis. The bishop must at all times reveal the presence of Christ in the world and, to be effective, he must be "up" on all these things. Archbishop Guerry's speech seemed to put into words what was behind many of the other interventions. The remaining speakers dealt with one aspect or another of the problem of adapting the episcopal office to modern times.

On Wednesday, after the debate had been closed, two final speakers were allowed, in the name of at least 70 Fathers. Bishop Greco, of Alexandria, Louisiana, spoke on the subject of confraternities, while Bishop Gonzalez Moralejo, auxiliary of Valencia, Spain, was one of the few to bring up the subject of episcopal nominations. He heartily approved of the last-minute changes in the text calling for freedom from control by the state in this matter. However, better criteria could be worked out governing episcopal nominations, including discussion by episcopal conferences and consulting the wishes of the clergy and even the laity.

Summary

September 14, 1964, Monday—SOLEMN OPENING OF THIRD SESSION.
—Mass concelebrated by Pope Paul VI.
—Address by Pope Paul.
September 15, 1964, Tuesday—80TH GENERAL CONGREGATION.
MASS: Bishop Vanuytven, former Vicar Apostolic in Congo.
MODERATOR: Cardinal Agagianian.
PRESENT: 2,170 Fathers.
ANNOUNCEMENTS: by Cardinal Tisserant, Dean of the Sacred College;
—by Cardinal Agagianian
—by the Secretary General, Archbishop Pericle Felici:* distribution of certain documents; reads revised Rules; no unauthorized distribution of pamphlets or texts in council hall or vicinity will be permitted; Periti admonished to abide by norms laid down by Secretary of State; speeches on Pastoral Office of Bishops must be submitted by today or tomorrow; plan for balloting on *De Ecclesia* will be voted on tomorrow; distribution of *votum* of Biblical Commission on collegiality; daily Congregations will ordinarily end by 12:30 and the coffee bar will not be open until 11:00.
BUSINESS: Schema on the Church, Chap. VII "The Eschatological Nature of our Calling."
SPEAKERS: *relator:* Cardinal Browne. 1. Cardinal Ruffini (Palermo, Sicily). 2. Cardinal Urbani (Venice, Italy). 3. Cardinal Santos (Manila, Philippines). 4. Cardinal Rugambwa (Bukoba, Tanganyika). 5. Archbishop Gori (Latin Patriarch of Jerusalem). 6. Archbishop Nicodemo (Bari, Italy). 7. Archbishop Darmajuwana (Semarang, Indonesia). 8. Archbishop Ziadé (Maronite Archbishop of Beirut, Lebanon). 9. Archbishop Hermaniuk (Ukrainian Archbishop of Winnepeg, Canada). 10. Bishop Pont y Gol (Segorbe-Castellón, Spain). 11. Archbishop Elchinger (Co-

---

* The Secretary General as a rule made nearly all the announcements during the course of each morning's Congregation, therefore it will not be necessary to note the fact each time. For the sake of convenience all the announcements are grouped together regardless of when they were made. For a fuller record, consult the Daily Press Bulletins, e.g. as published in *La Civiltà Cattolica* or *La Documentation Catholique*.

adjutor of Strasbourg, France). 12. Dom Butler (Superior of English Benedictines). 13. Archbishop Garcia de Sierra y Méndez (Burgos, Spain). 14. Archbishop Mathias (Madras and Mylapore, India).

September 16, 1964, Wednesday—81ST GENERAL CONGREGATION.
MASS: Archbishop Thiandoum of Dakar, Senegal.
MODERATOR: Cardinal Lercaro.
PRESENT: 2,204 Fathers.
ANNOUNCEMENTS: speeches on Religious Liberty and the Jews must be submitted by Friday, Sept. 18; today is the last day for summaries of speeches on Bishops.
PENDING BUSINESS: Schema on the Church, Chap. VII.
SPEAKERS: 1. Cardinal Suenens (Malines-Brussels, Belgium). 2. Bishop Ancel (Auxiliary of Lyons, France). 3. Bishop D'Agostino (Vallo di Lucania, Italy).
NEW BUSINESS: Schema on the Church, Chap. VIII "The Blessed Virgin Mary, Mother of God, in the Mystery of Christ and the Church."
SPEAKERS: *relator:* Archbishop Roy of Quebec, Canada. 1. Cardinal Ruffini (Palermo, Sicily). 2. Cardinal Wyszynski (Warsaw, Poland). 3. Cardinal Léger (Montreal, Canada). 4. Cardinal Döpfner (Munich, Germany). 5. Cardinal Silva Henriquez (Santiago de Chile). 7. Archbishop Djajasepoetra (Djakarta, Indonesia). 8. Archbishop Márquez Toriz (Puebla de los Angeles, Mexico). 9. Archbishop Mingo (Monreale, Sicily). 10. Bishop Ruotolo (Ugento, Italy). 11. Bishop Cambiaghi (Novara, Italy). 12. Bishop Hervás y Benet (Ciudad Real, Spain). 13. Bishop Abasolo y Lecue (Vijayapuram, India). 14. Bishop Necsey (Czechoslovakia).

VOTES: Plan of voting on *De Ecclesia* and Chap. I.
Relator: Bishop Charue.

	Total	Placet	Non placet	Placet iuxta modum	Invalid
Plan of voting	2,204	2,170	32	—	2
Chap. I*	2,189	2,114	11	63	1

* The results of this vote were not announced until the following day. This not infrequently was the case, but lack of space precludes mention of the fact each time in this short summary.

September 17, 1964, Thursday—82ND GENERAL CONGREGATION.
MASS: Bishop Angrisani of Casal Monferrato, Italy.
MODERATOR: Cardinal Lercaro.
PRESENT: 2,210 Fathers.
ANNOUNCEMENTS: Voting on Chap. III of *De Ecclesia* will begin
on Monday; Moderators have decided on following schedule:
summaries of speeches on Divine Revelation and Apostolate of
Laity must be submitted by Sept. 25 and 28, respectively, and
those on all other schemata must be handed in by Oct. 1;
criticisms of Schema 13 should be in accordance with the cri-
teria to be distributed today; although Chap. I of *De Ecclesia*
received more than the required ⅔ majority for approval, the
Commission will nevertheless take into account the *modi* submitted.
PENDING BUSINESS: Schema on the Church, Chap. VIII.
SPEAKERS: 1. Cardinal Suenens (Malines-Brussels). 2. Bishop Rendeiro (Faro, Portugal). 3. Bishop Sapelak (Ukrainian Visitor
Apostolic for Argentina). 4. Bishop Van Lierde (Curia). 5.
Archbishop Gawlina (Ordinary for Poles in exile). 6. Archbishop Jaeger (Paderborn, Germany). 7. Bishop Ancel (Auxiliary of Lyons, France). 8. Bishop Kempf (Limburg, Germany).
9. Bishop de Uriarte Bengoa (Peru). 10. Father Fernández (Master General of Dominicans). 11. Bishop Gasbarri (Auxiliary of
Velletri, Italy). 12. Father Monta (Prior General of Servites).
13. Archbishop Garcia y Garcia de Castro (Granada, Spain).
14. Archbishop Signora (Italy). 15. Bishop Le Couëdic (Troyes,
France). 16. Bishop Méndez Arceo (Cuernavaca, Mexico).

VOTES: Chap. II of *De Ecclesia*.
Relator: Bishop Garrone.

	Total	Placet	Non placet	Placet iuxta modum	Invalid
Art. 9-12	2,210	2,173	30	—	7(3)*
Art. 13	2,202	2,186	12	—	4(2)
Art. 14-16	2,099	2,048	48	—	3(1)
Art. 17	2,174	2,106	67	—	1

* According to the Rules, only *placet* and *non placet* votes were allowed
in voting on the individual Articles, in contrast to the voting on whole
Chapters, therefore the votes erroneously cast as *placet iuxta modum* were
counted as invalid. The first figure indicates the total invalid votes; the figure
in parenthesis, the votes erroneously cast as *placet iuxta modum*.

September 18, 1964, Friday—83RD GENERAL CONGREGATION.
MASS: Bishop Larrain Errázuriz of Talca, Chile.
MODERATOR: Cardinal Döpfner.
PRESENT: 2,190 Fathers.
ANNOUNCEMENTS: insurance policies on the Council Fathers have been renewed; distribution of schedule of 40 votes on Chap. III of *De Ecclesia* to begin on Monday and texts of 2 *relationes;* speakers on Pastoral Office of Bishops should confine their remarks to the new sections.
PENDING BUSINESS: Schema on the Church, Chap. VIII.
SPEAKERS (each in name of at least 70 Fathers): 1. Cardinal Frings (Cologne, Germany). 2. Cardinal Alfrink (Utrecht, Holland). 3. Bishop Castán Lacoma (Sigüenza-Guadalajara, Spain).
NEW BUSINESS: Schema on Pastoral Office of Bishops in the Church.
SPEAKERS: *relatores:* Cardinal Marella and Archbishop Veuillot. 4. Cardinal Richaud (Bordeaux, France). 5. Cardinal Browne (Curia). 6. Bishop Carli (Segni, Italy). 7. Bishop Rupp (Monaco. 8. Bishop Pildain y Zapiain (Canary Islands, Spain). 9. Archbishop Fares (Catanzaro-Squillace, Italy). 10. Archbishop Melendro (Anking, China). 11. Bishop Corboy (Monze, Northern Rhodesia). 12. Bishop Drzecnik (Maribor, Yugoslavia). 13. Bishop Foley (Lancaster, England). 14. Bishop Kaiser (Peru). 15. Archbishop Lucey (San Antonio, Texas). 16. Bishop McEleney (Kingston, Jamaica).

VOTE: Chap. II of *De Ecclesia* as a whole.

	Total	Placet	Non placet	Placet iuxta modum	Invalid
Chap. II	2,190	1,615	19	553*	3

* The SG announced that the Commission would consider the *modi*, although the Chapter had been approved by the required ⅔ majority.

September 21, 1964, Monday—84TH GENERAL CONGREGATION.
MASS: Bishop Donaghy of Wuchow, China (exiled).
MODERATOR: Cardinal Döpfner.
PRESENT: 2,220 Fathers.
ANNOUNCEMENTS: (by Cardinal Tisserant) distribution of pamphlets against this morning's *relationes* by certain members of Theological Commission deplored, and complaints of some bishops about conferences of certain *Periti;*
— (by SG) addition to text of Pastoral Office of Bishops dis-

tributed this morning; Pope will take part Wednesday in ceremony honoring relic of St. Andrew; at request of Theological Commission, Moderators have allowed Bishop Franic to speak first.

PENDING BUSINESS: Schema on Pastoral Office of Bishops.
SPEAKERS: 1. Cardinal Léger (Montreal, Canada). 2. Cardinal Confalonieri (Curia). 3. Bishop Nuer (Coptic auxiliary of Thebes, Egypt). 4. Bishop Compagnone (Anagni, Italy). 5. Archbishop Rossi (Ribeirão Prêto, Brazil). 6. Bishop Staverman (Indonesia).

VOTES: Chap. III of *De Ecclesia*
Relatores: Bishop Franic, Archbishop Parente, Bishop Henriquez Jimenez.

	Total	Placet	Non placet	Invalid
Art. 18	2,220	2,166	53	1
Art. 19	2,206	2,012	191	3(1)*
Art. 19-20	2,211	2,103	106	2(1)
Art. 20	2,207	2,091	115	1

*See p. 20 for meaning of parenthesis. And likewise for the following tables.

September 22, 1964, Tuesday—85TH GENERAL CONGREGATION.
MASS: Archbishop Roy of Quebec, Canada.
MODERATOR: Cardinal Döpfner.
PRESENT: 2,248 Fathers.
ANNOUNCEMENTS: reminder of deadline of Sept. 25 for summaries on Divine Revelation, and the discussion will be divided into three parts; discussion will begin tomorrow on Religious Liberty.
PENDING BUSINESS: Schema on Pastoral Office of Bishops.
SPEAKERS: 1. Bishop Guyot (Coutances, France). 2. Bishop Renard (Versailles, France). 3. Bishop Guilly (Georgetown, British Guiana). 4. Archbishop Urtasun (Avignon, France). 5. Bishop Barrachina Estevan (Orihuela-Alicante, Spain). 6. Archbishop Guerry (Cambrai, France). 7. Bishop Sauvage (Annecy, France). 8. Archbishop D'Souza (Bhopal, India). 9. Bishop Maziers (Auxiliary of Lyons, France). 10. Bishop Bednorz (Coadjutor of Katowice, Poland). 11. Archbishop Miranda y Gómez (Mexico City, Mexico). 12. Bishop Iriarte (Reconquista, Argentina). 13. Bishop Pluta (Poland). 14. Bishop Proaño Villalba (Riobamba, Ecuador). 15. Bishop Ruiz Garcia (Chiapas, Mexico). 16. Archbishop Ziadé (Maronite Archbishop of Beirut, Lebanon). 17.

Bishop Lopes de Moura (Portalegre-Castelo Branco, Portugal).
18. Archbishop Baraniak (Poznan, Poland). 19. Bishop Himmer
(Tournai, Belgium).

VOTES: Chap. III of *De Ecclesia*

	Total	*Placet*	*Non placet*	Invalid
Art. 20	2,248	2,198	50	—
Art. 21	2,246	2,201	44	1(1)
Art. 21	2,240	2,117	123	—
Art. 21	2,247	1,917	328	2(1)
Art. 21	2,243	2,088	156	2
Art. 22	2,243	1,918	322	3(1)
Art. 22	2,213	1,898	313	2(1)
Art. 22	2,205	2,114	90	1

II

The Declaration on Religious Liberty;
The Declaration on the Jews;
Debate on Divine Revelation;
Collegiality Approved

✠

THE DEBATE on the Declaration on Religious Liberty began Wednesday, September 23, with a report by the *relator*, Bishop de Smedt of Bruges, Belgium, who emphasized that the text had been greatly improved over the original, presented but not debated at the end of the Second Session, "thanks to the collegial discussions of the Fathers" who had submitted 380 amendments to the Secretariat. Man's fundamental dignity as God's creature, as well as the present development of human society, he said, made a conciliar statement on this theme imperative.

Despite the assurances of Bishop de Smedt that sufficient care had been exercised to ward off the dangers of subjectivism or religious indifferentism in treating this topic, Cardinal Ruffini rose to begin the discussion by claiming that this was by no means so. The declaration should be entitled "On Religious Tolerance," not "Liberty," because those in error had no rights. In his usual disconcerting fashion—a pose which the elderly cardinal thoroughly enjoys, for after such interventions he can be seen chuckling over the disturbance he knows he has caused—he laid it on the line that as the Catholic Church was the one and only true Church, it should be supported by governments; while no one should be forced to profess a religion, or have his conscience outraged, it was God's will that the Catholic Church should prevail. There was no denying that the cardinal presented the outdated pre-Johannine position with great candor.

The Spanish Cardinal Quiroga y Palacios, of Santiago de Compostela, adopted a similar although somewhat milder approach. He denounced the document as favoring liberalism and said that it seemed to be meant primarily for Protestant countries. Its adoption would mean a revolution in the Church, whereas Paul VI had called for a gradual reform. The tide of the debate was quickly turned, however, by an impressive run of speeches from Cardinals Léger Cushing, Bueno y Monreal, Meyer, Ritter, and Silva Henriquez. It was the first speech on the floor by the Boston cardinal and he was listened to with close attention and some expectancy. In flawless Latin, despite his disclaimers to any knowledge of the language, and in a high-pitched Bostonese accent that made it difficult for his continental hearers to grasp some of his words, though the purport of his message was perfectly clear, he asserted his joy that the Council was finally coming round to safeguard "a decent respect for the opinions of mankind." While not denying that the subject was complicated, he thought that the essence of the matter could be reduced to two principles: summed up by the traditional phrase which the Church was always claiming for herself, *libertas Ecclesiae,* and the principle of freedom for other Churches and for every human person, which she was now claiming also. His summation, including a quotation in English of Lord Acton's famous dictum, "Freedom is the highest political end," and his reference to Pope John's encyclical, *Pacem in Terris,* as the final word on the subject of human freedom won him a warm round of applause.

Cardinal Cushing made it clear that he approved of the present text only in a general sense, as a basis for further revisions. His remarks were mainly addressed to the idea of religious liberty as such, which he wanted to emphasize in the strongest possible terms. This was also, in the main, the line which other American speakers took. Cardinal Meyer explained that the text was acceptable to the American bishops primarily for three reasons: because men of today expected the Church to come out with a statement on behalf of religious freedom, which the text did; because it made clear that the act of faith must be freely made; and because a document on this subject would facilitate the Church's apostolate, for it would show that the faith was not to be spread by violence, conquest, or propaganda, but through freedom. A statement was necessary because of its implications for the ecumenical movement.

Cardinal Ritter's discourse caused some mild consternation. After accepting the declaration, in principle, as both pastorally oriented and necessary, he went on to say that the acceptance of the declaration itself did not necessarily mean acceptance of the reasons for it, as separated, and that a simple declaration be worked out merely stating the need for religious liberty without making any attempt to justify it. The Moderators, he said, might distinguish between these two points when putting the text to a vote. This seemed to be playing directly into the hands of the minority, who claimed that indiscriminate religious liberty could not be justified on theological grounds, and that the call for this document was purely an American or Anglo-Saxon move based on considerations of political expediency. The St. Louis cardinal was taxed with having used the wrong tactics, delivering the type of speech appropriate only for a stalemate, when it was time for compromise, not at the beginning when absolutes are laid down. He took the criticism in good grace. The American position was also represented by Archbishop Alter, of Cincinnati, speaking in the name of many American bishops. Unless the Church clearly proclaimed the right of religious liberty as an absolute, how could she insist that it be recognized by the totalitarian states?

When Cardinal Ottaviani rose to speak, the last speaker on the first day of the debate, he seemed to be seizing upon Cardinal Ritter's suggestion and it was expected that he would develop the idea, but instead he fell back upon the usual theological clichés. The schema was acceptable in general, but with reservations, one of these being the suppression of the paragraph on proselytism, which he felt might hinder the work of the missions. The Fathers were reminded that the Council was not an "assembly of philosophers." His assertion that governments were entitled to intervene in religious matters was immediately countered by Bishop Čekada, of Yugoslavia, who said that a declaration on religious liberty was a necessity in today's world when Marxist regimes were so actively engaged in the business of suppressing religion. "Yesterday it was Nazism, today it is atheistic materialism or communism. Religious freedom is the problem *par excellence.*" The bishop urged that the Council draft a message to the United Nations, insisting on the right of all men to religious liberty.

On the second day of debate, support for the declaration came from Cardinal König, of Vienna, who also wanted some mention of the fact that religious freedom was being denied in certain countries. Freedom of worship was not the sum total of religious liberty. The idea meant much more. In some countries, where there was suppression of true liberty, believers were reduced to a kind of second-class status and were subject to real discrimination. Public opinion should be alerted about this problem. His speech drew a round of applause.

A number of conservative speakers, taking up the suggestion of Cardinal Ritter, urged that the declaration be confined to a general statement of principles, leaving aside theological considerations about which there was disagreement. Cardinal Browne observed, first of all, that the present text was totally unacceptable to him because it seemed to accord the same rights to a right conscience as to an erroneous conscience. In attempting to interpret Pope John's statement that a man's conscience is the final arbiter of human liberty, he misquoted the Pope. Archbishop Parente, who followed, was more cautious. The present text seemed to be an "inextricable forest," a jumble of theology, law, sociology and politics. It should be reduced to a few simple principles about the dignity of man, freedom of conscience, the freedom of the Church to preach the Gospel everywhere and at all times, and finally the duty of the state toward religion.

The minority position having been laid down, by a curious coincidence, or what some American punsters described as a "Felicitous" bit of manoeuvering, a line-up of seven conservative speakers now rose to hammer away at the minority thesis, Archbishop Cantero Quadrado, Bishop Abasolo y Lecue, Archbishop Nicodemo, Bishop Lopez Ortiz, Bishop de Castro Mayer, Bishop Canestri, and Archbishop Lefebvre. The criticism of the text by Bishop Canestri, auxiliary of Rome, was particularly harsh and in strange contrast to the spirit of the Pope who had appointed him to his Roman post. Fortunately this impression was erased by a series of vigorous interventions by Father Buckley, American Superior of the Marist Fathers; Bishop Primeau, of Manchester, New Hampshire; Bishop Nierman, of Holland; and Archbishop Dubois, of Besançon, France. Father Buckley insisted that the text should state more clearly what it meant by freedom of conscience, while Bishop Primeau made a telling objection to the dichotomy that would recognize freedom of conscience, but deny external religious liberty. Both related to the dignity of man, he said, and were inseparable.

At their weekly meeting in the North American College

the previous Monday, the American bishops had prepared for this debate carefully. After listening to an address by the well-known Jesuit *peritus* and authority on the subject, Father John Courtney Murray, they had agreed that at least eight of their number would speak on the floor of the Council. The text of the declaration was unanimously accepted by the bishops, in spite of efforts by two conservative theologians, Monsignor George Shea of Darlington Seminary, New Jersey, and Father Francis J. Connell, C.Ss.R., emeritus professor of moral theology at Catholic University in Washington, to present objections.

On the last full day of debate, the curial Cardinal Roberti suggested a distinction between the idea of *freedom of conscience,* which he reprobated as a subjective right leading to religious indifferentism, and *freedom of consciences,* which he explained could be a proper expedient in modern society. This canonical fine point failed to impress most of the prelates.

Both Archbishop Garrone, of Toulouse, France, and Bishop Colombo, of the Milan archdiocese, delivered particularly noteworthy speeches, the former on the necessity for showing the continuity between the past and the present with respect to the Church's attitude toward religious liberty and how this has changed; the latter on the necessity for a more theological approach to the whole problem. Since Bishop Colombo is the Pope's private theologian, his words were listened to with a great deal of attention. He declared that in Italy the debate was considered a "turning point" for the Council. "Unless we have this declaration," he said, "there can be no dialogue with men of good will." But the whole problem of the theological foundations of religious liberty must be studied and worked out carefully. A general statement would not suffice. The three foundations of religious liberty must be: 1) the principle that man has a natural right to the search for truth, especially religious truth, which Cardinal Montini had emphasized at the First Session

in his Council speech of December 5, 1962; 2) the principle
that man has a natural right to follow his conscience; 3) a
principle of the supernatural order, namely the liberty and
nature of the Christian faith. If these three principles were
taken into account, it would not be difficult to work out a
satisfactory text on religious liberty. The only possible limits
were the rights of others and the common good.

Following this intervention, Cardinal Suenens called for
a standing vote on whether to end the debate and the motion
was carried overwhelmingly. The debate had been closed
somewhat early on Friday, depriving a number of American
speakers of their opportunity to be heard, because it was
necessary to give the floor to Cardinal Bea so that he could
introduce the next item on the agenda, the Declaration on
the Jews, before departing on Saturday with the relic of the
Apostle St. Andrew, which the Pope had ordered returned
to the Orthodox Church of Greece, 500 years after it had
been entrusted for safekeeping to the fifteenth century hu-
manist Pope Pius II by the last Byzantine prince fleeing from
the Turks.

Following the close of the debate on Religious Liberty,
on Friday, the floor was again given on Monday to four
prelates who asked to speak in the name of at least 70 Fathers.
Archbishop Heenan, of Westminster, England, pointed to
the Catholic experience in his country as an example of
the benefits that accrue from an uninhibited, frank recognition of the principle of religious liberty. In the 16th century,
he noted, England had been subject to violent religious persecution from which Roman Catholics had suffered. Ever since
the "Catholic Emancipation Act" of 1828, however, their
rights to complete religious freedom had been respected. Although the Church of England, of which the Queen was the
head, was still the established church, Catholics were not discriminated against. In fact they received the same support
from the state as other religions in regard to education. The
principle of religious liberty must be firmly proclaimed,

while the right of the state to intervene in religious matters on the grounds of protecting the common good must not be too freely acknowledged, for abuses were possible. All religions should be treated alike so far as the state is concerned. Bishop Wright, of Pittsburgh, developed the relationship between religious liberty and the common good, reading a long quotation from Maritain to the effect that the essential concern of the common good was to provide for the development of the human person, and therefore of human freedom. He pointed out the implications of the document with regard to the Church's missionary activity and its efforts to encourage the practice of religion. The only function of the state should be to see that the rights of religion were not infringed.

The discussion was wound up by two African bishops, Bishop Ddungu of Masaka, Uganda, and Archbishop Zoa of Yaoundé, Cameroun, who likewise requested a strong affirmation of the theological basis for religious liberty and pointed out that this was important in the struggle to protect African youth from the influences of non-Christian religions and atheistic materialism.

On Monday, September 28, the Council reached the controversial Declaration on the Jews. In his *relatio* the previous Friday, Cardinal Bea had begun by stating that it was "absolutely impossible" to think of abandoning a conciliar statement designed to improve relations with the Jewish people, as certain bishops had suggested, and he was warmly applauded when he urged the Fathers to adopt the present text as the basis for a conciliar pronouncement. The present document had no political overtones, he emphasized, by way of rejecting one of the most frequently heard arguments against it, particularly in Arab countries. Much of his speech was devoted to rejecting the thesis that the Jewish people as such could be accused of the charge of "deicide." His remarks were an open invitation to the Council to restore the

L'Azione
GIUDAICO - MASSONICA
nel
CONCILIO

IL CARDINALE BEA SEGUE LE ISTRUZIONI DEI B'NAI B'RITH

Fino al dicembre 1962 apparivano solo degli ecclesiastici come promotori della riabilitazione del popolo ebraico da parte della Chiesa Cattolica. Il primo a parlare dell'avvicinamento della Chiesa al giudaismo è stato il Vescovo di Cuernavaca (Messico) Sergio Mendez Arceo, discendente dei safarditi che tentarono di giudaizzare la popolazione di Cotija nel Messico. Egli estese la riabilitazione anche ai massoni e, sebbene le sue parole cadessero nel vuoto, riuscì utile agli ebrei per mettere in moto la campagna internazionale di stampa alla quale assistiamo e che ne parla come se il Concilio si fosse già pronunciato in loro favore.

Il piano degli ebrei, messo in azione dai loro rappresentanti ecclesiastici, sembrava procedere senza ostacoli fino a che, nei primi giorni del dicembre 1962, i Padri conciliari vennero messi al corrente di quanto accadeva per mezzo di un libro intitolato «*Complotto contro la Chiesa*», pubblicato da eminenti prelati di varie Nazionalità, sotto il pseudonimo di Maurice Pinay. Dobbiamo

Testo riservato esclusivamente ai Reverendissimi Padri Conciliari

Antisemitic propaganda pamphlet (title-page and excerpt), distributed to the bishops.

original, much stronger, statement contained in the version presented to the Council, but not debated, in December 1963.

The history of the version presented to the Council in September 1964 is interesting. No other conciliar document probably has been subject to so many influences and counter-influences. When postponement of the debate at the end of the Second Session was announced "because of lack of time," most observers regarded this as a mere pretext. Different reasons were alleged for this move: because the Pope was anxious not to compromise the reception he might receive in Jordan and Jerusalem on his intended pilgrimage; because of sharp Arab protests against the document made directly to the Vatican Secretariat of State through diplomatic channels; because of misgivings on theological grounds by some of the Pope's advisers, perhaps shared by Pope Paul; because of pressure exercised by the minority in the Council. The decision to postpone consideration was probably taken because of a combination of factors. However, as Cardinal Bea said, "What is put off is not put away." The Secretariat began its work of revision on the basis of the written observations of the Fathers. According to an announcement made in February 1964, the revised text was "much strengthened." In April, unfortunately, at a meeting of the Coordinating Commission, it was decided to order several changes in the document to make it more palatable to the theological minority and the Arab world. The text was broadened to include mention of the Moslems and other non-Christian religions so that it became a statement of the Church's attitude toward, and relationship to, all non-Christians. The most disturbing changes, however, were a watering-down of the passage exonerating the Jewish people of the charge of "deicide" and a certain emphasis on the idea of their "conversion" presented in such a way as to suggest that this was to be the dominant note governing Catholic-Jewish relations.

Word about the changes was leaked from Rome toward the beginning of May and greatly upset Jewish communities throughout the world, particularly in the United States. In an audience granted to the American Jewish Committee, on May 30, 1964, Pope Paul expressed sympathy for the "horrible ordeals" through which the Jewish people had passed, but made no allusion to any changes in the document. Publication of a report by the *New York Times,* on June 10, to the effect that the document had been "muted," as rumored, produced a communiqué from the Secretariat denying that any essential "watering-down" had taken place and attempting to take the edge off the controversy. Some days later, however, the Coordinating Commission formally approved the revised text and it was distributed to the bishops. In the course of the late summer, several bishops, including Cardinal Ritter (August 24), acknowledged that the text of the declaration had indeed been changed in the sense of the rumors, but he expressed the hope that when the Fathers re-assembled, they would restore the passages that had been "toned down."

The conservative minority, perhaps feeling the uselessness of further resistance on the floor of the Council, confined their opposition to the token speech of Cardinal Ruffini. Representing the Arab world, only Cardinal Tappouni and Archbishop Tawil spoke on the issue, both calling for rejection of the text as offensive to Moslems and dangerous for Christians living in that part of the world. All the other speakers were in favor of restoring what had been taken out. Cardinal Liénart made a strong appeal on behalf of the document as a just and charitable effort on the part of the Church to right the wrongs of centuries toward a people who had laid the foundations of the Christian religion. Cardinal Frings expressed his pleasure over the fact that more extensive treatment had been accorded the Moslems and other non-Christians in the revised document and urged restoration of the passage absolving the Jewish people of the charge of "deicide." Cardinals Lercaro, Léger, Cushing, König, Meyer and Ritter all called for the same thing and emphasized the bonds that existed between Jews and Christians.

As usual, Cardinal Ruffini's intervention amounted to an attempt to throw a monkey-wrench into the works. He praised what the text had to say about the Jews and agreed with Cardinal Bea that the term "deicide" should be abandoned because "no one can kill God," and he referred to the many Jews whom "we" had saved from the Nazis, as proof of the Church's goodwill toward them, but he suggested that the improvement of relations should be on a *quid pro quo* basis: the "deicide" charge should be dropped, but Jews should be exhorted to love Christians. Certain anti-Christian passages should be expunged from the Talmud, and he blamed the alleged Jewish anti-Christian inspiration of European Masonry as the motive-force behind anticlericalism.

The speakers on the following day, including Bishop Nagae of Japan, Bishop Elchinger of France, Bishop Leven of San Antonio, Texas, Bishop Stein of Germany, Archbishop Heenan of Westminster, England, Archbishop O'Boyle of Washington, Archbishop Shehan of Baltimore, and Archbishop Descuffi of Turkey, all urged acceptance and restoration of the text to its original form. The latter stressed greater efforts toward a dialogue with the Moslems, because, as he said, they were closer to us than the Jews. He also suggested that the declaration could be a fitting way to defend the memory of Pope Pius XII, which had been slandered because of his alleged failure to act vigorously enough during World War II in defending the Jews against the Nazis. After Bishop Descuffi had spoken, the Moderator, Cardinal Agagianian, called for a vote of cloture and the document was sent back to the Secretariat to be revised according to the sense of the debate.

Debate on the revised text of the schema on Divine Revelation was begun on September 30, 1964. Partial consideration of the original document at the First Session resulted in a crisis, causing Pope John to withdraw it from discussion and confide its revision to a mixed commission, consisting of members from the Theological Commission and Cardinal Bea's Secretariat for Unity. The present schema was completely rewritten and now represents a moderate position on many points, more satisfactory to modern biblical scholars and theologians than the older version which reflected the theological outlook of the minority only.

In a futile attempt to hold back the wheels of progress, the session's champion of lost causes, Bishop Franic, of Yugoslavia, demanded the right to make a summation of the minority position on Divine Revelation. Revealing once more a pitiful lack of understanding of the momentous mystery involved in the Church's reception, explanation and preservation of the Word of God as handed down by the apostles and disciples of Christ in the Scriptures, this facile, learned, but single-minded theologian appealed to every possible motive from honesty in ecumenism to his notion of traditional inerrancy to have the schema rejected—or at least his own antiquated concept of the relation between Scripture and Tradition accepted—by the Council. What is disturbing is to discover that men of this calibre, well trained in the arts of logic and technical thinking, widely read in theological literature and devoted to the constant search for religious truth through study and prayer, have deliberately cut themselves off from the obvious inspiration of the Holy Spirit at the present juncture in the Church's development. Mistaking a stubborn allusion to outmoded formulas and a misconception of the spiritual nature of Christ's teaching as theological consistency, they use every means possible to thwart the mind of the vast majority of the bishops who are giving witness to the mind of the Church now; what is worse, they do not hesitate to challenge the directives of two Popes, despite the fact that they are vociferous protagonists of papal supremacy.

What the new decree does is acknowledge that there is no

absolute manner of interpreting the Scriptures; that in each age the Church, under the inspiration of the Spirit and in keeping with the intellectual progress of mankind, can gain a more meaningful appreciation of the mysteries of divine revelation in relation to the facts of salvation, as they were achieved by Christ in His birth, death and resurrection. In the attempt to offset a divergent reading of the Scriptures by the 16th century reformers, the Fathers at Trent had insisted on the historical accuracy of the content of the sacred books and had attempted to explain the development of doctrine by appealing to Tradition as, for all practical purposes, a separate source of divine inspiration. The danger of this method had been recognized by a few of the scholars at Trent but was completely ignored owing to the polemical development of Catholic teaching during the next 300 years. Only when this matter came to a head at the First Session of the present Council were the entrenched minority in several Roman Congregations, and particularly the Holy Office, forced to so much as concede that a problem existed. Till then they had fiercely suppressed every effort of scholars to take an honest look at the problem and this despite the progressively more liberal documents of Pope Pius XII, beginning with *Divino Afflanto Spiritu* in 1943 and *Humani Generis* in 1951. The debate on this subject became so acute in the First Session that Pope John withdrew it from discussion, as we have said. Pope Paul decided to let it go over until the Third Session for final consideration, meanwhile engaging several mixed commissions in its revision. The architect of the new document was Archbishop Florit of Florence, who gave the majority report, explaining the committee work on the current text and stating unequivocally that the intent of the document was to deal with the essential fact of revelation, its nature, and its relation to the magisterium of the Church. It did not intend to settle any disputed theological points, but wanted to encourage the discussion of these matters rather than hamper or cut it off by false fears.

As usual, Cardinal Ruffini led the debate. He stated that the minority report expressed the constant teaching of the ordinary magisterium of the Church. He maintained that faith must be expressed mainly in intellectual concepts, and this was not done by the present text. It was precisely this point that Cardinals Doepfner and Meyer seized upon by way of lauding the document. "Faith should not be described in such a way as to make it too intellectualistic," said the Chicago prelate, "as this would be contrary to the spirit and general approach of St. Paul," as well as the Scripture authors generally. Here again fundamental disagreement on the basic approach to theological knowledge became apparent. The small minority continued to indulge in a sort of gnostic notion of their ability, by force of logic and a few philosophical axioms, to decipher not merely the meaning of Scripture but the historical process by which God must have revealed and transmitted revelation, using both Scripture and Tradition as separate and equal transmitters. This thesis has prevailed in scholastic circles since the 17th century as a counter-Protestant apologetic, but like the various attempts to reconcile impossibly irreconcilable historic statements in the Gospel, it has been forced out of business by modern research. The grave error which arch-conservatives make in this sphere is to consider the Church's doctrine compromised by their theories, which an indulgent magisterium has tolerated, whereas it should have branded their arrogant presumption with the charge of heresy as they have unhesitatingly done toward their opponents.

Cardinals Léger of Montreal and Landázuri Ricketts of Lima brought the full weight of modern research to bear on the notion of revelation, which is at the heart of the Christian religion, as well as at the center of the present attempt to reform the Church. In so far as the present schema tries to portray the genesis, reception and continuation of divine revelation in the historical perspective created by the Scripture witness to the Word of God, and the apostolic as well as primitive Christian tradition, it is a splendid document, and exhibits precisely what the function of the magisterium of the Church is, namely witnessing to the mind of Christ in a specific moment of history. Exaggerated claims to infallibility in dealing with revelation are both dangerous and unnecessary; they have not only cut the Church off from many of its proper brethren but have prevented the full appreciation of the Gospel message by many of its own members. Cardinal Landázuri-Ricketts called for a distinction between the Tradition that must be accepted by faith, and certain merely ecclesiastical or human elements in the life of the Church. Revelation is not merely a closed deposit but a living, dynamic reality.

Cardinal Browne rose to defend the position of the intransigent theologians, who he maintained had had a decisive role in handing down Tradition. Here, as a leading scholastic, he ran head on into the wall of divinely revealed fact. He quarreled with the text of the document which insists that revelation is contained in *deeds and words* because, said the Irish cardinal "words are prior as a means of expressing thought." Denying that "Tradition grows," he held that "Sacred Scripture is evolved in its expression, but not in its substantial content." Unconsciously the good cardinal revealed the fact that fundamentally he resembles the Platonists, whose concepts of ideas as the fundamental reality were rejected by early patristic theology in favor of the fact of God's existence, His providence in creating the world, and redemption of all of mankind through the salvific incarnation, death and resurrection of His Son, and the constitution of the Church with its guarantee of guidance by the Holy Spirit—all of which deeds are recorded as historical events in Holy Scripture. The cardinal also showed some irritation with the assertion that man can "experience" the religious value of faith through the witness of the Scripture, again basing his objection on the rigidly rational concept of psychology that led to the excesses committed in connection with the condemnation of Modernism. This scandal still haunts the "concept" theology of the old school.

The Armenian Patriarch Ignace Pierre XVI Batanian praised the schema but requested that norms of interpretation should be insisted on that would prevent "dangerous audacity" in Scripture study, while Bishop Kowalski of Poland asked for a condemnation of atheism in the text. Bishop Costantini of Sessa Aurunca, Italy, expressed doubts about the adequacy of the document's treatment of Tradition. But Archbishop Jaeger of Paderborn, Germany, took pains to meet the objections of Cardinals Ruffini and Browne by suggesting a clearer statement on the relation between divine revelation and the history of salvation. This could be done, he said, by introducing a parallel between the interior action of grace which follows the exterior preaching of God's Word in the Gospel and the activity of the Holy Spirit whose inspirational mission completes the mission of Christ. He quoted St. Thomas's teaching on the gift of wisdom in the *Summa Theologica* as a direct answer to Cardinal Browne's objection regarding the document's description of "the intimate experience of spiritual things" that follows from acceptance of the Gospel message.

Bishop Romero Menjibar, of Jaen, Spain, requested a strengthening of the salvational-history approach by an explicit linking of Moses and the Exodus of the Jewish people with the incarnation and the redemption; while Archbishop Shehan of Baltimore called for a clearer description of the part played by the human mind in receiving, interpreting, and transmitting divine revelation. Entering the problem carefully discussed by the late 2nd century theologian Clement of Alexandria and St. Augustine in the fifth century, he suggested that the passive sense of revelation was necessary to complete the theological and pastoral understanding of the Church's interpretation of God's Word, while Archbishop Vuccino, of France, called for more attention to the eastern approach to this problem, citing St. Athanasius as witness to the fact that revelation and apostolic tradition were identical. "From the beginning, the only source of the Church's preaching was her consciousness, formed by the Spirit independently of all written tradition. When tradition was put down in writing, only the apostolic tradition was expressed, and faith was put in the Scriptures because tradition was evident in them." In conclusion he asserted that the Church's right to call herself apostolic was based essentially on the fact that it possesses the whole apostolic Kerygma, that is, "the written or unwritten tradition is unfailingly preserved and infallibly interpreted in her with the assistance of the Holy Spirit."

Bishop Guano of Livorno, Italy, called for a more courageous assertion of the intimate relation between Scripture and Tradition, which embody all that the Church is, since inseparably they provide an encounter with Christ, and Archbishop Zoungrana of Ougadougou, Africa, said explicitly that "the very person of Jesus Christ is divine revelation"— the truth that conquered the ancient world, and was so much needed for the encounter with the existentially-conscious man of today. Despite the antiquated objections of the continual objector Bishop Compagnone, of Anagni, and Archbishop Ferro of Reggio Calabria, Italy, the remaining speakers showed general acceptance of the document and the discussion of the text as a whole was clotured after the debate on October 1.

During the session on Thursday, October 1, the text of the three chapters on Ecumenism were distributed and the following day the Fathers were asked to agree on a procedure for voting on this schema by paragraphs, beginning Monday, October 5. Likewise it was affirmed that when the Council came to discuss the schema on the Lay Apostolate and that on the Church in the Modern World, the pattern of a general debate on the whole of each document followed by a vote of acceptance or rejection would be resorted to, in accord with regular procedure. This had not been followed

in the discussion of the schemas on the Pastoral office of
Bishops or Divine Revelation because they had already been
debated in earlier sessions.

The debate on Chapters I and II of Divine Revelation began on Friday, October 2, and found a strong and determined majority in favor of the new approach to the Bible
achieved by contemporary biblical research and so hotly contested by the curial minority. The Dutch Bishop Van Dodewaard, of Haarlem, was joined by Archbishop Morcillo, of
Madrid, Bishop Rupp, of Monaco, and Archbishop Flahiff,
of Winnipeg, Canada, in supporting the position of Cardinals
Léger, Meyer and Landázuri-Ricketts, particularly by breaking away from the use of scholastic definitions in describing
the Tradition and magisterium of the Church residing in the
Pope and Bishops "built upon the foundation of the Prophets
and Apostles," according to the expression of St. Paul. Archbishop Beras, of Santo Domingo, utilized his intervention on
what seemed to be a return to old-fashioned notions of Tradition, to advertise the International Marian Congress being
organized in his archdiocese early in 1965. He was able to
employ this stratagem by announcing the theme of the Congress as "Mary in Sacred Scripture," and while most of the
prelates, including the Moderators, smiled in benevolent
toleration at this self-advertisement, it was not difficult to
trace the move to the Franciscan mariologist Father Balič,
one of Cardinal Ottaviani's henchmen, the organizer of the
Congress, who spent the summer of 1964 in the U.S.A. col-
lecting funds and voicing fierce opposition to the progressive
theology of the Council. At the same time rumors were
spread that Pope Paul was seriously considering making the
trip to Santo Domingo.

Toward 11:30 A.M., Bishop Van Dodewaard presented the
relatio on Chapters III to VI of the schema on Divine Revelation and stated that whereas the original text had concentrated attention on the so-called "founts of revelation" and
the "relationship between Scripture and Tradition," the new

text concentrates on the Sacred Writings themselves and their message. In so doing it was not being derelict in its duty but was actually avoiding a false problem which had needlessly divided the attention not only of the Council but of Christendom. The new emphasis allows for the validity of several modern theories and provides a reliable guide for understanding of the Word of God. The Old Testament (Chapter IV) is presented as the first part of the "History of Salvation" rather than merely as the story of the Chosen People; and the value of the witness offered by the Old Testament books is rightly centered not so much on their content as on the inspiration behind them. The section on the New Testament has been enlarged to include a consideration of all the books, while the special treatment of the historicity of the Gospels has been adapted from the Instruction of the Pontifical Biblical Commission issued on May 16, 1964. Finally, directives have been incorporated regarding the Scriptures as the source of the spiritual and theological life of the Church, and recommendations have been made for a cooperative effort, with our separated brethren, toward providing adequate vernacular translations, while the responsibilities and rights of Catholic exegetes and theologians are touched upon.

This latter point formed the basis of Cardinal Ruffini's intervention as soon as the new topic was thrown open to discussion under the moderatorship of Cardinal Doepfner. The Sicilian prelate blasted the "new freedom" allowed Scripture scholars and repeated his condemnation that the employment of literary forms in biblical exegesis was tantamount to admitting that the Church had not understood the Scriptures until modern times. In this respect, he was actually repeating his explicit criticism of Pope Pius XII's encyclical *Divino Afflante Spiritu,* on which he had been publicly challenged before the start of the Council.

Cardinal Koenig of Vienna delivering the last speech of the morning, courageously broached the central point of conflict between the two opposing conciliar sides, stating that

in keeping with the results of modern research in science and
natural history and particularly in Oriental studies, it must
be recognized that there are factual mistakes in both the Old
and New Testaments, which in no way interfere with either
divine inspiration or inerrancy. "Lest the authority of Scripture suffer, we must say sincerely and without fear that the
sacred writer's knowledge of historical matters was limited
according to the conditions of his time, and that God moved
him to write in keeping with his background and education.
In this way we see the complete condescension of the Divine
Word, making Himself conform in all things to human conditions, including the limitations of human speech." This
admission provoked the horror of the older school who felt
that every word, in both Testaments, was guaranteed by
divine infallibility, to the grave scandal of John Henry Newman, for one, when after his conversion in 1846, he consulted
the Roman theologian Fr. Perrone and was told that even a
detail such as the notion that "the dog wagged his tail" in the
book of Tobias had the stamp of divine authenticity upon it.
As one bishop remarked, Newman might have been spared
much trouble had he lived 100 years later. Now the book of
Tobias itself is no longer considered an historical account,
but rather an inspirational story.

The Council resumed business on Monday, October 5, as
Archbishop Martin, of Rouen, France, gave the *relatio* on
Chapter I of the schema on Ecumenism, in preparation for
the voting that would take place in the course of the morning's session.

Cardinal Meyer of Chicago began the discussion on Chapter III of Divine Revelation with the statement that while
the document contained excellent points, it failed to state
clearly or properly the nature of divine inspiration. It
seemed to consider inspiration confined to "the establishment of logical truths and to forming a series of propositions,
leading to the conclusion that its whole value consists in the
quality of inerrancy. The proper consideration of inspiration

should begin and end with the fact that it is "a personal communication to men of the Word of God which goes beyond merely manifesting concepts to another." The very idea of the Word of God means that some fact or object is being communicated by a Person speaking and looking for a response or reaction. As in the early Church, the proper manner of describing the Word of God as contained in Scripture, requires the acknowledgment that it is the heart of God that is revealed, not propositions; that it is not inerrancy that is guaranteed, but rather the means for *"educating and impelling to every good work,"* as St. Paul insists; finally, the reconciliation of inerrancy and inspiration must take into consideration human deficiencies and limitations as Cardinal Koenig pointed out. This speech, coming as the first of the day and from the Chicago cardinal, known as the Scripture scholar whose deep thought and calm objectivity have greatly impressed the Council, was listened to with rapt attention and greeted with applause.

It was followed by a similar speech by Cardinal Bea, who remarked that the schema's tone was in keeping with Pope John's desire for positive rather than condemnatory documents. He recommended a number of changes in both style and doctrine. Archbishop Weber, of Strasbourg, also a biblical scholar, described the different types of men whom God used to convey his message: Amos, the shepherd, Isaias, the noble, and Paul, formed in the Rabbinical schools. Yet unity of message and continuity of doctrine were guaranteed by the source of Divine inspiration. In interpreting the Bible, therefore, many factors must be employed including the context, Tradition, the analogy of faith, as well as the positive directions of the Church. He said that the recent Instruction of the Biblical Commission was intended to foster, not impede, biblical studies.

Bishop Simons, of Indore, India, stressed the fact that "we should distinguish between what God wished to say and what the sacred authors intended," since as is frequently evident,

there was a divergence between God's revelation in the Old
Testament which was directed toward the coming Redeemer,
but understood by the Jewish authors in a local setting. A
demurrer was offered by Bishop Gasbarri, of Grosseto, Italy,
who called for a ban on present-day exegesis that seemed
intent on emptying the Gospels of all historical meaning. He
cited the deliberately vague 1960 *monitum* of the Holy Office
on this matter, asserting that it could only be understood as
a condemnation of "modern exegetical techniques," for it
would be "foolish to think that the Holy Office was merely
dreaming." He was immediately contradicted by Bishop
Flores Martin, of Barbastro, Spain, who insisted that the
authors of the scriptural books should be called "true authors" who acted as "living instruments of God" and not as
automatons; while Bishop Maloney, of Louisville, Kentucky,
defended the use of "literary forms," citing Sts. Augustine
and Jerome as two early biblical scholars who understood
this process.

The Melkite Archbishop Edelby, of Edessa, put his finger
on the true weakness in the document by stating that the
timidity in dealing with Divine inspiration expressed in Article 12 was a leftover resulting from polemics with the Protestants in the post-Tridentine period. He called for a return
to the "intimate mystery of the Church" rejecting the too
juridical mentality in which both Protestant and Latin theology were enclosed. He described the Eastern attitude toward
Scripture as not a preoccupation with some written norm
but a liturgical and scriptural reality that captures the consecration of salvation history under the species of the written
word and is inseparable from the Eucharistic consecration in
which the Body of Christ is consumed. Tradition is thus the
Epiclesis or manifestation of the Holy Spirit in the salvation-
history of the world, without Whose presence Scripture remains a dead letter. Tradition is thus to be seen as essentially
liturgical, seen and lived in the Church through faith and
holiness. While Bishop Simons, of India, requested that the

"action of the Holy Spirit be extended to all who had a part in the editing of Gospels" conceding that the names given the authors need not be authentic, Bishop William Philbin, of Down and Connor, Ireland, the only Irishman to speak on the issue, expressed grave concern regarding the safeguarding of the historicity of the Gospels and deplored the justification of the employment of literary forms in exegesis, for all the world was determined, as an Irish proverb said, to prove that modern doubts about the validity of the term "the Isle of Saints and Scholars" were true, at least as far as the second category was concerned.

The debate on Revelation was closed on October 6, after ten more speakers had had their say, but not before Bishop Carli, of Segni, Italy, warned that "the Council will prove a great disappointment if it does not condemn the dangers threatening the Church from the *form-history* interpretation of the Scriptures," manifesting at once his lack of *rapport* with the mind of the Pope and the Church, as well as with modern biblical studies, regarding not merely the subject of Tradition but the nature of the Bible itself. While Bishop Cekada, of Yugoslavia, expressed doubts about certain aspects of the document, excusing himself as a simple pastor of souls, Abbot Butler, of Downside, England summed up the difficulties on both sides of the argument and attempted to allay the fears of the minority by assuring them that the historicity of divine revelation was not in jeopardy, rather the apologetic approach of previous Catholic biblical scholarship could now be supplemented by a wider and more factual consideration of the biblical witness to God's Word. "We do not want the childish comfort of averting our gaze from the truth, but a truly critical scholarship which will enable us to enter into dialogue with non-Catholic scholars."

The revision of the text proceeded satisfactorily during the remainder of the Session, but it was not possible to offer it for a final vote before the close. The schema has been held over until the Fourth Session. The revised version is regarded as even more satisfactory than the October version.

At the start of the Third Session, welcoming a group of Fathers from abroad, Pope Paul showed them a letter signed by some fourteen prelates, including cardinals of the Roman Curia and other Italian bishops. This letter asked that he remove the schema *De Ecclesia* from the Council's agenda, since in the minds of its signers it was replete with heresy. It was reported that Pope Paul pointed to one name, halfway down the list of signatures, and said, "This is the man responsible for this document. He unfortunately has neither the courtesy nor courage to acknowledge authorship."* When informed that the "remnant of Israel," as the small clique still opposing the Council's work of *aggiornamento* liked to think of itself, was praying for divine intervention, Pope Paul is reported to have remarked: "But the Holy Spirit has intervened. He inspired Pope John to summon the Council and He has given us the courage to carry out the directives of the divine will."

In a technical sense the doctrine of episcopal collegiality was the very core of Vatican Council II and, as the Pope said in his opening address, "will certainly be what distinguishes this solemn and historic synod in the memory of future ages." The doctrine meant that the bishops as successors of the Apostles form a college with the Pope as their head and share with him in the government of the Church. Never denied, this truth had tended to take a back seat, as it were, while emphasis was placed more and more on the Pope's authority. Even at the time when the papal primacy and infallibility were being defined at Vatican Council I in 1870

* It is possible that the document referred to by the Pope and another mentioned by Henri Fesquet were one and the same. The members of the Theological Commission each received a copy of a plea to the Pope opposing collegiality, signed by two Italian cardinals, one of whom was Cardinal Ruffini. The minority deserved commendation for its audacity and perseverance, if for nothing else. (Cf. *Le Monde,* October 9, 1964.)

it was realized by farsighted theologians and bishops that a corrective was needed, but plans had to be shelved because that Council was prorogued without finishing its business. Since then the conviction, amounting to a groundswell only in the last few years, has grown that the time was ripe for a definition, or at least a formal statement of collegiality. There is some slight plausibility in the charge of the minority that the doctrine was "immature" and not ripe for definition, to the extent that no doctrine, in modern times, or perhaps ever, had progressed in such a short time from a mere mooting of the point among theologians to formal definition —in the space of only a few years at most—but the doctrine was in no sense "new." The Church was merely returning to a more "primitive tradition." And the minority were at fault for not wanting to examine the claims of a thesis which they regarded on *a priori* grounds as being essentially dangerous and unpalatable. The doctrine has important implications with respect to church government in that it tends to promote respect for the ancient and vital principle of local autonomy, as well as the related principle of subsidiarity— that is, whatever can be done equally well by a lesser authority should not be undertaken by a higher authority. Its ecumenical potentialities are obvious.

This conviction was finally accepted by Archbishop Pietro Parente, Assessor of the Holy Office, who startled the Council Fathers with a turn-about that marked a critical moment in the history of Vatican Council II, when on the morning of September 21 he delivered the *relatio* on the amended text of Chapter III, dealing with collegiality. The speech of Archbishop Parente was not without its internal drama.

Before he gave the speech, Cardinal Tisserant announced that several of the *periti* and certain members of the Theological Commission had been accused of holding conferences and distributing literature in favor of collegiality against the conciliar rules. It turned out, however, that the complaint came from Spanish bishops who were being deluged by conservative pamphlets urging them to vote *against* collegiality, and the Cardinal President said nothing more of the matter. Then, by a decision of the Coordinating Commission, Bishop Franic, of Yugoslavia, also a member of the Theological Commission, was allowed to deliver a kind of "minority report" prior to Archbishop Parente's speech, summing up all the arguments of the minority against the doctrine of collegiality as expressed in the amended text of Chapter III, as well as the position opposing the sacramentality of episcopal consecration and the proposed restoration of a permanent diaconate. When Cardinal König rose next to present the positive, general introduction to the chapter, he made it clear that Bishop Franic's *relatio* was in no sense to be considered a real minority report, since the entire text had been approved by the full commission. It was rather allowed as a final courtesy extended to the minority. His Eminence then outlined the procedure which had been followed in revising the text and turned the rostrum over to Archbishop Parente.

The archbishop began by assuring the Fathers that he was not speaking as an official of the Holy Office but simply as a bishop. The very word *collegium,* he noted, had evoked no little terror (*non parvum terriculum* [sic!]) on the part of some prelates and theologians, who had immediately associated the idea with an attempt to strip the Roman Pontiff of his authentic jurisdiction. However, these fears were groundless and he advised the bishops to accept both the idea of collegiality and the amended text. It is known that Parente taught the doctrine as a professor of dogmatic theology at the Propaganda Fidei seminary in Rome some years ago, but when preparations for the present Council began he let himself be persuaded by zealots of papal supremacy, including the late Cardinal Tardini, Cardinals Ottaviani and Browne, and Archbishop Staffa of the Curia, that collegiality was "inopportune." This group acknowledged that while the theory of collegiality was theologically possible, it should not be admitted at the present time because of dangerous tendencies among many bishops and theologians toward decentralization of authority. In fact, they opposed Pope John's desire to have this doctrine discussed at the Council at all. Despite the fact that during its deliberations in the spring of 1964 the Theological Commission had approved the original text of the doctrine on collegiality (April 19, 1964) and had accepted the wishes of the majority of the Fathers as expressed in the vote of October 30, 1963 and their numerous petitions and suggested amendments, *nondum quies facta est*—peace was not yet achieved, Archbishop Parente observed. The contrast between Parente's and Franic's arguments was decisive. The impassioned Yugoslav prelate had given final voice to the juridical rationalizations that have hamstrung Latin theology during the last 300 years. By applying the axioms and concepts from Roman law, Aristotelian logic, and scholastic metaphysics to the mysteries of religion, they have reduced the doctrines of a supernatural faith to a series of logical propositions. To all of this Archbishop Parente bid a sharp and final *vale, valete*. "If there is difficulty in explaining the relation between the sacred powers of the pope and those exercised by the bishops," he said, "this is not to be wondered at *(mirum non est)*, since we are not dealing with a human society, but with the Church of Christ," a mystery, "that can only be elucidated by the theological vision of a St. Augustine and the early Church fathers, who adhered to the teaching of St. Paul concerning the Church as a mystical body, and thus came much closer to expressing the mind of Christ."

Finally, Bishop Henriquez Jimenez of Venezuela presented the *relatio* on the second half of the document dealing with priests and deacons and covering the main point at issue, namely the restoration of a married diaconate in those parts of the Church where it seemed called for.

Parente's historic discourse, coming from a prelate considered to be one of the leading conservatives during the Council's first two sessions, finally dissipated the pent-up fears and hesitations of numerous Anglo-Celtic and American bishops. When the voting began, it was not hard to predict the result on this central issue. The voting on Chapter III began on September 21 and continued through eight sessions. The articles of the text, nos. 18–29, were not voted on directly, but in the form of 39 propositions based on the essential points contained in them so that the Theological Commission would be facilitated in its work of revision. All the propositions were easily carried. Only those on the diaconate brought forth rather large negative votes, the final proposition, no. 39, on whether the diaconate could be conferred without any obligation to observe celibacy, not being carried at all. The key votes on collegiality resulted in only 328 negative votes at the most; this probably represented the full strength of the minority opposed to collegiality. The opposition was strongest against Proposition No. 8 (episcopal consecration confers full powers), Proposition No. 10 (pope and bishops form college), Proposition No. 11 (entrance to college through episcopal consecration), Proposition No. 13 (episcopal college is subject of full and supreme authority), Proposition No. 14 (power of binding and loosing given also to college of apostles), and Proposition No. 17 (exercise of collegial authority when pope approves or *accepts* collective action). Odd as it seems, the pattern of resistance had some hilarious results. Fifty bishops voted against the divine origin of the episcopate (No. 5), 44 voted against the episcopate as a sacrament (No. 6), 156 voted against the proposition that only bishops can confer episcopal consecration (No. 9). When it was announced that 90 bishops had voted against the supreme authority of the Pope (No. 12), the Council burst into laughter. Apparently some bishops had been instructed to vote again collegiality and did not know how to behave, voting simply negative throughout! Those voting *non placet* on these propositions were, by their own theology, at least material heretics. As one French bishop remarked, "So determined are the opposition, they are willing to risk heresy to prove their point!"

To make it possibe for those who might be opposed to the provisions restoring a permanent diaconate but were in favor of the part on collegiality, to vote favorably on Chapter III as a whole, the Moderators decided to divide the chapter into two sections and allow separate votes on Articles 18–23 and Articles 24–29. Normally all chapters are voted as a unit at this stage. The minority in the person of Bishop Carli immediately challenged the decision of the Moderators, who, in reply, at once called for a standing vote; their decision was overwhelmingly upheld. The large number of *placet iuxta modum* votes cast on September 30, 1964 on the two parts of Chapter III included some by the majority who wanted further changes made.*

Summary

September 23, 1964, Wednesday—86TH GENERAL CONGREGATION.
MASS: Cardinal Marella, preceded by procession in which Pope carried head of St. Andrew, sermon by Cardinal König of Vienna.
MODERATOR: Cardinal Suenens.
PRESENT: 2,254 Fathers.
ANNOUNCEMENTS: schedule of ceremonies in honor of St. Andrew.
PENDING BUSINESS: Schema on Pastoral Office of Bishops.
SPEAKERS: 1. Bishop Greco (Alexandria, Louisiana). 2. Bishop Gonzáles Moralejo (Auxiliary of Valencia, Spain).
NEW BUSINESS: Declaration on Religious Liberty.

* A record number of *modi* or amendments were submitted on the whole of Chapter III of *De Ecclesia*, totally 4,800 separate *modi*, of which 3,600 were concerned with collegiality and 1,200 with the diaconate. When voting *iuxta modum*, bishops are not restricted to submitting a single amendment but may offer as many as they wish. The Commission, therefore, had a formidable task ahead of it, sorting out and replying to all these suggestions. There was of course much overlapping. See p. 246. Cf. *Le Monde*, October 10, 1964.

SPEAKERS: *relator:* Bishop de Smedt (Bruges, Belgium). 3. Cardinal Ruffini (Palermo, Sicily). 4. Cardinal Quiroga y Palacios (Santiago de Compostela, Spain). 5. Cardinal Léger (Montreal, Canada). 6. Cardinal Cushing (Boston, Massachusetts). 7. Cardinal Bueno y Monreal (Seville, Spain). 8. Cardinal Meyer (Chicago, Illinois). 9. Cardinal Ritter (St. Louis, Missouri). 10. Cardinal Silva Henriquez (Santiago de Chile). 11. Cardinal Ottaviani (Curia). 12. Bishop Čekada (Skoplje, Yugoslavia).

VOTES: Chap. III of *De Ecclesia*

	Total	*Placet*	*Non placet*	Invalid
Art. 22	2,224	1,927	292	5(1)
Art. 22	2,254	1,943	307	4(1)
Art. 22	2,251	2,096	152	3
Art. 22	2,245	2,114	127	4
Art. 22	2,214	2,006	204	4(1)
Art. 23	2,220	2,163	56	1

September 24, 1964, Thursday—87TH GENERAL CONGREGATION.
MASS: Archbishop Cordeiro of Karachi, Pakistan.
MODERATOR: Cardinal Suenens.
PRESENT: 2,228 Fathers.
ANNOUNCEMENTS: deadlines for submitting summaries on Divine Revelation: Introd. and Chaps. I–II by tomorrow, Chap. III by Sept. 28, and Chaps. IV–VI by Sept. 30; votes on whole of Chaps. III, IV, V and VI of *De Ecclesia* will take place on Sept. 30 and *modi* should be ready.
PENDING BUSINESS: Declaration on Religious Liberty.
SPEAKERS: 1. Cardinal König (Vienna, Austria). 2. Cardinal Browne (Curia). 3. Archbishop Parente (Curia). 4. Archbishop Cantero Cuadrado (Zaragoza, Spain). 5. Bishop Abasolo y Lecue (Vijayapuram, India). 6. Archbishop Nicodemo (Bari, Italy). 7. Bishop López Ortiz (Tuy-Vigo, Spain). 8. Bishop de Castro Mayer (Campos, Brazil). 9. Bishop Canestri (Auxiliary of Rome, Italy). 10. Bishop Pohlschneider (Aachen, Germany). 11. Archbishop Lefebvre (Superior General of Holy Ghost Fathers). 12. Father Buckley (Superior General of Marists). 13. Bishop Primeau (Manchester, New Hampshire). 14. Bishop Nierman (Groningen, Holland). 15. Bishop Temiño Saiz (Orense, Spain). 16. Bishop Klepacz (Lódz, Poland). 17. Archbishop Dubois (Besançon, France). 18. Bishop Granados (Auxiliary of Toledo, Spain).
STANDING VOTE to close debate on Religious Liberty.

VOTES: Chap. III of *De Ecclesia*

	Total	*Placet*	*Non placet*	Invalid
Art. 23	2,226	2,162	64	—
Art. 23	2,228	2,205	23	—
Art. 23	2,226	2,147	77	2
Art. 24	2,225	2,189	35	1
Art. 24	2,221	2,177	43	1
Art. 25	2,203	2,152	51	—

September 25, 1964, Friday—88TH GENERAL CONGREGATION.
MASS: Archbishop Benni of Mossul, Iraq, Syro-Antiochene rite.
MODERATOR: Cardinal Suenens.
PRESENT: 2,198 Fathers.
ANNOUNCEMENTS: deadline for summaries on Apostolate of Laity now Oct. 2, for Schema 13 Oct. 5; Propositions were orginally to be voted without discussion, but Moderators have now decided to permit a brief discussion; *modi* may be submitted when these texts are voted point by point; deadlines for summaries on Propositions: Oriental Churches Oct. 10, Missions Oct. 11, Priests Oct. 12, Religious Oct. 13, Sacrament of Marriage Oct. 14, Preparation for Priesthood Oct. 15, and Catholic Schools Oct. 16.
PENDING BUSINESS: Declaration on Religious Liberty.
SPEAKERS: 1. Cardinal Roberti (Curia). 2. Archbishop Hurley (Durban, South Africa). 3. Bishop Cibrián Fernández (Bolivia). 4. Archbishop Melendro (Anking, China). 5. Archbishop Wojtyla (Kraków, Poland). 6. Archbishop Garrone (Toulouse, France). 7. Bishop Hoa Nguyen-van-Hien (Dalat, Vietnam). 8. Archbishop Alter (Cincinnati, Ohio). 9. Father Fernández (Master General of Dominicans). 10. Bishop Lucey (Cork and Ross, Ireland). 11. Bishop Colombo (Italy). Bishops still on list when Moderator cut off discussion by standing vote to allow Cardinal Bea's *relatio* today: Bishop Añoveros Ataún (Cadiz y Ceuta, Spain), Archbishop O'Boyle (Washington, D.C.), Bishop Dwyer (Leeds, England), Archbishop D'Souza (Bhopal, India), Bishop del Campo y de la Barcena (Calahorra, Spain), Archbishop Shehan (Baltimore, Maryland), Bishop Carberry (Lafayette, Indiana), Archbishop de Provenchères (Aix, France), Bishop Ona de Echave (Lugo, Spain), Bishop Flores Martin (Barbastro, Spain), Bishop Malanchuk (France), Abbot Prou (France), Bishop Hannan (Auxiliary of Washington, D.C.), Bishop Maloney (Auxiliary of Louisville, Kentucky), Bishop Wright (Pittsburgh, Pa.).
NEW BUSINESS: Declaration on the Jews. *Relator:* Cardinal Bea.
STANDING VOTE to close debate on Religious Liberty.

votes: Chap. III of *De Ecclesia*

	Total	Placet	Non placet	Invalid
Art. 25	2,198	2,134	63	1
Art. 25	2,192	2,159	32	1
Art. 25	2,187	2,140	46	1
Art. 25	2,187	2,139	46	2
Art. 25	2,180	2,155	25	—
Art. 26	2,162	2,139	21	2

*September 28, 1964, Monday—*89TH GENERAL CONGREGATION.
MASS: Bishop Tomášek of Czechoslovakia.
MODERATOR: Cardinal Agagianian.
PRESENT: 2,176 Fathers.
ANNOUNCEMENTS: Chap. III of *De Ecclesia* will be voted as a whole on Wednesday in two parts, at request of Theological Commission; *modi* must be presented individually, not collectively; explanation of tomorrow's votes on diaconate.
PENDING BUSINESS: Declaration on Religious Liberty.
SPEAKERS: 1. Archbishop Heenan (Westminster, England). 2. Bishop Ddungu (Masaka, Uganda). 3. Bishop Wright (Pittsburgh, Pa.). 4. Archbishop Zoa (Yaoundé, Cameroons).
NEW BUSINESS: Declaration on the Jews.
SPEAKERS: 5. Cardinal Liénart (Lille, France). 6. Cardinal Tappouni (Syrian Patriarch of Antioch). 7. Cardinal Frings (Cologne, Germany). 8. Cardinal Ruffini (Palermo, Sicily). 9. Cardinal Lercaro (Bologna, Italy). 10. Cardinal Léger (Montreal, Canada). 11. Cardinal Cushing (Boston, Mass.). 12. Cardinal König (Vienna, Austria). 13. Cardinal Meyer (Chicago, Ill.). 14. Cardinal Ritter (St. Louis, Missouri). 15. Archbishop Jaeger (Paderborn, Germany). 16. Archbishop Pocock (Coadjutor of Toronto, Canada). 17. Bishop Nierman (Groningen, Holland). 18. Bishop Daem (Antwerp, Belgium).

votes: Chap. III of *De Ecclesia*

	Total	Placet	Non placet	Invalid
Art. 27	2,176	2,088	86	2
Art. 27	2,169	2,155	14	—
Art. 28	2,164	2,125	38	1
Art. 28	2,168	2,157	11	—
Art. 29	2,152	2,055	94	3
Art. 29	2,148	1,903	242	3

September 29, 1964, Tuesday—90TH GENERAL CONGREGATION.
MASS: Archbishop Amissah of Cape Coast, Ghana.
MODERATOR: Cardinal Agagianian.
PRESENT: 2,229 Fathers.

ANNOUNCEMENTS: *modi* can be submitted only individually, and those submitted tomorrow will be taken into account by Commission even though approval by ⅔ majority does not require this; approval of text by general congregation does not mean conciliar approval; booklet on Cardinal Marella's Secretariat for Non-Christians will be distributed at the door.

PENDING BUSINESS: Declaration on the Jews.

SPEAKERS: 1. Cardinal Bueno y Monreal (Seville, Spain). 2. Archbishop Seper (Zagreb, Yugoslavia). 3. Bishop Plumey (Garoua, Cameroons). 4. Bishop Méndez Arceo (Cuernavaca, Mexico). 5. Bishop Satoshi Nagae (Urawa, Japan). 6. Bishop Nowicki (Gdansk, Poland). 7. Bishop Hoa Nguyen-van-Hien (Dalat, Vietnam). 8. Archbishop Elchinger (Coadjutor of Strasbourg, France). 9. Bishop Leven (Auxiliary of San Antonio, Texas). 10. Bishop Stein (Auxiliary of Trier, Germany). 11. Bishop Añoveros Ataún (Cadiz y Ceuta, Spain). 12. Archbishop Heenan (Westminster, England). 13. Archbishop O'Boyle (Washington, D.C.). 14. Bishop Sfair (Ordinary in Rome for Maronites). 15. Archbishop Parecattil (Ernakulam, India). 16. Archbishop Shehan (Baltimore, Maryland, who renounced his right to speak.) 17. Archbishop Attipetty (Verapoly, India). 18. Bishop Lamont (Umtali, Southern Rhodesia). 19. Bishop Podestà (Avellaneda, Argentina). 20. Archbishop Tawil (Syria). 21. Archbishop Descuffi (Smyrna, Turkey). Debate on Declaration closed by Moderator.

VOTES: Chap. III of *De Ecclesia*

	Total	*Placet*	*Non placet*	Invalid
Art. 29	2,228	1,523	702	3
Art. 29	2,229	1,598	629	2
Art. 29	2,211	839	1,364	8(2)

September 30, 1964, Wednesday—91ST GENERAL CONGREGATION.
MASS: Bishop Rodríguez Rozas of Pinar del Rio, Cuba.
MODERATOR: Cardinal Lercaro.
PRESENT: 2,242 Fathers.

ANNOUNCEMENTS: distribution of booklet containing *Adnexa* to Schema 13, which will not be discussed; the Eucharistic Congress in Bombay will begin on Nov. 28th, as planned; there will be a preliminary standing vote on whether there will be two ballots on Chap. III of *De Ecclesia* as a whole; *modi* must be submitted with the ballot, however if received by tomorrow they will be accepted, but not later.

PENDING BUSINESS: Declaration on the Jews.

SPEAKER (on behalf of at least 70 Fathers): 1. Bishop Gahamanyi (Butare, Ruanda).

NEW BUSINESS: Schema on Divine Revelation, Introd. Chaps. I–II.

SPEAKERS: *Relatores:* Bishop Franic (minority) and Archbishop Florit (majority). 2. Cardinal Ruffini (Palermo, Sicily). 3. Cardinal Döpfner (Munich, Germany). 4. Cardinal Meyer (Chicago, Ill.).

VOTES: Chap. III of *De Ecclesia* as a whole

	Total	Placet	Non placet	Placet iuxta modum	Invalid
Art. 18-23	2,242	1,624	42	572	4
Art. 24-29	2,240	1,704	53	481	2

VOTES: Chaps. IV, V and VI of *De Ecclesia*

Also, whether matter on Religious should form separate chapter. *Relator* for Ch. IV: Bishop Wright. *Relator* for Chaps. V and VI: Abbot Gut.

	Total	Placet	Non placet	Placet iuxta modum	Invalid
Chap. IV	2,236	2,152	8	76	
Religious separate	2,210	1,505	698	–	7(4)
Chap. V	2,177	1,856	17	302	2
Chap. VI	2,189	1,736	12	438	3

October 1, 1964, Thursday—92ND GENERAL CONGREGATION.

MASS: Bishop Campelli of Cagli and Pergola, Italy.

MODERATOR: Cardinal Lercaro.

PRESENT: 2,169 Fathers.

ANNOUNCEMENTS: statement about *Adnexa* to Schema 13 being merely a private document, later modified by SG, with admission that they were a conciliar document but would not be formally discussed; voting procedure on Ecumenism will be proposed tomorrow.

PENDING BUSINESS: Schema on Divine Revelation, Introd., Chaps. I–II.

SPEAKERS: 1. Cardinal Léger (Montreal, Canada). 2. Cardinal Landázuri Ricketts (Lima, Peru). 3. Cardinal Browne (Curia). 4. Patriarch Ignace Pierre XVI Batanian (Lebanon). 5. Bishop Kowalski (Chelmo, Poland). 6. Bishop Costantini (Sessa Aurunca, Italy). 7. Archbishop Jaeger (Paderborn, Germany). 8. Bishop Romero Menjibar (Jaen, Spain). 9. Archbishop Shehan (Baltimore, Maryland). 10. Archbishop Vuccino (France). 11. Bishop Reuss (Auxiliary of Mainz, Germany). 12. Bishop Compagnone (Anagni, Italy). 13. Archbishop Ferro (Reggio Calabria, Italy). 14. Bishop Guano (Livorno, Italy). 15. Bishop Wilczynski (Poland). 16. Archbishop Zoungrana (Ouagadougou, Upper Volta). 17. Bishop Arattukulam (Alleppey, India). 18. Archbishop Fares (Catanzaro and Squillace, Italy). 19. Archbishop Attipetty (Verapoly, India). 20. Bishop Rougé (Nîmes, France).

VOTES: none.

October 2, 1964, Friday—93RD GENERAL CONGREGATION.

MASS: Bishop Farren of Derry, Ireland.

MODERATOR: Cardinals Lercaro and Döpfner.

PRESENT: 2,119 Fathers.

ANNOUNCEMENTS: plan for voting on Ecumenism in 14 ballots; schedule of votes on Ecumenism beginning Monday; usual procedure of general discussion and vote of acceptance for Apostolate of Laity and Schema 13, to be followed by detailed debate on chapters, if favorable.

PENDING BUSINESS: Schema on Divine Revelation, Chaps. I–II.

SPEAKERS: 1. Bishop van Dodewaard (Haarlem, Holland). 2. Bishop Morcillo Gonzales (Madrid, Spain). 3. Archbishop Beras (Santo Domingo, Dominican Republic). 4. Bishop de Castro y Silva (Auxiliary of Vila Real, Portugal). 5. Bishop Temiño Saiz (Orense, Spain). 6. Bishop Argaya Goicoechea (Mondoñedo-Ferrol, Spain). 7. Archbishop Nicodemo (Bari, Italy). 8. Bishop Alba Palacios (Tehuantepec, Mexico). 9. Bishop Rupp (Monaco). 10. Bishop García Martínez (Spain). 11. Archbishop Baldassari (Ravenna and Cervia, Italy). 12. Father Rubio (Prior General of the Augustinians). 13. Dom Butler (Superior of English Benedictines). 14. Archbishop Calabria (Benevento, Italy). 15. Archbishop Marty (Rheims, France). 16. Archbishop Flahiff (Winnepeg, Canada).

NEW BUSINESS: Schema on Divine Revelation, Chaps. III–VI.

SPEAKERS: *Relator:* Bishop van Dodewaard. 17. Cardinal Ruffini (Palermo, Sicily). 18. Cardinal König (Vienna, Austria). STANDING VOTE on voting procedure for Schema on Ecumenism.

October 5, 1964, Monday—94TH GENERAL CONGREGATION.
MASS: Archbishop McKeefry of Wellington, New Zealand.
MODERATOR: Cardinal Döpfner.
PRESENT:2,112 Fathers.
ANNOUNCEMENTS: death of Father Janssens, S. J., General of the Jesuits.
PENDING BUSINESS: Schema on Divine Revelation, Chaps. III–VI.*
SPEAKERS: 1. Cardinal Meyer (Chicago, Ill.). 2. Cardinal Bea (Curia). 3. Archbishop Weber (Strasbourg, France). 4. Bishop Simons (Indore, India). 5. Bishop Gasbarri (Italy). 6. Bishop Flores Martin (Barbastro, Spain). 7. Bishop Maloney (Auxiliary of Louisville, Ky.). 8. Archbishop Morcillo Gonzales (Madrid, Spain). 9. Archbishop Edelby (Syria). 10. Bishop Schick (Auxiliary of Fulda, Germany). 11. Archbishop Garcia y Garcia de Castro (Granada, Spain). 12. Bishop Philbin (Down and Connor, Ireland). 13. Bishop Heuschen (Auxiliary of Liège, Belgium). 14. Archbishop Cordeiro (Karachi, Pakistan). 15. Bishop del Rosario (Malolos, Philippines).

VOTES: Schema on Ecumenism, Chap. I
Relator: Archbishop Martin (Rouen, France).

	Total	*Placet*	*Non placet*	Invalid
Art. 1	2,111	2,094	16	1
Art. 2	2,112	2,081	30	1
Art. 3	2,110	2,051	57	2
Art. 4	2,107	2,056	50	1

October 6, 1964, Tuesday—95TH GENERAL CONGREGATION.
MASS: Archbishop Santos of Tegucigalpa, Honduras.
MODERATOR: Cardinal Döpfner.
PRESENT: 2,161 Fathers.
ANNOUNCEMENTS: a certain number of parish priests have been invited to be present at the Council.
PENDING BUSINESS: Schema on Divine Revelation, Chaps. III–VI.
SPEAKERS: 1. Archbishop Fares (Catanzaro-Squillace, Italy). 2. Bishop Carli (Segni, Italy). 3. Bishop Caminada (Ferentino,

---

* According to announcement on Sept. 24, discussion was to take place in three stages, but speakers today began to deal with all remaining chapters.

Italy). 4. Bishop Barrachina Estevan (Orihuela-Alicante, Spain). 5. Bishop Čekada (Skoplje, Yugoslavia). 6. Bishop Volk (Mainz, Germany). 7. Father Ferreira (Portuguese Guinea). 8. Bishop Boillon (Verdun, France). 9. Archbishop Maccari (Mondovi, Italy). 10. Dom Butler (Superior of English Benedictines). Following in name of at least 70 Fathers: 11. Bishop Martínez González (Zamora, Spain). 12. Archbishop Muñoz Duque (Nueva Pamplona, Colombia). 13. Bishop González Arbeláez (Colombia).

NEW BUSINESS: Schema on Apostolate of Laity.
SPEAKERS: *Relator:* Cardinal Cento.

VOTES: Schema on Ecumenism, Chap. I as whole, and Chap. II
Relator for Chap. II: Bishop Helmsing.

	Total	Placet	Non placet	Placet iuxta modum	Invalid
Chap. I as whole	2,166	1,926	30	209	1
Art. 5-6	2,166	2,120	46		
Art. 7	2,168	2,076	92		
Art 8	2,166	1,872	292		2
Art. 9-12	2,161	2,099	62		

III

The October Crisis;
Debates on Apostolate of the Laity,
Priestly Life and Ministry,
Eastern Rite Churches

✠

DURING THE FIRST THREE WEEKS of the Third Session, a wave of concern swept through the basilica corridors almost every time Archbishop Felici rose to make announcements. His penchant for framing almost every statement in such a way as to favor the conservative minority was galling to the majority of the prelates, and even some conservatively-inclined bishops began to suspect his motives. For example his repetition of the formula on how to vote *non placet* when explaining the proposition on the married diaconate, and his frequent interpolations about submitting *modi* when describing the propositions on collegiality, were regarded as going far beyond the call of duty. It was clear that the minority had a spokesman in an important position to steer the Council to their advantage.

Having been outmaneuvered and outvoted on collegiality, the same minority now concentrated its efforts on sidetracking or hampering the revision of the Declarations on Religious Liberty and the Jews, with a view to preventing a final vote, if possible, and eventually burying both. In their next move, they overreached themselves. Their maneuver gave rise to the phrase, *magno cum dolore,* with which historians may accurately characterize the Third Session. The background of their move was this: Council rules provide that texts presented for discussion by a commission ordinarily remain within the competence of that commission right through until final promulgation. Nevertheless, at a meeting of the conservatively-dominated Coordinating Commission on Wednesday, October 7, under the presidency of Secretary of State Cardinal Cicognani, the channel through whom most of the minority intrigues were mounted, it was decided to take action regarding the two declarations. With regard to the text of the R.L. document, the suggestion had previously been made apparently in the presence of the Pope that it should be given to a new mixed commission charged with responsibility for working out its theological basis. Accordingly, Secretary General Felici, armed only with the authority of Cicognani, and without the knowledge of other members of the Coordinating Commission, including the council Moderators, it seems, proceeded to draft two letters to Cardinal Bea. In his letter regarding the Jewish Declaration, Felici appealed to a decision of the Coordinating Commission that this document be turned over to a subcommittee of the Theological Commission for incorporation in the schema on the Church. In the letter on Religious Liberty, on the other hand, the Secretary General referred to "a desire of the Holy Father that the text be reconsidered and reworked" by a new special mixed commission and then proceeded to appoint the new commission himself including, along with Bishop Colombo (the Pope's Theological adviser), a number of prelates noted for their opposition to the very idea of religious liberty

(Cardinal Browne, Archbishop Lefebvre, Father Fernandez, O.P.). Word of the latter names caused the greatest concern, and this ultimately led to the discovery of the whole "plot." News circulated that the decision to minimize the text on the Jews had been communicated to the five Oriental patriarchs in a meeting in the office of Cardinal Cicognani, on Thursday or Friday, October 8 or 9, at which they were informed that, because of "political and diplomatic" complications, it had been decided to divide the Jewish Declaration into three parts, incorporating the different sections in the schema *De Ecclesia,* Schema 13 and *De Oecumenismo.**

On Friday evening, October 9, and during the next morning indignant phone calls from Bea's Secretariat informed the stunned bishops and *periti* of the letters and warned them that a slick move was afoot to defy the authority of the bishops and tamper with the rules of the Council. Under those rules only the four Moderators or the Pope could reassign conciliar documents.** Since the Moderators had taken no action, it became imperative to know the precise degree, if any, to which Pope Paul had been involved in Felici's move. Bea accordingly confronted the archbishop and demanded to know whether the letters had come from the Pope. When Felici said, "No, but that is what the Pope means," Bea replied: "Well, I cannot accept that as final," and proceeded to appeal directly to the Pope, from whom he learned that there had indeed been talk about a mixed commission, but that nothing definite had been decided about names. (Fortunately the Theological Commission was not too keen on having the Jewish Declaration foisted on it, because this would have upset the balance of the text on the Church, the revision of which was proceeding smoothly.)

The majority leaders now understood the importance of mounting a counteroffensive of their own immediately. On Sunday evening, October 11, a group met in the residence of

---

* *Il Messaggero,* October 15, 1964.
** *Orientierung,* October 31, 1964.

Cardinal Frings, including Cardinals Alfrink, Doepfner, Koenig, Léger, Lefebvre, Liénart, Landázuri-Ricketts, Meyer and Ritter, some fourteen in all.* Though Cardinal Suenens had returned in haste from Brussels when he learned what was happening, he could not be present; however, both he and Cardinal Lercaro, who was also unable to attend, gave this group their support. The petition they addressed to Pope Paul is interesting for its firmness of tone and for the fact that it does not hesitate to deplore the "appearance of a violation of the rules of the Council." Starting with the famous phrase, *magno cum dolore,* the letter went as follows:**

Holy Father:
 With great sorrow we have learned that the declaration on religious liberty, although in accord with the desire of the great majority of the Fathers, is to be entrusted to a certain mixed committee . . . three of whom appear to be opposed to the orientation of the Council in this matter.
 This news is for us a source of extreme anxiety and very disquieting. Countless men throughout the world know that this declaration has already been prepared, and they also know the sense in which it has been drafted. In such an important matter, any appearance of a violation of the rules of the Council, and its freedom, would be extremely prejudicial to the whole Church in the light of world opinion.
 Impelled by this anxiety, we ask Your Holiness with great insistence that the declaration be returned to the normal procedure of the Council and dealt with according to the existing rules, so that there may not result from it great evils for the whole People of God. However, if Your Holiness feels that a mixed committee is necessary, in our humble opinion it should be formed from

---

* The letter which resulted is said to have been signed by 17 cardinals: Frings, Alfrink, Doepfner, Koenig, Meyer, Ritter, Léger, Lefebvre, Richaud, Liénart, Silva Henriquez, Landázuri-Ricketts, Quintero, Suenens, Rugambwa, probably Lercaro, and a seventeenth cardinal whose name is unknown. Cardinal Tisserant may have had some knowledge of, or something to do with, Archbishop Felici's letters to Cardinal Bea. Cf. *Le Monde,* October 17, 1964.
** Text disclosed by *Le Monde,* October 17, 1964, through an indiscretion on the part of one of the cardinal signers.

the conciliar commissions, as provided in Article 58, Paragraph 2, of the rules.

The letter, with the seventeen signatures, was taken to the Pope by Cardinal Frings, apparently Monday morning.* The Pope is said to have been much disturbed by the affair, but it was not made clear whether the letter or the Secretary General's maneuver caused the greater distress. Not only was Felici's plan to announce the composition of the mixed committee at the Council the next morning nipped in the bud by this quick action on the cardinals' part, but the final suggestion in their letter was adopted by way of compromise. The Pope assured Cardinal Frings (Tuesday) that both the Declarations on the Jews and Religious Liberty would remain under the jurisdiction of Cardinal Bea's Secretariat—the important thing—but that the latter would be "examined" by a committee made up in accordance with the Council's rules. The rules, and an important principle, were thus upheld.

On October 16, the Pope directed Cardinal Cicognani to write a letter to Cardinal Bea, conveyed to the latter by the same Archbishop Felici, and also a letter to Cardinal Ottaviani, asking them each to appoint two members of their respective commissions to form a joint mixed commission to consider ways in which the text on Religious Liberty could be improved. The Pope then chose five from among these twenty members, adding five names on his own, to form a consultative commission to review the text on Religious Liberty. The name of Archbishop Lefebvre, Superior General of the Holy Ghost Fathers, did not appear on the list; it did contain the names of Cardinal Browne, Bishop Pelletier of Trois-Rivières, Canada, Archbishop Parente, Bishop Colombo, etc.

The two essential differences between the old arrangement and the new were: 1. the declaration on Religious Liberty remained under the jurisdiction of the Secretariat for Unity, and the new commission was merely to make suggestions;

---

* Monday, not Sunday, according to the Abbé Laurentin.

2. the list of twenty members which served as a basis for the mixed commission was drawn up by the presidents of the interested conciliar commissions. In this way the stipulations of Article 58 of the rules were fully respected.

No decision was taken regarding the ultimate fate of the Declaration on the Jews, which was treated as a kind of theological football tossed back and forth behind the scenes, but never actually leaving the jurisdiction of the Secretariat. At the final business meeting of the session, on November 20, it was presented for a vote as an appendix to *De Ecclesia*. The text on Religious Liberty, on the other hand, was presented as a separate *"Schema* of the Declaration on Religious Liberty."

Another principle, freedom of the press, was grossly violated in connection with these maneuvers, however. News about the cardinals' letter was given to the world in a release by the press officer of the Latin American Documentation Center, on Monday, October 12 (the text was disclosed later in the week by *Le Monde*). Angered by these reports of maneuvers involving himself, Archbishop Felici ordered Archbishop O'Connor, formerly rector of the North American College in Rome and principal architect of the heavily criticized decree on Communications Media issued by the Council in 1963, to investigate the "unlawful publication of conciliar documents" and to prepare a statement for the press. When this statement appeared in *L'Osservatore Romano*,* the following sentences caused a furor among journalists in Rome: "On the basis of deplorable and unusually one-sided indiscretions, certain press organs have indulged in a series of conclusions without any basis in fact, and referring to non-existent maneuvers aimed at preventing the proper progress of the Council's work. The [Press] Commission condemns this method of providing information, a method in conflict with the truth, involving an injustice toward individuals and organs connected with the Council." Two days later the

* *L'Osservatore Romano,* October 23, 1964.

French journalist, Henri Fesquet, challenged the veracity of this statement in his newspaper *Le Monde*. On the same day, following a press conference by Bishop Wright of Pittsburgh, he had a lively personal confrontation with Archbishop O'Connor and the latter's press officer, Monsignor Fausto Vallainc. M. Fesquet stated for all the newsmen to hear, and emphasizing his remarks with sweeping gestures, that he considered Archbishop O'Connor's communiqué so "improbable" that he had asked several bishops, members of the Press Commission, whether they concurred in the published statement. Since they had assured him that they had not even seen this communiqué, the inference was that the wording was Archbishop Felici's. While Monsignor Vallainc offered the lame explanation that Archbishop O'Connor had acted on his own "but in the sense of" the whole Press Commission, the American archbishop turned red in the face and said nothing. It is said that Archbishop O'Connor is being considered to head a new Vatican press office after the end of the Council. Later, in *Le Monde*, Fesquet made an impressive statement about the great chasm existing between Truth, the central concern of an ecumenical Council, and the utterances of curial officials, when their maneuvers are exposed to the press. This contrast was also the theme of an audacious conference given here two weeks earlier by Father Hans Kueng, the German theologian. After American journalists protested against the aspersions of the Press Commission with regard to their professional integrity, the Commission issued a second communiqué, denying any such intention but retracting absolutely nothing and incidentally expressing renewed confidence in its president, Archbishop O'Connor, and its secretary, Monsignor Vallainc.

About midway during the Third Session, as the Council was entering its Fourth Week, the question arose whether it would be possible to bring the Council to a close in 1964 or whether a Fourth Session would be necessary. The prob-

lem was debated at a meeting of the Coordinating Commission on October 7. There may also have been some disagreement between members of the Commission and the
Moderators, or between the Moderators themselves, about the
proper course to follow. A feeling of euphoria had been generated by the rapid progress being made in the debates, and
it did not seem unreasonable to suppose that if the commissions buckled down and produced revised texts in time,
everything could be wound up by the end of November.
But the reasoning was wholly unrealistic. The debate on
the Apostolate of the Laity and other documents would
soon show how much work remained to be done. The minority did their best to propagate the opinion that the Third
Session could be the last, but to no avail. Various meetings
of the national hierarchies were held to decide whether to
petition for a Fourth Session or not. The English bishops
were in favor of doing so, while the Canadian bishops voted
to end the Council in 1964. The American bishops were
divided: Archbishop Krol argued in favor of seeking an end
with the Third Session, but a majority, under the leadership
of Cardinal Meyer, was mustered on behalf of a Fourth
Session. Most of the other hierarchies were of the same mind.
Cardinal Doepfner, it is said, endeavored to persuade the
German bishops to change their minds about a Fourth Session, but without success. It was the rejection of the so-called
"Doepfner Plan"—of reducing many of the remaining
schemata to a series of propositions, ordered in January 1964
by the Coordinating Commission—that tilted the scales in
favor of a prolongation of the Council, and incidentally saved
certain highly important documents from oblivion.

Consideration of the schema on the Apostolate of the Laity
which the Council took up on Wednesday, October 7, and
debated for five days, marked a turning point in the Council
in more than one sense. It was the first time, incredibly, that
official attention had been given by the Church to the corpo-

rate function of the laity as forming an integral part of the People of God. Canon law defines a layman as one "who is not a cleric," and it is well to remember that the general clericalist Italian attitude toward the layman is *"prega, paga, e zita"* (pray, pay, and shut up). As one bishop pointed out, laymen constitute over 99% of the fatihful and it was therefore high time that some consideration was given to them. Cardinal Suenens was in the chair as Moderator.

The schema was introduced by Cardinal Cento, as chairman of the conciliar Commission on the Apostolate of the Laity, who apparently assumed that the text he was presenting would be accorded a benevolent treatment and then accepted without much discussion. To his amazement, following the somewhat less sanguine *relatio* by Bishop Hengsbach, of Essen, Germany, a member of the commission, one speaker after another rose to condemn it. The document suffered from two fundamental defects: though it was supposed to deal with the laity, practically no layman had been consulted about it until the eleventh hour; and the material was badly arranged. The reason for the latter defect in this case is that while the Commission had resisted the order of the Coordinating Commission in January 1964 to reduce the existing schema to a set of propositions, it was deprived of some of the essential parts of its text: the theological portion was incorporated into *De Ecclesia,* while Schema 13 received the part about lay activity in the modern world. The result was a document that was bound to be a great disappointment to the laity, according to Bishop De Roo of Victoria, Canada, because it sidestepped any real discussion of their character or the spirit of their vocation.

The lack of theological perspective and general formlessness were the themes of many interventions. Cardinal Ritter, in a blast, noted that it suffered from three basic defects: clericalism, juridicism, and favoritism. By the latter he meant that it tended to favor Catholic Action too much at the expense of other forms of Catholic lay activity, as we shall see below. He proposed a new plan: the document should speak first of the importance of the apostolate in the life of the Church and then go on to distinguish various forms, not in accordance with their relations with the hierarchy, as the present text did, but according to their specific ends, finally dealing with holiness and the spirituality of the laity. Bishop Laszlo, of Eisenstadt, Austria, brought smiles when he declared that he had looked up the word "layman" in an old theological dictionary and found the directive, "see clergy." The schema lacked "punch," said Bishop Leven, auxiliary of San Antonio, pronouncing the word in English because there was no Latin equivalent. The lay apostolate should be inspired by a spirit of dialogue. There could be no dialogue when a bishop spoke to the laity as he did to his doctor or his housekeeper. Every bishop should have a lay "senate" consisting of laymen on whom he could call for advice and to explain to him the desires and wishes of the laity. A dialogue of this kind was really called for today, especially by thinking people. It was a "sign of the times." We must not stifle the charisms by which the Holy Spirit acts through the laity. A similar idea was suggested by Archbishop Seper, of Zagreb, Yugoslavia, who called for weekly meetings of laymen representing each parish in every diocese to discuss current problems. In this connection several of the Eastern-rite prelates noted that the cooperation of the laity was much more of an assured thing in the East than in the West, which tended to overemphasize the juridical (e.g. Father Kabbouchi and Archbishop Ziadé). The apostolate must be a group-affair, quasi-collegial, said Bishop Bettazzi, auxiliary of Bologna, because of the nature of the Church as a mystical body, not because of purely utilitarian reasons.

The theme that the apostolate must be a dialogue was well brought out by Archbishop Duval, of Algiers who focused his attention not so much on internal relations, as on the impact which the Church could be expected to make on those outside, for example on the Moslems. He said that it was important not to limit the boundaries too much. The Church must not be limited by visible frontiers. There were worthwhile values among other religions and other peoples. Christians can give much, but they can also receive much. Bishop Caillot, of Evreux, France, also wanted a more open attitude toward the role of laymen among non-believers, and noted that the ordinary daily life of the layman constituted the foundation on which the Gospel was built. A broadening of the concept of the lay apostolate was also the theme of the speeches by Archbishop Veuillot, Bishop McGrath, and Bishop Charbonneau, who agreed that the definition of the apostolate in the schema was too hidebound and conventional.

In this connection, a number of speakers pointed out that the schema did not bring out clearly enough that the real basis for the lay apostolate was the royal priesthood of Christ, in which all shared through baptism and confirmation (De Vito, Lucknow). Bishop Rastouil of Limoges, France, deplored the lack of a developed theology of confirmation in the Church, while Bishop De Roo, in the name of 15 Canadian bishops, called for a more theologically-oriented preface stressing the dual vocation of man: to build the world and to build the Church, a point more fully developed in Schema 13. Christian concern for the world was not merely humanitarian in inspiration, but authentically religious. The two principles were inseparable. Archbishop Hurley of Durban, South Africa did not agree. He thought that it was unwise to attempt to treat theological aspects in the present schema, which should concentrate on more practical matters.

The sections of the original schema on the apostolate and the missions had been sent to the Commission on Missions and were incorporated in the schema on missionary activity, observed Bishop Lokuang, but since the latter text had been reduced to propositions, almost nothing was left of this theme. It would therefore be appropriate to include a few words, particularly about the heroic action of many of the laity, in certain countries, as witnesses to the faith when the clergy had been hindered or exiled.

Quite a few speakers, following the lead of Cardinal Ritter, taxed the document with betraying a spirit of "clericalism." "Clericalism is the enemy," said Archbishop Kozlowiecki of Lusaka, Northern Rhodesia, "clericalism is the No. 1 enemy in the Church." The schema has been "conceived in the sin of clericalism," according to Bishop Carter of Sault-Ste-Marie, Canada. By the time the laity had been invited to take part in the work of preparing the schema, in the spring of 1963, it was already too late, he said. The present text amounted virtually to a document in which the clergy were speaking to the clergy. The laity would not be inspired by reading it. It scarcely took note of any associations except those that were clerically approved. The present text was a sort of *summa* of existing clerical lore on the subject, little more. The document should cause the laity to exclaim: *Nostra res agitur!*—"This is what we want to hear!" They will never be inspired to say this about a document dominated by a clericalist outlook, according to Bishop Tenhumberg, auxiliary of Münster, Germany, who spoke in the name of the German and Scandinavian bishops. Bishop De Vet of Breda, in the name of the Dutch bishops, warned against giving the impression that what the Church really wanted was to build a "clericalist" civilization. The role of the layman in the world was too neglected.

Perhaps the most detailed exponent of the anticlericalist view was Archbishop D'Souza, of Bhopal, India. It was time, he said, to start considering the laity as grown-ups. The principle quoted in the text: "Let nothing be done without the bishop," a quotation from St. Ignatius of Antioch, an early Father of the Church, must not be abused. Doubtless nothing should be done *against* the bishop and due order should be preserved, but there was much that could be done without his immediate cooperation. The People of God were not a totalitarian state. He objected particularly to the totalitarian implications of Catholic Action, as practiced in certain Latin countries, where no other outside activities by the laity were countenanced unless they fit into this scheme. "We are now going through a period of reform in the Church," said Archbishop D'Souza, "and one of the prime attributes calling for reform is the spirit of clericalism. Laymen must be treated as brothers by the clergy and the latter must no longer attempt to usurp responsibilities which properly belonged to the former. Why could they not represent the Church in international organizations, why could there not be laymen in the Roman Congregations, and why could not laymen even serve in the diplomatic service of the Holy See?" he asked. "The missionary work of the Church will fail," he declared, "unless there is much re-thinking along this line."

Several thoughts of Archbishop D'Souza were echoed by Cardinal Rugambwa, who wanted the principle of subsidiarity, mentioned in *Mater et magistra,* widely applied in the field of the lay apostolate, with everything being left to lesser or lower organizations that was possible. This would tend to promote a greater respect for spiritual freedom among the laity.

In contrast to this irenic approach, Bishop De Smedt of Bruges sounded a warning against those laymen who were not very respectful of the rights of others in pursuing the work of the apostolate. He spoke of their "frenetic propaganda," their abuse of the means of communications, and pressures on public opinion. This was equally wrong; what men of today wanted was to be entirely free to embrace the truth without being compelled to do so. No doubt he had in mind some of the pressure tactics not infrequently employed to induce Catholics to join different organizations and associations. Laymen, however, were not the only ones occasionally indulging in such tactics.

A further controversial question claiming a great deal of attention in the debate was the nature and role of Catholic

Action, or the organized form of the lay apostolate generally understood by that term. Although the expression has a generalized meaning and is often used in this sense in papal encyclicals, for example, it is usually taken as referring to certain types of organizations or associations which have been approved by the hierarchy and function under their close supervision. The schema attempts to straddle the fence between different meanings of the term and does not succeed very well. Article 16 defining the nature of Catholic Action, as understood by the schema, and Article 18 on the close relationship with the hierarchy, read as follows:

16. For some time now the laity in various countries, devoting themselves with greater frequency to the work of the apostolate, have joined together in activities and associations of various kinds. These associations, have pursued goals that are immediately and properly apostolic, maintaining a close connection with the hierarchy.

Among these and other similar older institutions, those particularly deserve to be mentioned which have borne much fruit for the Kingdom of Christ while following its own pattern of operation; which have rightly been commended and promoted by the supreme pontiffs and many bishops, which have received from them the name of "Catholic Action"; and which have all been characterized by presence of the following marks, all of which must be verified simultaneously for a movement to receive this title:

a) The immediate aim of these organizations is the general goal of the apostolate of the Church, namely the evangelization and the sanctification of men, and the formation of their conscience so that they can impregnate their milieu with the spirit of the Gospel;

b) Cooperating in their own proper fashion, the laity assume the responsibility for the organization of the group, the evaluation of the situations in which their activity is to be exercised, and for the drawing up and the execution of their programs;

c) In these associations the laity act as an organized group. This is a clear manifestation of the ecclesial community and renders the apostolate more effective;

d) Whether freely offering their services or called to action
and direct cooperation with the apostolate of the hierarchy, the
laity act under the higher direction of the hierarchy itself.
The hierarchy can also sanction this collaboration by means of
an explicit mandate.

Organizations which in the judgment of the hierarchy really
have all these marks, may assume various forms, whether they
be known as Catholic Action or have some other name in accordance with the requirements in different countries.

18. It is the task of the sacred hierarchy to promote the apostolate of the laity, formulate its principles, provide spiritual assistance, issue whatever directives are needed, and exercise a role
of vigilance.

When there is question of temporal activity, the role of the
hierarchy is to interpret authentically for Catholics and to
formulate moral principles. It also pertains to the hierarchy after
weighing the matter and consulting experts, to decide if a particular undertaking or institution is in keeping with moral principles, or if a particular project can produce results from the supernatural viewpoint.

The schema then goes on to describe and define four types
of relationship with the hierarchy, ranging from those associations organized by the laity on their own, to those having
a "mandate" from the hierarchy, and those finally whose
functions are purely pastoral and completely under clerical
control (e.g. catechetical, liturgical functions, etc.).

In general, while the term Catholic Action is looked upon
with favor in Latin countries (particularly in Italy, Spain
and South America, also France), it is regarded with less favor
by German Catholics, and with no enthusiasm at all by Catholics in English-speaking countries, as implying too much dis-
tasteful, compulsory organization. In Italy it has turned out
to be little more than a flag-waving, anticlerical-provoking,
hierarchically-dominated wing of the conservative bishops.
The French follow a middle course, retaining the name without the compulsory, political overtones associated with the

talian brand. Papal statements on the subject have not always lisplayed a proper sense of balance, sometimes tending to onfuse the forms of Catholic Action in Latin countries with he ideal form of the lay apostolate.

By attempting to steer a middle course, the schema tended o please neither side. It was not surprising that Archbishop Maccari, former head of Italian Catholic Action, should have noted, with regret, that the text did not bring out the "defensive nature" of Catholic Action and generally disapproved of its loose language. Bishop Ruotolo of Ugento, Italy, expressed the belief that all Christians should be bound in conscience to belong to one of the forms of Catholic Action, while Bishop Soares de Resende of Mozambique called for he establishment of an institute in Rome to train clergy and aity in the work of Catholic Action. "Those who live by the Church should have the sense of the Church," said Bishop D'Agostino of Vallo di Lucania, Italy, a phrase often repeated in documents of the magisterium on the apostolate of he laity where the word "Church" often seems to be used in he exclusive sense of "clergy." The bishop recalled an ambiguously worded phrase of Pope Paul VI: "Catholic Action belongs to the constitution of the Church." Cardinal Caggiano of Buenos Aires also recalled that Pope Paul had referred to Catholic Action as the "royal road" for the apostolate of the laity. He was particularly grateful that the schema seemed to accord its rightful place to Catholic Action, but he was disappointed in not finding any quotations from the encyclicals of Pius XI and Pius XII which defined this form of the apostolate. In many countries, he observed, the clergy and laity had shown themselves faithful to these directives.

The principal intervention on this subject was delivered by Cardinal Suenens on October 9. While still an auxiliary bishop of Malines-Brussels, the cardinal had proposed certain points for investigation with a view to arriving at a better definition of the term Catholic Action, proposals which had been made at the Second Congress for the Apostolate of

the Laity. Pope Pius XII had adopted some of them in his
discourses. Cardinal Suenens was dissatisfied particularly
with the treatment of Catholic Action in the schema. He said
it was not a question of persons, but of doctrine. The definition proposed in the text was ambiguous. Catholic Action
properly was a *genus,* not a specific form of activity. Some
countries did not use the term for organizations which nevertheless fulfilled the four conditions. It was not of advantage
to the Church to have such widely varying views about Catholic Action. He mentioned specifically the Legion of Mary. In
some countries this was considered Catholic Action, in others
not. As if the organization changed its nature depending on
countries! The difficulty was, he said with emphasis, that the
term Catholic Action had been monopolized by certain forms.
Was the close association of these forms with the hierarchy
sufficient reason for doing this? This was to look at matters
from a purely external and juridical point of view. Such an attitude was not in accordance with the theology of the laity as
developed in *De Ecclesia.* Such an explanation would have
been logical if the usual forms of Catholic Action were the
only ones in existence, but there are other forms, and tomor
row there will be still more, which cannot be comprised
under this heading. These forms are *fully entitled* (he pro
nounced these words in French) to be called Catholic Action
the bishop retaining his right to accept or reject certain types
as he sees best. Some common term should be found that
would cover all forms of the apostolate and a proper juridical
definition be worked out. It would be absurd to be more strict
in this regard with the laity than the Church was with the
forms of religious institutes. By showing a proper spirit of
freedom toward the laity, the Church would be showing
greater respect for the freedom of the Holy Spirit who in
spires and sustains the whole apostolate.

The debate continued on Monday (October 12) with at
tention being concentrated on Catholic Action. Cardinal

Suenens' suggestion that the notion needed broadening was not favorably received by bishops from countries where it was traditional. France being one of the countries where Catholic Action had proved to be successful, it is not surprising that Cardinal Liénart found this suggestion unacceptable. "I can see no reason for broadening the term," he said, "so that it can be applied to any type of apostolic action whatsoever." Catholic Action has always implied a close association with the bishop in the work of evangelization. The forms were not fixed, the bishop could accept the cooperation of any groups that he wished. It would be better for the schema to say so clearly, rather than pass this point over in silence. He also thought that the text should bring out more clearly the distinction between the apostolate of the laity and that of the clergy, and he wanted special mention made of the part that youth could play in the apostolate.

Both Archbishop Nicodemo of Bari, Italy, and the Military Vicar for Spain, Bishop Alonso Muñoyerro, insisted that greater stress must be placed on the subordination of Catholic Action to the bishop and its complete dependence on the hierarchy, in accordance with repeated papal recommendations. The present text gave too much latitude to local bishops to establish whatever forms they pleased under this title. Greater conformity was needed to avoid confusion. "The schema gravely wounds Catholic Action, which should be saved for the good of the Church." Bishop Del Pino of Lerida, Spain, professed himself shocked by allegations on the floor that the text was too "clerical." His solution was to banish all such thoughts by considering that ultimately everybody, including the laity, was subject to the Pope and "without the Pope there is no apostolate." When he embarked on a diatribe about religious liberty, denouncing it as a "liberty to sin," he was called to order by the moderator, but had difficulty getting back on the track.

Exception was taken to Cardinal Suenens' strictures by Bishop Padin, the auxiliary of Rio de Janeiro, who offered

the support of the Brazilian episcopate on behalf of Cathol
Action, which "had done great things for some countries.
It was idle to accuse the movement of having claimed
privileged name. Should the name of the Jesuits or that of th
Holy Office be changed simply because we all live in th
society of Jesus or because the Church is *per se* holy? It w;
pointless to fight over names. The important thing was to r
spect the freedom of the laity which we have been preachin
He also suggested that the clericalism implied by the u
of the word "cooperate" with reference to the part which th
laity were to play in the proposed Secretariat, should k
avoided in favor of a direct summons to responsibility.

For Bishop Donze of Tulle, France, the text did not pa
sufficient attention to the object of the lay apostolate, name
the persons to whom it is directed. They were all referred t
in the abstract. Instead they should be treated concretely, ;
social beings sharing in the life of their communities, an
Catholic Action itself must be collective, must work in team
to make the apostolate effective. Bishop Hoeffner of Münste
Germany, detected an undue note of optimism and a negle
of what the Bible had to say about the effects of original si
The times were evil and would remain evil until the end (
the world, according to the teaching of theology, in spite (
efforts toward perfection. He thought it unwise, also, t
lump cooperation with other Christians and non-Christiar
together at the end. Different motives were applicable in eac
case. Bishop Civardi, connected with Italian Catholic A
tion, regretted the absence of any treatment of the notio
of Social Action, which had been present in an earlier draf
Schema 13, on the Church in the Modern World, was onl
concerned with the principles of social order, not with soci;
action. This was the place to deal with this topic, of speci;
interest in countries like Italy, where workers belonged t
marxist-dominated or tinged associations, not from convi
tion, but from economic necessity.

A fundamental defect for Bishop Renard of Versaille

France, was that the schema lacked any clear-cut definition of the lay apostolate based on Scripture. The sociological reflections in Article 1 were useful, but did not take the place of a more fundamental teaching based on the Bible. The apostolate must be viewed as proceeding from faith and leading men to faith. Bishop Larrain of Talca, Chile, insisted strongly on the idea of the apostolate as bringing Christ to the world. "The apostolate must be 'incarnated' concretely, but not over-institutionalized" lest too much attention be given to the material side. The lay apostolate must be a bridge between the Church and the world. We must listen attentively to the "signs of the times," and not be too bound by existing forms. The frontiers of the apostolate are vast and Christians must see themselves as missionaries. The present is the hour of the laity, he concluded. A somewhat clerical and conservative note was struck by Bishop Bäuerlein of Srijem, Yugoslavia, advocating that as regards the apostolate of the Christian family, the schema should state that the principal duty of married people was the procreation of Christian children, but he sounded a well-deserved warning about the necessity of paying more attention to "public opinion." "What is needed in some cases," he said, "is recourse to public opinion. Without fear of such exposure the absolutist spirit of the local councils which the schema proposes cannot be quenched."

Archbishop Heenan of Westminster clearly summed up the position with regard to Catholic Action so far as Anglo-Saxon prelates were concerned. He said simply: "It would be better in certain countries if the expression were not used. I hope that each regional conference will be left free to speak of the apostolate rather than of Catholic Action." His final remarks bore on the subject of the proposed Secretariat about which he had some interesting comments:

This is something which is bound to fail unless the laity is fully consulted. This Secretariat will be unique among the secretariats of the Holy See. It would be a disaster to model it on any

of the departments already existing in the Roman Curia. Most
of the members of the Secretariat must be chosen from the laity.
Let me stress that the faithful take it very badly if decisions over
matters in which they are well versed are taken without any
word of advice being asked from them. Before setting up the
Secretariat it is important, therefore, to enquire from the laity
themselves how they think it should be set up and how it ought
to be run. Many of our Catholic laity know much more than
we do about public affairs . . . The proper thing for us to do
is to learn from them. It is obviously necessary for this Secretariat
to have the guidance of competent ecclesiastics. But this does not
mean that all the business must be conducted by prelates or that
laymen would not be capable of presiding at any of its meetings
. . . The people to choose for this Secretariat are the men and
women who in their own countries have taken a lead in the lay
apostolate . . . We do not want to send to Rome only old
gentlemen who are loaded down with ecclesiastical honors. We
must also choose some of our young men and women who have
to earn their daily bread.

It was typical of the text of the schema that it was long on
the details of Catholic Action and dependence on the
hierarchy, but had almost nothing at all to say about the
proposed Secretariat. The ideas of His Grace must have
struck practiced Roman hands as either absurd or alarming, boldly suggesting as they did an end to clerical domination in this field.

After the last speaker on Monday, the Moderator called
for a vote of cloture on the debate on the lay apostolate, and
the motion was approved by an overwhelming majority. The
Secretary General then announced that the following day the
floor would be taken only by those speakers who wished to
speak in the name of at least 70 Fathers, and that the debate
would be concluded with a speech by one of the Lay Auditors.

Archbishop Guerry of Cambrai, France, directed his attention particularly to Article 11. All expressions must be
avoided which could be interpreted as implying that the
Church desires to dominate the temporal order. The au-

tonomy of temporal society must be preserved in its own area, but at the same time the transcendence of the Church in its mission of service to mankind must be asserted. The traditional cooperation between priests and laity in the East was held up by Archbishop Zoghby, patriarchal vicar for Egypt, as an example for the West. In every town where there is a parish, he said, with regard to the Melkites, there exists a patriarchal commission, two thirds of whose members are elected by the people, and one third appointed by the patriarch. The commissions had a hand in all kinds of activities, helping with education, acting as a church court, managing church property and parish gatherings. The faithful do not try to impose their will, but offer help and advice, but those bishops who disregarded this advice would soon lose their authority over the faithful.

The Lay Auditor turned out to be Patrick Keegan, president of the International Catholic Workers' Movement. He spoke in English, the first time that any layman had ever addressed a modern ecumenical council during the course of one of its business sessions, since the addresses of Jean Guitton and Vittorio Veronese in 1963 took place on a special day. The tenor of Keegan's remarks was "unexceptional." The loud applause which greeted him at the end was due, no doubt, more to the rhetorical flourish with which he had delivered his remarks than to what he had said. The effect of his remarks was frankly disappointing to those who had expected greater fire from the first layman to have something to say in public on a subject so much criticized by the clergy; his speech appeared to have been "clericalized."

Bishop Hengsbach wound up the discussion by promising to improve the text, in the name of the Commission, on the basis of the many suggestions made. He apologized for the defects, especially as regards the "clerical" treatment of Catholic Action. The schema on the Lay Apostolate should be a sort of pendent to the one on the Church in the Modern World which could be expected to give definitive form to many of the basic ideas only dealt with cursorily and tentatively in the present text. He called for time to revise the text and spoke of the need to consult more laymen. His emphasis upon the "time" necessary to complete the work of revision naturally caused all thoughts to turn to the necessity for a fourth session and he was warmly applauded on concluding. The schema was not submitted to a vote, the general sentiment in favor of a thorough revision being so obvious.

On Tuesday, October 13, the Council took up the first of the schemata reduced to a series of propositions earlier in the year, on orders of the Coordinating Commission, according to the so-called "Doepfner Plan." The assembly was to have taken up Schema 13 on the Church in the Modern World next, but the *relationes* were not ready, the Secretary General assured the anxious assembly, so the intervening time would have to be spent in considering several of the Propositions.

The schema *De clericis,* distributed to the Fathers in May 1963, had been revised on the basis of their suggestions submitted in writing and was given a new title, *De sacerdotibus,* in January 1964. It was then decided to reduce it to a series of propositions, extracted from the revised text. The propositions along with the text of the revised *De sacerdotibus* were distributed to the bishops, after their approval in April 1964. The text which the Fathers had before them in October 1964 when the debate began was in two parallel columns. The first contained the propositions distributed in the spring of 1964; the second, a revised and slightly expanded series of propositions, amended on the basis of the suggestions sent in meanwhile. The chief change was the introduction of a paragraph on celibacy (inserted in Proposition 2), "at the urgent request of 70 bishops, disturbed by so many confusing voices raised regarding a possible abolition of this law." The original text had contained no mention of this subject because it was meant for both the Eastern and Western

Churches which had different disciplines. The wording was such that it was applicable to both cases:

2. Let priests preserve and sincerely love holy chastity, and let those who, on the recommendation or by the command of the Church, have made a vow of celibacy, trusting in the grace of God, be faithful to their vow with their whole heart and rejoice that they are united with Christ directly in this way and can serve the family of God with greater freedom. Let them remain and progress in this state with strength and rectitude, so that they may become more and more able to serve and may acquire more fully a fatherhood in Christ.

Another passage was added at the beginning (Prop. 1), at the request of German and Scandinavian bishops, explaining the theology and mission of the priesthood more fully and relating it to what was said in *De Ecclesia*. Other notable changes were the addition of a sentence in Prop. 2 stating that priestly obedience (to bishops) was different from that of religious and the laity, because priests shared in the episcopal mission through the sacrament of orders; they were advised to cultivate an "ascetical spirit in fulfilling their pastoral ministry" and to practice contemplation (Prop. 3); wherever possible they were to establish a common form of life (Prop. 4); they were to show a "solicitude for all churches" and to be ready to undertake work in other dioceses according to need (Prop. 7)—this opened the door to a very considerable change from the traditional incardination of priests in one diocese; and they were warned against appropriating ecclesiastical property for their own personal use or using it for gain, and to avoid all "cupidity and carefully to refrain from engaging in any kind of commercialism" (Prop. 9). The title of the propositions, now numbering 12, which were handed to the Fathers in October 1964, was "Concerning the Priestly Life and Ministry," a more apt description. The approach was mainly practical and pastoral.

In his introduction Archbishop Marty of Rheims, France, after giving an outline of the various vicissitudes through

which the text had passed, referred to one rather radical
change being recommended, not so far mentioned, namely
the abolition of the time-honored system of benefices stemming from the Middle Ages, "lest the Church be accused of
feudalism and lest it lead to setting up social classes among
priests," as of course it had long since done. The old system
was to be abolished, wherever it was in effect, and replaced
by a more equitable salary system. The tone of the debate was,
if anything, more critical and censorious than in the case of
the preceding schema. The "crisis" through which the Council had just passed undoubtedly helped to whet some appe-
tites for blood.* The "blood" in this case was not that of
the members of the Commission that had drafted the text,
who had perhaps done as well as they could and in any case
displayed no eagerness to defend their work, but the "higher
authority" that had ordered the reduction of the original
schema to a series of propositions. The impression was inevitable that priests were being downgraded as compared
with bishops. For whatever reason, the members of this Commission as well as those of the other commissions whose texts
had been reduced to propositions, had not had the backbone
or "nerve" of the Commission on the Apostolate of the
Laity, which had earlier in the year refused outright to adopt
this procedure.**

Cardinal Meyer set the tone of discussion with a critical
appraisal of the aims of the propositions. The purpose, as
announced by Archbishop Marty, was to relate the life and
ministry of the priest to the conditions and needs of today's
world, but this was hardly evident from what followed. There
had been full discussion of the apostolate of bishops and
also of the apostolate of the laity, and there should also be
a full discussion of the apostolate of priests, but the present
text did not do justice to the idea. The propositions speak
almost exclusively about the obligations of priests, but have

* See p. 63 ff.
** Disclosed by Msgr. Higgins in the Bishops' Press Panel.

little to say about anything that should encourage them to fulfill their duties. The text was badly organized. It was not clear whether the aim was to lay down norms to be followed now, or norms for a future revision of the Code of Canon Law. Mention of the relations between priests and the laity in the first proposition following the preface was not appropriate, since priests were first of all men of God before they were men among men. Insufficient attention was paid to the subject of the mass, in Proposition 3, "the greatest work and source of the priestly apostolate." Finally, after criticizing the treatment of the "common fund" mentioned in Proposition 12, the cardinal concluded: "A full schema and a full discussion are desired in order to respond to the pastoral aim of the Council and to the expectations of so many priests." His speech was greeted with a wave of applause.

The following speaker, Bishop Théas of Lourdes and Tarbes, observed that while the number of bishops was always becoming greater, the number of priests was continually diminishing, in contrast to the needs of a constantly growing population. The words in the schema on the apostolate of the laity, "nothing without the bishop," can be applied to priests. We should say, "nothing without the priests." This was true both for bishops and the laity. We should also react against a tendency today which sees in the priest a mere man. Priests share in the priesthood of Christ and are "other Christs." The close relationship between the bishops and the priest should be brought out more clearly. Cardinal de Barros Câmara of Rio de Janeiro expressed himself as in agreement with the sentiments of Cardinal Meyer and Bishop Théas on the schema. The text must be restored to juster proportions.

The present document was declared to be basically satisfactory by the conservative Cardinals Ruffini and Quiroga y Palacios who, however, criticized it on minor points, mostly with regard to the arrangement of the material. This was also the view of Archbishops Rosales of the Philippines and

Evangelisti of Meerut, India, though the latter wanted more emphasis on the missionary responsibilities of priests. The former felt that it was a good idea to refer to celibacy and obedience at the beginning, as the text stood, while Archbishop Fares of Catanzaro, Italy, was of the opinion that the passage on celibacy had been badly formulated, implying, by the use of the word "vow," that the Church had decided the controversy over whether celibacy was a matter of "law" or a "vow." He approved of what L'Osservatore Romano had recently said about the Church's determination to maintain the requirement of celibacy and disapproved of speculation in the press about the subject.

The notion of the *presbyterium,* or college of priests gathered around the bishop in each diocese which assists him in the government of his see, a concept going back to the earliest days of the Church, needed to be stressed more, according to the Maronite Archbishop Ayoub of Aleppo in a constructive speech. The idea does not imply that priests are the "slaves" of the bishop, but rather that they form a "family" around him and consider one another as "brothers" and "co-workers." The schema smacked too much of paternalism and gave advice and commands to priests as if they were "not yet of age."

The idea of a "priestly senate" was still further explored by Archbishop Baldassari of Ravenna, Italy. Some mention should be made of the rights of priests to share in church administration. While much had been said about the rights of bishops, almost nothing was said about the *rights of priests,* according to Bishop Garaygordobil of Ecuador, their rights particularly when faced by an arbitrary exercise of authority on the part of bishops. "Pardon me for having to say this," he said, "but we are not yet confirmed in sanctity." Priests should be considered the true collaborators of bishops and not merely the latter's assistants. His proposal that in each diocese there should be set up a *Coetus Presbyterorum* to act as consultors to the bishop and the bishop should govern in accordance with their advice was much the same as Archbishop Ayoub's recommendation.

Quite a few of the interventions bore on the theme of priestly holiness. A certain minimalizing of the means to holiness was detected by Bishop Añoveros Ataún of Cadix y Centa, Spain, who felt that there was not enough emphasis on the mass, the divine office, and an examination of conscience in this connection. The establishment in each diocese of a spiritual director for priests was recommended by Bishop Kuharic, auxiliary of Zagreb, Yugoslavia, who noted that continued spiritual counseling after priests left the seminary was an important element in keeping up their fervor. He said also that the Church should not merely "leave behind" but "reject outright" the outmoded and harmful system of ecclesiastical benefices, which had been the ruin of many priests, was a "scandal to the faithful," and had turned many away from the Church. Bishop Latusek, auxiliary of Breslau, Poland, noted that there was little said about the apostolic, dynamic, missionary spirit which a priest today was required to have in keeping with the times through which we were passing, of "thinking with the Church," of reducing differences in outlook between the older and the younger clergy, and between pastors and curates. The need for spiritual directors and priestly associations was emphasized by Bishop Kowalski of Poland. Bishop Nowicki of Gdansk, Poland, wanted frequent confession mentioned among the means of holiness and a new paragraph added to Proposition 2 giving some norms on the conduct of priests in the political field, and also with regard to their own families, along the lines of Pope John's splendid example. Coadjutor-Archbishop Ferreira de Macedo of Brazil said that the text should begin with the principle *"sacerdos alter Christus"* rather than simply list priestly virtues, and fuller treatment should be given to the virtues of charity, humility and self-denial. The schema rightly took note of the "signs of the times," according to Bishop Sanchez Moreno Lira of Peru, and stressed the necessity of breaking down the wall or barrier between priest and community, by requiring study of pastoral needs, greater mobility and other things in accordance with *aggiornamento*.

The three Spanish bishops, Masilla Reoyo of Ciudad Rodrigo, Gonzalez Martin of Astorga, and Castan Lacoma of Siguenza-Guadalajara, all spoke on some aspect of the question of priestly holiness. The first wanted the need for specific ascetic-pastoral courses, annual retreats and the like, spelled out and not left to postconciliar commissions or not mentioned at all; the second thought that priests should have a certain year, like the third year of a novitiate, for spiritual renewal some years after their ordination, not immediately afterward; the third wanted priestly associations, which had proved successful, given recognition in canon law like lay organizations. In conformity with the rather dour attitude generally taken by the Yugoslav clergy, who seemed to think that the world had not progressed much since the days of Pius X, Bishop Cekada of Skoplje painted a dark picture of the inroads of "laicism" and "modernism" among some of the clergy, "which increases everyday and is a sign of the times." According to him some priests are degrading the confessional by watering down the seriousness of sins against the Sixth Commandment and downgrading confession generally; by bringing into the sanctuary "boys and girls, singing and dancing"; by trying to abolish ecclesiastical precepts or disregarding the rules for clerical attire. "Imagine such things thirty years ago!" he said.

The two questions of the "common life" and support for priests from a common or diocesan fund naturally came in for considerable comment. With regard to the former, the objection was made that there were many vocations to the secular priesthood precisely because individuals wished to preserve their individuality and not be bound by any form of life resembling the monastic. There was a place for both types in the Church and the two forms should not be confused. Several bishops raised the point of exactly what was meant by a "common life"? The question of adequate financial support for the clergy was mainly one of interest to Latin American and certain European countries. Contrasting views for example were advocated by Bishop Corripio Ahumada of Tampico, Mexico, and Bishop Pereira, auxiliary of Coimbra, Portugal. The former held that priests should have as much protection as modern employers would give to their employees, while the latter saw danger in going too far along this line and said that the present text seemed to deprive the priest of control over certain categories of property or income which had been traditionally recognized as theirs by right, patrimonies, quasi-patrimonies, parcimonials. "The schema will cause anxieties and scruples for many clerics on this score."

On the subject of poverty, Bishop Komba of Tanganyika observed that it was not a "fair trick" for the Council to recommend this virtue to priests, when nothing had been said about it in the schema on bishops. What was good for the latter was also good for the former. Regarding the subject of priestly remuneration (Proposition 9), Bishop Hiltl, auxiliary of Regensburg, Germany, was of the opinion that there could also well be some mention of the need for priests to pay a fair wage to their domestics and some word about the "social security" of the latter. It was not enough to repay the services of housekeepers by holding out the hope of some legacy or bequest in a priest's will, they needed some guarantee for the future, otherwise maids would continually be looking elsewhere for employment.

The section recommending greater flexibility in the transference of priests from one area to another was welcomed by the South American prelate, Bishop Rodriquez Ballon of Arequipa, Peru, and he thanked those episcopally sponsored bodies which were working to this end, but he pointed out the need for a more equitable distribution of personnel and for training the latter in the customs of the country where they were going. The impression must be avoided that they

were a foreign group in the country. One of the chief difficulties encountered by the some 4,000 American clergy
(priests and nuns) working in Latin America has been this
problem of "adjusting" to local conditions, without compromising the efficacy of their apostolate. Some progress was
being made in Latin America, however, according to Bishop
Proano Villalba of Ecuador, who announced the establishment of a pastoral institute for Latin America formed by
CELAM to travel from country to country in that part of the
world. Special mention should be made of priestly associations, he said, for these had proved very helpful where they
existed. And "the Pope should be asked to stop bestowing
merely honorific titles since these are a cause of division and
envy" among the clergy, he insisted. It should be remembered, that for all practical purposes, it will be the priests who
will make the decrees of the Council a success after they have
been enacted.

The loneliness and rather solitary pastorate of the country
priest was brought up by Archbishop Perris of Naxos, Greece.
More attention should be paid to their plight. Everything
seemed to be keyed to the needs of the city parish.

A problem brought to the fore particularly by World War
II was that of the psychologically or neurologically unbalanced priest, who was a victim of the war. Bishops had often
reacted to the appearance of these ills by assigning such persons to virtual ecclesiastical jails, instead of recognizing the
problem and trying to help them medically and enabling
them to return to their work. The text should refer to this
problem, and not merely to "psychological adjustment to
modern times" (Prop. 5), according to Bishop Donovan,
auxiliary of Detroit, Michigan.

The most notable intervention of the second day, and the
one which helped seal the doom of the schema, was that delivered by the Brazilian Archbishop Gomes dos Santos of
Goiania. "The text even in its revised form is a great disappointment to us and to many of the Fathers," he said, speak-

ing in the name of 112 Brazilian and other bishops. "The text is almost an insult to our priests . . . We praise the good intentions of the editors, but we deplore the result which does not give true consideration to either the secular or religious clergy. It is paternalistic and urges on priests things which we dare not impose on ourselves, e.g. poverty, the common life, clothing, the renunciation of titles and honors . . ." He asked the Moderators not to submit the text to a vote now, but to send it back for revision, with the vote to be postponed until the Fourth Session. His remarks were greeted by two outbursts of applause.

At the beginning of the congregation that day, Archbishop Felici had announced that a vote would be taken on different sections of the schema the following days, Thursday and Friday. At the end of the session, about 12:30, however, he withdrew this and announced that the vote had been postponed "because the list of speakers was not yet exhausted." This was because Cardinal Meyer had protested to the Moderators against following this procedure when so many of the Fathers were against the schema.

During the first part of the congregation, Thursday morning, seven more speakers were more or less insistent that the schema must be rewritten. Cardinal Alfrink stated that while the present text represented an improvement over the previous version, it did not come up to the expectations of priests because it did not describe an image of the priest which the modern world could recognize. The Council should adopt a more forthright attitude toward the "crisis" with regard to priestly celibacy by bringing out more clearly the biblical and traditional background of the subject. "Perhaps some consolation and encouragement could be added," he remarked, "for those priests who see celibacy as a burden" and not a "joy." The present text would be a great disappointment to priests today and must be rewritten to provide consolation, strength and hope. There was applause following his intervention. Bishop Koestner of Gurk, Austria, and

Archbishop Sartre of Cameroun followed him in offering
general criticisms and calling for a complete revision. Archbishop Modrego y Casaus of Barcelona, Bishop Gugic of
Dubrovnik and Bishop Flores Martin of Barbastro, Spain,
confined their attention to specific points. Bishop Jenny,
auxiliary of Cambrai, France, favored neither approval nor
rejection, but revision, if possible, before the end of the
present session.

At this point the Moderators called for a standing vote on
whether to close debate. The motion was carried by a narrow
majority, thus indicating that many of the Fathers still felt
that the subject had not been sufficiently exhausted. The only
other speaker, Cardinal Lefebvre of Bourges, France, who
spoke in the name of at least 70 Fathers, was for revision with
more attention being paid to the relationship of priests to
the priesthood of the laity, so much emphasized these days.
Archbishop Marty then summed up in the name of the Commission, stating that the members were at the service of the
Council and expressing a desire that the Fathers manifest
their wishes by *iuxta modum* votes rather than a negative
vote, so as to give better guidance to the Commission. He
also referred expressly to the desire of many Fathers that
more emphasis should be placed on the notion of the *presbyterium,* or the close bonds which ought to prevail between
bishops and priests. The Commission also hoped that the
Moderators would allow expansion of the propositions into a
full-fledged schema again. Any suggestions for the solemn
message to priests, which it was still intended to issue, should
also be sent in.

Later that day the Coordinating Commission met to consider the question of voting on the propositions, in the likelihood that other texts would elicit the same unfavorable reaction as the present one. The Moderators also had their usual
audience with the Pope. As a result of these consultations it
was announced on Friday by Secretary General Felici:

A number of Fathers having asked the Moderators to remand to commission after discussion the schemata reduced to propositions, the Coordinating Commission has decided that after a brief discussion in general congregation the Council will vote on the motion as to whether these schemata should be submitted for an immediate vote. If an absolute majority (half the votes plus one) is favorable, the vote will take place at once. If it is unfavorable, the schemata will be sent back to be revised as rapidly as possible.

The decision, while saving face, amounted to a tacit acknowledgment of the contention of most Fathers that the texts under question were far too important to be reduced to mere propositions and should be restored to their original form—though no decision was apparently taken regarding this latter point as yet. The first test of the new procedure came when the propositions on the Priestly Life and Ministry were put to a vote on Monday, October 19. The result was a large majority in favor of returning the document to commission at once.

On Thursday, October 15, the Council took up the second of the schemata reduced to propositions, that on the Eastern Churches (*De Eclesiis Orientalibus*).* There were now 30 Propositions as compared with 54 articles in the text debated in 1963, but the length was approximately the same. However, while the material had been considerably re-arranged and the tone and emphasis changed for the better, it was obvious from the ensuing debate that the Latinizing tendencies which had presided over the destiny of this document from the beginning were still in evidence. They are even apparent in the final version promulgated as a council decree on November 21, 1964. Anyone comparing the successive stages through which the document passed on its way from the rough draft first presented to the Fathers in 1962 to the final version would be likely to hail the progress made. But it was never possible to free it entirely from a certain conde-

* Ordered by the Coordinating Commission on January 15, 1964.

scending attitude toward the Eastern Churches or do full justice to Eastern conceptions when there were important divergences in outlook between East and West, because of an instinctive inability on the part of some of the framers to adopt an objective approach, to abandon some of the preconceptions inherent in *romanità*. This attitude has been typical of the Cardinal Secretary of State, Amleto Cicognani, in particular, both during the years when he presided over the Congregation for the Oriental Churches and later as president of the corresponding conciliar commission which drafted the texts. He has been supported, of course, by a number of prelates (of both rites), who find it difficult to rid themselves of their prejudices. On the other hand, for many years, a number of prelates and specialists in the oriental field, professors and students at the Oriental Institute and in the various colleges in Rome and elsewhere, have been raising their voices in protest against this outmoded curial outlook, but they have generally not been listened to, or their ideas have been adopted only in part. The classic example of Roman ineptness in this field is the Code of Canon Law for the Oriental Churches, promulgated under Pius XII. The result of many years of diligent work and painstaking research on the part of experts in eastern canon law and theology, allegedly, it turned out to be nothing more than a pale image of the already outmoded Code of Canon Law for the Latin Church and now awaits drastic revision with a view to eliminating its many Latinisms.

The picture has been complicated by divided loyalties among the Uniats, or those Christians of eastern rite in communion with the Apostolic See. Formerly, these bodies were subject to strong Latinizing pressures, not only from without but in some cases from within their groups, urging them to conform as much as possible to the Latin pattern of church government and the teaching of theology by abandoning their time-honored traditions and customs. Lately, the trend has, on the whole, been the other way, toward carefully preserving and reviving and purifying their authentic traditions and especially their autonomous status within the fold of the Catholic Church. These divided loyalties played a part in the ultimate fate of the document up for consideration. A final factor was the unquestioned lack of interest in it on the part of the majority of the Fathers, except for those who were concerned on an ecumenical basis or as ordinaries for the various groups of Eastern-rite Catholics in their midst.

The propositions were introduced by Cardinal Cicognani, who said that three points in particular had caused difficulty for the members of the commission, and that the majorities reached on these points were far from unanimous. These were the three points around which much of the debate would revolve, namely:

1. When Eastern Orthodox Christians were converted to Catholicism, they were to retain the same rite in the Catholic Church which they had followed in the Orthodox Church, with provision being made for an appeal to the Holy See in special cases. (This article was later eliminated from the final text in accordance with a vote.)

2. The presence of a Catholic priest at a marriage between two Eastern Christians was necessary for the liceity, but not the validity, of the marriage, unless a dispensation had been granted (Proposition 18). This provision reversed a ruling of Pius XII in a Motu Proprio of 1949.

3. Eastern-rite Catholics could make use of Orthodox sacraments provided no Catholic priest were available, and the Orthodox could, under certain circumstances, be admitted to receive Catholic sacraments (the so-called *communicatio in sacris,* Propositions 26–29).

Archbishop Bukatko, who followed the cardinal, read the report of the Commission. The text before the Fathers had been approved in April 1964, and few changes had been made after that date on the basis of suggestions sent in by the Fathers. Those received recently were printed as an appendix and not incorporated in the text itself.

Cardinal Koenig of Vienna, speaking as ordinary for Eastern Catholics in Austria, led off the debate with three fundamental objections, reiterated by subsequent speakers, which reflected the inveterate pro-Latin outlook of certain circles in Rome: 1. The non-Catholic Eastern Churches were not honored sufficiently as Churches. 2. The Eastern Churches were practically identified with the Churches united with Rome (Uniats), and relations with the Orthodox were viewed under the guise of conversion to the Catholic Church. 3. There was a discrepancy between the outlook in Chapter III of the decree on Ecumenism and the present text. Its language should be brought into line with the former. The Eastern Churches should be viewed not so much with regard to their "separateness" as to the things they hold in "common" with the Catholic Church. Further, he found fault with Prop. 2–4 which regarded only the Eastern Churches as "particular churches," whereas there were also particular Churches in the West. He objected to the use of the term "mixed" when referring to mixed marriages, between Orthodox and Catholics, because it was virtually meaningless in such cases, and he felt strongly that because *communicatio in sacris* meant intercommunion, or at least a beginning along this path, it was necessary to come to some kind of an agreement with the separated Orthodox Churches through conferences. He was dissatisfied also with the description of the patriarchates in the document.

The cardinal was followed by the Coptic Patriarch of Alexandria, Stephanos Sidarouss I, who was in general satisfied with the text and hoped that it would receive a large majority. While disapproving the provision that Orthodox converting to Catholicism were to retain their native rite, he was in favor of abolishing the legislation of Pius XII regarding eastern marriages. But the speaker of the morning who caused the most stir was the doughty Melkite Patriarch of Antioch Maximos IV Saigh, who spoke last and in French, according to his custom. This was his first speech during the Third Session and he was listened to with rapt attention.

After praising the progress shown in the disciplinary portions of the document, he castigated its doctrinal or ecumenical presuppositions:

The preamble praises the Catholic Church for having always held the institutions of the Christian East in great esteem. It thereby contrasts or distinguishes between the Catholic Church, which addresses this praise, and the Eastern Church, to whom this praise is addressed. This leads one to believe either that the Catholic Church is identical with the Latin Church, which is not exact, or that the Eastern Churches do not belong essentially to the Catholic Church, which is also equally inexact.

But the portion which came in for his greatest ire and sarcasm was the section dealing with the patriarchal office:

Of all the chapters of the present schema, the weakest is incontestably that devoted to the Patriarchs (nos. 7–11). This chapter as it is presented to us is inadmissible. It cocks a snook at history and in no way prepares for the future. For the institution that is the most venerable of the hierarchy after the Roman primacy, the schema has only succeeded in giving scholastic definitions (which furthermore are incomplete) and Platonic aspirations, most often repeating recent canon-law texts, as if Vatican II had not been summoned to make a certain advance but ought to content itself with the prescribed *status quo.*

There are four important remarks to be made:

(1) It is false to present the patriarchate as an institution peculiar to the East. It is an institution common to the Caholic Church which considers itself honored to have at its head the due successor of Peter in the Roman See. The premier Patriarch of the Catholic Church is the Bishop of Rome, as has so many times been affirmed by Ecumenical Councils, as is to be found among the Pope's official titles in the *Annuario Pontificio,* as is confirmed by the very name of this *Patriarchal* Basilica of St. Peter where we are gathered, as we are reminded also by the name of the Bishop of Rome's residence at the Lateran Palace, a

name perpetuated in the records and in stone—*Patriarchium*. Successor of Peter in his universal primacy over all the Church, and Bishop of Rome, the Pope is also Patriarch of the West. Patristic tradition and Ecumenical Councils have always regarded him as such, without ever believing that this could be prejudicial to his primacy. The Pope does not feel himself diminished by the fact that he is Bishop of Rome and in virtue of *this* equal to the bishops: why should he feel himself diminished by the fact that he is *also* Patriarch of the West and in virtue of *this*, on *this* level, the colleague of the Patriarchs of the East? Today the conception of the Patriarchate of the West has been too much forgotten, and its place has been filled by the institution of several honorary patriarchates. These latter institutions ought to disappear in order to make way for the true conception of the patriarchate, a conception that is absolutely necessary for the serenity of the dialogue with Orthodoxy. Why deny these facts, as if that could erase them from history?

(2) The patriarchate is not an anonymous institution. The Ecumenical Councils, to which the schema appeals, acknowledged this dignity in the case of definite sees which they cited by name, and this was done for precise motives peculiar to these sees. These sees ought to be cited again, even if the list ought to be completed by the names of other patriarchal sees of more recent creation. One cannot talk of the Patriarchates of the East without once citing, for example, the Holy Roman See or the Ecumenical See of Constantinople, the incumbent of which represents, quite apart from any consideration of numbers or temporal effectiveness, the premier dignitary of the Orthodox Church regarded and honoured as such His Holiness Pope Paul VI. As far as the editors of the schema are concerned, one could say that that historic meeting of His Holiness Pope Paul I and His Holiness the Ecumenical Patriarch Athenagoras did not represent anything.

(3) If one wishes to be faithful to history, which is like the action of the Holy Ghost in the Church, it cannot be forgotten that the incumbents of the patriarchal sees were closely linked to the universal care of all the Church entrusted to Peter and to his successors. Popes and Eastern Patriarchs were, at the time of union, the summits of the universal episcopate. As soon as he

was elected, the Bishop of Rome sent his profession of faith to
the four Patriarchs of the East. And these latter, on their en-
thronement, did the same exclusively between themselves and
with regard to the Pope. Thus there was constituted in the
Church, a patriarchal college, a "summit," as we would say today,
of universal care, by which, while safeguarding entirely the inalienable and personal rights of the successor of Peter, there took
place the visible collegial communion of all the Churches, of
all the episcopate, as is attested by itself by the exchange of
"irenic" letters (to use the terminology in use among the Orthodox), without mentioning the exchange of the pallium, sent both
by the Patriarchs to the Pope and by the Pope to the Patriarchs,
and the commemoration, by each of the Patriarchs, of the Bishop
of Rome and of the other Patriarchs.

The supreme authority in the Church is without doubt able to
renew or to rejuvenate these forms of the ancient ecclesial communion. But the principle that underlies them should not be
passed over in silence if it is wished to offer our Orthodox
brothers a preliminary draft of the charter of union.

(4) Finally, the patriarchate is not only a simple honorary dignity. Its dignity ought to be only the external expression of its
effective importance. Moreover, it ought not to be a question of
covering the Eastern Patriarchs with honour and granting them
precedence in order to go on to treat them as subordinates whose
authority is limited, in the smallest details, by numberless compulsory appeals, both before and after, to the dicasteries of the
Roman Curia. Without infringing the prerogatives of the successor of Peter, the Patriarch, with his Holy Synod, ought normally to be the [court of] last instance for all the affairs of his
patriarchate. It is this internal canonical autonomy which has
saved the Christendoms of the East from all sorts of vicissitudes
throughout history. It could be an interesting formula to be en-
visaged for other ecclesial groups existing in special conditions.
It could also act as the foundation of union between the Catholic
Church and other Churches, of the West as well as of the East.

Venerable Fathers, when one talks of the East one ought not to
think solely of those who humbly represent it today in the bosom
of Roman Catholicism. A place must be kept for what is absent.
The circuit of Catholicism must not be confined to a dynamic

and conquering Latinity on the one hand, and on the other a fraction of the East, a fraction that is more or less weak, assimilated, and absorbed. The circuit must be left open. Let us make Catholicity loyal to its solemn affirmations, to its definition of Catholic in universality. Let us make it great, not for us humble individuals and communities in fortunate communion with Rome, but so that our Churches of origin may find their home there, when it shall grow, in fact as by right, in the realisation of love, to the dimensions of the universe. *Dixi.*

The speech of this venerable dissenter from *romanità* is so typical, and makes the essential points so well, that it deserved to be quoted in full. Pope Paul rewarded the aged patriarch by naming him first on the list of cardinals elevated in his recent consistory (February 25, 1965).

Support for the right of a convert to choose whatever rite he pleased, when changing from Orthodoxy to Catholicism, came from Cardinal de Barros Câmara of Rio de Janeiro, Brazil, and Archbishop Gori, the Latin Patriarch of Jerusalem. The latter's enthusiasm for free choice in the matter of rite is perhaps explicable in view of his position. As a Latin-rite patriarch in the East, he is regarded as an interloper and Trojan Horse of Latinism by the Orthodox clergy and he could therefore hardly be expected to admit the justice of the other side. Typical of him were his constant appeals to Leo XIII's encyclical *Orientalium Dignitas,* as the last word in the matter. He was answered by Archbishop Tawil, Melkite patriarchal vicar for Damascus, who pointed out that the restoration of the Latin Patriarchate of Jerusalem in the last century evoked many bitter memories. For the good of the whole Church, he said, it was necessary to put an end to "Latinization," meaning the Latin Patriarchate. By contrast the Armenian Patriarch of Cilicia, Peter XVI Batanian was all for retaining the reading of the text which prohibited a choice of rite. "Like every law," he said, "the text limits freedom but with good reason: a son of a family coming back to his home town should return to his own family." Most of his talk was taken up with the subject of mixed marriages. A return to the pre-1949 legislation was necessary, because the remedies applied by Rome, for example the invalidation (*sanatio*) of a previously invalid marriage, were not working well. The only solution was recognition of all the marriages in question as valid.

The attention of Major Archbishop Slipyi of the Ukraine was focused almost entirely on the, to him, apparently, overriding problem of how to protect the Eastern Churches from the inroads of Latinization. "Everyone is aware of the destructive setbacks which Orientals have suffered in the course of history, but the diminished numbers of Oriental faithful are also due to the imprudence of Latin Catholics who try to convert Orientals to their rite." Let the Council learn a lesson from the friendly meeting between Patriarch Athenagoras I and Pope Paul VI in Jerusalem. "Have mercy on us," he said, facetiously, in conclusion, "because we are Orientals!" In response to the archbishop's appeal in 1963 for recognition of a Ukrainian patriarchate, he must have noted with pleasure the paragraph in the text (No. 10) which stipulates that for all practical purposes "major archbishops" have the status of patriarchs.

Enthusiasm for the patriarchate likewise marked the intervention by the Coptic Bishop Ghattas of Thebes, Egypt. As the Coptic patriarch his superior had done, he asked whether it was really necessary to have a separate document on the Oriental Churches at all, and why these could not be dealt with in a special section of *De Ecclesia?* "How good it would be if our patriarchs could only return home as members of the Church's senate and with the right to elect the Pope!" His wish was to be fulfilled in part sooner than he realized, on February 25, 1965, to be exact.

The Fathers were treated to a bit of a lecture by Archbishop Zoghby, Melkite patriarchal vicar for Egypt. He agreed with the theological objections to the schema raised by Cardinal Koenig and Patriarch Maximos IV. His princi-

pal contribution was an excursion into the field of history.
At the time of the Patriarch Photius, he said, in the ninth
century, when the patriarch had been restored to the throne
of Constantinople with Roman approval (879), the relationship between the two churches was defined as a sort of co-
existence. The primacy of the Pope was recognized, as well as
his right to preside over ecumenical councils, and the right
to appeal to him in matters of controversy, but for all practical purposes East and West respected each other's canonical
autonomy, and there was no feeling of separation among the
faithful at large. The disputes were regarded as local affairs,
between pope and patriarch, or among theologians. It was only
gradually, in response to certain events, that the two sides
drew apart definitely, and the sense of belonging to the same
Church was lost. The present text still reflects the latter-day
feeling of alienation in its attitude toward the Eastern
Churches. He concluded by referring to the rigorous Cardinal
Humbert, the Cardinal Ottaviani of his day, who in 1054, as
the emissary of Pope Leo IX, laid a bull of excommunication
on the altar of Haghia Sophia in Constantinople, excom-
municating the patriach and formally breaking off discussions
between the two Churches. "If Cardinal Humbert were here
. . ." At this point he was interrupted by the moderator who
reminded him that he had gone beyond his time, but he managed to finish, "If Cardinal Humbert were here, many of us
would be excommunicated!"

There followed a series of interventions on particular
points. Maronite Bishop Doumith was frankly disappointed
by the text. "This schema destroys the hopes that many had
placed in the Council." The text said nothing about how
lines of authority were to be established among oriental
hierarchies outside the East. A multiplicity of jurisdictions
had created only confusion. The visitor for Rumanians living
in exile, Bishop Cristea, evoked the doleful plight of those
Catholics of Byzantine rite living in Rumania and the
Ukraine. Since 1948 their hierarchies and Churches had been

suppressed. It was discouraging to find no mention of their plight in the present text. A note of haste and superficiality was detected by Bishop Stangl of Würzburg in parts of the schema, particularly the sections relating to *communicatio in sacris*. The matter had not been thoroughly thought out. The treatment betrayed a certain timid and "canonical" approach, he felt. Future generations would not judge the Council by whether it had gone through three or four sessions, but by how valuable its decrees were, he reminded the Fathers.

The speeches on Monday by Cardinal Lercaro and Abbot Hoeck, the latter a Benedictine and member of the Commission for the Oriental Churches, were important as pointing to a possible way out of the vexing problems of conflicting jurisdictions, precedence, prestige and differing notions about ecumenism in which the Council found itself as a result of having decided to deal with the Oriental Churches as a separate item on its agenda. Both stressed the necessity of a realistic approach toward the institution of the patriarchate, which must be regarded as an integral part of the structure of the Church, and not something merely applying to the East, as a normal thing, not a mere oddity. Both suggested that a general statement of desires and some practical points should be substituted for the present normative and juridical decree, and that the terms of a directory dealing with matters in greater detail should be worked out by a secretariat or mixed commission which would weigh each aspect carefully. Cardinal Lercaro referred expressly to the Orthodox Church and said: "The hierarchy not yet sitting with us here should be heard before legislation is drawn up, and their consent sought." Abbot Hoeck pointed out that it was impossible for the Orthodox to agree to union with Rome as long as the status of their hierarchy was not regulated vis à vis the Curia and the Cardinalate. Their patriarchs would never agree to be dependent on the Curia. Cardinal Lercaro seemed to say that the question of the ultimate place of the patriarchs in the hierarchy should be left to a decision of the Pope, since it concerned the supreme authority. This was in conformity with his recommendation regarding the "episcopal senate" in the Second Session. Abbot Hoeck, however, was for having the autonomy of the patriarchates proclaimed by the Council. He concluded his remarkably outspoken speech by saying: *"Dixi et salvavi animam meam"*—I have spoken to relieve my conscience.

Archbishop Vuccino of France was for replacing the term "separated brethren" wherever it occurred by "Orthodox," to avoid all suspicion of favoring Latinization, and also because the Orthodox have been extraordinarily faithful to their traditions. He recalled the words of Athenagoras I to Maximos IV when the latter paid a visit to Constantinople in January 1964: "You were the voice of the East in the Council. You were the voice of our common hopes."

Not all the Eastern prelates shared the above fervor for the patriarchate. Bishop Bidawid, in the name of the Chaldean bishops, stressed that the office of patriarch was not of divine but of human origin, and that there was room for reforming the institution. The Church was a living body. Why not increase the number of patriarchs, just as the number of cardinals was increased? This remark was greeted by applause. The Armenian Bishop Bayan of Alexandria saw danger in exalting the person of the patriarch at the expense of the patriarchal synod. A return to the past would not inevitably solve all difficulties. The applause which followed the remarks of Bishop Bidawid may also have been due to the fact that he was the last speaker. A number of other prelates spoke earlier, but they added nothing significant to the debate. At this point the moderator, Cardinal Lercaro, called for a standing vote on whether to close debate. The motion was carried overwhelmingly.

The following day, Tuesday October 20, three more speakers were allowed to address the assembly in the name of at least 70 Fathers each. Bishop Hakim of Israel pleaded for

SACROSANCTUM OECUMENICUM CONCILIUM
VATICANUM SECUNDUM

DECRETUM DE ECCLESIIS ORIENTALIBUS CATHOLICIS

TYPIS POLYGLOTTIS VATICANIS

Title-page of Decree on Eastern Rite Churches

acceptance of the schema. "A negative vote would throw out everything, good and bad," he argued. "It is true that the text is not perfect. But what text hitherto presented in Council has been perfect? An Arab proverb states, 'Only God is perfect.' " He was followed by Archbishop Baudoux of St. Boniface, Canada, and Archbishop Athaide of Agra, India. The *relator*, Archbishop Bukatko, then summed up the debate and also put in a plea for acceptance of the text, as a basis for revision. The feeling had been that in view of the highly critical tone of the discussion, the *Non placet* votes might carry the day, but when the votes were counted they were in favor of an immediate vote on the several parts of the text. The final appeals for acceptance undoubtedly counted for something in swaying the Fathers. In the voting on the individual propositions which followed on October 21 and 22, all the propositions were carried, except group 2–4, which failed to achieve a majority because of dissatisfaction with the ruling that converts were to have no choice of rite. When the result of this vote was known, Archbishop Felici announced: "The text has not been adopted," but he later corrected himself and explained that when *iuxta modum* votes amounted to less than a third of the total, the Commission was not "obliged" to consider them, but when they came to more, the Commission was "morally bound" to take them into consideration. The provision was omitted from the final version of the decree.

Summary

October 7, 1964, Wednesday—96TH GENERAL CONGREGATION.
MASS: Archbishop Signora, Prelate Nullius of Pompeii, Italy.
MODERATOR: Cardinal Suenens.
PRESENT: 2,133 Fathers.
ANNOUNCEMENTS: booklet containing amendments to Schema on Priests being distributed and this is text that will be debated later.
PENDING BUSINESS: Schema on Apostolate of Laity.
SPEAKERS: *Relator:* Bishop Hengsbach. 1. Cardinal Ritter (St. Louis, Missouri). 2. Cardinal Browne (Curia). 3. Bishop De Roo (Victoria, Canada). 4. Bishop Charbonneau (Hull, Canada). 5. Bishop Sani (Den Pasar, Indonesia). 6. Archbishop Fernandes (Coadjutor of Delhi, India). 7. Archbishop Duval (Algiers, Algeria). 8. Bishop Rubio Repulles (Salamanca, Spain). 9. Archbishop Maccari (Mondovi, Italy).
STANDING VOTE to proceed with debate on Apostolate of Laity.

VOTES: Schema on Ecumenism, Chap. II as whole, and Chap. III
Relatores for Chap. III: Archbishop Hermaniuk (Arts. 13-18) and Archbishop Heenan (Arts. 19-24).

	Total	Placet	Non placet	Placet iuxta modum	Invalid
Ch. II					
as whole	2,174	1,573	32	564	5
Art. 13	2,177	2,154	21		2
Art. 14-18	2,162	2,119	39		4(4)
Art. 19-24	2,133	2,088	43		2(2)

October 8, 1964, Thursday—97TH GENERAL CONGREGATION.
MASS: Bishop Pedicini of Avellino, Italy.
MODERATOR: Cardinal Suenens.
PRESENT: 2,169 Fathers.
ANNOUNCEMENT: anniversary of death of Pius XII tomorrow.
PENDING BUSINESS: Schema on Apostolate of Laity.
SPEAKERS: 1. Archbishop D'Souza (Bhopal, India). 2. Bishop de Smedt (Bruges, Belgium). 3. Bishop D'Agostino (Vallo di Lucania, Italy). 4. Bishop Barela (Czestochowa, Poland). 5. Arch-

bishop Wojtyla (Kraków, Poland). 6. Bishop Bettazzi (Auxiliary
of Bologna, Italy). 7. Archbishop McCann (Capetown, South
Africa). 8. Archbishop Ziadé (Maronite Archbishop of Beirut
Lebanon). 9. Archbishop Mosquera Corral (Guayaquil, Ecua-
dor). 10. Bishop Caillot (Evreux, France). 11. Bishop Lever
(Auxiliary of San Antonio, Texas). 12. Bishop De Vet (Breda
Holland). 13. Archbishop Conway (Armagh, Ireland). 14
Bishop De Vito (Lucknow, India). 15. Bishop Tenhumberg
(Auxiliary of Münster, Germany). 16. Bishop Van Lierde
(Curia). 17. Archbishop Enrique y Tarancon (Oviedo, Spain)
18. Archbishop Veuillot (Coadjutor of Paris, France).

VOTE: Schema on Ecumenism, Chap. III as a whole

	Total	Placet	Non placet	Placet iuxta modum	Invalid
Chap. III as whole	2,169	1,843	24	296	6

October 9, 1964, Friday—98TH GENERAL CONGREGATION.
MASS: Archbishop Mar Zaya Dachtou of Urmya and Salmas, Iran,
Chaldean rite.
MODERATOR: Cardinal Suenens.
PRESENT: 2,070 Fathers.
PENDING BUSINESS: Schema on Apostolate of Laity, in general and
Chap. I.
SPEAKERS: 1. Cardinal Caggiano (Buenos Aires, Argentina). 2.
Cardinal Rugambwa (Bukoba, Tanganyika). 3. Cardinal Sue-
nens (Malines-Brussels, Belgium). 4. Archbishop Hurley (Dur-
ban, South Africa). 5. Archbishop Kozlowiecki (Lusaka, North-
ern Rhodesia). 6. Bishop Barbero (Vigevano, Italy). 7. Bishop
McGrath (Santiago-Veraguas, Panama). 8. Bishop Lokuang
(Tainan, Formosa). 9. Bishop Cazzaro (Chile). 10. Bishop Carter
(Sault Ste. Marie, Canada). 11. Archbishop Seper (Zagreb,
Yugoslavia). 12. Bishop Rastouil (Limoges, France). 13. Father
Capucci (Superior General of Basilians of Aleppo). 14. Bishop
de Orbegozo y Goicoechea (Peru). 15. Bishop Quarracino
(Nueve de Julio, Argentina). 16. Bishop Pironio (Auxiliary of
La Plata, Argentina). Following on Chap. I: 17. Bishop László
(Eisenstadt, Austria). 18. Bishop Soares de Resende (Beira,

Mozambique). 19. Bishop Ruotolo (Ugento, Italy).
VOTES: none.

October 12, 1964, Monday—99TH GENERAL CONGREGATION.
MASS: Archbishop Ferreira de Macedo, Coadjutor of Aparecida, Brazil.
MODERATOR: Cardinal Agagianian.
PRESENT: 2,065 Fathers.
ANNOUNCEMENTS: (by Moderator) limit debate to Prologue and Chap. I of Apostolate of Laity; (by SG) a Lay Auditor will speak tomorrow; *relationes* for Schema 13 not yet ready, so next item will be propositions on Priesthood; after Priesthood, propositions on Oriental Churches.
PENDING BUSINESS: Schema on Apostolate of Laity, Prologue and Chap. I.
SPEAKERS: 1. Cardinal Liénart (Lille, France). 2. Archbishop Pluta (Poland). 3. Bishop del Pino Gómez (Lerida, Spain). 4. Bishop Padin (Auxiliary of Rio de Janeiro, Brazil). 5. Bishop Renard (Versailles, France). 6. Bishop Llopis Ivorra (Coria-Caceres, Spain). 7. Bishop Power (Antigonish, Canada). 8. Archbishop Heenan (Westminster, England). 9. Bishop Larrain Errázuriz (Talca, Chile). 10. Bishop Bäuerlein (Srijem, Yugoslavia). 11. Bishop Donze (Tulle, France). 12. Bishop Höffner (Münster, Germany). 13. Bishop Ch'eng (Auxiliary of Taipeh, China). 14. Bishop Civardi (Italy). 15. Bishop Alonso Muñoyerro (Spain). 16. Bishop Fougerat (Grenoble, France). 17. Archbishop Nicodemo (Bari, Italy).
STANDING VOTE about noon to close off debate on Apostolate of Laity.

October 13, 1964, Tuesday—100TH GENERAL CONGREGATION.
MASS: Bishop Mason of El Obeid, Sudan.
MODERATOR: Cardinal Agagianian.
PRESENT: 2,152 Fathers.
ANNOUNCEMENT: welcome to parish priests.
PENDING BUSINESS: Schema on Apostolate of Laity.
SPEAKERS (each for at least 70 Fathers): 1. Archbishop Guerry (Cambrai, France). 2. Bishop Quadri (Auxiliary of Pinerolo, Italy). 3. Archbishop Zoghby (Melkite Vicar for Egypt). Patrick Keegan, Lay Auditor. *Relator:* Bishop Hengsbach.
NEW BUSINESS: Propositions on the Priestly Life and Ministry.
SPEAKERS: *Relator:* Archbishop Marty (Rheims, France). 1. Cardi-

nal Meyer (Chicago, Ill.). 2. Bishop Théas (Tarbes-Lourdes, France). 3. Archbishop Rosales (Cebù, Philippines). 4. Archbishop Evangelisti (Meerut, India). 5. Bishop Añoveros Ataún (Cadiz y Ceuta, Spain). 6. Archbishop Fares (Catanzaro-Squillace, Italy). 7. Archbishop Ayoub (Maronite Archbishop of Aleppo, Syria). 8. Bishop Hiltl (Auxiliary of Ratisbon, Germany). 9. Bishop Komba (Tanganyika). 10. Archbishop Rodriguez Ballón (Arequipa, Peru). 11. Archbishop Perris (Naxos, Greece). 12. Bishop Donovan (Auxiliary of Detroit, Mich.). 13. Bishop Casullo (Brazil). 14. Bishop Kuharic (Auxiliary of Zagreb, Yugoslavia).
VOTES: none.

October 14, 1964, Wednesday—101ST GENERAL CONGREGATION.
MASS: Bishop Brizgyz, Auxiliary of Kaunas, Lithuania.
MODERATOR: Cardinal Agagianian.
PRESENT: 2,119 Fathers.
ANNOUNCEMENTS: revised version of Propositions on Training of Priests distributed; schedule of voting tomorrow and Friday on propositions on Priestly Life and Ministry has been delayed; a message to the priests of the world, now being prepared (proposed last session), will accompany text on Priestly Life and be submitted for approval but will not be debated; *relationes* on Schema 13 have been completed but not yet printed, they will be distributed on Friday and debate will begin that day or Monday.
PENDING BUSINESS: Propositions on Priestly Life and Ministry.
SPEAKERS: 1. Cardinal de Barros Camara (Rio de Janeiro, Brazil). 2. Cardinal Ruffini (Palermo, Sicily). 3. Cardinal Quiroga y Palacios (Compostela, Spain). 4. Bishop Bank (Hungary). 5. Archbishop Baldassari (Ravenna, Italy). 6. Bishop Ferreira de Macedo (Auxiliary of Aparecida, Brazil). 7. Bishop Sanchez-Moreno Lira (Auxiliary of Chiclay, Peru). 8. Bishop Latusek (Auxiliary of Wroclaw, Poland). 9. Archbishop Gomes dos Santos (Goiania, Brazil). 10. Bishop Pereira (Auxiliary of Coimbra, Portugal). 11. Bishop Kowalski (Chelmo, Poland). 12. Bishop Mansilla Reoyo (Ciudad Rodrigo, Spain). 13. Bishop Garaygordobil (Ecuador). 14. Bishop Nowicki (Gdansk, Poland). 15. Bishop Čekada (Skoplje, Yugoslavia). 16. Bishop Gonzalez Martin (Astorga, Spain). 17. Bishop Proaño Villalba (Ecuador). 18. Bishop Corripio Ahumada (Tampico, Mexico). 19. Bishop Castán-Lacoma (Siguenza-Guadalajara, Spain).
VOTES: none.

October 15, 1964, Thursday—102ND GENERAL CONGREGATION.
MASS: Bishop Moro Briz of Avila, Spain.
MODERATOR: Cardinal Agagianian and Cardinal Lercaro.
PRESENT: 2,130 Fathers.
ANNOUNCEMENTS: burden of granting permissions to attend the daily conciliar mass.
PENDING BUSINESS: Propositions on Priestly Life and Ministry.
SPEAKERS: 1. Cardinal Alfrink (Utrecht, Holland). 2. Bishop Köstner (Gurk, Austria). 3. Bishop Jenny (Auxiliary of Cambrai, France). 4. Archbishop Modrego y Casaus (Barcelona, Spain). 5. Bishop Gugic (Auxiliary of Dubrovnik-Ragusa, Yugoslavia). 6. Archbishop Sartre (Malagasy Republic). 7. Bishop Flores Martin (Barbastro, Spain). After closing of debate, in name of at least 70 Fathers: 8. Cardinal Lefebvre (Bourges, France). *Relator:* Archbishop Marty (Rheims, France).
NEW BUSINESS: Propositions on Oriental Churches.
SPEAKERS: *Relatores:* Cardinal Cicognani and Archbishop Bukatko (Belgrade, Yugoslavia). 1. Cardinal König (Vienna, Austria). 2. Patriarch Stephanos I Sidarouss (Coptic Patriarch of Alexandria). 3. Patriarch Maximos IV Saigh (Melkite Patriarch of Antioch).
STANDING VOTE to close debate on Priestly Life and Ministry.

October 16, 1964, Friday—103RD GENERAL CONGREGATION.
MASS: Concelebrated by Bishop Hakim and other eastern-rite prelates, Byzantine rite.
MODERATOR: Cardinal Lercaro.
PRESENT: 2,092 Fathers.
ANNOUNCEMENTS: distribution of amended text of Chap. VII of *De Ecclesia,* to be voted on Monday; Coordinating Commission has decided that each of texts reduced to propositions will have preliminary vote immediately after discussion, and if accepted by simple majority council will proceed to vote on individual propositions, otherwise text will be remanded to Commission for revision; preliminary vote will be taken on Monday on Priestly Life and Ministry; distribution of new Instruction on liturgy; schedule of meetings: no general congregations on Nov. 1, Nov. 2 and Nov. 3.
PENDING BUSINESS: Propositions on Oriental Churches.
SPEAKERS: 1. Cardinal de Barros Camara (Rio de Janeiro, Brazil). 2. Archbishop Gori (Latin Patriarch of Jerusalem). 3. Patriarch Ignace Pierre XVI Batanian (Lebanon). 4. Archbishop Slipyi (Lwów, Ukraine). 5. Archbishop Ghattas (Thebes, Egypt).

6. Archbishop de Provenchères (Aix, France). 7. Archbishop Zoghby (Egypt). 8. Bishop Doumith (Lebanon). 9. Bishop Cristea (Roumanians in exile). 10. Bishop Stangl (Würzburg, Germany).
VOTES: none.

October 19, 1964, Monday—104TH GENERAL CONGREGATION.
MASS: Archbishop Descuffi of Izmir, Turkey.
MODERATOR: Cardinal Lercaro.
PRESENT: 2,135 Fathers.
ANNOUNCEMENTS: preliminary votes on acceptance or rejection of propositions will be by simple majority, as stated; three more days will be allowed for submitting *modi* on the Priestly Life and Ministry; discussion will begin on Schema 13 tomorrow; vote tomorrow on Oriental Churches.
PENDING BUSINESS: Propositions on Oriental Churches.
SPEAKERS: 1. Cardinal Lercaro (Bologna, Italy). 2. Archbishop Tawil (Syria). 3. Archbishop Scandar (Egypt). 4. Abbot Höck (Superior of Bavarian Benedictines). 5. Bishop Bayan (Egypt). 6. Bishop Costantini (Sessa Aurunca, Italy). 7. Archbishop Vuccino (France). 8. Archbishop Edelby (Syria). 9. Bishop McDevitt (Auxiliary of Philadelphia, Pa.). 10. Bishop Kocisko (Passaic, New Jersey). 11. Archbishop Ayoub (Syria). 12. Archbishop Sfair (Turkey). 13. Bishop Sipovic (Finland). 14. Bishop Bidawid (Amadiyah, Iraq).

VOTE: Acceptability of Priestly Life and Ministry (for immediate voting)

	Total	*Placet*	*Non placet*	Invalid
Priestly Life	2,135	930	1,199	6(2)

VOTES: Revised Chap. VII of *De Ecclesia*
Relator: Cardinal Santos (Manila, Philippines).

	Total	*Placet*	*Non placet*	Invalid
Art. 48	2,135	2,099	20	16(16)
Art. 49	2,132	2,121	8	3
Art. 50	2,121	2,104	8	9(9)
Art. 51	2,077	2,067	8	2(1)

VOTE: standing vote to close debate on Oriental Churches.

IV

The Debate on
"The Church in the Modern World"

✠

TUESDAY, OCTOBER 20, 1964, was a red-letter day in the history of the Council, because the Fathers finally reached the long-awaited, controversial Schema on the Church in the Modern World. It has been more commonly known as "Schema 13," because this was the number which it acquired in the list of seventeen schemata to which the seventy original conciliar documents were reduced. This designation was unofficial, of course; there was no set numbering of the schemata.

Schema 13 almost failed to make the floor, however. Rumors spread on October 8 that it would be withdrawn from debate in order to allow the Council to end with the Third Session. The suggestion was discussed at a meeting of the Coordinating Commission the day before, but no decision was reached. It was obvious that there was a certain amount of stalling during this weekend of the *magno cum dolore* "crisis," when there was momentary confusion in the reaches of higher authority. The Council was scheduled to take up the schema after debating the Apostolate of the Laity, but Archbishop Felici suddenly announced that this would be followed by a brief discussion of several of the propositions, because "the *relationes* for Schema 13 were not yet ready." Needless to say, hardly anybody believed that this was the full story, but in a few days it became apparent that the debate would be held after all. The strong protest to the Pope drafted by the cardinals on October 11 may have had something to do with reaching a positive decision on going ahead with Schema 13. It is unthinkable that Pope Paul himself can have seriously entertained the idea of side-tracking the document, since he, as Cardinal Montini, along with Pope John and Cardinal Suenens, had been one of its prime movers from the very start.

A mixed commission, headed by Cardinal Cento and Cardinal Ottaviani, presidents respectively of the Commission for the Apostolate of the Laity and the Theological Commission, had been responsible for preparing the schema. The drafting was actually done by a subcommission presided over by Bishop Guano of Livorno, Italy, of which the Redemptorist moral theologian, Father Bernard Häring, was secretary. There were a number of other subcommissions responsible for different parts of the document. The draft schema before the Fathers was worked out by the subcommission in the early spring of 1964 and received final approval from the Coordinating Commission in June. Probably no other conciliar document had gone through so many stages before reaching its final form. It now consisted of four chapters and five appendices called *Adnexa,* containing in part earlier versions of the schema that had been discarded as formal texts but retained as explanatory matter, helpful to an understanding of the schema itself. Archbishop Felici, the Secretary General, had overconfidently announced on

October 1 that the *Adnexa* were "private documents" with no official standing, but he was obliged to retract these words, at the direction of the Moderators, and explain that they were "conciliar documents" but would not be debated.

The Secretary General announced that there would first be debate on the schema as a whole, after which the Fathers would be asked to vote on whether the document should be accepted for further discussion or sent back to commission. If the vote were favorable to continued debate, the latter would take place in three stages: the Introduction and Chapter I; Chapters II and III; Chapter IV. Since the final chapter covered so many topics, the discussion of it would proceed by paragraphs.

In an optimistic and enthusiastic tone, the schema was introduced by Cardinal Cento, who appeared quite unabashed by the rough treatment accorded the earlier document he had introduced, on the Apostolate of the Laity. "No other document had aroused so much interest and raised so many hopes," he said. "It was evident that Mother Church had not become senile and was not suffering from hardening of the arteries, but had preserved the youthful freshness of her Founder, Christ." Bishop Guano, who followed, delivered the report of the subcommission and entered into more detail. He stressed in particular the novelty of the schema and its lack of perfection. It was not offered as a final text but as a first draft and should be received as such. The Fathers must not be put off because of the differences in tone and content from other conciliar documents. It was not a definitive or exhaustive statement, but one intended to inaugurate a "dialogue," to discuss some of the burning problems of today and the Church's reaction to them. "The Church cannot remain closed up within herself as in a fortress, intent only on defending her own interests and members. The Church recognizes that she is living in the world, sharing the life of men in order to give them the life of God, existing among men and for men." One of the difficulties encountered

in preparing the text was in finding a correct balance between the great principles of the Gospel and an adequate description of present-day conditions to be discussed in the
light of these principles. Another was the difficulty of finding
the right language. Some people would be put off by the
unaccustomed terminology; others would find it still too
traditional and ecclesiastical. Another was that people would
probably expect too much from the document and Bishop
Guano warned against this over-optimism. With regard to the
Adnexa, he explained that they remained as working documents under the jurisdiction of the subcommission which
had prepared them, but they were being submitted to the
Fathers now for comment, rather than for debate. The subcommissions would reconsider them at their leisure in the
light of the comments in writing, with the decision about
their ultimate fate to be made later.

The debate was led off with an impressive barrage from
the "big-guns" Cardinals Liénart, Spellman, Lercaro, Léger,
Doepfner, Meyer and Silva Henriquez the first day. Cardinal
Ruffini managed as usual to interject a discordant note, but
he could only rate third place on the list this time. The
salvoes continued the following day with volleys from Cardinals Landázuri-Ricketts, Suenens and Bea, and a host of
smaller shots. The reception was on the whole overwhelmingly favorable. The subcommission was delighted. Cardinal
Liénart found the schema good in essentials, but the style
was too much that of a sermon: "The text proceeds by way
of constant exhortations and seems lacking in humility";
and there was not a sufficiently clear distinction drawn between the supernatural and the natural orders in the Preface and Chapter I. He said the schema moved indiscriminately from one order to the other without making that fact
clear at all times.

In his first speech at the Council following an illness that
had prevented him from attending the first part of the session, Cardinal Spellman termed the schema "admirable." He

said that it came up to the Council's expectations and should not be weakened in any way. It manifested the will of the Church for service and dialogue. A condition of dialogue, however, was a proper sense of obedience, of obedience to ecclesiastical authority. He wished that the document would deal with this subject and show that "true filial obedience is fully consonant with liberty."

The importance of the schema was fully acknowledged by Cardinal Ruffini of Palermo, but he found the treatment wholly inadequate of the questions it raised. Some statements seemed to smack of "situation ethics" which the Church had already condemned. He was particularly critical of the section on the family. "Some statements are either wrong, or else I don't understand them," he admitted, with refreshing candor. When reminded by the Moderator, Cardinal Doepfner, that he was wandering from the subject under discussion (the schema as a whole), he replied that he knew that, but his speech had been prepared before it was known what the order of discussion would be, and he went right on with his talk. "I am not against ecumenism, I believe, but *ne quid nimis!*" he exclaimed. The schema should be completely rewritten and based on the papal social encyclicals of the present century.

A plea for a full discussion of the schema was put in by Cardinal Lercaro, who observed that experience had shown that it was possible to arrive at a satisfactory text only on the basis of a generous airing of views in the Council hall (e.g. the schemata on the Church and Divine Revelation). This was necessary in order to avoid too European or Western an outlook. It was unwise to proceed with too much haste. Even a Fourth Session held in 1965 might not find the text ready for final approval. He warned, too, against expecting too much from the present discussion. The world press had become so wrought up over the question, there was danger of a let-down (applause). The approach of Cardinal Léger was similar to that of Cardinal Liénart: while approving of the schema in general, he felt that the distinction between man's terrestrial and his celestial vocation was not made sufficiently clear; however, its avoidance of sterile condemnations marked progress. Speaking in the name of 83 bishops, Cardinal Doepfner surmised that the text could not be discussed and revised in the remaining five weeks of the Council, and that enough time must be allowed so that it could be perfected, "to make it the real crown of this Council." He regretted that not enough space had been devoted to the problem of modern atheism, especially dialectical materialism.

The same sentiments were shared by Cardinal Meyer of Chicago, whose intervention was along more theological lines. The schema appeared to fear the "contagion" of the world too much: this was because of an insufficient emphasis on the theology of salvation and the bonds which redemption has established between God and man, according to St. Paul. Man's work in the temporal order is part of the transformation which God plans for the world. Every act of his fits into this divine plan. The compenetration of the Church and the world could be better explained if these points were brought out more fully. Cardinal Silva Henriquez saw the schema as a step in the formulation of a "Christian cosmology" and he was pleased that it showed the need for a dialogue with contemporary humanism, especially atheism, along the lines of Pope Paul's encyclical, *Ecclesiam suam*. Modern atheism derived its strength from its emphasis on the temporal order and the Church must be prepared to engage in conversation with it on its own ground.

Several speakers found the language inexact and vague. One of the terms most frequently criticized was "world": sometimes it seemed to be used in a favorable sense and again as something opposed to the Church; the word "Church" was also used ambiguously. These points were brought out by Cardinal Landázuri-Ricketts, who felt also that insufficient attention had been paid to the problem of famine in the world today.

While concurring in what his fellow-moderators had said, in a "spirit of fraternal collegiality," Cardinal Suenens made several points of his own. It was not stated explicitly enough that the Church "does not evangelize by civilizing, but civilizes by evangelizing," as Pius X had observed. Further consideration should be given to militant atheism. We must ask ourselves why men are atheists and question our own way of speaking about the faith, otherwise we make the idea of God obscure for them. Some of the material in the *Adnexa* could profitably be introduced into the text, particularly the parts on the international order and conjugal love. Cardinal Bea admitted that when he had first read the schema it had seemed to be superficial, but in a second reading he decided that it dealt with profound and difficult matters after all. But he thought the text could be helped if there were more arguments from the Bible, from the fonts of faith, rather than from mere rational principles. It was addressed, primarily, to Christians.

The tone of the document was too individualistic to suit the Maronite Patriarch Meouchi, and he detected a subordination of the supernatural goal of the Church to earthly ends, probably stemming from an insufficient theological outlook. But the text was good as a basis for discussion. Bishop Mathias of India regretted the absence of any mention of the notion of Providence, while the Italian Bishop Vairo of Gravina was particularly severe, because the teaching of Thomas Aquinas seemed to be ignored in favor of a method of carrying on a dialogue with the modern world, on too relativistic a basis. The Archbishop of Madrid declared flatly, and rather surprisingly, *non placet*, because it was not clear to whom the schema was intended to be addressed, whether Christians or non-Christians. The same defect was pointed out by Archbishop Conway of Armagh, Ireland, who stated further that it was a serious lack not to find in it anything

about the widespread commercialism of sex nowadays, for
which even the Marxists reproach us. The downgrading of
moral values and of life itself, which was continually being
encountered today, according to Bishop Elchinger of Strasbourg, France, could only be counteracted by a stronger
emphasis on the importance which the Church attached to
life. He agreed with Cardinal Suenens that some of the material which was better stated in the *Adnexa* should be introduced into the text of the schema itself. Archbishop Wojtyla
of Krakow, Poland, hailed what he called the "heuristic
method" employed by the schema, that is, its attempt to appeal to non-believers on grounds which they could understand.

On the third day of the debate the temperature suddenly
plunged toward zero and it seemed, momentarily, as if all
might be lost owing to a chorus of criticisms. Archbishop
Heenan of Westminster, England, was the first speaker of
the day. His beginning was innocuous enough, with praise
for a Commission that had labored so hard, but when he
referred to the document as "unworthy of a general Council,"
and "a set of platitudes," ears began to prick up. He soon
launched into the heart of the matter.

I must speak plainly. This document is going to dash the hopes
of everyone who has been waiting for it. Its authors do not seem
to realize even to whom the message is directed . . . The whole
treatise reads more like a sermon than a Council.

He objected strenuously to the advice given that the Council
should read the schema in the light of the *Adnexa* or supplements. "The fact is that the schema even read with the
supplements remains obscure and misleading; read on its
own, it could be dangerous and misleading." The Council
had been told to debate the schema and pass over the rest
without comment, but this would be fatal, because it would
leave the mind of the Council to be interpreted by "experts"
who helped draw up the documents.

God forbid that this should happen! I fear specialists when they are left to explain what the bishops meant. (*Timeo peritos adnexa ferentes.*)

Between sessions of this Council, the Church of God has suffered a great deal from the writings and speeches of some of the specialists. They are few in number but their sound has gone forth to the ends of the earth. These few specialists care nothing for the ordinary teaching authority of the bishops—nor, I regret to say, for that of the Pope. It is idle to show them a papal encyclical in which a point of Catholic doctrine is clearly laid down. They will immediately reply that a Pope is not infallible when writing an encyclical. It really does not seem worth while for the Pope to write any more encyclical letters since they can apparently no longer be quoted in support of the Faith.

We must protect the authority of the Teaching Church. It is of no avail to talk about a College of Bishops if specialists in articles, books and speeches contradict and pour scorn on what a body of bishops teaches. Until now it has not been a doctrine of the Church that the theologians admitted to the Council are infallible. The theories of one or two must not be mistaken for a general agreement among theologians which has, of course, special authority.

Archbishop Heenan went on to say that the Commission should perhaps not be too much blamed for the document since they "were in fact denied the help of experts who really knew their subjects." In dealing with problems of social life, it was necessary to consult those who knew and lived in the world. "These scholars often have a childlike trust in the opinions of men in the world. Certainly they are simple as doves, but they are not always wise as serpents." The section on marriage was singled out as a particularly glaring instance of misinformation, in the archbishop's opinion, and of the harm that could be done by leaving too many decisions to the *periti:*

If you are looking for examples of all this, you need only study the section on matrimony. Everyone knows that doctors all over the world are busily trying to produce a satisfactory contraceptive pill. This special kind of pill is to be a panacea to solve all sexual problems between husbands and wives. Neither the treatise itself nor the supplements hesitate to prophesy that such a pill is just round the corner. Meanwhile, it is said, married couples and they alone must decide what is right and wrong. Everyone must be his own judge. But, the document adds, the couple must act according to the teaching of the Church. But this is precisely what married people want to be told—what *is* now the teaching of the Church? To this question our document gives no reply. For that very reason it could provide an argument from our silence to theologians after the Council who wish to attack sound doctrine.

The document thus blandly addresses husbands and wives: "Some practical solutions have made their appearance and there are more to come." This is no way for a document of the Church to be composed. When our children ask us for bread, we should not give them a stone.

In conclusion, he strongly urged that the document be given to a new Commission, on which specialists of the day and priests with pastoral experience were represented, and suggested that three or four years might be necessary to produce a really satisfactory text.

The majority was obviously stunned by the vehemence and unexpected nature of Archbishop Heenan's attack. The speech, of course, evoked a round of applause for its display of rhetorical skill. Cardinal Ruffini was seen to grasp the hand of the archbishop, who looked somewhat embarrassed and uneasy over support from this quarter. Apparently Heenan had momentarily allowed resentment and irritation to get the better of good judgment. His blanket condemnation of *periti* was widely interpreted as an attack on Father Bernard Häring, who had had much to do with the formulation of the schema and was involved in a controversy with the English hierarchy in the spring of 1964 over the question of birth control. It was not true, of course, that competent experts had not been consulted when the document was drawn up, but it is possible that not enough divergent views had been canvassed, a criticism that could be levelled against most of the other Commissions as well. If the archbishop really was irritated, he soon got over his pique. Meeting Father Häring later, he invited him to speak to the English hierarchy at the English College. When someone remarked to the Redemptorist, "You must have suffered this morning during the congregation," he replied: "No, I expected something like that . . . It is not we who are important, but the work which each one should do humbly in his place." Bishop Wright of Pittsburgh perhaps summed up the general impression of Heenan's speech at a press conference two days later, when asked for his comment: "It is clear that the archbishop felt very deeply and personally about what he had to say—whatever it was he had to say."

The following day Abbot Reetz, superior of the Beuron Benedictines in Germany, amused the Fathers by replying humorously to Archbishop Heenan. "It is with fear and trepidation," he said, "that I speak to the Fathers, because we heard yesterday that it is useless for the Council to call upon men from religious houses, seminaries and universities. I, a monk and abbot, who hardly knows the world, am now addressing the assembly, speaking with the simplicity of the dove rather than the asperity of a serpent." He went on somewhat ironically: "Perhaps the 40 monks once sent to make *angels* of the *Angli* didn't know very much about the world. But it was a monk who was the first primate of England, St. Augustine of Canterbury; and it was a monk, St. Benedict, whom the Pope will proclaim as the Patron of Europe, tomorrow, at Montecassino." This remark was followed by applause, which the Moderator stifled by saying, *"Ne fiant plausus."* The monk's flight from the world was not a flight from the Church and the apostolate, Abbot Reetz went on. History proves how much those who have been monks have contributed to the Church and to mankind. Father Teilhard de Chardin was currently enjoying a great influence, especially over the young. The beauty of his can-

ticle to matter has been compared to the famous canticle of
St. Francis of Assisi. But Father Teilhard did not pay enough
attention to the presence of sin in the world. The schema
must be praised for avoiding this pitfall. Archbishop Heenan,
typically, was delighted by the *riposte* and sent a letter to the
abbot, saying *"Touché"* and inviting him to dinner at the
English College. (Some time after the close of the session,
Abbot Reetz was unfortunately killed in an automobile
accident.)

The name of Teilhard de Chardin was also brought up by
Archbishop Hurley of Durban, South Africa, in connection
with what he called "the central theological problem of the
century," the value of the natural order in its relation to
man's supernatural end. He approved of Teilhard's splendid
vision, "at once religious, scientific, evolutionary and eschatological," and suggested the setting up of a special commission
to study this fundamental question, along the lines of the
intervention of Cardinal Meyer and in the light of the doctrine of Thomas Aquinas on the presence of God in the
world, so that concrete problems could be decided on the
basis of this guidance. He added, slyly, "there must still be
some experts left who could be called upon for this." Bishop
Charue of Namur also came to the support of the *periti:*
"The schema is premature; it needs a good incubator. The
commission has *excellent* experts; if others are added, the
results will be good."

Reference to the name of Teilhard de Chardin naturally
suggested the propriety of mentioning the name of John
Henry Newman in connection with Schema 13. This was
done by Archbishop Shehan of Baltimore, who felt that the
document should refer, as did Pope Paul's encyclical *Ecclesiam suam,* to the problem of the Church's progress in its
doctrines and institutions. "The Church must advance more
and more in the consciousness of its task," the Pope had said.
Newman in his *Essay on the Development of Doctrine* had
made the comment, "A power of development is proof of
life."

The schema was praised by Bishop Gonzalez Moralejo of Valencia, Archbishop Roy of Quebec, Archbishop Duval of Algiers, Bishop Stimpfle of Augsburg and some other prelates, but a few of the Latin-speaking bishops took a cautious or fear-laden line. The Bishop of Campos, Brazil, regretted that there was no mention of the devil, "who nevertheless exists"; and Bishop Barbieri of Cassano, Italy, found that the schema said nothing about "the greatest evil today, the loss of any feeling for God." The same prelates also found it displeasing that so little was said about the threat of communism (e.g. Archbishop Bolatti of Rosario, Argentina), a judgment in which the exiled Archbishop of Nanking, Yu Pin, quite naturally concurred. He called for an entire new chapter on the subject.

The questioning of the authority of the *magisterium,* which Archbishop Heenan had brought up earlier, was mentioned again by Archbishop Beck of Liverpool, England, who felt some uneasiness over the document's treatment of marriage and its implied downgrading of *Casti connubii.* He thought also that the arrangement of the material could be improved by starting out with more practical and concrete questions, including many topics dealt with in the *Adnexa.*

Toward 11 o'clock on Friday, October 23, the moderators decided that debate on the schema had been sufficiently exhausted and called for a standing vote on whether to close off discussion. The assembly being willing, the Fathers were then asked to cast their ballots on whether to continue discussion of the various parts of the schema. The results were overwhelmingly favorable: 1,579 to 296. About 200 bishops were either in the bars or had left the Council hall, not expecting a vote that morning. Bishop Guano could not be located at once to sum up the debate, so that the Secretary General, Archbishop Felici, was obliged to fill in with some remarks about the likelihood of some of the Fathers becoming saints, as had happened to one of the bishops at Vatican Council I, St. Anthony Mary Claret, whose feast day it was. He hoped that the secretary general of the next ecumenical

council would be able to announce that some of the present
Fathers had been canonized, but he, Pericle Felici, would
surely be in purgatory expiating his sins. The rumor spread
that the reason Bishop Guano could not be found was that
he had been to see the Pope; there was naturally considerable
interest in his remarks, therefore, when he disclosed that
while it would not be possible to bring back the schema to
the floor before the end of the present session, it was hoped
there would be a vote on certain urgent questions such as
poverty, hunger, peace and atheism—but he did not elaborate on this. Bishop Guano reminded the prelates that since
a special commission of experts had been appointed by the
Pope to consider the question of birth control, the schema
remained somewhat vague on details because it would be
unwise to anticipate the results of this body's recommendations. The Holy Father had reserved to himself a final decision in this matter.

Earlier, at the beginning of the congregation, Archbishop
Felici had confirmed that the Third Session would definitely
end on November 21 with a concelebration ceremony by the
Pope and 24 prelates from countries with Marian shrines.
He also had some warm words of praise for the "hard-working *periti*" and expressed the hope that the commissions
would have some documents ready in time so that they could
be proclaimed on the final day. He continued: "The next
session of the Council will be held"—and then paused, as all
ears were strained to catch the all-important words—"when
the Holy Father decides." A Fourth Session was inevitable.

There was a noticeable relaxation of tension at the end of
the meeting on October 23. The mood of the Council seemed
to change from pessimism to one of cautious optimism and
even excitement over the prospect of achieving the essential
goals this session.

Keeping up its rapid pace, the Council covered considerable ground in the next two weeks, debating a new section
of Schema 13 practically every other day. Some held that the

pace was too fast and that justice was not being done to important topics, but there was no alternative under the circumstances. It seemed vital to allow every item on the agenda to come to the floor however briefly, so that the commissions could get on with the work of revising the texts in the light of the interventions, oral and written. Above all it was deemed necessary for the Council to express its wishes with regard to the drafts at least by a preliminary vote. Experience had shown that drafts accepted to be voted on in detail, and amended in accordance with the wishes of the Council (*modi*), were more likely to retain their identity, for the commission was then morally bound to respect the wishes of the assembly in such cases. But the rules of the Council were purposely made vague by their framers, so that even when texts had been "registered" in this way, they were still liable to behind-the-scenes pressures and drastic alterations in the name of "higher authority." The experience of the first two sessions amply demonstrated this. There could be no certainty of a document's integrity until it had finally been promulgated. The text* of the schema:

PREFACE

1. (*The Church in Council and mankind*). The joys and sorrows, hopes and anguish of men of this time, of the poor and afflicted especially, are the anguish and hopes, the sorrows and joys of the Council. For we are all men, the members of an immense people, created by God, inhabiting the earth, which God entrusted to us . . . Moreover we have all been called to be one family of the sons of God in Jesus Christ, who pursues all men regardless of race or language, country or condition, with the same love, and came into the world to free all from the misery and discord of sin and gather them together and rule them by his commandment of love, unity and peace.

* The translation of key passages is based on the copious extracts printed by *Le Monde* (October 13, 14, 15, 1964) and in various diocesan newspapers, e.g. *The Catholic Reporter* (October 23, 1964) and therefore can be said to belong to the public domain. Comparison has been made with the Latin text of the schema.

2. (*The Church searches the "signs of the times"*). The times are a sign and a voice, for the Church and for men, either of the presence of God or, unfortunately, of the absence of God . . . We should listen to the voice of God, therefore, in the voice of the times . . . The Church recognizes that many things have been well done by the men of our times, it notes the growing feeling that all men are members of one family . . . it rejoices in the growth of learning and the technical sciences which corresponds to the will of God . . . But it will escape no one that mankind is far from a true solution of the grave problems which are an obstacle to the progress of civilization today. Progress has not been proportionate in wisdom and the technical sciences . . . Nor can there be true peace, which is the fruit of charity and justice, truth and liberty, so long as many men are deprived of due liberty, or others are suffering from hunger or some other disability because of an inadequate distribution of the goods of this earth . . .

. . . The Council recognizes, however, in the various events which concern the whole of mankind, the work of the Holy Spirit . . .

3. (*Those for whom the present Schema is intended*). . . . We invite all men who ask us concerning the hope that is in us, to consider with us what man is and what his vocation and task are in this world. Let them be assured of the sincere intention of Christians to cooperate in the building of a truly fraternal city . . .

4. (*Christ the Light of the World*). The Council . . . only wishes to present Christ, true God and man, as the Light and Savior of the world. . . . Christians, individually and in communities, should manifest Christ in the midst of His brethren by a generous and sincere cooperation with all men, in a spirit of brotherhood, poverty and service. And the Council urges all Christians to tackle the most urgent problems of our time with vigilance and promptness.

CHAPTER I
The Vocation of the Whole Man.

5. (*Introduction*).

6. (*The value of earthly things*). . . . The Word of God, by

assuming a human nature in the incarnation, has not only raised the whole man, body and soul, but also all of creation, matter itself, to a higher dignity, and has caused everything, earthly tasks as well, to stand in a relationship with God which surpasses the nature of man. . . .

7. (*The vocation and dignity of man must not be diminished*) . . . But the Council observes with sadness the blindness of those who, either in their teachings or their actions, reduce the life of man to its mere terrestrial dimensions. Christ has severely reprimanded and accused of being worshipers of Mammon those who have an inordinate attachment to the goods of this earth. . . .

8. (*Man the sinner needs the Savior*) . . . Man is not only born with a tendency toward evil, but is tempted by the very conditions of life, as it were, to misbehave toward God, toward his brethren, and toward the world. Mankind is continually experiencing how prosperity is destroyed by injustice, lying and violence. . . . Man is in need of the gifts of God, not only to attain eternal bliss, but also to be able to build the earthly city on a solid basis of justice and charity. . . .

9. (*The tension and harmony in the vocation of the whole man*). The two reasons for the vocation of man—namely that he first seek the kingdom of God and faithfully build the earthly city—are not opposed to each other. An earthly culture which denied its goal and divine help, would be sterile; while, on the other hand, those who pursued their vocation by spurning divine gifts in renewing the world, would be seeking God in vain. . . . Christians . . . practice in the world the love of God by alleviating the living conditions and suffering of their brethren. . . . No one should doubt that a sincere complete conversion to God demands continual concerted efforts, so that the order of charity and justice will become more and more apparent in earthly things and men will be freed from the want and bonds which prevent them from acting morally and raising their minds to higher things. . . . Let no one who is engaged in earthly occupations fail to thank God or forget how important it is to know God; let no one, likewise, who has consecrated himself to God, despise earthly occupations. All should remember that man has need of both spiritual and material food.

The Preface and Chapter I were debated for part of two
mornings (October 23 and 26). Most of the speeches dealt
with points already brought out in the general discussion.
The two themes which claimed most attention were atheism
and the relationship between the supernatural and the natural orders, or the Church and the world. The schema had
purposely avoided involvement in a detailed explanation and
condemnation of the phenomenon of widespread disbelief
today, contenting itself with listing the "absence of God" as
one of the "signs of the times," in accordance with Pope
John's recommendation, following St. Paul, "to conquer evil
by good" and with a view to initiating a dialogue with those
behind the Iron Curtain, advice which Pope Paul VI repeated in his encyclical *Ecclesiam suam*. There was no point
in stressing differences if a dialogue were to be carried on
successfully. What must be brought out were the things that
people had in common, their common aspirations and ideals,
while at the same time an attempt was made to get at the
roots of ideological differences objectively, with a view to
reaching some kind of a common understanding. But this
rather benign and philosophical approach to the problem
of atheism was not to the liking of a certain number of prelates, who spoke out in favor of a more forthright attitude,
one, however, which took into account Pope John's distinction between "atheists" and atheistic systems as "historical
movements." There were no speeches that could be labelled
as sterile calls for condemnation, pure and simple.

Taking a lead from Cardinals Suenens and Doepfner, the
auxiliary of Madrid, Bishop Guerra, asked for fuller treatment of atheistic communism. The true character of atheistic
communism must be explained in such a way that both the
simple-minded and the educated person could understand it.
The idealistic humanism to be found in theoretical communism was a very powerful force, and communism had its own
eschatology: it preached an earthly paradise, devoted to the
development of all man's potentialities. Communism ac-

cepted mankind's aspirations and did not enclose itself in skeptical agnosticism; therefore it was possible to initiate a dialogue with it.

The Archbishop of Ljubljana, Yugoslavia, called for a more positive development of atheism as one of the "signs of the times." He noted that encyclicals like *Mater et magistra* were too often neglected by Catholics and bishops, whereas in his country they were carefully studied by the communist authorities. "If God has permitted this great apostasy, it is because of the cosmic dimensions of sin, including our own sins, and with a view to our correction and perfect conversion to God," he observed. These notions should be brought out more clearly in the Preface.

This insistence on a fuller treatment of atheism inevitably caused uneasiness among the observer-delegates, both Protestants and Orthodox. Did it mean that the Catholic Church was about to abandon the wise precepts of Pope John? The former feared any relaxation of the spirit of reform and self-criticism; the Russian delegates, in particular, saw a danger to their own position if the Council laid too much stress on this theme, for it had been stipulated as one of the conditions for their attendance that there were to be no stereotyped condemnations of communism at the Council. It is just possible that the tone of the first week's debate on Schema 13 influenced the Russian delegation at the Pan-Orthodox Conference of Rhodes, headed by Metropolitan Nikodim, to change its mind and push for a more cautious approach on the establishment of a dialogue with the Roman Catholic Church, a policy which eventually triumphed.

Several speakers complained about what they called a lack of vision in the first part of the schema. According to the Archbishop of Rennes, the Preface lacked a broad cosmic vision of the differences between light and darkness in the world. The language was weak and anemic; the text seemed to have been written by men living in peace, not by those having a part in the world's anxieties. It was poorly devised to arouse much hope. A renewed vision of the world was necessary, according to Bishop Pietraszko, auxiliary of Krakow, Poland, because in some parts of the world man had lost a theological outlook and regarded man himself as the absolute master of everything. The reality of the world should be presented more in the light of its creation by God, redemption by Christ, and transformation by the work of man.

Speaking in the name of the bishops of Holland, Bishop De Vet of Breda found the text lacking in a definition of the world in the modern and Christian sense. The world is presented as something too extraneous to the Church, with good and bad elements. The Preface and first three chapters need revision to bring out a more concrete vision of the world. Another objection was that the term "Church" sometimes seemed to be something existing outside men, and sometimes was identified too closely with the hierarchy.

A particularly suggestive approach was offered by Bishop Schmitt of Metz, France. The schema seemed to pay too little attention to what was "new" about the modern world. He offered an impressive analysis of the situation today, as he saw it. The world was not merely human society and its institutions, but a whole new complex which had arisen in the last four centuries, marked by technical progress, an enormous broadening of horizons, a stirring of the masses, socialization, contrasting ideologies, constant changes. The danger was that the world had grown without any effective collaboration on the part of the Church and in open hostility to it. The world was claiming its own autonomy. What was the attitude of the Church to this new phenomenon to be? It should seek to take its place in the world. Too long it had been suspicious of humanism. In order to be missionary, the Church must exist in the mainstream of world progress. It must function in what he called "dynamic solidarity with the world's progress."

The whole vocation of man must be explained synthetically, the Archbishop of Burgos, Garcia de Sierra y Mendez, maintained. Chapter I must show how the Church makes the problems of the world its own and above all explains its view of man, the only sound view, in the face of the many false concepts about man prevalent today. A new plan was proposed by Bishop Romero Menjibar of Jaen, Spain. The schema should open with a presentation of the Church as a community of salvation, made up of men and intended by God to continue the mystery of the incarnation. Then deal with the world's problem, etc. And he wanted more emphasis on the reality of sin.

Archbishop Del Rosario of the Philippines objected to what he called "the squirrel-cage mentality" according to which man is viewed as being on probation in the world until such time as he finally gets his reward like an angel. He is always running but never gets anywhere, until God plucks him out of the cage through death. His actions remain meaningless. Chapter I contained some confusion along this line which needed straightening out. The Latin language, he observed incidentally, was not suitable for speaking about modern subjects intelligently: a modern language should be used.

Worry was expressed by the Auxiliary Bishop of Münster that the Church might not always recognize the "signs of the times," as had happened in the past. For example, the orders founded by Ignatius of Loyola and other saints, were not recognized immediately. To recognize the signs of the times the Church should cultivate a renewed theology of the Holy Spirit, be on the lookout for His presence in the Church, and ecclesiastical authority must adopt a new attitude of observing, judging and acting along more Biblical lines, acknowledging charisms. The "signs of the times," according to Archbishop Ziadé of Beirut, can be recognized only by faith, particularly in the light of the Resurrection, the greatest sign of them all, which looks toward Christ's Parousia. The

Resurrection helps us to understand all the other signs. We need prophets to help us read the signs of the times.

The speech of Cardinal Léger stressed the primacy of the supernatural vocation of man over the temporal order which he wanted made clearer, but the text seemed to imply also that the only danger to the Christian was in despising earthly things and taking refuge in the supernatural. This danger certainly existed, but there were others as well. One of them was the general crisis today over "religious practice," he said, citing the difficulty of prayer as Christians were more and more immersed in worldly affairs. While busy about such matters, they should be strengthened by meditation. The correct proportion between earthly and religious duties should be brought out in the first chapter. There was the problem also of the Christian notion of suffering. Something could be said about this.

The speech of Bishop De Roo of Victoria, Canada, impressed his hearers by its obvious sincerity and spirit of charity. The temporal responsibilities of man must be insisted on, but he warned against any dichotomy between his supernatural and natural ends. Man's vocation was an immersion and real incarnation in the world, he maintained, with all its tensions, aspirations, and victories. Man is like a vicar of Christ in the midst of the world.

One of the younger Italian bishops, Quadri of Pinerolo, who had himself been a *peritus* last session, addressed his remarks to the experts primarily. He declared that there should be a special paragraph on the topic of work. A spirituality of work must be developed, especially with regard to the final end of man and the world. A number of speakers stressed particular points, like that of Quadri. Unless there is some treatment of the immortality of the soul, felt Bishop Schoiswohl of Graz-Sechau, Austria, man's hopes will inevitably gravitate toward earthly things. Because men no longer believed in immortality there was such widespread disbelief today, hence the point should be stressed, but not with outmoded philosophical arguments. Abbot Prou of Solesmes objected to the theological implications of the statement that "all creatures," both spiritual and corporal, were intrinsically raised to the supernatural order. It was sounder, he thought, to hold that "only a spiritual creature, and on earth only the human soul, can be elevated to the supernatural order." This was intended as an indirect criticism of Teilhard de Chardin and Père de Lubac.

Debate on Chapters II and III of the schema occupied a day and a half (October 26–27), and involved such widely different topics as Church and State, the renewal of the Church, the guidance of the hierarchy, the spirit of brotherhood and poverty, and participation in international institutions. The text:

CHAPTER II

The Church in the Service of God and Men.

10. (*Introduction*). Although the Church which finds itself in this world is not of this world, it is bound by innumerable mutual ties with the world, that is with all men, their institutions and their tasks. These mutual relations are fruitful for the Church itself and for the world, notwithstanding certain differences and inevitable difficulties. Many of these difficulties can be removed or at least diminished, if all understand properly how the Church interprets the mission which it has received from the Lord with regard to the world. . . .

11. (*The proper task of the apostles and their successors*).

12. (*How the Church is related to earthly powers*). . . . The Church itself uses temporal things to the extent that its own mission requires. Nevertheless it puts no hope in the privileges offered by civil authority. Moreover, it would willingly renounce the exercise of certain rights legitimately acquired, if it were convinced that because of the use of such things the purity of its witness could be called into doubt, under changed circumstances. . . . The Church is particularly concerned to promote, with the aid of all men of good will, a true spirit of liberty, excluding any use of force which would offend the dignity of the

human person or compromise a sincere faith. For the gospe
calls for the free response of man, is opposed to any merely ex
ternal assent, but on the contrary demands a sincere interna
conversion and new life in Christ. . . . Freedom is an essentia
part of the common good. The Church teaches that the tw•
powers, the spiritual and the temporal, are to be distinguished
and that Christians are bound by the just laws of the tempora
powers, saving for the duty of preaching the gospel, professin;
the faith, and observing the divine law in all things. Pastors
moreover, while fulfilling their mission sometimes have to pas
judgment on temporal matters because of faith or morals, bu
they should never mix in the proper sphere of the tempora
authority. For they know that their task is not to intervene ir
temporal matters as such. . . . The clergy should be concernec
with their sacred task of unique service to God and the salvatior
of men, they should not be distracted by any desire for ruling
but they should not forget that temporal things are subject tc
God and the laws of His wisdom, which bind all consciences. . .
By divine providence, pastors are daily less and less involvec
in looking after temporal matters owing to present conditions.

13. (*How the Church is helped by the world*). . . . Witl
simplicity the Church listens to those who find fault with the
sins of its members, of their lack of an evangelical spirit. For i
knows that the Holy Spirit has been given to it to give His gift:
to the world, but also that it consists of men, whose ignoranc•
and sins can often impede a ready response to the prompting•
of the Spirit, and that the need for a continual renewal has beer
imposed on the Church until the end of time. . . .

14. (*The Church helps the earthly city*). . . . The people o•
God, especially in these changing and difficult times, must con
tinually ask what it is that the signs of the times demand. In
this the pastors and the rest of the faithful should help one an•
other: pastors by interpreting in accordance with their apostolic
task the teaching of the gospel and what is essentially connected
with it; the faithful, by helping in accordance with their own
role and their sense of the faith, the pastors, either by advice
or in practical ways. All moreover should value the intelligence
and prudence of those who are outside the Church. The faithful,
however, must not think that their pastors are either competent or

alled to give them an answer to all the questions, even the
erious ones, and tell them what has to be done here and now;
and besides, it is no wonder that even the church's magisterium,
n new and very difficult questions, where it is a matter of apply-
ng the principles of current teaching to changed conditions of
ife, does not immediately have prompt and ready answers or
olutions. But if in such a situation, where there are no direc-
ives issued by ecclesiastical authorities, the faithful must never-
heless do something, let them be bold enough on their own
esponsibility to take matters into their own hands and according
o the dictates of their own conscience, guided always by that
Christian prudence that is inherent in the truth of the gospel
and the Church's moral teaching, and which always takes note
of the individual circumstances in which man must act, and let
t be aided also by all the human sciences that have a bearing
on the several problems. Of course disagreements quite often
arise as to whether the decision reached is the right one. Nevertheless let them remember that at all costs there must be unity in
regards to a doctrine definitely proposed, but in many other
things free inquiry and difference of opinion, even among the
faithful, are perfectly valid; but in all things charity and the
humble search for God's will must shine forth. . . .*

CHAPTER III

The Conduct of Christians in the World.

15. *(Introduction)*.
16. *(Primary conditions for confronting the world)*.
17. *(Promoting brotherhood in a spirit of poverty)*. . . . The
spirit of poverty, which all the structures of the Church should
express, is the royal road for all Christians. . . .
18. *(The dialogue and its conditions)*. Christians should pursue a dialogue with all men of good will by promoting mutual
knowledge and esteem through fraternal communion. A firmness
of faith and spirit of brotherhood compel us to engage in friendly
colloquy and cooperate with all, wherever Christian prudence
permits. . . . The formation of separate temporal institutions

---

* The Latin reads: Meminerint tamen in doctrina definitive proposita
unitatem omnino adesse debere, in multis aliis vero liberam valere investi-
gationem et diversitatem opinionum etiam inter fideles: in omnibus vero
caritas atque humilis perscrutatio voluntatis Dei elucescat oportet.

should be avoided whenever it appears that cooperation with
other men of good will, especially the separated brethren, can
be accomplished within the framework of a common institution.
. . . In specifically Christian institutions, however, sometimes
necessary, let them take care that a spirit of charity and the zeal
for social work may always be thriving and apparent; moreover, such institutions should be open to all who are desirous
of cooperating in the same spirit. Christians should also be
active in international institutions, which are increasing today
in such numbers, both individually and collectively . . .

The present text of Chapter II seemed to be incomplete,
according to Bishop Ancel of Lyons. It did not show how the
interest of the Church in temporal matters proceeded from
its total mission, which was the evangelization of man. The
Church would be failing in its spiritual mission if it neglected
or ignored temporal things. Modern man expected the
Church to declare what it stood for and why it was interested
in temporal matters. People would listen, if the Church
avoided any appearance of moralizing or proselytizing.

Cardinal Frings called for greater accuracy in the use of
such words as "world," "progress," "salvation." Those who
accused the Church of a certain Platonism because of its
aloofness from the world were not wrong, but it should be
remembered that salvation did not come from the world.
The true liberty of the Christian would be safeguarded only
if account were taken of the three doctrines of the Creation,
the Incarnation, and the Cross and Resurrection.

We must find a new way of presenting the Church to the
world, said Archbishop Marty of Rheims. The Church is
too western, too hidebound by the past. During the Middle
Ages the western world was under the Church; today the
modern world extends far beyond the confines of the Church
and has its own contours. The Church must be in the world
like leaven mixed in flour. This is the only possible way. And
we must be careful not to say that the laity are a bridge between the Church and the world, for on the one hand this

implies that the Church is not in the world, which is false, and on the other that the laity are outside the Church, which is equally false. The Church must be present *as a body,* clergy and laity.

An intriguing point was raised by the next speaker, Bishop La Ravoire Morrow of India. "How," he asked, "can the men and women of our time understand that God is good if we continue to teach them that those who do not abstain on Fridays go to hell? They do not see any proportion between the Church's precepts and God's commandments. How can eating meat on Friday deserve the same punishment as committing adultery or murder? This causes the moral sense of people to become blunted and ecclesiastical authority to be despised. I do not propose that the Church's precepts be abolished, but they should be simplified. No precept should be imposed lightly under pain of mortal sin. Religion is not fear, but love." The bishop's remark about Friday abstinence was only incidental to his general thesis, but it quite naturally caused a stir outside the confines of the Council hall, resulting in such headlines as "CHURCH TO ALLOW MEAT ON FRIDAYS?"

In his usual forthright style, Patriarch Maximos IV rose on October 27 and lambasted some of the more glaring maladjustments of the Church to the modern world. "The Church should take an interest in all the problems of her children," he began. "It must consider them not as servants, but as friends." The important thing was to train the faithful in love of Christ and develop a sense of responsibility. He said:

We are no longer living in the Middle Ages, a time when mankind was young. Today man is grown up. We must not impose any laws on him unless we can explain the reason and positive purpose. Our method of teaching morality must be radically transformed. Teaching, especially since the seventeenth century, has been entirely too legalistic and conducive to the immaturity of a closed and absolutistic society. We are still too much influenced by juridicism. Christ should be the center of morality. Even in the East, we have been contaminated by Roman juridicism.

Take, for example, the catechism. We make it an obligation for the faithful to abstain on Fridays and to assist at Mass on Sundays under pain of mortal sin. Is this reasonable, and how many Catholics believe this? As for unbelievers, they merely have pity on us. Even in connection with the sacrament of penance there are some things which need revision.

A revision is necessary. All the commandments have been laid down for the sake of love. Let us not give orders, but act from love. A mother does not like having to chastise her child with a stick. Modern man rebels against the use of force. I propose the creation of a large commission of theologians to make a general study of the teaching of morality and the precepts of the Church with a view to making the necessary adaptations to our modern way of life.

The patriarch received a long round of applause when he had finished.

Wholehearted concurrence in the views of Bishop La Ravoire Morrow and Patriarch Maximos IV was voiced by Bishop Mendez Arceo of Cuernavaca, Mexico. One of the principal signs of the present times was the growth of a sense of responsibility and freedom. The Church must appear not only as a defender of religious liberty, but of liberty itself. It must preach a spirit of liberty and love. But the multiplication of church laws was hardly in accordance with the spirit of liberty. What the schema said was good, but deeds were more important. The numerous penalties imposed under pain of mortal sin were ridiculous. Yet seminarians were taught that they must observe a host of things under this threat. Catholics were threatened with hell if they so much as took one drop of water before taking communion. All trace of rigorism should be avoided, for it has brought the Church into disrepute. In our manuals, for example, it is said that no sin is involved in embroidering on Sunday, but that if a woman knits for several hours she is committing a

.n. This type of attitude *makes* people sinners, he stated. Turning to the subject of poverty, Archbishop Golland 'rindade of Botucatú, Brazil, put forth a strong plea for the :hurch "to come down from its thrones and rid itself of its rnaments." He remarked that the Secretary General fre- uently addressed the Fathers as *"patres ornatissimi."* This 'as true in one sense. But people understood the words in nother sense. Catholic bishops were loaded down from head ɔ foot with ornaments, as anyone could see, daily, on the treets of Rome. Bishops looked wealthy, but they were often ery poor. The Communists, numbering some seven million 1 Italy alone, see this and rejoice, for it is a symbol of the nmense distance they fondly believe exists between the ishops and the faithful. He pleaded that, with the permis- ion of the Pope, the bishops should be allowed to come to heir daily congregations dressed in black.

Bishop Fourrey of Belley, France, was also of the opinion hat it was necessary not only to profess a spirit of poverty, ut to manifest it by deeds, beginning with religious orders nd other collective institutions. He warned against the sin f usury today, particularly among trusts which exploited nderdeveloped countries.

Also speaking on the topic of poverty, Cardinal Silva Ienriquez of Chile, distinguished between its two meanings: he poverty of the Gospel or spirit of poverty, and misery or uffering. The latter was something that should be eliminated nd it could be if Christians of the world would unite to mploy the wealth of the world properly. He referred to the iggestion made some time ago by the Protestant theologian nd observer-delegate, Oscar Cullmann, professor at the Sor- onne, for an annual ecumenical collection to be taken up y each Church and devoted to the poor of another Church nd said that he highly approved of it. The Church would do 'ell, said Archbishop Zoghby, to imitate the spirit of poverty y abandoning the pompous titles which it used, for example he phrase *feliciter regnans* applied to the Pope, because

this smacked too much of temporal rule. We should be ani
mated by the spirit of Pope John XXIII, who said at the
end of his life: "I have loved all those whom I have met in
the course of my life."

Bishop Himmer of Tournai, Belgium, called for a clearer
distinction between the poverty of the Church and the pov
erty of Christians and wanted the role of poverty in building
up the Kingdom of God emphasized. "Poverty is the key to
the whole schema," he insisted. All problems, such as those
of the family and of hunger, can be solved in a spirit of
poverty. On the other hand, Cardinal Caggiano of Bueno
Aires felt that paragraph 17 should not begin with Christ'
mandate of evangelical poverty, but with mention of natura
justice. The Council should call for justice everywhere, in
cluding within the Church, and should urge governments to
pass just laws. Emphasis should be placed first on justice
before going on to charity and the spirit of poverty, which
help to build up brotherhood.

The question of Church and State was briefly touched on
by Bishop Cule of Mostar, Yugoslavia, who stated flatly
"The Church must avoid every trace of clericalism, an
suggestion of caesaro-papism, any spirit of domination." N
political party should presume to act in the name of the
Church. The Church had no need for privileges and should
ask for none from the state, only the freedom which be
longed to her. No freedom of conscience was possible with
out the Church or the autonomy of the human person. This
autonomy was based on the transcendence of God. However
for the Church's witness to God to be effective in the world
it must be practiced by the Church's members. Unfortu
nately the West was setting a bad example in this respect a
compared with the East. The fact that Bishop Cule wa
practically the only speaker to touch on this vital topi
seemed to indicate that the carefully phrased section in th
schema dealing with it was generally satisfactory.

The schema treated the relationship between the Church
and the scientific world well, according to Bishop Spülbeck

f Meissen, Germany. However there was not enough empha-
is on the effects of the profane sciences. The Church must
ccept the legitimate findings of science if it wants to carry
n a dialogue with the world. In certain communist coun-
ries the Church appears to be ignorant of some of the dis-
overies of science, and this brings religion into disrepute
vith the atheists. The great influence of the books of Teil-
ard de Chardin is due to the fact that, as a priest, he tried
o understand the language of science. Therefore the com-
nunists regard him as particularly dangerous, lest he should
be influential in reconciling the discrepancies between sci-
nce and religion. A dialogue between the Church and the
modern scientific world should be expressly encouraged in
paragraph 13. The condemnation of Galileo was wrong, and
his should be admitted.

On the other hand Bishop Klepacz of Lodz, Poland,
ounded a warning note against the evils resulting from mod-
rn "scientism" or the glorification of scientific discovery and
esearch and the resulting apotheosis of man, which has built,
one might almost say, a new Tower of Babel and confused
man with its false optimism and nihilism. A more optimistic
view was voiced by Auxiliary Bishop Kuharic of Zagreb,
Yugoslavia, who pointed out that the Pontifical Academy of
Sciences was evidence of the Church's interest in science and
its support for scientific progress and that it saw no contradiction between science and religion.

A remarkably frank intervention by Bishop Huyghe of
Arras drove home the point that before the Church could
expect to carry on a dialogue with those outside its borders,
there must be a dialogue within the Church itself. This
meant that all members of the Church must be in dialogue
with each other. They must learn to listen, to look for the
voice of the Holy Spirit. The Holy Spirit was given to the
whole community on Pentecost. We should do away with all
administrative jealousy or authoritarian practices, anything
that inhibited a dialogue between subjects and superiors in
the Church. For example, the condemnation of books by the

Holy Office without giving the author a hearing was co
trary to the dignity of the children of God. "Let us beg
by instituting a dialogue of friendship, confidence and li
erty within the Church before we approach the world
Bishop Huyghe was warmly applauded for these remarks.

The *Index Librorum* also came in for some caustic r
marks from Bishop Cleven, the auxiliary of Cologne, wl
said that it created a kind of "Catholic ghetto image" th
was the very opposite of the image of trust and freedom th
we were trying to create. The *Index* was particularly o
noxious to the young, he noted. The Church had nothing
fear from science. Science would not bring about salvatio
of course, but the Church had a long way to go to catch u
on its generally backward attitude on this score.

The Fathers were amused by the intervention of Italia
Bishop Garneri of Susa. Speaking the name of 84 bisho
from different countries, he entertained them with a discour
on the importance of tourism as a typical expression of mo
ern life, mentioning it as a useful instrument for the dialogu
Last year, he noted, some sixty million Western Europea
travelled outside their own countries. Taking care of the
called for special pastoral efforts and presented opportuniti
for promoting peace and ecumenism which should not l
missed.

On October 28, Wednesday, the Council embarked on
discussion of what was perhaps the most controversial part
Schema 13, Chapter IV. The decision to deal with each one
its paragraphs separately, by causing the speakers to conce
trate on one or two points at most, undoubtedly gave the d
bate more coherence than usual; it also helped to sustai
public interest, which could hardly fail to be aroused by suc
provocative subjects as civil rights, the place of women, ma
riage, birth control, concentration camps, prostitution, an
nuclear bombs, as well as the more sedate topics of cultura
progress, economic growth, alleviating poverty, internationa
solidarity and peace.

Expectations were momentarily dampened when the Moderator, Cardinal Agagianian, suddenly announced that, because of their delicate nature, "certain points" would not be discussed on the Council floor. This measure was intended to forestall possible misunderstanding outside the Council, he said. Written communications could be submitted by the Fathers as usual and all comments would be carefully weighed and considered by the commission. The statement was interpreted as a move on the part of conservative forces to exercise some kind of a restraining hand on the course of the debate, but since the lists of speakers were already drawn up and the content of the remarkably bold speeches that would be made on the following days must already have been known to the Council authorities, to the moderators in particular, who were among those dealing some of the heaviest blows, Agagianian's remarks must have been meant primarily *pro forma*. They may have been nothing more than an awkwardly-worded reminder to the bishops that the Pope had reserved a final decision on the delicate subject of birth control to himself, as everybody knew.

The discussion opened with a fine, carefully balanced *relatio* on Chapter IV as a whole, delivered by Bishop Wright of Pittsburgh, who said that it dealt with certain cardinal questions that he called "the masterknots of fate," peculiar to our times:

Regarding particular points, it is not our business to give quick and ready—but sometimes equivocal and deceptive—answers. Nor is it our intention to scrutinize each and every sign of the times, a task which would require many years of consultation with experts, as Archbishop Heenan indicated. But fortunately we have had and *do have* competent clerical and lay advisers to assist us in an accurate analysis of the major fears, aspirations, and desires of men today. Only thus can we bring the Church's wisdom and perennial norms of morality to bear on the entirely new situations faced by Christian consciences.

In no way, however, does this chapter intend to be exhaustive or definitive; it states not a concluding but an opening word in

a completely new dialogue to be carried on by the bishops an
by the faithful for many years . . .

We humbly request that not too much be demanded from thi
schema, which is without conciliar precedents though not with
out great hope for the future.

He concluded by noting that Article 20 had logically bee
placed at the beginning of the Chapter, "because man hold
the position of primacy among earthly creatures" and be
cause every attack upon the right social order is sooner o
later directed against the dignity of the person. The funda
mental purpose of the section was to "state the principle
bearing on the Christian's role in restoring and promotin
the personal dignity of man," in view of the many ways i
which the dignity of man was being degraded today.

There were two speakers on Chapter IV as a whole. Bisho
Gonzalez Martin of Astorga, Spain, who gave up his epis
copal palace in order to move into a humbler dwelling, sug
gested that the text could be improved with a somewha
different perspective and concluded with the call: "Befor
the Church can hope to be heard by those outside, she mus
devote herself earnestly to renewing herself within!" Th
Coptic Archbishop Ghattas of Thebes, Egypt, may have bee
speaking more or less for the record when he observed tha
the schema seemed to take too materialistic a view of th
nation. Although exaggerated nationalism was a disease t
be healed, genuine patriotism of Christian inspiration wa
something to be commended. The recognition of new na
tions by the Church should not be a question of opportunism
but the acknowledgment of a true Christian reality in whicl
men have been freed from the yoke of imperialism.

CHAPTER IV

The Chief Duties of Christians Today.
    19. *(Introduction).*
    20. *(Promoting human dignity).* Men of today hesitating be
tween hope and anxiety, desire above all that the dignity of th

human person should be recognized, by all and among all, without regard to any discrimination according to race or sex or social condition, not by mere words alone, but also by deeds, and especially by just laws. They desire that the social and the economic order should favor the cessation of any unjust slavery and promote true moral, intellectual and cultural progress, as well as security in work and leisure, so that the whole of public and private life may reflect the dignity of the human person.

The Church recognizes those desires and studies as a good seed, implanted by Him who created all things through the Word and vivifies them by His Spirit. This seed will bear mature fruit, if it is nourished by the full light of the Gospel. There are already many signs of progress on account of this; progress however has been slower in being realized than in being recognized: many people are daily engaged in rooting out the last traces of slavery; in many parts of the world the equal dignity of woman and her peculiar contribution not only to family life but to society and government are gradually being more and more acknowledged; access is being made available to higher studies and a higher degree of culture, whereas formerly these things were the privilege of a few; the dignity and rights of workers are being more and more recognized in many countries, especially the right to work and to proper conditions of labor. . . .

But it is far from true that conditions of life today are promoting a real increase in human dignity for all. Deplorable obstacles stand in the way of this goal. . . . Monstrous crimes have been perpetrated in our century or are still being perpetrated: concentration camps, where men are not only deprived of their liberty, but of almost all human rights without any recourse to justice; deportations, physical and mental torture, the infamous selling of women for the pleasure of depraved men, and the frequent depriving of unborn children of their right to live. . . .

Consideration of Articles 19 and 20 was begun by Cardinal Ritter. The treatment of human dignity was not entirely satisfactory, he thought. The cardinal wanted more stress on what Christians could do to manifest this dignity by witnessing in their lives to the transcendence of God and assuming their responsibilities. Christians, by shirking their individual and collective responsibilities, were doing real harm to the dignity of the person. The description of human dignity in the schema appeared to be based too much on psychology and technical considerations, in the opinion of Bishop Barrachina Estevan of Orihuela-Alicante, Spain. The rights of man are founded on nature enlightened by the Gospel. In contrast to the man-god, Christianity teaches the mystery of the God-man, he said. The mild tone of Chapter IV was good, declared Bishop Schick of Fulda, Germany, but the impression must not be given that the Church was offering men simply another ideology. There must be more emphasis on Scripture and theology. In some twelve pages of text there were only four quotations from the Bible. The Book of Acts could be profitably drawn on, because it was an account of the action of the Holy Spirit in the world. Auxiliary Bishop Béjot of Rheims concurred and wanted dignity expressed more clearly in terms of the Gospel. Men today attributed a great value to life, everything was done in order to save it, to find out all that could be found out about its laws, etc. But the Christian view that man was not an end in himself must be brought to bear to counteract the excessive glorification of mankind as such.

There were crimes against liberty of the human person other than unjust coercion, noted Bishop Laszlo of Eisenstadt, Austria. Liberty could be abused through excess as well as by restriction. An example of the former would be the widespread sensuality found today; an example of the latter, the tendency to avoid doing what one should do as a matter of justice. Even more pointed was the observation of Bishop Stimpfle of Augsburg that the more freedom there was in education, science, and the administration of the Church, the more human freedom would be assured in all walks of life. As a sort of rider, Bishop Barthe of Fréjus-Toulon, added that there was really no such thing as absolute liberty: the freedom of some was an evil for others. Full liberty could only be found in voluntary subjection to the will of God. The bishop felt that Article 20 should contain some criteria for judging the dignity of man today.

Three speeches which aroused the greatest interest on the first day were clarion calls for the Church to take a firm stand on the present-day issue of racial injustice and discrimination. Archbishop Athaide of Agra, India, speaking first, deplored racial segregation, *apartheid,* which exists even in countries that profess to be Christian. It is almost incredible, but such things as slavery and the buying and selling of people still are practiced. The world expects the Council to take a stand on this. "I do not ask that countries be condemned by name, but we must arouse the consciences of the world. A magnificent example has been set in this respect by such people as Gandhi, who went about barefoot attempting to get landowners to share their property with the landless, and President Kennedy, who spoke out on behalf of racial justice. Recently Pope Paul VI received Martin Luther King and praised him for his great work of passive resistance in this regard, following the example of Gandhi." (Applause.) "It is a scandal to see parishes deserted," said Bishop Grutka of Gary, Indiana, "whenever Negro families move in. The Council must proclaim the absolute opposition of the Church to all forms of racial discrimination."

Archbishop O'Boyle of Washington, rising to address the assembly in the name of all the American bishops, called for the insertion of a special paragraph in the schema dealing with the problem of discrimination not from the viewpoint of sociology and economics, but on moral and religious grounds. "The statement need not be long, but it should flatly condemn all forms of racial discrimination on the grounds that all men are equal and brethren because they are the sons of God. Our experience in the United States," he added, "suggests that this is one area of social action which calls for close cooperation between Catholics, Protestants, Jews, and all men of good will." His remarks were also greeted with applause.

A number of speakers wanted the rather brief reference to women's rights in the schema spelled out in more detail The evils of racism, tribalism, and the custom of regarding women as mere chattel in Africa was deplored by Archbishop Malula of Leopoldville in the Congo. The Pope's recent canonization of the Uganda martyrs had brought great joy to African Christians. Tribalism was merely racism on a minor scale (applause). The most detailed talk on the role of women was delivered by Bishop Coderre of St. John, Quebec, Canada, who insisted that the Council should state that woman has her own God-given personality and therefore a specific and necessary task to perform in society and in the Church. Until now woman has been prevented from fulfilling her true role, but as one of the signs of the times she is being accorded her place more and more. Bishop Coderre spoke in the name of 40 Canadian bishops. There are some three million handicapped children in France alone, nearly a quarter of all French children. The Church should have something to say about this problem, Monsignor de la Chanonie, the Bishop of Clermont, ventured to suggest. The verdict passed on Chapter IV by Bishop Bäuerlein of Srijem, Yugoslavia, was *placet iuxta modum*. He got ahead of himself somewhat by pronouncing on the treatment of marriage in Article 21 before that subject was taken up, and insisted that it was an "error" to place so much emphasis on conjugal love as the primary factor in marriage. One sensed that the private opinion of the dour and usually very conservative Yugoslav bishop was not entirely favorable to an increased role for women. On the other hand, the opinion expressed by Auxiliary Bishop of Cologne Frotz to the effect that the rise and fall of civilizations could be attributed to the public esteem which women either enjoyed or failed to enjoy, represented something of an oversimplification of history, though a highly attractive theory, it must be admitted. Modern women expected to be treated as the quals of men, the bishop held, but the Church had not yet caught up with the idea. This was something of an understatement.

Bishop Quadri of Pinerolo, Italy, wanted a fuller description of the social teaching of the Church inserted in the text at this point, one avoiding any trace of "feminism" or "anti-feminism," however. He said that the old text had a good passage along this line. The Italian bishop was not the only one to fear the perils of an unrestrained "feminism." There were many feminists in Rome for the Third Session, no doubt there to look after their rights. When Archbishop Roberts, S.J., was asked by one such feminist at a press conference—ostensibly on the twin subjects of contraception and nuclear war—whether he still believed that women should agitate in behalf of their rights, as he had apparently written somewhere in an unguarded moment, the archbishop candidly replied: "I hope that I have not heard the question, but I'm afraid that I have."

Since the close of the Third Session there has been a noticeable tendency among certain American prelates to issue statements minimizing or playing down the import of the discussion in the Council on marriage, birth control and similar "delicate" topics. The attempt to scotch the idea that the Church is ever likely to revise its traditional teaching on any essential point, and the effort to placate consciences and keep the lid on the pot by making such statements, is indication enough that people are aroused. In defense of the American bishops, it can be said that their reaction is partly explainable by the rebuff they received at the hands of the Pope during the last days of the session; their mortification has resulted in an understandable re-emphasis of the "don't rock the boat" line. Appeal is usually made to the Pope's statement in June 1964 calling for restraint in the public discussion of delicate subjects, but neither the indefinite postponement of TV programs on birth control, nor the censoring or banning of articles can disguise the fact that people today, Catholics included, are caught up in a movement of intense concern over the related problems of over-population, birth control methods, the procreation of children, their education and their future in a highly uncertain world. One American bishop is quoted as saying: "In my diocese, I *know* that people do not sit around talking about birth control." Whether people talk about these things or not, they are certainly doing a great deal of thinking and acting. In France, for example, loosely regarded as a "Catholic country," a recent survey has shown that 30 percent of women questioned, mostly young women, had had one or more abortions. More than half the sample were Roman Catholics, and among these nearly one-quarter were practicing Catholics. In another survey, 69 percent of the women questioned had used contraceptive methods at some stage in their lives; the older they were, the higher the percentage of such use; among those 37 years or older there were none who had not used such methods. In the United States these methods are used on a much wider scale, as investigations have proved. Both in the United States and France surveys have shown that a large to very large proportion of Roman Catholic women use methods forbidden by the Church. In Italy, where the public advertisement of birth control methods is prohibited by law but not the distribution of contraceptives because of a regulation laid down by Mussolini, there is ample evidence that the pattern is the same. In the face of overwhelming evidence of the increasing use of these devices by Catholics, as well as by people generally, the statement of one American bishop that he was "certain" the conservative position condemning the use of mechanical contraceptives would remain "the true Catholic position," sounds like a prejudgment of the issue.*

Other bishops have been more guarded in their pronounce-

---

* The English theologian, Father Charles Davis, has pointed out that, while this may very well be the case, doubts have been raised by "eminent churchmen" about the traditional doctrine, and the matter cannot be regarded as settled. He is of the opinion that a profound change in the theology of marriage has probably already occurred in the Church and that this will, in time, bear fruit if theological discussion can be kept open. Cf. *The National Catholic Reporter,* February 24, 1965.

ments, referring to the essential distinction that has to be made between what is fundamental and what can be changed, thus leaving themselves a convenient loophole for escape. That this has proved to be the wiser policy since the Council began its public sessions was never more amply demonstrated than by the memorable, all too brief but very much to the point discussion, on Thursday and Friday, October 29–30, 1964, of Article 21 of Schema 13. The fundamental weakness of the conservative position, as has frequently been pointed out, is that it does not allow for making this distinction. According to the conservative "all or nothing" school, if the Church has been wrong in permitting a certain type of teaching during the past four hundred years, then the Church has failed, *quod est absurdum*. Therefore, that teaching must be correct. The fallacy here is the naïve equation of the terms: Church of God = Roman Catholic Church = Curia = Lateran University (or any Catholic school teaching the conservative line). Fortunately, the new Constitution on the Church and the Decree on Ecumenism will help to dispel misconceptions and make the necessary distinctions.

Paragraph 21 is as follows:

21. (*The dignity of marriage and the family*). 1) (The supernatural ends of marriage). 2) (Marriage is based on genuine love).

3) . . . Marriage is not a mere instrument of procreation, but its nature of an indissoluble bond between persons and especially the good of the offspring demand that the spouses truly love one another; and if there are no offspring, marriage is not deprived of its fundamental value and indissolubility. Nevertheless the nature of conjugal love is such that marriage is by its nature ordained to procreation and education. Therefore true conjugal love and the whole pattern of family life arising from it are meant to dispose the spouses to cooperate generously with the love of the Creator and Savior, who by means of them enlarges and endows His family.

With regard to the number of children, Christian couples know that they are not subject to a blind instinct, but that they truly glorify God and perfect themselves in Christ if they strive to fulfil their function of procreating with full awareness of their responsibility toward the gifts of God and the norms of a true love. In this matter it is not without prayer and without a joint effort that they will arrive at a prudent judgment, not on one occasion only but at all times, on each particular occasion seeking to determine the educational and economic conditions, the health also of mind and body, and in addition to the good of the family and the Church that of the needs of society as well.

4) Turning to spouses, the Council recognizes that they are laboring under many grave economic, socio-psychological and civil difficulties, which make it extremely difficult for the strength of conjugal love, the preserver of faith and perfecter of persons, to be preserved, except in the case of those who are endowed with great personal gifts. In particular, the Council recognizes the frequent difficulty in reconciling on the one hand the sense of responsibility that forbids at least for a time an increase of offspring, and on the other hand the tender fostering of love, without which married people often become like strangers to one another. As a consequence of this, the good of fidelity is endangered and the good of offspring is defeated, both as regards the rearing of children already born, and as regards the maintaining of a strong and open mind in regard to the procreation of children in the future, when circumstances are more favorable.*

Mother Church recognizes all these facts and urges spouses not to be discouraged if her ministers, when inculcating God's law, seem not to solve the conflicts between that law and their concrete difficulties, for such difficulties often arise from grave social defects and from human frailty or malice.

Nevertheless the Church, when teaching God's law and holding up the example of chastity, is defending the family and true conjugal love and happiness. She therefore exhorts all experts in the anthropological, psychological, medical and sociological sci-

* In paragraph 23 there is a further remark about the limitation of families, and in Appendix II it is stated: The ultimate decision and practical application of universal principles belongs to the spouses themselves. However they should act according to a conscience formed in accordance with the teaching of the Church.

ences, and married people themselves trained by their own experience and virtue, to collaborate with theologians in exploring daily more deeply the complicated order imposed upon nature by Providence. Out of this, practical solutions for many conflicts have already appeared in some measure, and others can still be hoped for, which will nevertheless not make the crucifixion of Christ meaningless.

The discussion on marriage was opened with a *relatio* by Archbishop John F. Dearden of Detroit, in which this sensitive prelate spoke of the "principle of conscious and generous procreation" without mentioning the hackneyed formula, "procreation is the primary purpose of marriage." The treatment in the text was not intended as a full doctrinal statement of the Church's position on marriage, he declared, but was a synthesis presented with a view to stating those things which would help the faithful today to appreciate more fully and deeply the nature and dignity of marriage and family life. Marriage was presented as an institution oriented to God, the specific love of the married, and the procreation of children (in that order). Conjugal love must be understood within the context of a stable, sacramental union. Couples could, "for sufficiently grave reasons," regulate the number of their children, but they were not authorized to use any means for regulating family size: "Nothing can be permitted which is opposed to the natural orientation of the marital act or which destroys the conjugal act's expressiveness of personal and marital love," he declared, choosing his words carefully. The schema avoided the specific question of the use of progesteron (birth control) pills, because this was not a question that could be decided in the Council hall and because the Pope had reserved it to himself.

The discussion revolved around the key questions of the ends of marriage, procreation and conjugal love, and whether birth control was permissible or not. Cardinal Léger of Montreal was the first of four speakers to challenge accepted notions. He pointed out that many of the faithful today were worried about marital problems and were not satisfied with the answers given them. "Pastors, confessors particularly, are assailed by doubts and uncertainties and, many times, no longer know what they can or should reply to the faithful. Many theologians feel more and more strongly the need to examine more deeply in a new way the fundamental principles concerning marriage." Though there were some who feared all renewal in the theology of marriage, on the grounds that it would lead to acquiescence in popular wishes, the final end of such renewal was actually to "enhance the holiness of marriage by a deeper insight into the plan of God" and to find out what contribution recent biological, psychological and sociological discoveries could make to a solution of marital problems. He continued:

A certain pessimistic and negative attitude regarding human love, attributable neither to Scripture nor to Tradition, but to philosophies of past centuries, has prevailed and this has veiled the importance and legitimacy of conjugal love in marriage . . . The authors of the present schema . . . have avoided the difficulty of putting into opposition the primary and secondary ends of marriage. However the schema . . . fails to present conjugal love and mutual help as an end of marriage and does not in any way touch on the problem of the purpose of expressions of love in marriage . . .

It should clearly present human conjugal love . . . as a true end of marriage, as something good in itself, with its own characteristic and its own laws. The schema is too hesitant on this point. There is no point in the schema's avoidance of the term "secondary end" if it does not present love as being at the service of procreation . . . Otherwise the fears which have for so long paralyzed our theology would remain. Conjugal love is good and holy in itself and it should be accepted by Christians without fear . . . In marriage the spouses consider each other not as mere procreators, but as persons loved for their own sakes.

It is not sufficient to establish clearly the doctrine which concerns marriage as a state. Unless the problem of the purpose of the actions themselves is dealt with in its most general principles, the difficulties which occupy spouses and pastors cannot be solved . . . It must also be stated that the intimate union of the spouses also finds a purpose in love. And this end is truly the end of the act itself, lawful in itself, even when it is not ordained to procreation.

The inclusion of a statement along this line would be entirely in accordance with the principle recognized by the Church for centuries, that the union of spouses is considered lawful even when procreation is known to be impossible. The important thing was to proclaim clearly the two ends of marriage "as equally holy and good."

While the Fathers were catching their breaths, Cardinal Suenens rose to deliver another salvo. He called first for a conciliar commission to work in close collaboration with the commission appointed by the Pope to study marriage problems, and suggested that the names of its members should be known so that they could receive the widest possible information. He then proceeded to lay down some of the guidelines for the work of such a commission. The first task of the commission should be in the area of faith, namely,

to study whether up to now we have given sufficient emphasis to all aspects of the teaching of the Church on marriage. To be sure, it is not a question of modifying or of casting doubt on the truly traditional teaching of the Church. That would be folly! It is a question of knowing whether we have opened our hearts completely to the Holy Spirit in order to understand the divine truth.

The Bible is always the same. But no generation can take pride in having fully perceived the unfathomable riches of Christ. The Holy Spirit has been promised to us to introduce us progressively to the fulness of the truth. Thus the Church has never to repudiate a truth that it once taught, but according as, and in the measure that, she progresses in a deeper study of the Gospel, she can and she must integrate this truth in a richer synthesis, and bring out the fuller fruitfulness of the same principles. In this way, the Church draws from her treasure things new and things old.

This established, it is important to examine whether we have maintained in perfect balance all aspects of the teaching of the Church on marriage. It may be that we have accentuated the Gospel text "increase and multiply" to such a point that we have obscured another text, "and they will be two in one flesh." These two truths are central and both are scriptural; they must illuminate each other in the light of the full truth that is revealed to us in our Lord Jesus Christ. St. Paul in effect has given to Christian marriage, as a prototype, the very love of Christ for his Church. This "two in one" is a mystery of interpersonal communion, gratified and sanctified by the sacrament of marriage. And this union is of such profundity that divorce can never separate two whom God unites as one.

Also, it is for the commission to tell us whether we have excessively stressed the first end, procreation, at the expense of another equally important end, that is growth in conjugal unity. In the same way, it is up to this commission to deal with the immense problem arising from the population explosion and over-population in many areas of the world. For the first time we must proceed with such a study in the light of the faith. It is difficult, but the world, whether consciously or not, waits for the Church to express her thought and to be a "light for the nations."

Let no one say that in this way we open the way to moral laxity. The problem confronts us not because the faithful try to satisfy their passions and their egotism, but because thousands of them try with anguish to live in double fidelity, to the doctrine of the Church and to the demands of conjugal and parental love.

He proposed that the second task of the commission be to study whether "classical doctrine, especially that of the manuals," takes sufficient account of the new knowledge achieved by modern science, for example, with respect to "the complexity with which the real or the biological interferes with the psychological, the conscious with the subconscious. New possibilities are constantly being discovered in man of his power to direct nature. This gives rise to a deeper understanding of the unity of man. We have made progress since Aristotle (and even since Augustine)," he noted. Studies of this kind would help us to understand better "what is according to nature and what is not."

Then, with special emphasis, he pronounced the following words:

> I beg of you, my brother bishops, let us avoid a new "Galileo affair." One is enough for the Church.

It should not be said that the new synthesis called for amounted to giving in to "situation ethics." The explanation of doctrine, which remains unchangeable in its principles, must take into account contingent factors and changes in the course of history. This is what the Popes did in writing *Rerum Novarum*, *Quadragesimo anno* and *Mater et magistra*. They attempted to express the same principles more precisely in terms more in keeping with new times. In conclusion, he recalled the words of Scripture: "The truth—both natural and supernatural—will set you free."

The speech of Cardinal Suenens was followed by a long round of applause.

Some days later, speaking on another topic, the Belgian cardinal took the unusual step of clarifying his previous remarks on the subject of marriage, "owing to certain reactions of public opinion." It had not been his intention to call into doubt doctrine "authentically and definitively proclaimed by the Church's magisterium" he said, but to suggest a study to formulate a synthesis of "all principles governing this subject"; and as regards discipline, to suggest that the commission's findings would have to be submitted to the Pope and judged by his supreme authority. The methods to be followed in these studies and what was done with the research would depend solely on his authority. It is not clear what prompted this clarification: whether an article appearing in a French journal misinterpreting his thought, or some remarks made by fellow bishops in the Council hall, or word from the Pope himself. In any case the cardinal can hardly be said to have retracted anything; his purpose may have been merely to dissipate an impression that he was presuming to dictate to the Pope.

The next speaker was the 87-year-old Patriarch Maximos IV Saigh, whose intervention was probably the most revolutionary of all—certainly the most outspoken—on this theme. It was directed particularly to the "agonizing and burdensome" problem of birth control:

It is an urgent problem because it lies at the root of a great crisis of the Catholic conscience. There is a question here of a break between the official doctrine of the Church and the contrary practice of the immense majority of Christian couples. The authority of the Church has been called into question on a vast scale. The faithful find themselves forced to live in conflict with the law of the Church, far from the sacraments, in constant anguish, unable to find a viable solution between two contradictory imperatives: conscience and normal married life.

On the other hand, on the social plane, demographic pressures in certain countries of particularly heavy population, prevent any increase in the standard of living and condemn hundreds of millions of human beings to unworthy and hopeless misery. The Council must find a practical solution. This is a pastoral duty. It must say if God really wishes this enfeebling and unnatural impasse.

Venerable Fathers, be aware in the Lord, who died and rose again for the salvation of men, of the really sad crisis of conscience of our faithful, and have the courage to tackle this question without prejudice.

Frankly, can the official positions of the Church in this matter not be reviewed in the light of modern theological, medical, psychological and sociological science? In marriage, the development of personality and its integration into the creative plan of God are all one. Thus, the end of marriage should not be divided into "primary" and "secondary." This consideration opens new perspectives concerning the morality of conjugal behavior considered as a whole.

And are we not entitled to ask if certain positions are not the outcome of outmoded ideas and, perhaps, a bachelor psychosis on the part of those unacquainted with this sector of life? Are we not, perhaps unwillingly, setting up a Manichaean conception of man and the world, in which the work of the flesh, vitiated in itself, is tolerated only in view of children? Is the external biological rectitude of an act the only criterion of morality, independent of family life, of its moral, conjugal and family climate, and of the grave imperatives of prudence which must be the basic rule of all our human activity?

Secondly, does modern exegesis not require of us greater care in the interpretation of the two passages from Genesis—"increase and multiply," and that concerning Onan, so long used as the classic scriptural support for the radical condemnation of contraception.

How relieved the Christian conscience felt when Pope Paul announced to the world that the problem of birth control and family morality "is under study, a study as extensive and deep as possible, that is, as serious and honest as the great importance of this problem requires. The Church must proclaim this law of God in the light of the scientific, social and psychological truths which, in recent times, have been the object of study and scholarship."

Further, given the extent and gravity of this problem which concerns the whole world, we ask that this study should be conducted by theologians, doctors, psychologists and sociologists, to find its normal solution. The collaboration of outstanding married Christians is also necessary. In addition, is it not following the ecumenical line of the Council to open a dialogue on this subject with other Christian churches and even with the thinkers of other religions? . . . Are we not here face to face with a problem common to all humanity? Shouldn't the church open itself to the non-Christian as well as the Christian world? Is it not the leaven that is to make the dough rise? So it must come, in this area as in all other matters of interest to humanity, to positive results giving peace to the conscience.

Far from me to minimize the delicacy of and the gravity of the subject, or of eventual abuses: but here as elsewhere, isn't it the duty of the Church to educate the moral sense of her children, to form them in moral responsibility, personal and communitarian, profoundly rooted in Christ, rather than to envelop it in a net of prescriptions and commandments, and to demand that

they purely and simply conform to these with their eyes closed?
For ourselves, let us open our eyes and be practical. Let us see
things as they are and not as we would like them to be. Otherwise
we risk speaking in a desert. What is at stake is the future of the
mission of the Church in the world.

Let us loyally and effectively put into practice the declaration
of Pope Paul opening the Second Session of the Council: "Let
the world know this: The Church looks upon the world with
profound understanding, with a sincere admiration, with a sincere intention not to subjugate but to serve it, not to despise it
but to appreciate it, not to condemn it but to support and
save it."

Applause began when the patriarch had finished, but it was
at once stifled by the Moderator, who gave the floor to the
Spanish Bishop Beita of Santander. The burden of his talk
was that marriage should be presented as a contract. The
schema seemed to say that the sacrament of marriage depended on love, but the divine law might require heroic
sacrifices when it was impossible, at least temporarily, to
reconcile the responsibility of spouses to each other with the
desire not to have children. All problems could not be solved.
Uneasiness was expressed also by Archbishop Botero of
Medellin, Colombia, over the way in which the schema admitted the difficulty of reconciling the teaching of the Church
with practical difficulties without offering any solution.
Priests and people wanted practical solutions; it was not
enough to leave the question to the experts, much less, to
married people to decide for themselves. The question of
birth control seemed to be considered mainly from the economic point of view. The Church's position on birth control
should be stated much more clearly. Bishop Rusch of Innsbruck pointed to divorce as the reason why there were so
many parentless children, and said that insistence on the
indissolubility of marriage would help to ward off this evil.
A petition which 182 professional laymen from various
countries had recently sent to the Pope and the Council ask-

ing that "the teaching of the Church place less emphasis on certain formulations of her doctrine which are largely products of their historical context," and that "a way be opened for new scientific and philosophical discoveries in this field to be integrated with the theology and living thought of the Church," was mentioned by Bishop Staverman of Indonesia. The document stated that the laymen who had signed it were responding to Pope Paul's call in his recent encyclical for a dialogue within the Church.* The bishop cited it in support of his thesis that marriage was continually evolving historically toward a more and more authentic form and that the Church should accept this transformation. Merely to repeat the traditional teaching was not acting in a pastoral spirit. A true pastoral approach involved a continual updating of doctrine.

Earlier Cardinal Ruffini had sounded his usual warning note about the failure of the schema to say anything very much about the true nature of Christian marriage as a sacrament, signifying unity and indissolubility, according to St. Paul. The fact that the document is addressed to all men should not be used as an excuse for overlooking this central idea or being obscure about Catholic teaching. Unless this is clearly brought out, how can polygamy, divorce, and sexual excesses be regarded as wrong? As for the affirmation that it was up to couples to decide about the number of children they would have, he found this a "hard, obscure and ambiguous" saying. He cited St. Augustine in reproof of selfish sexuality which was rampant today. To meet the needs of our day it was only necessary to quote Pius XI's *Casti connubii* and Pius XII's "Allocution to Midwives." "I hope that the experts who revise the text will follow the teaching of the *magisterium*," he concluded.

The heat generated by the debate on Thursday, as well as word which leaked out that a cloture vote was imminent,

* The petition was dated October 17, 1964. *The Pilot,* October 24, 1964.

resulted in a number of last-minute requests to speak on
Friday. Cardinal Alfrink came to the support of Cardinals
Léger and Suenens. He said that all priests are well aware
of the pastoral difficulties involved in advising people about
marriage problems and why so many people are leaving the
Church. The Church cannot of course change the divine law,
just because difficulties arise, nor can it condone situation
ethics. The Church teaches that sacrifice, the Cross, belongs
to the essence of Christianity. However the joy of the Resurrection also pertains to its essence, and God does not take
pleasure in the difficulties of man. Cardinal Alfrink said:

Indeed, the difficulties of married life are often of such a kind
that in fact a serious problem arises between two values of marriage, namely on the one hand the value of procreation, and on
the other, the value of human and Christian education of the
children.

This conflict can be avoided only when there is conjugal love
between the parents, being sustained and increased by sexual
intercourse. This conflict is not between two distinct values. For,
without the love and fidelity of the spouses, strengthened by the
fostering of love (as the schema rightly calls it) the very motive
of procreation is morally endangered.

The real question is this: Given the moral conflict in performing one and the same act, if in this act the spouses wish to
preserve the biological end, their human duty of educating their
future and even their existing children in a proper Christian
way is harmed. If, however, they wish to preserve the fidelity of
the marriage and the duty of educating their children, the question is whether, besides periodic continence (which many married people practice with great Christian virtue but which more
often is attempted with great difficulty) or by complete continence (which demands, among other things, of spouses a greater
moral strength than they are normally supposed to have) only
one solution is available—namely, performing the act and excluding offspring, at least in this particular set. If the excluding
of offspring is brought about by the use of means which are undoubtedly intrinsically bad, the Church can never admit the

sacrifice of a particular value in marriage in order to preserve the total value of marriage.

But with the new anthropological knowledge, especially the growing recognition of the essential distinction between a mere biological sexuality and human sexuality, an honest doubt is arising among many married people and also among scientists and some theologians regarding at least the arguments used to prove that the only efficacious moral and Christian solution to such conflicts in the married life of the faithful of good will is complete or periodic continence.

The situation or the state of the problem is too serious to permit the Church to decide this real conflict hastily and perhaps prematurely. The Church must be careful to preserve the purity of divine law, but she must also be solicitous about human problems.

The Church must investigate in a holy and diligent way so that all Christians may know that whatever the answer should be it will be stated with great charity and by all the means which the various sciences can supply. Therefore, it is right to rejoice at the establishment of a commission of selected experts who are dealing with this question.

Only if there is real certainty regarding the knowledge of the true content of divine law can and must the Church bind or free the consciences of her faithful.

Finally, because of the very rapid progress of science, particularly medicine and the other sciences which concern human life by which scientific progress brings new ethical and moral problems to light day by day, the question can be asked whether the Church does not need nowadays a permanent commission of experts in philosophy and theology and also in the field of science. Because of her pastoral solicitude this commission would follow up the evolution of these sciences immediately, lest the Church would come to consider and attempt to solve these problems to late.

The next impromptu speaker was Cardinal Ottaviani, whose remarks were mainly by way of introducing the Dominican Cardinal Browne of the Holy Office, principal spokesman for conservative theology. The secretary of the

Holy Office spoke with considerable emotion, however. "Ex-cuse me," he said, "if I speak *ex abrupto*. I had not expected to speak until tomorrow. I am not pleased with the statement of the text that married couples can determine the number of children they are to have. This has never been heard of before in the Church. Are we to think that the precept, 'In-crease and multiply,' is contradicted by the precept 'They shall be two in one flesh'?" This was a specific reference to the intervention of Cardinal Suenens. Continuing in a more intimate vein, he said of himself: "The priest who speaks to you is the eleventh of twelve children, whose father was a laborer in a bakery. I purposely say laborer, not the owner of a bakery. My parents never doubted Providence. Their motto was: 'Look to the birds of the air and the lilies of the field . . .' Cardinal Browne will now speak on the doctrinal question. But I issue a warning to you bishops, you who have proclaimed the infallibility of the Pope and of the bishops with the Pope: a doubt has been raised with regard to the Church's teaching on marriage. Can the Church possibly have erred for so many centuries?"

The intervention of Cardinal Browne was listened to with marked attention as he set forth the classical scholastic doc-trine on the primary and secondary ends of marriage.

I thought that the Council discussion would throw light on the text, but I find now that I must bear witness to the tradi-tional doctrine on marriage which has been called in doubt. The primary end of marriage is procreation and the education of the children. The secondary end is, on the one hand, the mutual aid of the spouses, and on the other a remedy for concupiscence.

What about love, you may say? Love forms part of marriage, but we must distinguish between the love of friendship which desires the welfare of another, and the love of concupiscence which seeks what is good for oneself. The kind of love required for the stability of marriage is the conjugal love of friendship. There is an element of sensual pleasure in the marital act which often causes the love of concupiscence to predominate. We must be careful, therefore, in vindicating the rights of conjugal love. Conjugal love is good when the spouses act with due regard for the ends of marriage: the begetting and education of children, fidelity in rendering the debt, and the sacrament which renders married life holy. For the conjugal act to be naturally licit, it suffices that the good of fidelity is present in rendering the debt.

He then cited Leo XIII's *Arcanum*, Pius XI's *Casti connubii*, and Pius XII's "Allocution to Midwives."

Difficult problems remain, particularly with regard to the sterile periods. But this is now being studied by true experts. We can do nothing but await the outcome of their studies. I say nothing with regard to other problems, namely that of the pill, because the *relator* has told us that the Pope has reserved this to himself. If the Council should wish to consider this question, it seems to me that this could be done only by a restricted commission which would present its conclusions to us.

Of the eight speakers who followed, four spoke out in support of Cardinals Léger, Suenens and Alfrink—Bishop Reuss of Mainz, Archbishop Urtasun of Avignon, Bishop Nkongolo of Luebo (Congo), and Bishop Fiordelli of Prato, Italy. Two were inclined to favor stricter adherence to the position of Cardinal Browne, Bishop Del Campo y de la Barcena of Calahorra, Spain, and Bishop Hervás y Benet of Ciudad Real, Spain. The two remaining, Bishop Rendeiro of Faro, Portugal, and Archbishop Yago of Abidjan, Ivory Coast, dealt with particular topics, the latter seconding Bishop Malula's condemnation of African tribalism and polygamy in an earlier session.

At 11:15 A.M., when many of the Fathers were in the bars, Cardinal Agagianian suddenly called for a standing vote to close the debate on Article 21. More than the usual number of bishops remained seated, but the motion was declared to be carried anyway. The essential points had been made.

Two days after the session ended, Cardinal Ottaviani, in a world-wide television interview, again serenely assured his interrogator that the Church's doctrine on marriage could never change because it was based "on the natural law *and several scriptural texts.*"

The doctrine of the Church is actually based on divine revelation and has little to do with the natural law, as was pointed out in the course of the debate; for it begins and ends in a great mystery. St. Paul tells husbands: "Love your wives as Christ loves the Church," and Christ Himself repeated the commandment recorded in Genesis, "You shall be two in one flesh," adding the injunction, "What God has joined together, let no man put asunder."

It was precisely here that a fundamental issue was bared in the Council. The forward-looking prelates, representing the vast majority, rejected outright any conception of the Church as a natural society whose teaching authority was represented by a juridically-structured doctrine interlaced with the axioms of Roman law, the antiquated guesses of Stoic anthropology, and the so-called truths of the natural law. The Constitution on the Church says explicitly that the Church as a society is a mystery, distributing sacramental grace and witnessing to the presence of Christ in the world. Hence the Church's teaching on marriage is in need of a drastic overhaul, if it is truly represented by the thinking of such men as Cardinals Ottaviani and Browne.

After the challenges thrown down in the debate on Thursday, one *peritus,* a frequent spokesman for the new theology of marriage, summed up his impressions in the following words: "It was the death of *Casti connubii!*"

The abruptness with which the discussion of marriage was terminated—no doubt motivated in part by fears over the public repercussions that might be expected from too detailed and too prolonged a treatment—became symptomatic of the course of the final three weeks of the session, with new topics for debate, texts to be voted on, para-conciliar activities, and rumors of behind-the-scenes maneuvers succeeding one another at a kaleidoscopic pace. Presiding over all was the iron-willed determination on the part of the Council authorities to get through the agenda by the end of the session at all costs, with just enough time being allowed each item so as to finish by the deadline, provided there were no set-backs. As happened during the Second Session, however, the more relaxed spirit of *romanità* managed to assert itself in particularly galling ways at the last moment. Though time was so precious, it was still thought necessary to devote two full days to the "long weekend" of November 1—no con-gregations were scheduled for November 2 and 3; while it was announced later that one full day—November 13—would be devoted to liturgical exercises, with Patriarch Maximos IV concelebrating in the presence of the Pope. The ultimate intention here, no doubt, was to display some kind of feeling of solidarity with the prelates at the Pan-Orthodox Confer-ence of Rhodes which was then ending, as well as to honor the Melkite patriarch, but the question inevitably arose whether the means were proportionate to the end. The in-terruption of debate on Article 24 of Schema 13, in order to take up the propositions on Missionary Activity (November 6, 7 and 9), by distracting the attention of the Council away from the subject under consideration, also proved to be an irritating and rather pointless move.

During the remaining portion of the morning of October 30 and through the session on November 4, attention was focused on Article 22 of Schema 13, on promoting culture—with much time out for announcements, reports and voting on texts having nothing to do with the subject under debate. Father Ferreira, Apostolic Prefect for Portuguese Guinea, the first speaker on this topic, put his finger on one of the weaknesses of the text when he noted that the word *"cultura"* was used 23 times in the schema but not always in the same sense. The Latin word was quite inadequate to distinguish between "culture," properly speaking, and what we call "civilization," a much broader concept. Hence the ambigui-ties of the text.

22. *(Promoting human culture)*. 1) (Following the commandment of God). 2) (The hierarchy of values). 3) (Dialogue and mutual respect for cultures).

4) (Cultural function of the Church). . . . The Church of the Incarnate Word, having its origin at a particular time and place in history but directed to all men, is tied to no particular cultural system, but faithful to a living tradition, it maintains contact with all of them, giving and receiving. In order for this dialogue to be fruitful for every culture and for religion itself, it is necessary for the standardbearers of the faith to come to know the riches of a given cultural tradition, for the heralds of the Word to study the values of all cultures. . . . Those who devote themselves to the work of evangelization, particularly pastors and theologians, should learn how to interpret revealed truth according to the words and forms of the culture where they are serving the gospel, and to be conscious of the limitations of their own culture.

Several speakers objected to the title of the Article, "The Promotion of Culture." The implications seemed to be much too optimistic, said Archbishop de Provenchères. The poor had not yet benefited from any such promotion. It was wrong to assume that great progress had already taken place, so long as "actual discrimination, ignorance and poverty keep most of mankind from cultural achievement." The text must pay more attention to existing inequities. Everything the Council has to say about the human person, culture, and liberty will be useless as along as men do not have the means necessary for a decent human existence, both on an individual, family and social level, observed the Master General of the Dominicans, Father Fernandez. With reference to the "right order of values," he wanted it spelled out that spiritual values take precedence over material values, and in the enumeration of the different aspects of human culture, mention should be made of philosophy and theology. For these were the "high point" of human culture. Bishop Proaño Villalba, of Ecuador, pointed out that "in Latin America, more than 80 million people did not know how to read or write, and more than 15 million children failed to attend school. Because of the increasing birthrate, some 250,000 new classrooms should be built each year. There was need for 600,000 new teachers. These facts were a scandal, for society has never been so blessed with means as now."

A theme which kept constantly cropping up was that it was not enough for the Church to declare its regard for culture, it must prove this by deeds. It was not a sign of evangelical poverty, said Cardinal Lercaro, to cling to the cultural forms of the past, such as philosophical and theological systems or ecclesiastical institutions. The Church should speak less triumphalistically of these things, which repelled more men than they attracted. True poverty implied an awareness on the part of the Church of her own inadequacies, joined with boldness in making the necessary adaptations demanded by a true sense of history and a spirit of humility. The Church should act on contemporary life by way of being a leaven. The Church's claim that she is tied to no culture was more theoretical than factual. And he favored a return to the "ancient custom" favoring the scientific study of theology by laymen.

As a way for the Church to prove its good intentions, decisively, Bishop Elchinger (Strasbourg, France) suggested the rehabilitation of Galileo. Such a decision if taken by the supreme authority in the Church would be a fitting climax to the current fourth centenary of his birth. He said that many people believed that the Catholic Church was fearful and on the defensive with respect to modern culture. The action taken by the Church's *magisterium* in dealing with modernism still caused suspicion and uneasiness, and some concrete act was needed, therefore, to dispel these misgivings.

Showing a proper respect for other cultural traditions really meant keeping our Western culture from swallowing up the East. It was now an accepted principle of missionary work, said the Chinese Bishop Lokuang of Tainan, to recognize

the validity of all cultures and to see that the Church was
firmly rooted in those cultures, so that it would not disappear
when persecutions arose. But while much had been done to
win over the masses, little attention had been paid to reaching the educated. It was sad that after so many years of missionary work in Asia, learned men in all branches of knowledge there knew so little about Christianity. There was
danger that Africa might lose its own sense of religious values,
commented Archbishop Zoa of Cameroun, while absorbing
Western science. There should be cultural and theological
institutes to help the Africans achieve a proper synthesis and
the text should mention Christ as the norm and measure of
such a cultural synthesis.

Bishop Carli of Segni, Italy, commented that the study of
law, while regarded by some as "pseudo-charismatic," should
nevertheless be mentioned along with other liberal studies.
The text seemed to give first place to scientific studies. He
also wanted some of the dangers of modern culture pointed
out.

Judging by the number of bishops who spoke on Article
23, on "Economic and social life,"—debate on which began
at 11:45 on Wednesday, November 4 and lasted only until
11:15 the following morning—this important section of the
schema was hardly accorded the attention which was its due,
but there were a great many written communications making
up for this deficiency. As the extracts show, the text adopts a
stand not likely to endear it to proponents of the laissez-faire
school of capitalism or rugged individualism in sociological
matters. It marks a return to the economic and social teaching
of the Church common to the Church Fathers and the Middle
Ages, but which has become progressively obscured ever since
the sixteenth century. As the Abbé Laurentin has pointed
out, the Roman conception of *ius utendi et abutendi* (the
right of use and abuse) and the modern conception of capitalism became so dominant in the nineteenth century as to

cause the thought of St. Thomas Aquinas to be virtually ignored. According to Aquinas and the traditional teaching of the Church: 1) God gave the goods of the earth to all men; but 2) for their proper use, they were to be divided among men. The right of private property is therefore neither primary nor absolute, but subject to the first consideration. The poor, accordingly, have a claim on the "common patrimony" which cannot be denied.

Leo XIII, in his famous enyclical *Rerum novarum,* or rather the drafters of it, in their attempt to restore a proper social outlook, claimed that "private property" was a divinely decreed right, whereas St. Thomas spoke only of the "common destination" as decreed by divine right. This misinterpretation of tradition naturally resulted in underestimating the rights of the poor, and over-exaggerating the rights of private property. The return to a sounder tradition took time and was not accomplished without difficulty. Pius XII was the first to refer to the matter in one of his discourses. Further steps were taken by John XXIII in his encyclicals *Mater et magistra* and *Pacem in terris.* The Council's text, by restoring the original conception, of course has no intention of downgrading private property or denying its place or efficacy, but is determined to assert that its rights are subject to a higher law. And the Abbé notes that this reassertion of the claims of the "common destination" willed by God for the benefit of all comes just at a time when men are so preoccupied about the problem of the unequal distribution of wealth.* The principle may be put in a nutshell, according to the Abbé, by saying that, while a man who steals a piece of bread when he is dying of hunger may be condemned by the state as a criminal, he has a right to do so according to the Church.

23. (*Economic and social life*) . . . A certain socialization, that is, the interdependence and mutual influence of men on each

* *Le Figaro,* November 5, 1964.

other in all fields, economic and social, is increasing and daily
becoming more widespread. . . . Mankind is becoming more and
more conscious of its unity and of its common will. . . .

1) (Control of wealth). If economic progress is not to oppress
man, it must remain under his control and subject to prudent
guidance. The profitable organization of this progress requires
that as many people as possible, from all ranks of society, should
have an active part in promoting this growth, lest a few persons
(whether experts, groups, or particularly powerful nations) divert
the economy for their own selfish ends or use it to harm
others. . . .

2) (Distribution of wealth). Progress rightly organized should
be esteemed, and should be promoted so as to benefit all men
and all societies, with no discrimination as regards race or region
of the world. Economic progress should not be left to itself, as if
the amassing of wealth, ambition or power, or an ever greater
production of goods were a law or an end in itself. . . .

3) (Obligations of developed countries).

4) (Mutual aid a duty). God has given the goods of the earth
as a common patrimony for all of mankind. He has left the
method of distributing them to the wisdom of peoples. The forms
and institutions devoted to the appropriation, production and
distribution of property can vary considerably. The Church is
therefore not bound by any one economic system. . . .

5) (Protection of rights). . . . Every effort should be made,
without injuring the rights of the human person and by taking
into account the nature of each country, to lessen social injustices
as rapidly as possible, with a view to eliminating them eventually.

6) (Responsibilities of business and labor). . . . It is very important for the process of production and working conditions
to be in accordance with the higher needs of the human person,
and not vice versa; for workers to be truly and effectively associated in the common life of the enterprise . . . ; for them to have
a part, both within and without the enterprise, at all levels,
especially by their representatives freely chosen, in the economic
and social decisions on which their lot and that of their children
depends so much. . . .

7) (Christian responsibility).

8) (Catholic participation).

Most of the speakers purposely avoided going into any detail when dealing with this section, and concentrated instead on such general principles as the need for pointing out more clearly the evil effects of economic systems which denied moral principles, "whether of free enterprise or collectivism." Like several other Fathers, Cardinal Wyszynski thought that the Council should "praise and approve" all the social encyclicals of the Popes, as containing "the authentic teaching of the Church on social questions." But as we have just seen the drafters of the text wisely avoided any such blanket commendation. The tone of Cardinal Wyszynski's speech was rather on the conservative side. He hit out at certain modern "progressive Catholics"—apparently referring specifically to the Pax group of Catholics in Poland who are in favor of close collaboration with the Communist government and who have been his constant critics—"who defame the Church as if it neglected the lot of the workers."

Cardinal Richaud of Bordeaux, nevertheless, felt that it was advisable to go into some detail in laying down rules for a dialogue between management and labor, to ensure a smooth functioning of the economy, for example, with regard to avoiding lay-offs and worker-training. Bishop Zambrano of Colombia, a South American prelate, declared that he was not satisfied with the treatment of the distribution of wealth. Many people have abandoned the Church because they believed that it was hopelessly indifferent to their needs. More must be said about the moral issue and the duties of owners. Unless a fuller treatment was given of the inequities of the present system, based on the law of supply and demand, the assumption would be that the Council approved of the inequities inherent in this system. A rather detailed analysis, replete with statistics, was offered by Bishop Benitez Avalos of Paraguay of the economic situation in Latin America and he wanted certain conclusions with regard to it incorporated in Article 23 as a "sign of the times."

The questioning of papal encyclicals by recent speakers

and what he fancied to be the disrespect being shown for
the teaching of the *magisterium,* so exercised Bishop Alba
Palacios of Tehuantepec, Mexico, that he never did come
to the point of his speech; he had to be reminded by the
Moderator that the topic under discussion was Article 23, not
Article 21 or 24.

As an earnest of the Church's concern for the poor and for
the relief of worldwide poverty, numerous bishops suggested
that a special effort be made to focus international attention
on the plight of the millions of people still in danger of star-
vation. James Norris, an American lay auditor at the Council, who has been dealing with relief and population problems in all parts of the world for some twenty years, proposed
that a recognized expert introduce Article 24, on world
solidarity, with a special *relatio.* He suggested as an ideal
candidate the well-known author and correspondent of *The
Economist* Barbara Ward, who is known in private life as
Lady Jackson. After several weeks of intensive campaigning,
which involved the buttonholing of cardinals, bishops, and
Vatican officials, Norris seemed well on the way to success, but
then he was suddenly informed by Archbishop Felici's office
that despite the Council's welcome to women auditors (fif-
teen of them, including Sister Mary Luke, of Kentucky,
head of the Conference of Major Superiors of Women Religious in the United States, and Mlle. Marie-Louise Monnet,
sister of Jean Monnet, the father of the Common Market, attended the session in this capacity), it was felt that it would
be "premature" to have a woman address the assembly. Obviously, the thought was still too much for the masculine-ori-
ented, Italian-dominated bureaucracy of the Council. Instead,
Norris was told to take on the job himself. Also, he was asked
to deliver his report in Latin. He did so, on only six hours'
notice. This was a precedent-shattering act in itself, for no
layman had yet been entrusted with such an official responsibility.

RELATIO

IACOBI I. NORRIS DE PAUPERTATE MUNDIALI
IN SCHEMATE DE ECCLESIA IN MUNDO HUIUS TEMPORIS
CAP. IV, PAR. 24

(Sub secreto)

TYPIS POLYGLOTTIS VATICANIS
MCMLXIV

Title-page of *Relatio* delivered by James J. Norris
on November 5, 1964.

On Thursday, November 5, 1964, about 11:30, Norris mounted the rostrum and delivered his talk in excellent, clearly enunciated Latin and he was listened to with marked attention until the end. This was the first occasion, one might say, that any layman had succeeded in making a lasting impression on the Fathers:

In the last decade the problem of poverty—one of the oldest and deepest that confronts the Christian conscience—has taken on a new shape, new dimensions and new urgency. "The poor you have always with you"—yes, but today the poor are with us in a new and revolutionary context, because modern science, medicine and technology have helped to bring about a single economy, a neighborhood that is interdependent, but largely lacking the institutions and the policies that express solidarity, compassion and human obligation.

In this lopsided community, one small group of nations have become immensely wealthy. These nations represent 16 per cent of the world's peoples, and they own 70 per cent of its wealth. They are the nations grouped around the North Atlantic, . . . Meanwhile, three-quarters of the human race live in a state of poverty bordering on or below the subsistence level.

The gap between the rich and the poor is rapidly widening— side by side the rich grow richer and the poor grow poorer, in a single world community. This is a wholly unprecedented historical fact, and it presents the Christian conscience of the western nations with a challenge, because for the first time in history it is accepted as a fact that, given time, the western nations have the means to wipe out poverty in the rest of the world.

There will be no meaning to their Christian profession or humane traditions if they forget that wealth is a trust and that property carries social obligations and that riches on the scale of the West's modern riches must be redeemed by generosity. . . .

World poverty will not be wiped out speedily, nor will the problem of development be solved in anything short of several generations. Our Christian peoples must not become weary of well doing.

But the goal will be reached if in each wealthy country there is brought into being a strong, committed, well-informed and courageous group of men of good will who are prepared to see world poverty as one of the great central concerns of our time and press steadily and vocally for the policies in aid, in trade and in the transfer of skills, that will lessen the widening gap between the rich and the poor.

This problem is not only the concern of the wealthy nations. In our complex 20th century world, the developing nations, to progress effectively, need the capital, the knowledge, and the technical assistance of the more economically developed countries, but as wise leaders in those countries insist, the development must come from the local resources, both material and human, which God has given these lands.

Recently a bishop from one of these lands said to me, "My people live not only in poverty but in permanent misery." This type of utter poverty brings with it other human sufferings. The first is hunger—a constant, gnawing hunger that is never satisfied day or night. Poverty brings diseases that cannot be cured because there are no medical services. Poverty brings illiteracy in lands where the great majority of people cannot read or write. Poverty brings bad housing "slums" that breed crime and sin. Poverty means that a mother looks at her new-born infant knowing that it will probably die before the year is out. For millions of people, poverty means that life expectancy is 35 years. For millions of people, living in this kind of poverty, death is a sweet release.

A loving human family does not permit its members to suffer in this way. When all the members of our Christian family become aware of the extent of suffering and privation among the poor of the world, surely they will make certain that their wealthy lands will not fail to respond to their Christian obligation.

From this Ecumenical Council could come a clarion call for action which would involve the creation of a structure that would devise the kind of institutions, contacts, forms of cooperation and policy, which the Church can adopt, to secure full Catholic participation in the world-wide attack on poverty.

This great gathering of bishops represents every continent and every country on earth. Since world poverty affects all humanity, the great contribution of our universal Church can be a world-encircling manifestation of brotherly love, bringing effectively to bear the social teaching of the Church on the problem which our

beloved Holy Father discussed in his Christmas message last
year when he said that hunger is the principal problem in the
world today:

". . . We make our own the sufferings of the poor. And we hope
that this our sympathy may itself become capable of enkindling
that new love which, by means of a specially planned economy,
will multiply the bread needed to feed the world."

Warm applause greeted Norris when he finished. His suggestion about concerted effort was immediately seconded
by Cardinal Frings, who called for the setting up of episcopal
committees, on a national and international scale, to promote
projects designed to alleviate world poverty. Every year col-
lections should be taken up during "the penitential season,"
and the money collected from each nation should be distributed through a commission of bishops with the aid of a
secretariat responsible for examining the projects proposed
and with the help of lay experts. The delegates should meet
together at least once a year to review their efforts, and the
minutes of these meetings should be forwarded to the Holy
See. As a token of the seriousness of their intentions, he suggested that the bishops should give up "their triumphalistic
vestments."

24. (*Promoting the solidarity of the human family*). 1) (Economics and spiritual progress). 2) (Dissipation of wealth). 3)
(Principle of subsidiarity).

4) (Obligations of wealthier countries). . . . It is certain that
a grave responsibility of justice and charity rests on those nations
which have drawn heavily on the common patrimony and abound
in material wealth, but are also powerful because of technical
and scientific resources. . . .

5) (Family limitation). . . . So that families and countries may
continue to develop in a sound way, the wealth of the earth
should be expended necessarily on all of mankind. As regards
the number of children that people should have, the ultimate
decision belongs to the couples themselves. Solutions should
not be proposed or imposed by states which show little or no
respect for morality or amount to an attempt by any means to

put an end to the increasing population of the world or of any country. . . . 6) (Freedom of opportunity). 7) (International co-operation).

The following intervention of Cardinal Alfrink on promoting solidarity among the family of nations was really on Article 25 rather than the article under discussion, however, he was not interrupted. He said that he agreed with the proposals of Cardinal Frings. Then turning to the subject of the Church's attitude toward communism, he laid down that, while atheism and communism must certainly be rejected, the rejection must not be done in such a way as to make it impossible to meet the promoters of those ideologies, "who are seeking the truth with good will," in a spirit of charity. The Church should avoid any new sterile condemnation of communism, as some speakers had demanded. This has already been done often enough and it would be useless to repeat what has been declared once and for all. Instead, the Council should promote a dialogue with all people of good will, including communists. No good could come from closing the doors to a dialogue.

Several other speakers were able to offer a few remarks before the end of the morning. Bishop Rupp of Monaco felt that the schema should attack not only the evils of famine and injustice, but the very roots of these evils. The text appeared to him to be too prudent, too diplomatic, too "feminine." In its present form it would not attract the attention of the world. The incompatibility of the unequal distribution of wealth with Christian principles, as enunciated by Thomas Aquinas, especially his principle "in necessity all things are common," was the theme of the intervention of Bishop Pildáin y Zapiáin of the Canary Islands. The American Bishop Swanstrom, Director of the U.S. Bishops' Relief Program, observed that while the text talked largely about what governments and the laity should do to alleviate poverty, it might also say something about the role which Catholic bishops and priests could play in promoting concerted action. The final speaker on Thursday, Bishop Thangalathil of India, dwelt on the moral and spiritual consequences of the increasing gap between the have- and have-not nations.

Debate on Article 24 was concluded on Monday, November 9, with interventions by Cardinal Rugambwa, Archbishop Seper of Zagreb, Yugoslavia, Bishop Begin of Oakland, California, Cardinal Richaud, and Father Mahon, Superior General of St. Joseph's Society for Foreign Missions, Mill Hill, U.S.A., who noted that Vatican Council I, convened two years after Karl Marx published the *Communist Manifesto,* had had nothing to say about social justice. Today the proletarian classes have been succeeded by proletarian nations. "We cannot remain silent about social justice. The Church is not a mere spectator of the world's miseries, it is not called on to save disembodied souls but men." He gave wholehearted approval to the Secretariat proposed by James Norris and Cardinal Frings.

The advent of nuclear weapons is unquestionably *the* most important scientific achievement in recent years and their use and effects have revolutionized traditional concepts of warfare. It remains less clear, however, just what their effects have been on traditional Catholic notions of a "just war." The highly controversial matter is still under debate among Catholic theologians and no consensus of opinion has yet been reached. The drafters of Schema 13 were therefore under a particular disadvantage when they came to deal with Article 25 on peace and war. The debate on this issue revealed a rather neat cleavage between Continental bishops and theologians on the one hand, and some British and most American bishops and theologians on the other. The former, representing nations for the most part without access to the "bomb," were decidedly in favor of banning all nuclear weapons. It is significant that "ban-the-bomb" movements seem to have much more of an attraction for Europeans than for Americans; the latter, representing nations possessing the bomb, were more guarded in their statements and distinctly unfavorable to any categorical and unconditional condemnations of nuclear warfare so long as the discussion of the "just war" remained up in the air. Without presuming to decide this controverted issue, the text of Article 25 had been drafted in such a way as to give more satisfaction to the Continental school. The opposition between the two schools must not be pressed. The views of individual speakers were often highly nuanced, but in general this distinction is valid. Since the debate produced no clear-cut consensus of opinion, the framers of the draft will have a difficult task working out a text capable of winning the approval of the assembly at the Fourth Session. They may have to sidetrack the issue altogether.

25. (*The consolidation of peace*). . . . Differences between nations should not be settled by force of arms but by agreements. Although, after exhausting all efforts at peaceful discussion, it may not be illicit to defend by the use of force rights unjustly injured in an unjust aggression, nevertheless, the use of arms, especially nuclear weapons, whose effects are greater than can be imagined and therefore cannot be reasonably regulated by men, exceeds all just proportion and therefore must be judged before God and man as most wicked.

Every honest effort, therefore, must be made so that not only nuclear warfare may be solemnly proscribed by all nations and alliances as an enormous crime, but also so that nuclear arms of others of a like destructive force may be utterly destroyed and banned.

The Council denounces the uncontrolled armaments race, which threatens peace, harmony and confidence between countries, endangers the lives of many people, and dissipates the wealth needed for better things.

As decisive as the present text of Article 25 is in its condemnation of all nuclear warfare, it was still not clear enough, in the opinion of Archbishop Roberts, S.J., a frequent spokesman on the subject, mainly because it avoided going into the related moral problem of conscientious objection. In a press conference on October 21, 1964, at the Dutch Documentation Center, he maintained that the use of weapons capable of destroying millions of innocent people posed a new problem, that conscientious objection should be recognized by the Church and people ought not to be forced to fight. He drew attention to the fact that it was countries with an English law, or possibly Protestant, tradition behind them which had proved to be sensitive to the importance of this issue, rather than countries with a predominantly Catholic tradition. The principle of conscientious objection had first come to the fore in Britain during World War I and had been recognized by parliament and other legislative bodies following the common law tradition.

A number of speakers, while favorable to Article 25 in general, pointed out that they regarded it as a "retreat" compared with the more explicit condemnation of nuclear warfare found in Pope John's *Pacem in terris*. Cardinal Feltin of Paris, anticipating the discussion by speaking on October 29 because he had to leave Rome, stated that Catholics, and the hierarchy in particular, should be more active in promoting peace, in preaching and in catechetics, "lest the oft lamented divorce between papal encyclicals and Catholic life continue." Peace should be presented as a true apostolate to be furthered by dialogue and cooperation with non-Christians. He called for the establishment of a special commission of theologians and scientists to study the present state of the question regarding peace and war. Cardinal Alfrink, for his part, noted that the Johannine encyclical "speaks more positively than the schema on the subject of disarmament." It was more specific, in particular, with regard to two important conditions for disarmament, namely reciprocity and simultaneity. The present text must not fail to mention this. As for the so-called ABC weapons (atomic, biological, chemical), the text declared that their effects are greater than can be calculated, but in contrast to the "dirty bomb" scientists have produced a "clean bomb" whose effects can be controlled and calculated, both as to duration and area. The language of the text, as drafted at present, seemed to suggest that nuclear weapons were criminal only because their effects were incalculable, and that they ceased to be so if the effects could be calculated. Therefore if the intention of the Council was to condemn the use of all nuclear weapons indiscriminately, the language should be tightened up. The cardinal questioned whether there should be any mention of a "just or unjust war" in the schema at all. What people expected from the Church was an outright condemnation of *all* war, nuclear warfare specifically. "It is not for us to go into the question of whether a war can be just or not," he said, "but to propose the abolition of war altogether." He quoted the saying of President Kennedy: "Unless we destroy weapons, weapons will destroy us." The primary solicitude of the Church should be to exhort men to peace.

The same thought was echoed by Bishop Ancel, the auxiliary of Lyons, who insisted that the primary task of the Church was not to become involved in technical details, but to state moral principles. What the schema only insinuated should be brought out more clearly, namely that the good of the human family required that all nations "must renounce the right to war and armaments," retaining only those arms necessary for internal security, and that an international organization be given the means to suppress war.

Another forceful speaker on the Continental side, Bishop Guilhem, of Laval, France, the author of a bold letter on nuclear disarmament, added his opinion that since the Church is the "Light of the World," its primary function in this important matter was to stir up public opinion, to get the faithful and all men of good will, generally, involved in the (gradual) movement to abolish the arms race and nuclear weapons in particular. Like Bishop Ancel and Cardinal Alfrink, he felt that the apparent contradiction in the text, between the condemnation of war, especially nuclear war, and the legitimacy of a defensive war, should be eliminated. It was wrong, he maintained, to imply that peace could be maintained by a military balance or through fear of the effects of nuclear weapons. Peace must be based on mutual respect, and a dialogue was therefore necessary to eliminate misunderstandings and differences. Patriarch Maximos IV Saigh was also for issuing a more solemn condemnation of all nuclear, chemical and bacteriological warfare, and for revising the traditional concept of a just war. The intervention of 2,000 bishops from all parts of the world, he said, should be capable of bringing about some change in the course of world history and defending the rights of humanity. The interventions of Bishop Hengsbach of Essen, Germany and Bishop Hakim of Israel were along the same line.

The American-British position was represented by Auxiliary Bishop Hannan of Washington and Archbishop Beck of Liverpool. Neither spoke in the names of their respective hierarchies, so that it is somewhat inaccurate to imply that they were voicing an agreed "American-British" consensus. The former said that if the Church was going to appeal to the principles of a just war, in its treatment of the morality of warfare, it should consult theologians who were competent in this field and were familiar with the facts about modern weapons, including nuclear weapons. He objected to the easy assumption that all nuclear weapons were automatically incalculable in their effects, as implied in the text. Cardinal Alfrink had stated that this was not true. The trouble was that the schema "apparently ignores the traditional teaching of the Church on conducting a just war." He concluded with a statement approving the principle that a dialogue was necessary to avert war, but made the following pertinent comment:

Article 25 implies that all nations have been equally negligent in working for international peace. This is cruelly unfair to many nations and statesmen, and particularly to nations now suffering under unjust aggression. The world knows the source of this aggression; it would be ridiculous for the Council to pretend that it does not know. In order to have a dialogue with materialistic atheists, we must enjoy full liberty; slavery would render such a dialogue impossible. Therefore, we should praise those who defend freedom, and especially those who have died for it.

Bishop Hannan called for a complete rewriting of the section.

If the speech of Bishop Hannan succeeded in slightly jolting some of the Fathers, that by Archbishop Beck frankly frightened others. Without mincing words, he declared that while the text condemned the use of any weapon whose effects could not be estimated and controlled, as Pius XII and John XXIII had done, it was nevertheless important to "make clear that this is not a univeral condemnation of the use of nuclear weapons. There may well exist objects which in a just war are legitimate targets of nuclear weapons even of vast force (e.g. an attack against a ballistic or satellite missile in the outer atmosphere). Responsibility for the use of nuclear weapons rests with those who exercise supreme authority in the state, and the Council should express sympathy for those who carry this heavy burden. The government of a country has a grave duty to do all it can to prevent war, but in certain circumstances, it may well be true that peace can be assured only by a 'balance of terror,' i.e. by the threat of the use of nuclear weapons as a deterrent against unjust aggression. Let us not too readily condemn these governments which have succeeded in keeping the peace, however tentative, in the world by the use of such means. Let the Council make clear that it does not demand of governments that they decide on a unilateral abandonment of nuclear weapons because of a possibly proximate danger that these weapons may be used in an immoral way."

The interesting question arises why, if these two speakers

really were voicing a representative opinion about Article
25, they were not supported by other bishops?

The debate on Schema 13 closed with some general remarks
by Bishop Rigaud of Pamiers, France, in the name of 80
bishops, on international organizations; a regret by Bishop
Yanez Ruiz Tagle of Los Angeles, Chile, in the name of 70
bishops, that nothing special was said in Chapter IV about
social justice; a recommendation by Bishop McGrath of
Panama, in the name of 70 bishops, that the effectiveness of
the document could be improved by expanding the introductory paragraphs to each section of Chapter IV as well as to
Chapters I-III and by the inclusion of more emphasis on
the application of principles to actual problems; and by an
intervention by the Argentinian Lay Auditor, Professor Juan
Vasquez. Bishop Guano summed up by proposing a slightly
different plan for the revision. The schema would start out
with the "signs of the times"; this would be followed by a
fuller treatment of what the Church thinks about the world
with Chapters I-III probably lumped together, and by an
expanded treatment of Chapter IV at the end, enriched by
the inclusion of material from the *Adnexa*. He repeated his
earlier suggestion that the Moderators might decide to put
certain points to a vote so that the commission would have
better guidance, but no action was taken on this motion at
the Third Session.

Summary

October 20, 1964, Tuesday—105TH GENERAL GONGREGATION.
MASS: Archbishop Wojtyla of Kraków, Poland.
MODERATOR: Cardinal Döpfner.
PRESENT: 2,191 Fathers.
ANNOUNCEMENTS: after discussion of Schema 13 in general, there will be vote on acceptance of text as basis for discussion: if results are favorable, discussion will proceed in three parts.
PENDING BUSINESS: Propositions on Oriental Churches.
SPEAKERS (each supported by at least 70 Fathers): 1. Bishop Hakim (Israel). 2. Archbishop Baudoux (St. Boniface, Canada). 3. Archbishop Athaide (Agra, India). *Relator:* Archbishop Bukatko (Belgrade, Yugoslavia).
NEW BUSINESS: Schema 13 on the Church in the Modern World.
SPEAKERS: *Relatores:* Cardinal Cento and Bishop Guano. 1. Cardinal Liénart (Lille, France). 2. Cardinal Spellman (New York, N.Y.). 3. Cardinal Ruffini (Palermo, Sicily). 4. Cardinal Lercaro (Bologna, Italy). 5. Cardinal Léger (Montreal, Canada). 6. Cardinal Döpfner (Munich, Germany). 7. Cardinal Meyer (Chicago, Ill.). 8. Cardinal Silva Henriquez (Santiago de Chile).

VOTE: Chap. VII of *De Ecclesia* as a whole

	Total	Placet	Non placet	Placet iuxta modum	Invalid
Chap. VII as whole	2,184	1,921	29	233	1

VOTE: Acceptability of Oriental Churches (for immediate voting)

	Total	Placet	Non placet	Invalid
Oriental Churches	2,180	1,911	265	4(1)

October 21, 1964, Wednesday—106TH GENERAL GONGREGATION.
MASS: Bishop Cristea of the Curia, in Roumanian rite.
MODERATOR: Cardinal Döpfner.
PRESENT: 2,176 Fathers.
ANNOUNCEMENTS: propositions on Missionary Activity will be next item on agenda after Schema 13.

PENDING BUSINESS: Schema 13 on Church in Modern World.
SPEAKERS: 1. Cardinal Landázuri-Ricketts (Lima, Peru). 2. Cardinal Suenens (Malines-Brussels, Belgium). 3. Cardinal Bea (Curia). 4. Patriarch Meouchi (Syria). 5. Bishop A. Mathias (Chikmagalur, India). 6. Bishop Vairo (Gravina and Irsina, Italy). 7. Archbishop Morcillo Gonzales (Madrid, Spain). 8. Archbishop Conway (Armagh, Ireland). 9. Archbishop Elchinger (Coadjutor of Strasbourg, France). 10. Archbishop Zoghby (Egypt). 11. Archbishop Hermaniuk (Winnepeg, Canada). 12. Archbishop Wojtyla (Kraków, Poland).
VOTES: Propositions on Oriental Churches

	Total	Placet	Non placet	Pl. iux. mod.	Invalid
Prop. 1	2,176	1,790	119	265	2
Prop. 2-4*	2,170	1,373	73	719	5
Prop. 5-6	2,172	2,005	31	136	—
Prop. 7-11	2,167	1,790	183	186	8
Prop. 12-18	2,146	1,920	103	118	5

* Did not receive required majority.

October 22, 1964, Thursday—107TH GENERAL CONGREGATION.
MASS: Archbishop Printesis of Athens, Greece.
MODERATOR: Cardinal Döpfner. PRESENT: 2,157 Fathers.
ANNOUNCEMENTS: distribution of commemorative medals.
PENDING BUSINESS: Schema 13 on Church in Modern World.
SPEAKERS: 1. Archbishop Heenan (Westminster, England). 2. Archbishop Roy (Quebec, Canada). 3. Bishop Stimpfle (Augsburg, Germany). 4. Bishop Soares de Resende (Beira, Mozambique). 5. Bishop Franic (Split, Yugoslavia). 6. Archbishop Muñoz Vega (Coadjutor of Quito, Ecuador). 7. Bishop de Castro Mayer (Campos, Brazil). 8. Archbishop Hurley (Durban, South Africa). 9. Archbishop Hamvas (Csanád, Hungary). 10. Bishop Charue (Namur, Belgium). 11. Archbishop Shehan (Baltimore, Maryland). 12. Father Fernandez (Master General of Dominicans). 13. Archbishop Duval (Algiers, Algeria). 14. Archbishop Beck (Liverpool). 15. Bishop Barbieri (Cassano all' Ionio, Italy).
VOTES: Propositions on Oriental Churches

	Total	Placet	Non placet	Placet iuxta modum	Invalid
Prop. 19-23	2,157	2,104	22	27	4
Prop. 24-29	2,154	1,841	111	195	7

October 23, 1964, Friday—108TH GENERAL CONGREGATION.
MASS: Archbishop Sangaré of Bamako, Mali.
MODERATOR: Cardinal Döpfner and Cardinal Suenens.
PRESENT: 2,076 Fathers.
ANNOUNCEMENTS: appendix to propositions on Religious distributed today will not be discussed; present session will end on Nov. 21 with concelebration by Pope and 24 Council Fathers from countries with Marian shrines, and an afternoon ceremony in St. Mary Major's; hope that Commission members and hard-working *Periti* will prepare texts for final approval so there can be a public session.
PENDING BUSINESS: Schema 13 on Church in Modern World.
SPEAKERS: 1. Archbishop Tchidimbo (Conakry, Guinea). 2. Bishop Von Streng (Basel and Lugano, Switzerland). 3. Abbot Reetz (Superior of Beuron Benedictines). 4. Archbishop Yu Pin (Nanking, China). 5. Bishop Gonzales-Moralejo (Auxiliary of Valencia, Spain). 6. Archbishop Bolatti (Rosario, Argentina). 7. Archbishop Darmajuwana (Semarang, Indonesia). *Relator:* Bishop Guano.
NEW BUSINESS: Schema 13 on Church in Modern World, Introd. and Chap. I.
SPEAKERS: 8. Archbishop Gouyon (Rennes, France). 9. Bishop Schmitt (Metz, France). 10. Bishop Romero Menjibar (Jaen, Spain). 11. Bishop De Vet (Breda, Holland). 12. Archbishop del Rosario (Zamboanga, Philippines). 13. Bishop Schoiswohl (Graz-Seckau, Austria). 14. Archbishop Garcia de Sierra y Mendez (Burgos, Spain).
STANDING VOTE to close debate on Schema 13 in general.

VOTE: Acceptability of text of Schema 13 as basis for discussion

	Total	*Placet*	*Non placet*	Invalid
Schema 13	1,876	1,579	296	1

October 26, 1964, Monday—109TH GENERAL CONGREGATION.
MASS: Archbishop Alvim Pereira of Lourenço Marques, Mozambique.
MODERATOR: Cardinal Suenens.
PRESENT: 2,007 Fathers.

194 THE THIRD SESSION

ANNOUNCEMENTS: concelebrations on Oct. 28 and Oct. 29.
PENDING BUSINESS: Schema 13 on Church in Modern World, Prologue and Chap. I.
SPEAKERS: 1. Cardinal Léger (Montreal, Canada). 2. Bishop Pietraszko (Auxiliary of Kraków, Poland). 3. Abbot Prou (Superior of French Benedictines). 4. Bishop Guerra (Auxiliary of Madrid, Spain). 5. Archbishop Pogacnik (Yugoslavia). 6. Bishop Tenhumberg (Auxiliary of Münster, Germany). 7. Bishop De Roo (Victoria, Canada). 8. Bishop Quadri (Auxiliary of Pinerolo, Italy). 9. Archbishop Ziadé (Beirut, Lebanon).
NEW BUSINESS: Schema 13, Chaps. II and III.
SPEAKERS: 10. Bishop Ancel (Auxiliary of Lyons, France). 11. Bishop La Ravoire Morrow (Krishnagar, India). 12. Bishop Cule (Mostar, Yugoslavia). 13. Bishop Hacault (Auxiliary of St. Boniface, Canada). 14. Archbishop Marty (Rheims, France). 15. Bishop Spülbeck (Meissen, Germany). 16. Bishop Klepacz (Lódz, Poland). 17. Archbishop Golland Trindade (Botucatu, Brazil). 18. Bishop Fourrey (Bellay, France).
VOTES: none.

October 27, 1964, Tuesday—110TH GENERAL CONGREGATION.
MASS: concelebrated by Bishop Abed, Maronite Bishop of Tripoli, Lebanon.
MODERATOR: Cardinal Suenens.
PRESENT: 2,042 Fathers.
ANNOUNCEMENTS: revised Chap. VIII of *De Ecclesia* distributed today and vote on whole chapter will be taken Oct. 29; tomorrow discussion will begin on Chap. IV of Schema 13.
PENDING BUSINESS: Schema 13, Church in Modern World, Chaps II and III.
SPEAKERS: 1. Cardinal Frings (Cologne, Germany). 2. Cardinal Caggiano (Buenos Aires, Argentina). 3. Cardinal Silva Henriquez (Santiago de Chile). 4. Patriarch Maximos IV Saigh (Syria). 5. Bishop Gand (Coadjutor of Lille, France). 6. Archbishop Zoghby (Egypt). 7. Bishop Himmer (Tournai, Belgium) 8. Bishop Garneri (Susa, Italy). 9. Bishop Kowalski (Auxiliary of Chelmo, Poland). 10. Bishop Kuharic (Auxiliary of Zagreb, Yugoslavia). 11. Bishop Volk (Mainz, Germany). 12. Bishop Cleven (Auxiliary of Cologne, Germany). 13. Archbishop Nicodemo (Bari, Italy). 14. Bishop Pourchet (Saint-Flour, France). 15. Bishop Sorrentino (Bova, Italy). 16. Bishop

Méndez Arceo (Cuernavaca, Mexio). 17. Bishop Huyghe (Arras, France).
VOTES: none.

October 28, 1964, Wednesday—111TH GENERAL CONGREGATION.
MASS: concelebrated by Archbishop Felici and 12 parish priests.
MODERATOR: Cardinal Agagianian.
PRESENT: 2,077 Fathers.
ANNOUNCEMENTS: (by Cardinal Agagianian) there will be no public discussion of "certain points" dealt with in Chap. IV of Schema 13, written observations will receive full consideration by the Commission; (by SG) distribution of brochure containing *modi* on Chap. I of *De Ecclesia*, there will be vote on Commission's work on Friday.
NEW BUSINESS: Schema 13 on Church in Modern World, Chap. IV as whole.
SPEAKERS: *Relator:* Bishop Wright (Pittsburgh, Pa.). 1. Bishop González Martin (Astorga, Spain). 2. Archbishop Ghattas (Thebes, Egypt).
NEW BUSINESS: Schema 13, Chap. IV, Arts. 19-20.
SPEAKERS: 3. Cardinal Ritter (St. Louis, Missouri). 4. Archbishop Athaide (Agra, India). 5. Bishop Bejot (Auxiliary of Rheims, France). 6. Bishop Grutka (Gary, Indiana). 7. Bishop Lourdusamy (Auxiliary of Bangalore, India). 8. Bishop Barrachina Estevan (Orihuela-Alicante, Spain). 9. Archbishop O'Boyle (Washington, D.C.). 10. Bishop Coderre (St.-Jean, Canada). 11. Bishop Bäuerlein (Srijem, Yugoslavia). 12. Bishop Schick (Auxiliary of Fulda, Germany). 13. Bishop de la Chanonie (Clermont, France). 14. Archbishop Malula (Leopoldville, Congo). 15. Bishop László (Eisenstadt, Austria).
VOTES: none.

October 29, 1964, Thursday—112ND GENERAL CONGREGATION.
MASS: concelebrated by Cardinal Döpfner of Munich, Germany.
MODERATOR: Cardinal Agagianian.
PRESENT: 2,092 Fathers.
ANNOUNCEMENTS: distribution of brochure containing *modi* on Chap. II of *De Ecclesia*, vote on this and Chap. I tomorrow.
PENDING BUSINESS: Schema 13, Chap. IV, Art. 19-20.
SPEAKERS: 1. Bishop Stimpfle (Augsburg, Germany). 2. Bishop Quadri (Auxiliary of Pinerolo, Italy). 3. Bishop Frotz (Auxiliary of Cologne, Germany). 4. Bishop Barthe (Fréjus-Toulon,

France). On Art. 25, because of his imminent departure from Rome: 5. Cardinal Feltin (Paris, France).

NEW BUSINESS: Schema 13, Chap. IV, Art. 21 on Family.

SPEAKERS: *Relator:* Archbishop Dearden (Detroit, Mich.). 6. Cardinal Ruffini (Palermo, Sicily). 7. Cardinal Léger (Montreal, Canada). 8. Cardinal Suenens (Malines-Brussels, Belgium). 9. Patriarch Maximos IV Saigh (Syria). 10. Bishop Beitia (Santander, Spain). 11. Archbishop Botero (Medellin, Colombia). 12. Bishop Rusch (Innsbruck, Austria). 13. Bishop Staverman (Indonesia).

VOTE: Revised Chap. VIII of *De Ecclesia*
Relator: Archbishop Roy (Quebec, Canada).

	Total	Placet	Non placet	Placet iuxta modum	Invalid
Chap. VIII	2,091	1,559	10	521	1

October 30, 1964, Friday—113TH GENERAL CONGREGATION.

MASS: Bishop Gay of Basse-Terre and Pointe-à-Pitre, Guadaloupe.

MODERATOR: Cardinal Agagianian and Cardinal Lercaro.

PRESENT: 1,929 Fathers.

ANNOUNCEMENTS: no general congregations on Monday and Tuesday, but there will be one on Saturday of next week; distribution of amended Schema on Pastoral Office of Bishops, and voting will begin Wednesday, Nov. 4.

PENDING BUSINESS: Schema 13, Chap. IV, Art. 21.

SPEAKERS: 1. Cardinal Alfrink (Utrecht, Holland). 2. Cardinal Ottaviani (Curia). 3. Cardinal Browne (Curia). 4. Bishop Reuss (Auxiliary of Mainz, Germany). 5. Archbishop Urtasun (Avignon, France). 6. Bishop del Campo y de la Barcena (Calahorra, Spain). 7. Bishop Nkongolo (Luebo, Congo). 8. Bishop Rendeiro (Fàro, Portugal). 9. Bishop Fiordelli (Prato, Italy). 10. Bishop Hervás y Benet (Spain).

NEW BUSINESS: Schema 13, Chap. IV, Art. 22 on Culture.

SPEAKERS: 11. Monsignor J. Ferreira (Portuguese Guinea). 12. Bishop Johan (Agen, France). 13. Bishop Bejze (Auxiliary of Lódz, Poland). 14. Bishop Lokuang (Tainan). 15. Father Fernández (Master General of Dominicans). 16. Bishop Muñoz-Vega (Coadjutor of Quito, Ecuador).

STANDING VOTE to close debate on Article 21 of Schema 13.

VOTES: Approval of Commission's revisions of Chaps. I and II of *De Ecclesia*

	Total	*Placet*	*Non placet*	Invalid
Chap. I	1,924	1,903	17	4(3)
Chap. II	1,915	1,893	19	3(2)

November 4, 1964, Wednesday—114TH GENERAL CONGREGATION.
MASS: Cardinal Forni of the Curia, in the Ambrosian rite.
MODERATOR: Cardinal Lercaro.
PRESENT: 2,011 Fathers.
ANNOUNCEMENTS: distribution of volume on pilgrimage of Pope Paul VI to Holy Land; Fathers asked to remember Orthodox Conference of Rhodes in their prayers; at request of Moderators, the SG assured the Fathers that the final text of Pastoral Office of Bishops would conform to definitive text of *De Ecclesia*.
PENDING BUSINESS: Schema 13, Chap. IV, Art. 22.
SPEAKERS: 1. Cardinal Lercaro (Bologna, Italy). 2. Bishop Carli (Segni, Italy). 3. Bishop Talamás Camandari (Ciudad Juárez, Mexico). 4. Archbishop de Provenchères (Aix, France). 5. Archbishop Zoa (Yaoundé, Cameroons). 6. Archbishop Elchinger (Coadjutor of Strasbourg, France). 7. Bishop Proaño Villalba (Riobamba, Ecuador).
NEW BUSINESS: Schema 13, Chap. IV, Art. 23 on Economic and Social Life.
SPEAKERS: 8. Cardinal Wyszynski (Warsaw, Poland). 9. Cardinal Richaud (Bordeaux, France). 10. Bishop Herrera y Oria (Malaga, Spain). 11. Bishop Zambrano Camader (Facatativa, Colombia).
VOTES: Revised text of schema on Pastoral Office of Bishops, Preface and Chap. I
Relatores: Archbishop Veuillot and Bishop Gargitter.

	Total	*Placet*	*Non placet*	*Placet iuxta modum*	Invalid
Art. 1-3	2,011	1,908	101		2
Art. 4	2,010	1,782	225		3
Art. 5-7	1,996	1,912	81		3(2)
Art. 8	1,963	1,880	81		2(1)
Art. 9-10	1,968	1,889	78		1
Pref. & Ch. I as whole*	1,965	1,030	77	852	6

* The Preface and Chap. I as a whole failed to get the required ⅔ majority and therefore will have to be submitted again for a vote.

November 5, 1964, Thursday—115TH GENERAL CONGREGATION.
MASS: Bishop Kabukasansha, Auxiliary Bishop of Fort Rosebery, Zambia.
MODERATOR: Cardinal Lercaro.
PRESENT: 2,063 Fathers.
ANNOUNCEMENTS: interruption tomorrow of Schema 13 to allow debate on Missions at which Pope will be present; Holy Father will receive bishops in national groups before their departure from Rome.
PENDING BUSINESS: Schema 13, Chap. 14, Art. 23.
SPEAKERS: (in name of at least 70 Fathers each): 1. Bishop Benitez Avalos (Auxiliary of Asunción, Paraguay). 2. Bishop Alba Palacios (Tehuantepec, Mexico). 3. Archbishop Zoungrana (Ouagadougou, Upper Volta).
NEW BUSINESS: Schema 13, Chap. IV, Art. 24.
SPEAKERS: *Relator:* Mr. James J. Norris. 4. Cardinal Frings (Cologne, Germany). 5. Cardinal Alfrink (Utrecht, Holland). 6. Bishop Rupp (Monaco). 7. Bishop Pildain y Zapiain (Canary Islands, Spain). 8. Bishop Swanstrom (New York, N.Y.). 9. Bishop Thangalathil (Trivandrum, India).
STANDING VOTE (at beginning of congregation) requested by Moderator to end debate on Art. 23 in favor of 3 Fathers who would speak in name of at least 280 others, although eight were still on list to speak.

VOTES: Schema on Pastoral Office of Bishops, Chap. II
Relatores: Bishop Carli (Part I) and Bishop Jubany (Parts II and III).

	Total	Placet	Non placet	Invalid
Art. 11-18	2,062	2,040	22	—
Art. 19-20	2,063	2,055	8	—
Art. 21	2,044	1,986	57	1
Art. 22-24	1,993	1,979	12	2(1)
Art. 25-26	2,005	1,982	22	1(1)
Art. 27-29	1,981	1,956	25	—
Art. 30-32	1,964	1,950	14	—
Art. 33-35	1,985	1,801	172	12

November 6, 1964, Friday—116TH GENERAL CONGREGATION.
MASS: Bishop Cahsay of Adigrat, Ethiopia, in Ethiopian rite.
MODERATOR: Cardinal Döpfner.
PRESENT: 2,129 Fathers.

ANNOUNCEMENT: discussion will continue tomorrow on Missionary Activity.
PENDING BUSINESS: Propositions on Missionary Activity of the Church.
SPEAKERS: *Relatores:* His Holiness Pope Paul VI*, Cardinal Agagianian and Bishop Lokuang. 1. Cardinal Léger (Montreal, Canada). 2. Cardinal Tatsuo Doi (Tokyo, Japan). 3. Cardinal Rugambwa (Bukoba, Tanganyika). 4. Cardinal Bea (Curia). 5. Monsignor M. Legarra (Panama).

VOTES: Propositions on Pastoral Office of Bishops, Chap. II as whole, and Chap. III
Relator: Bishop Schäufele (Freiburg-im-Breisgau, Germany).

	Total	Placet	Non placet	Placet iuxta modum	Invalid
Chap. II**	2,129	1,219	19	889	2
Art. 36-37	2,014	2,000	11		3(2)
Art. 38	2,021	1,948	71		2(1)
Art. 39-41	2,025	1,998	27		–
Art. 42-43	2,065	2,053	11		1
Art. 44	2,074	2,049	15		10(9)
Chap. III	2,070	1,582	15	469	4

November 7, 1964, Saturday—117TH GENERAL CONGREGATION.
MASS: Archbishop Jurgens of Cuzco, Peru.
MODERATOR: Cardinal Döpfner.
PRESENT: 1,911 Fathers.
ANNOUNCEMENT: conclusion of discussion of Missionary Activity Monday and preliminary vote.
PENDING BUSINESS: Propositions on Missionary Activity.
SPEAKERS: 1. Cardinal Frings (Cologne, Germany). 2. Cardinal Alfrink (Utrecht, Holland). 3. Cardinal Suenens (Malines-Brussels, Belgium). 4. Bishop Yougbare (Koupela, Upper Volta). 5. Archbishop Gantin (Cotonou, Dahomey). 6. Bishop Geise (Bogor, Indonesia). 7. Bishop Lamont (Umtali, Southern Rhodesia). 8. Bishop Kihangire (Auxiliary of Gulu, Uganda). 9. Bishop Massa (Anyang, China). 10. Bishop Carretto (Thailand). 11. Bishop Moors (Roermond, Holland). 12. Bishop

---

* The Pope's talk was in the nature of a *relatio*, hence he has been included among the *relatores*.
** Chap. II was not approved.

Velasco (Hsiamen, China). 13. Monsignor Grotti (Brazil). 14.
Bishop Gahamanyi (Butare, Ruanda). 15. Bishop Riobé
(Orléans, France). 16. Bishop Moynagh (Calabar, Nigeria). 17.
Bishop Lokuang (Tainan, China).
VOTES: none.

November 9, 1964, Monday—118TH GENERAL CONGREGATION.
MASS: Cardinal Masella, Archpriest of the Lateran Basilica.
MODERATORS: Cardinals Döpfner and Suenens.
ANNOUNCEMENTS: vote tomorrow on revised Introduction and
Chap. I of schema on Ecumenism; (by Moderator) agenda for
discussion of remaining texts: propositions on Religious,
Priestly Formation, Catholic Education and Matrimony.
PENDING BUSINESS: Propositions on Missionary Activity.
SPEAKERS: 1. Bishop Picachy (Jamshedpur, India). 2. Bishop
Geeraerts (Belgium). 3. Archbishop Garcia de Sierra y Mendez
(Burgos, Spain). 4. Archbishop Zoghby (Egypt). 5. Archbishop
Amissah (Cape Coast, Ghana). 6. Bishop Sheen (Auxiliary of
New York, N.Y.).
NEW BUSINESS: Schema 13, Chap. IV, Art. 24 on human solidarity.
SPEAKERS: 7. Cardinal Rugambwa (Bukoba, Tanganyika). 8.
Father Mahon (Superior General of Missionary Society of St
Joseph). 9. Archbishop Seper (Zagreb, Yugoslavia). 10. Bishop
Begin (Oakland, California). 11. Cardinal Richaud (Bordeaux,
France).
NEW BUSINESS: Schema 13, Chap. IV, Art. 25 on war and peace.
SPEAKERS: 12. Cardinal Alfrink (Utrecht, Holland). 13. Bishop
Ancel (Auxiliary of Lyons, France). 14. Bishop Ntuyahaga
(Usumbura, Burundi). 15. Bishop Guilhem (Laval, France).
STANDING VOTE to end debate on Missionary Activity. Relator
Bishop Lokuang.

VOTE: Propositions on Missionary Activity: whether agreeable to return
text to Commission for revision

	Total	Placet	Non placet	Invalid
Missionary Activity	1,914	1,601	311	2(1)

November 10, 1964, Tuesday—119TH GENERAL CONGREGATION.
MASS: Archbishop Mathias of Madras-Mylapore, India.
MODERATOR: Cardinal Suenens.
PRESENT: 2,119 Fathers.

ANNOUNCEMENTS: vote tomorrow on Chap. II of Ecumenism; distribution of Commission report on *votum* on Matrimony; will be general congregation on Saturday of this week; Maximos IV will concelebrate on Friday.

PENDING BUSINESS: Schema 13, Chap. IV, Art. 25.

SPEAKERS: 1. Patriarch Maximos IV Saigh (Syria). 2. Bishop Hengsbach (Essen, Germany). 3. Bishop Hannan (Auxiliary of Washington, D.C.).

NEW BUSINESS: Schema 13, Chap. IV in general.

SPEAKERS (in name of at least 70 Fathers): 4. Bishop Arrieta Villalobos (Tilaran, Costa Rica). 5. Archbishop Beck (Liverpool, England). 6. Bishop Rada Senosiain (Guaranda, Ecuador). 7. Bishop Hakim (Akka, Israel). 8. Bishop Rigaud (Pamiers, France). 9. Bishop Yáñez Ruiz Tagle (Los Angeles, Chile). 10. Bishop McGrath (Santiago de Veraguas, Panama). 11. Bishop Nguyen-Khac-Ngu (Long-Xuyen, Vietnam). Lay Auditor: Juan Vazquez. *Relator:* Bishop Guano.

NEW BUSINESS: Propositions on Religious.

SPEAKERS: *Relator:* Bishop McShea (Allentown, Pa.). 12. Cardinal Spellman.

VOTE: Revised text of Schema on Ecumenism, Introduction and Chap. I

	Total	*Placet*	*Non placet*	Invalid
Introd. & Chap. I	2,119	2,068	47	4(1)

V

The Debates on Missionary Activity, Religious, Priestly Formation (Seminaries) Christian Education, Marriage

✠

THE THIRD SESSION MADE HISTORY when Pope Paul put in a
appearance at one of the working sessions of the Council, an
took his place not on his throne but at the head of the Coun
cil Presidents' table. According to canon law, the Pope is th
head of the Council, but modern Popes have studiousl
avoided giving the impression that they were interfering i
any way with the Council's freedom of discussion by absen
ing themselves from all purely business sessions. Perhaps th
Pope wanted to symbolize more clearly the close relationshi
between Pope and Council, in keeping with the spirit c
collegiality, than was possible by daily behind-the-scenes co
tacts and appearances at solemn public sessions. On the oth
hand, it has been suggested that his appearance was symbol
of something other than the spirit of collegiality, namely

lesire to impress on the Fathers, in case any were inclined to
orget, that the prerogatives of his office must not be over-
ooked, but this seems an unlikely way of making the point.
The Pope was under some pressure, it seems, from various
quarters to make a personal appearance, and the idea may not
have originated with him at all. The question that had to
be decided was *when* he should appear. Debate on Schema 13
vas already underway, and while the reception accorded the
first two schemata reduced to propositions was not very en-
ouraging, a choice nevertheless had to be made, so it was
rranged that he should help introduce the text on missionary
ctivity, as the least controversial of the remaining documents.
The discussion of Schema 13 had to be interrupted to allow
his. Time was running out and the agenda was already over-
rowded. The decisions about the James Norris *relatio* and
he appearance of Paul were apparently made suddenly, on
he spur of the moment. The Pope was also badly advised
y Cardinal Agagianian, who misled him about the character
f the text on missions and the reception that it might expect
o receive at the hands of the bishops. Instead of turning out
o be a wise move, the papal visit proved to be symptomatic
f the inauspicious happenings during the final days of the
Third Session.

On Friday, November 6, 1964, after hearing a mass cele-
rated according to the Ethiopian rite from a chair placed
n front of the conciliar altar, the Pope took his place at the
able of Council Presidents, sitting in the middle between
Cardinals Tisserant and Tappouni, at the place normally
ccupied by the former, as Dean of the Sacred College and
anking cardinal. A minor incident occurred while the Pope
vas being seated, or shortly after he was seated. Archbishop
Dante, who as papal master of ceremonies normally hovers
ear the papal side on all occasions, wanted to remain stand-
ng behind his chair at the Presidents' table, but this was too
uch for Cardinal Tisserant who sternly ordered him away
-after a similar warning by Archbishop Felici had failed to

do the trick. The Pope was now in safe hands and there was no need for monitors. In the course of a short speech introducing the missionary text, Pope Paul referred to the importance and seriousness of the missionary problem today and made the specific recommendation: "We hope that, while you may decide on improvements in some parts, you will approve the present text." Cardinal Agagianian then rose to deliver his *relatio* as president of the conciliar commission on commissions, referring to Pope Paul, in fulsome terms as *"qualis et quantus missionarius,"* in view of his announced intention to go to Bombay. His Holiness then got up, gave his blessing, walked slowly toward the side aisle of the basilica, greeting various persons and groups on the way, and finally disappeared from view.

The debate on Missionary Activity occupied two and a half days, Friday and Saturday, November 6 and 7, and Monday, November 9. When the Pope had left, Bishop Lokuang of the conciliar commission that had drafted the schema, read the commission's report. He pointed out that the present 13 propositions had been extracted from the seven chapters of the original schema. The discussion of this text was extremely well orchestrated: the African secretariats were called upon to provide their quota of speakers; Cardinal Bea, a friend of the Africans and Asians, was pressed into service to help support the views of the missionary bishops, as well as other leading bishops. Everything was done to make the essential points on the floor. The outcome, as one observer put it, was "a resounding Yes for the missions; a resounding No for the skeleton of a schema" which the bishops were asked to accept. The propositions were adjudged wholly unsatisfactory as an adequate expression of the Church's views about such an important topic.

Cardinal Léger of Montreal, who led off the debate, put his finger on an essential point. He said that it was hoped that the Council would give a new impetus to the missionary *élan* of the Church by directing attention to this vital part of the

ostolate. A new plan was called for. There were encourag-
g signs that a new approach was possible, because of more
neral recognition in the Church of the principle of diver-
ty and the necessity of adapting the Church's methods to
cal conditions; because of the restoration of a permanent
aconate; because of a hoped for dialogue with non-Chris-
an religions, but on this score the text had nothing to say;
ecause of a new awareness on the part of the bishops of their
sponsibilities toward the universal Church. With regard
 the central commission proposed by the schema, the cardi-
al was in favor of a body within the framework of the Con-
regation for the Propagation of the Faith, but as a supreme
uncil over all the parts. What was desirable, according to
ardinal Frings, was a kind of "senate" of missionary and
ther bishops, or "missionary strategy board," fully repre-
ntative of all areas, to be assisted by experts, both theoreti-
l and practical. He was applauded when he called for the
writing of the schema and its presentation at the Fourth
ssion. Applause also greeted the Irish-born Bishop Lamont
 Umtali, Southern Rhodesia, when, in the course of a
ighly rhetorical speech, he quoted Isaiah, characterizing the
ropositions as so many "bare bones" which needed to be
vivified in a worthy schema, one that would set on fire not
nly the bishops, but also religious superiors and the whole
hurch with the missionary spirit of Pentecost. The Modera-
r's warning to the speaker to be less rhetorical naturally
nly caused the Fathers to be more generous with their ap-
ause when he finished.

The vision of the present text was too limited, according
 Archbishop Zoghby, patriarchal vicar for Egypt, and its
utlook too Western. The Eastern Churches were capable of
ggesting new approaches to the missions, even though they
ad not been very active along this line in recent centuries.
e referred in particular to the close connection between
e missions and the mystery of the Trinity, the mystery of
hrist as being "sent" by the Father, and the mystery of the

"seed of God's word" being sown in men through the actic of the Holy Spirit, according to a "divine pedagogy."

Cardinal Alfrink's reminder was of a more practical n ture. He noted that the work of evangelizing the world h; scarcely begun. There are two billion men who have not y received Christ's message, but while the needs are vast, tl number of missionaries has been steadily declining for year New churches flourish, but they are short of priests. Aft twenty centuries it is shameful to admit these facts, but v must.

The dimensions of the missionary problem were rath well brought out by Cardinal Bea, who cited the words St. Paul to the effect that missionary activity should be c rected to uniting all people with Christ and with each othe It was sometimes said that because of the shortage of pries and the need for missionary work at home, as well as tl fact that the hierarchy was now established among near all nations, that it was no longer vital to support foreig missions, properly speaking. But it must not be forgotte that the *first* obligation of the Church was to bring Christ message to those who had never heard it. And it was not tru of course, that because the hierarchy had been establishe in certain areas that there was no longer any need there fc outside help. The intervention of Cardinal Suenens also bor on this general point, namely the need for not taking too r stricted a view of the laymen's role, as presented in the eight proposition. In accordance with their role of helping to coi secrate the world, laymen have a place in missionary worl but they should of course be well prepared for the tasks the will be called on to undertake. They can help with catechet cal work, cooperate in the parochial apostolate, and furthe the work of various apostolic organizations.

Quite a few Fathers insisted on the necessity of disassoc ating missionary work from the implication that it was merel a form of spreading Western culture, or the long arm c Western capitalism, or that any such mercenary goal was i nded. Speaking in the name of the bishops of Africa and adagascar, Archbishop Gantin, of Dahomey, said that the d prejudices about the missions as an attempt to dominate ere still very much alive. Everything must be done to dissi- te this misunderstanding, by promoting a cultural dialogue d the establishment of higher institutes, on a "give and ke" basis. Speaking in French, he said: "The Church is pranational. It transcends all regimes."

The Brazilian Father Grotti, prelate nullius of Acre and urus, delivered a rather fiery intervention against the whole nor of the propositions, which he characterized as "pater- listic exhortations and generalizations." The *periti* who ew them up should be sent to the field to learn the true eaning of "mission." He reminded his hearers of the saying: Rome also is a missionary territory!"

Father Grotti was opposed to the establishment of a cen- al commission under, or part of, the Congregation for the ropagation of the Faith. It should be established within e Consistorial Congregation, and missionary churches ould cease to be called "missionary"; rather it was better speak of them as "new churches," and of Propaganda itself the "Congregation for New Churches."

Bishop Geise, of Bogor, Indonesia, speaking in the name the Indonesian Episcopal Conference, announced that e Conference and many other Fathers would vote *Non lacet* on the propositions and demanded that they be sent ack for a thorough revision; while Bishop Riobé, of Orleans, rance, a member of the Missionary Commission itself, sub- ribed to the same thesis. He observed that their Commis- on had been torn for three years between a theological and juridical view of the missions and that the just requests of many bishops for a full-fledged schema should be satisfied. nly in this way could justice be done to the many sugges- ons sent in by the bishops, which "lie sleeping in the files." ishop Moors of Roermond, Holland, and Bishop Moynagh Calabarra, Nigeria, spoke in the same sense.

The last speaker was Bishop Sheen, auxiliary of Ne
York, who approved the proposal for the formation of a ce:
tral commission, which would be able to cut corners an
satisfy legitimate needs without regard to juridical conside
ations. He closed with the thought that, while chastity ha
been the fruit of the Council of Trent, and obedience that c
Vatican Council I, poverty ought to be the fruit of Vatica
Council II.

In the face of such overwhelming and insistent demanc
for a drastically revised, ampler schema, Bishop Lokuang lo:
no time in his final summation in assuring the Fathers tha
they would be presented with a better schema at the Fourt
Session, according to their wishes.

The vote on the motion, "Does it please the Fathers t
send the text back to Commission?"—framed, it should b
noted, in keeping with the critical tone of the debate—pro
duced the desired result. The text on missionary activity wa
ordered sent back to commission (1601 *placet* to 311 *no*
placet). Ordinarily, the question would have asked whether i
pleased the Fathers to vote on the propositions at once.

On November 11 and 12, the Council took up the nex
schema to be considered, entitled "On the Adaptation an
Renewal of the Religious Life." The debate was actuall
begun the day before, toward the end of the session on Nc
vember 10, with a reading of his *relatio* by Bishop McShea, c
Allentown, Pennsylvania, and one intervention by Cardina
Spellman. The present text of four pages comprising 2
propositions was extracted from the thirty pages of the ful
text of the schema on religious orders, which, in turn, ha
been condensed from an original schema of some 100 page:

The debate revealed two tendencies. Those favoring
wider view of the religious apostolate were clearly for a r
jection of the present text, which appeared to them to b
too conservative and narrow. Representative speakers amon
this group were Cardinals Richaud, Doepfner, Suenens, Bea

Bishop Charue, Father Buckley, Father Lalande, and Bishop Huyghe. The opposing group were either in favor of the text or strongly opposed to any drastic alterations in religious life. Representative speakers here were Cardinals Landázuri-Ricketts and Ruffini, Father Fernandez, Master General of the Dominicans, Father Anastasius, Superior General of the Discalced Carmelites, and Archbishop Perantoni, of Lanciano, Italy.

The most critical evaluation of the schema came from Cardinal Doepfner, who said that it was weak, not because it had been abbreviated, but because it failed to come to grips with the basic problems of religious renewal, of the accommodation of religious life to modern times, of the preparation of religious for their vocation, and because it took too restricted a view of religious institutes. Too many religious congregations were doing the same work. Women religious, particularly, he said, often found themselves torn between "a quasi-monastic regimen and over-demanding work." As to contemplatives, he was even blunter: "In contemplative communities, there is an institutional narrowness which is psychologically unbearable; hence, of many contemplative vocations few persevere." A longer schema was not necessarily recommended, but one including consideration of the above points.

The address of Cardinal Suenens repeated points that he had frequently made in lectures, and in his controversial book on women religious. He confined himself to this theme, beginning with the words: *"Schema non placet."* It was necessary to cease regarding nuns as children or minors and treat them as adults, and they must have freedom to engage in apostolic work. Theologians must elaborate a "spirituality of the active life for them," so that they can get away from "the traditions and mentality of the cloister." Without abandonment of any of the essentials of the religious life, what the cardinal wanted was that the religious apostolate should be directed more to the work of "evangelization," with more

frequent contacts between religious and the laity. The role
of the nun should be to help inspire the laity in their apostolate. Apart from this theoretical or doctrinal consideration,
he called for drastic reforms in practical matters. Nuns should
begin acting as "adults" and display a sense of responsibility
by working in cooperation with others. "We should give up
the habit of treating nuns as minors, an attitude so typical
of the nineteenth century, which is still found in many religious congregations today," he said. "This emphasis on in-
fantilism is matched by another disgraceful trait: the exhibition of maternalism on the part of mother superiors. Let us
abandon these customs which perpetuate a feeling of inferiority among women religious. They are based not on consideration for the requirements of the religious life, but on
outmoded ideas about society. As for cloistering active orders,
this serves for the most part as an obstacle to their effectiveness; it prevents nuns from being the leaven in the loaf which
they ought to be." He called for canon lawyers and competent
nuns to elaborate rules for a more balanced organization of
religious orders; for a change in the system of electing superiors; for general chapters to be more truly representative of
the order; and for the abandonment of outmoded forms of
garb, anachronistic customs and the like. Everything must be
eliminated that helped give nuns an inferiority complex. The
text should be rejected and a new one drawn up. The cardinal was seconded by Bishop Moors of Roermond, Holland.

Several speakers, like Cardinal Bea, referred overtly to the
"crisis" in the religious life now being experienced. According to the cardinal, it was not sufficient, as the schema did, to
urge a renovation primarily in the juridical sphere. This was
important, but the most vital element, ways whereby the
spiritual outlook of religious could be renewed, were hardly
mentioned by the text at all. The first requirement was the
accommodation of the nature and scope of the religious life
to a modern mentality. The text should point out that the
consecration of the religious regarded not only the indi-

vidual Christ, but the whole Christ, that is, the Church, as pointed out in *De Ecclesia*. Each institute had its own rule and scope, but all the institutes were related to the Church and were dedicated to the service "of the whole human family." There was too much striving to preserve the spirit of the separate orders, and not enough effort being expended on ways in which to participate in the changing circumstances of the world around them. The religious should be encouraged to take an active part in all the movements, biblical, liturgical, missionary and ecumenical, which were animating the Church at the present time.

Current speculation over the place in the apostolate of the contemplative orders, devoted wholly to prayer, was reflected in the concern shown by a number of speakers that there must be no downgrading of their importance in any plans for a renewal of the religious life. Greater emphasis must be placed on such orders, said Cardinal Landázuri-Ricketts. He also observed that one reason why there were so many defections from religious orders today was that the candidates who entered them were more interested in apostolic work than in holiness or submitting to the discipline of the evangelical counsels. More insistence should be placed on religious institutes as "schools of sanctity."

The schema in its reduced form was generally satisfactory to Cardinal Spellman, who felt that it contained the essential points that ought to be made. But he warned about any renewal of religious orders which would impose on religious any kind of apostolate inconsistent with the functions which they normally performed. He was referring to the suggestions often made by Cardinal Suenens. Many superiors of religious orders, Cardinal Spellman said, had spoken to him about their anxieties with regard to this recommendation. Instead of promoting an observance of their rules, it would mean a further departure from them. It was sufficient for religious to do whatever they were normally required to do, for example, teaching, nursing, or leading a purely contemplative life. With regard to the last point, Cardinal Spellman said that he was worried lest the contemplative life might be smothered "by the onrush of activism."

Cardinal Ruffini expressed himself as worried about the flat recommendation in the text that religious orders should renew themselves. He felt that this ought to be toned down, as there was danger that it might produce imprudent demands for reform. In any case, nothing should be done toward accommodating or renewing religious life without consulting the Holy See, otherwise changes might be introduced which would make it more difficult for religious to lead a life of perfection. He was also opposed to anything that might draw contemplatives away from their form of life, by way of requiring them to take part in active apostolic works. His recipe for all dangers to the vow of chastity, was to recommend that "religious should be urged to implore the grace of chastity, for the preservation of purity amid so many dangers is a great gift." The cardinal was applauded by the conservative benches when he finished.

It was strange, said Bishop Charue, of Namur, Belgium, that nothing was said about the relations between conferences of religious superiors and bishops, in Proposition 19, and nothing about the relations between religious and diocesan clergy on the parish level. He also noted, in the name of the Belgian hierarchy, that the warning about observing the norms laid down by the Holy See was a good thing because there had been abuses in such things as the recruitment of novices. Some religious, in their zeal for recruiting students for their schools or in speaking to youths about the life of perfection, had given the impression that it was impossible to reach evangelical perfection outside the monastery or cloister. While regretting the impossibility of submitting a "really good and proper schema," Bishop Sol of Indonesia, in the name of the Indonesian Episcopal Conference, indicated acceptance of the present text as a working basis, however, he made it clear, in his remarks, that he agreed with what Cardinals Doepfner and Suenens had said by way of its inadequacy.

Disturbed by so much adverse criticism Archbishop Perantoni, O.F.M., of Lanciano, Italy, former General of the Franciscans Minor, speaking in the name of 370 Fathers, rose to give his approval to the text. He said that he was alarmed "in the face of the rumors being circulated these days by some who are saying that religious do not want the schema retained." As member of the Conciliar Commission on Religious which had drafted the text, he proceeded to defend his handiwork against the intrigues which he said were being directed against it "even from those in high places."

There followed a number of Fathers speaking in the name of rather large groups: Archbishop Sartre of Cameroun, in the name of 265 Fathers; Bishop Guilly, of British Guiana, in the name of 265 Fathers; Father Buckley, Superior of the Marist Fathers, in the name of 130 Fathers; Archbishop Athaide, O.F.M. Cap., of Agra, India, in the name of the National Conference of India; Father Lalande, Superior General of the Holy Cross Congregation, in the name of more than 140 Fathers; Bishop Carroll, Auxiliary of Sydney, Australia, in the name of 440 Fathers, the largest ever; Archbishop Baraniak, of Poznan, Poland, in the name of the Polish hierarchy; and Bishop Fiordelli, of Prato, Italy, in the name of 82 Fathers. Two other superior generals also spoke, in their own names: Father Hoffer, Superior General of the Marianists, and Father Van Kerckhoven, Superior General of the Missionaries of the Sacred Heart. Sartre, Guilly, Carroll and Hoffer were favorable to the present text, to which number should be added Bishop Cekada, of Skoplje, Yugoslavia, but all the rest, including Bishop Huyghe, of Arras, France, were highly critical. Particularly outstanding interventions were delivered by Father Buckley, Bishop Huyghe, and Father Lalande. They pointed out that while the conservatively-oriented Congregation of Religious had been "pushing" for the adaptation of religious orders ever since 1950, nothing important had been done and the present text, which was intended to accomplish this purpose, should be completely rewritten. Touching on the delicate subject of relations between orders and bishops, Father Buckley called for a gesture of friendship toward the diocesan clergy, to be included in the new draft. He went on: "We religious may be worried about the greater authority that bishops want to have over us; but we ought to face up to the fact that some of our habits irritate the diocesan clergy, such as our tendency to talk as if we were the only ones in the state of perfection. The sound spirituality of diocesan priests should be recognized. In fact, religious priests of the active life are closer to diocesan priests than to contemplative religious. The canonical distinction, while necessary, should not be insisted on in practice; for what unites us is more important than what separates us." He declared that Pope John had expressed agreement with these sentiments in a private audience which he had granted him. He called further for the dropping of the distinction between Orders and Congregations. As for the "crisis in obedience" about which religious superiors were always talking, it was his feeling that the crisis was with the superiors, not with the religious under them. The truth was that "today's young people don't swallow archaic formulas like 'the will of the Superior is exactly the same as the will of God.' "

Bishop Huyghe called for the cooperation of mother superiors in drafting a new schema, referring particularly to the mother superior who had been appointed one of the Council's Lay Auditors, Sister Mary Luke, of the American order of the Sisters of Loretto. The bishop noted that it was unfortunately customary for legislation regarding religious to be drawn up by men only. As a matter of fact, no woman religious had been consulted by the conciliar commission which drew up the present draft, at least to the extent that lay auditors and experts had been consulted on the document on the Apostolate of the Laity. This was declared, expressly, by Sister Mary Luke in an interview at the bishops' press panel. While understandably cautious in her remarks about the conservative nature of the conciliar commission and the likelihood that a better document could be produced by them, she expressed it as her fervent hope and as the desire of many women religious that a new text would: a) modernize theological teaching with regard to the religious life in accordance with the aims and goals of *aggiornamento;* and b) provide for the representation of women religious on ecclesiastical bodies which governed them. It is known that Sister Mary Luke has taken an active part in the work connected with the revision of Schema 13.

Bishop McShea's defense of the text in summing up the debate—his remark that "those who offered suggestions accepted the schema in substance" was hardly in conformity with the facts—played an important part in saving the text, when the question was put to the Fathers whether it was pleasing to proceed to an immediate voting on the several propositions (1155 *placet* to 882 *non placet*), for it is an almost invariable rule that when a commission defends its own text, the Fathers are unlikely to reject it outright. A factor in support of retention was unquestionably the massive concerted action on the part of many conservatively-inclined bishops and religious to save the text, which they regarded as at least a satisfactory basis for revision and a safeguard against too much reform. Sensing what the outcome might be, Cardinals Doepfner and Suenens marshalled a massive attack of their own, so that when the individual propositions were put to a vote, Propositions 1–13, representing the weakest portion of the text, were not carried because of the large number of *iuxta modum* votes submitted. In this way they forced the commission to give consideration to their demands and come up with a more radically revised text than would otherwise have been the case. In this in-

stance, the majority showed that they had learned something
from the tactics of the minority.

The short series of propositions entitled "On the Formation of Priests," that is, on priestly training in all its aspects,
was taken up on Thursday, November 12, and debated for
four days until November 17, with time out for the ceremony
on Friday, November 13, when the Pope laid his tiara on
the altar as an offering to the poor. It had originally been
a schema totalling sixty pages in 1962; it was now reduced
to 22 propositions, comprising four pages.

The text was one of the few sets of propositions that were
adjudged favorably. The need for a statement of principles
had been fulfilled very well by the Conciliar Commission on
Seminaries, the author of the document, which had somehow
managed to escape from the predominately conservative influence of the curial Congregation on Seminaries and Universities and keep that influence at arm's length. It was almost
inevitable that the bishops would approve of it heartily, for
the very first Proposition boldly announced the principle
that programs for the training of the clergy were to be
adapted to local conditions in accordance with plans drawn
up by the local episcopal conferences:

So that the general rules may be adapted to each people and
to each rite, episcopal conferences are to prepare a program for
the formation of their priests. This program is to be constantly
brought up to date and submitted for the approval of the Holy
See. Thus universal laws will be adapted to the needs and char-
acteristics of individual peoples and all countries, in such a way
that the formation of their priests will harmonize with the
spiritual needs of the country.

The net effect of this ruling, if finally enacted, would be to
take much of the initiative in controlling and standardizing
the training of priests, in the broadest sense of the term, away
from the Congregation of Seminaries in Rome and out of

the hands of the conservative prelates there who have dominated this sector of ecclesiastical life for so long. It is understandable that the spokesmen for that body, particularly Archbishop Staffa and Cardinal Bacci, both of the Curia, as well as Cardinal Ruffini, expressed themselves as unhappy with the text.

The text stressed the idea of developing a sense of responsibility, proper freedom, and wider outlook among seminarians. Seminarians must come to know more about the world, they must be better acquainted with the various branches of knowledge, and in particular with the Bible, as modern scriptural exegesis understands it. The schema was declared a "masterpiece" by Cardinal Léger of Montreal, who hoped that it would become a solid foundation for the transformation of seminaries, imbuing them with a new dynamism, as had happened after the Council of Trent. The Cardinal of Rio de Janeiro concurred in Cardinal Léger's judgment regarding the effectiveness and success of the schema. The principles laid down were good; further practical measures should be left to the judgment of local bishops and local episcopal conferences. Cardinal Meyer, for his part, welcomed the provision for adjusting programs locally. One of the defects of seminary training has been that too much uniformity has been imposed. There were other ways of exercising the priesthood beside those assumed to be normal for the Latin clergy and the schema should make this point, to be consistent with Proposition 1.

The schema was also praised by Bishop Charue, of Namur, Belgium, because it recommended principles that were sound, viable and productive, not excessively severe or impractical. Bishop Weber of Strasbourg, with 25 years behind him in the seminary at Paris, also gave his approval to the text. It avoided the tendency to throw over everything that the Council of Trent had decreed, while at the same time undertaking the renewal demanded by the changed times and mentalities of today. He put in a word about seminary rectors and hoped that they would be chosen from priests who were well fitted and trained for the job, and they should form a "college" of their own, conducting the seminary on family lines, under the direction of the bishop.

Cardinal Meyer brought out the important point that a priest should be trained not only to be a mediator between God and men but to be a man *per se*. These were the two principles which should form the basis of seminary training. Connected with the latter point, was the need for training priests to be good Christians, of course. Seminary students should be trained in the ethical field as well as in the purely ecclesiastical sciences.

The point made by Cardinal Meyer was also stressed by Archbishop Colombo of Milan, the brother of the Bishop Colombo who is the Pope's theological adviser. He pointed out that unless seminary students received the proper kind of training calculated to develop their personalities, they might turn out to be immature, excessively passive, with too detached a feeling toward human society, which would hinder them in their apostolate. The schema was to be praised for recognizing these dangers and making recommendations to counteract and avert them, particularly by its emphasis on the "Christo-centric" formation which every priest should receive, a point frequently mentioned by Pope Paul VI in his discourses and by other advocates of *aggiornamento*.

Could a vocation always be recognized? The Cardinal Archbishop of Seville felt that the words in the text were too specific when it spoke of the "signs of a vocation"; it was better to omit this phrase altogether and refer simply to the fact that a vocation was a grace from God. It was useless to argue over the "signs" of a call from God; a vocation would become apparent in time if a person offered himself with the right disposition. On the other hand, Bishop Drzazga of Poland maintained that it was desirable to spell out more clearly such signs. His intervention was rather typically on the conservative side. In his opinion the text should be sent back to the commission and "made worthy of an ecumenical Council."

On a more practical plane, there was considerable discussion, both inside and outside the council hall, on the merits of maintaining a minor seminary in each diocese to prepare boys for the major seminary, or seminary proper. Were such schools duplicating parochial schools really necessary? The Cardinal Archbishop of Seville tended to minimize their importance in his intervention, claiming that, to some extent, it was true that boys had a "more natural and perfect seminary in their own homes" and that they could overcome the crises of youth with the help of a prudent priest. Minor seminaries were therefore not strictly necessary. Cardinal Doepfner also agreed. While minor seminaries were good, they were not the only way to prepare youth for the seminary and priesthood. He observed that in Germany many candidates for the priesthood came not from the minor seminary, but from those who have already completed their examinations in the public high school for the university and there was an advantage in this, because the candidates were very often more well-rounded, since it was "in the nature of man" to prefer family life. Something should be said about this in the text so that Christian families would become conscious of their responsibility to foster vocations for the priesthood more than they do at present. Cardinal Ruffini, on the other hand, was very definitely of the view that minor seminaries were the *only* way to train students for the priesthood and that where there were none to be found, they should be opened immediately in accordance with the wishes of the Council of Trent, which laid it down that vocations were to be fostered *"inde a teneris annis."* The text should state also that Pontifical or Catholic schools were to be preferred when selecting students for special studies. This, of course, is diametrically opposed to the tendency nowadays for bishops to send their gifted students and priests to study at secular universities, with a view to broadening their training in specialized fields.

An interesting proposal was made by Cardinal Suenens of Belgium, who called for the establishment of a special commission to study programs for the renewal of seminaries. For a pastoral renovation to be effective, it was not sufficient to publish conciliar texts, since the fruits of the Council's work would depend on the men who put these ideas into practice. The hopes of the Council were closely connected with the formation of priests, therefore it was important to go into this matter thoroughly and make recommendations on the basis of an investigation of local conditions and problems. Opposition to this proposal was at once voiced by Cardinal Bacci of the Curia, who termed it wholly unnecessary and "very inopportune," since this was the proper function of the Congregation of Seminaries. If such a commission were established, it would have to be within the framework of the Congregation or directed by it. Apparently, in the thinking of people like Cardinal Bacci, the various organs of the Curia, as they exist at the present time, are eternal. His categorical dismissal of the idea was symptomatic of the outlook and fears of the Curia.

A warning was sounded by Bishop Pawlowski of Poland that all changes in seminaries must be gradual. It was dangerous to alter a system that had borne fruit for centuries. Those who were most critical today of the traditional training in seminaries, he noted with some satisfaction, were from countries that had the fewest vocations. It did not seem to have occurred to him that this was precisely why they were criticizing the present structure. He concluded by calling for the need to increase devotion to Mary among seminarians.

If the suggestion of Cardinal Suenens was likely to upset the Congregation of Seminaries and Universities, that made by Archbishop Garrone, of Toulouse, France, was calculated to cause dismay, for it was nothing less than an indictment of that citadel of conservatism in the Curia, similar to the indictment of the Holy Office by Cardinal Frings during the Second Session. The archbishop was commenting on Proposition 1, calling for decentralization and an increase in the authority of episcopal conferences over seminaries. This meant, he said, that the duties and rights of the Congregation of Seminaries in Rome would be changed. He suggested that to ensure that this took place, it might be a good idea to lay down certain norms for a renovation of the central body in Rome. His remarks summed up the two chief criticisms most frequently levelled against the Congregation: "It must take more account of the necessities and needs of local countries. To accomplish this it must no longer be behind the times or negative in its approach, but should be organically joined to the Congregation dealing with priests, and it should have as members men from all over the world, so that it would be better acquainted with the conditions of priestly life. Secondly, it should be more open to progress and change in the sciences which pertain to seminary training. Hence, the Congregation should use the experience of men who are true experts in every field of higher learning." The commission may be spared the trouble of having to look into this highly congenial subject, for by the time the Fourth Session begins, a plan for the reorganization of the Curia may have been announced, so that it will no longer be necessary.

Considerable attention was focused also on the problem of how much time should be devoted to pastoral work, during seminary years. Cardinal Suenens was of the opinion that the whole of the seminary period should be marked and dominated by preparation for pastoral work; others thought that a year should be set aside, others that enough practical experience could be gained during summer vacations, etc. There was no consensus of opinion. Two Fathers brought up the subject of priestly celibacy, Bishop Reuss of Mainz and Bishop Mendez Arceo of Mexico. Both wanted a more positive presentation of the idea of celibacy, so that it would not be presented to students only as a renunciation, something that had to be agreed to primarily as a step before ordination.

Much attention was given the problem of the correct intellectual formation of the priest. The issue was rather clearly joined between, on the one hand, the advocates of a more open attitude, represented by the text of the propositions, and those who favored strict adherence to the existing scholastic norms, on the other hand. A middle view was represented by Archbishop Hurley, of Durban, South Africa, who agreed with Cardinal Suenens that the present manner of teaching philosophy in seminaries should be examined, but he thought that scholasticism, as such, could not be brushed aside. Some of its themes were "very essential for the Catholic mind." Nevertheless he was in favor of having students learn to develop their philosophical ideas in the light of man's growing knowledge and to express their ideas in modern language, so that a dialogue would be possible. One of the resolute defenders of the status quo, Cardinal Ruffini, was shocked that St. Thomas Aquinas was not mentioned in the section on philosophical studies and was named only "timidly" in connection with theology. Other men need not be ignored just because St. Thomas was given his proper place, he declared.

Cardinal Léger objected to the habit of calling scholastic theology "perennial" (*philosophia perennis*) and wanted the term dropped from Proposition 15 dealing with the curriculum of faculties and universities. He said that use of the adjective seemed to be contrary to the nature of philosophy itself, which should be concerned, according to St. Thomas, not with what authors have said, but with things in themselves. It was not for the Council to propose a particular philosophy but to lay down rules, in accordance with the requirements of faith, for the valid philosophical instruction of the students. It was disadvantageous to seem to impose scholastic philosophy, not only because there was really no such thing as "scholastic philosophy" *tout court,* there were various schools of scholastic philosophy; but also because it was unwise to give the impression that the Church was imposing scholastic philosophy on non-Occidental students, who had valid philosophical traditions of their own which they might prefer. The cardinal was glad that the schema did not "dwell ponderously on the teaching of St. Thomas" in Proposition 16, not, he maintained, because his works were to be avoided, but because it was advisable not to give any impression of exclusiveness. The important thing was to recommend not so much the doctrinal ideas of St. Thomas, as his scientific and spiritual approach which was to use the ideas of his day to illustrate and extol the Gospel.

Such liberalism was anathema to Archbishop Dino Staffa, Secretary of the Curial Congregation of Seminaries and Universities, a ruthless spokesman for the official line on Thomism. Speaking in the name of "bishops of both the West and East"—it would be interesting to know who the latter were—Staffa indignantly and categorically rejected the imputation of Cardinal Léger that St. Thomas was not all that the Thomists had claimed him to be. Dialogue with the world of today must be "steeped" in the philosophical and theological sciences, with St. Thomas as the leader. Progress in knowledge could not be made apart from truth. Apparently, according to Staffa, Aquinas was synonymous with truth. The teaching of St. Thomas should be preserved in seminaries, in accordance with papal encyclicals. After Staffa, the next most spirited defender of Thomism, the Curial Cardinal Bacci, had his say. He was troubled, he declared, by what he had heard several days before about the dethroning of St. Thomas from his primacy. He did not think that the Fathers wished to belittle St. Thomas, whom Popes ever since the 13th century had praised so highly. If anyone dared to do this, he would be placing the Council not only above the Pope, but *against* the Pope—which no one among the Fathers would surely think of doing. On the other hand, he admitted that philosophy, like everything else progresses and needs perfection. Therefore those who defend the "perennial" or Thomistic philosophy today, do so with the knowledge that other philosophers are also approved by the Church and are not to be neglected. Other philosophers are to be studied, and if they have taught anything that is new and more perfect, "if it corresponds to right reason, is to be proposed for the study of seminarians." Proposition 15 should certainly state that the "perennial philosophy" is to be held in the greatest honor by our seminarians, but it should be said that the works of other Doctors are not to be neglected, as long as error is separated from truth, so that philosophical studies will better correspond to the needs and mentality of modern men. The speech of Cardinal Bacci represented a backing down from the rather extreme statements of previous speakers, particularly those of Archbishop Staffa, regarding the exclusive role which Thomism is supposed to play in seminary instruction. However the arrogance of his insinuation did not escape his hearers.

As the last speaker, Bishop Reuss, summed up the general impression that the schema accomplished its purpose of stating general principles and he recommended a vote of *placet,* with some *modi,* as a gift from the Council to rectors and students of seminaries. The official *relator,* Bishop Carraro, then summed up. By a vote of 2,076 to 41 the schema was easily accepted for immediate voting. Since the final voting on the several propositions produced no upsets, the text was sent back to commission to be revised in accordance with the wishes of the majority.

After Bishop Carraro had spoken, and before the Council went on to the next topic, on November 17, the floor was given to one of the parish priests invited to be present at the Third Session, Father Marcos, of Madrid, Spain. Instead of being the conventional bow to the powers that be in gratitude for the privilege of being able to address the assembly, with a few truisms and platitudes thrown in, his speech turned out to be a highly articulate voicing of the desires of parish priests almost everywhere. He called for emphasis on the idea of a diocesan *presbyterium* in the schema on the priesthood, that is the notion that bishops were to govern with the advice of their parish clergy. More specifically, he wanted wider permission to be granted to parish priests to confirm, as clergy of the eastern rites were able to do, and for greater flexibility in the hearing of confessions, at least within the confines of one country.

On Tuesday, Wednesday and Thursday, November 17–19, the Council took up the very short schema in the form of propositions, entitled "Declaration on Christian Education." The original document had been a full-fledged schema "On Catholic Schools," but the Coordinating Commission had ordered this shortened to a series of propositions along with other texts. When the propositions were distributed to the Fathers, in May 1964, they met with considerable criticism, so in the course of the summer the Commission on Seminaries revised them and changed the name to the present title, as more representative of the contents of the document.

The propositions were introduced by Bishop Daem, of Antwerp, Belgium, a member of the commission. Their purpose was to state some of the broad principles governing the subject, not to go into too much detail. Consequently the commission proposed, in the revised Preface, that a post-conciliar commission be set up to study all problems in greater depth.

The debate, punctuated by the many exciting events and interruptions of the final days of the Session, quickly showed that there was a general consensus among the bishops in favor of retaining the present draft as a basis for revision. The text was evidence of the progress that could be made when conciliar commissions paid attention to what the bishops really wanted, instead of attempting to impose on them ideas favored by the curial faction, as some commissions had

done. The main differences which emerged were between the
American and Continental bishops. While the former urged
immediate acceptance with a minimum of discussion, the
latter were more critical in their approval of the text and
wanted numerous points to be aired for the benefit of the
commission. Cardinal Léger, of Montreal, seemed to voice
the Continental view when he said: "We should not approve
too hastily what will be the *Magna Carta* of Christian Education." By contrast, Archbishop Cody, of New Orleans, speaking in the name of most American bishops and as president
of the National Catholic Education Association, declared:
"The Council cannot refuse to approve the Declaration, because it is closely connected with other schemata already
approved. Moreover the failure of the Council to make a
pronouncement on Catholic education would deeply offend
countless lay Catholics who, often with great sacrifice, support the Church in its education work." Cardinal Ritter,
Cardinal Spellman, and Bishop Malone, Auxiliary Bishop of
Youngstown, Ohio, also gave it their wholehearted approval.
About the only concrete improvement suggested by the
American bishops was the proposal of Cardinal Spellman for
an additional paragraph stressing the right of parents to be
free to choose the school of their choice for their children and
for the state, in due measure, to provide for the support of
such schools. Since it was a commonly recognized principle
in Europe, and elsewhere in the world, for the state to support private schools—in England, for example, all Catholic
children in parochial schools receive some kind of support
from the government—the suggestion was not likely to meet
with any opposition from that quarter, but some questioned
whether it was altogether wise and expedient, from the viewpoint of American politics, to inject into the conciliar debate
an issue that was still so highly controversial in the United
States. Would the original wording of the schema not have
sufficed?

Not all comments were so entirely favorable, however.

Bishop Elchinger, of Strasbourg, noted that the present text had been drawn up, essentially, before account could be taken of the important schemata discussed in the Third Session and that it therefore needed a complete overhauling. In the process of revision he wanted a more ecumenical spirit introduced, more emphasis placed on the spiritual or religious side of teaching as a witnessing to the Christian life, and a clearer delineation of the responsibilities of parents. Archbishop Gouyon, of Rennes, found the text deficient in spelling out the specific end of Christian education, namely the development of a deep personal faith. Cardinal Léger found that it said nothing about the coordination of Catholic universities. He proposed that the main function of the Congregation in charge of studies in Rome should be to promote such coordination, by the convocation of scientific congresses and by urging Catholic universities to pay greater attention to urgent problems confronting Catholic doctrinal and scientific life. His hearers were well aware that the Congregation of Seminaries and Universities has consistently done the very opposite. The schema should proclaim, prudently but clearly, the freedom of investigation which ought to prevail in all the sacred sciences, particularly in the liturgical, biblical and ecumenical fields.

A rather discouraging view of Catholic education was painted by Bishop Henriquez Jimenez, of Caracas, Venezuela, who questioned whether the schema had really come to grips with the basic problem of coping with education on a mass scale. Most Venezuelan children were in public schools. The number of Catholic children was steadily increasing, but there was a great disparity between the number and those who could expect to receive a Catholic education. "Our schools," he said, "are lovely 'enclosed gardens' cultivated with much loving care, but whose fruits for the evangelization of the world seem to grow less with each passing day." The absence of the Church from the public school was a pressing problem. No attempt had been made to train Catholic teachers for such schools. The same anxieties were expressed by Bishop Muñoz-Vega, of Quito, Ecuador.

Five bishops from Nigeria, one from Vietnam, and one from Indonesia, developed the idea of the close connection between schools and missionary work. After launching into a discourse on the meaning of the term "Catholic universities," the Master General of the Dominicans, Father Fernandez, was soon treating the Fathers to a sermon on St. Thomas as "the Master to be imitated"—the text speaks of him as "the Master who reconciled faith and reason, both divine and human science"—going on at length about the unique role of Thomism and throwing out such far-fetched statements as, "The authority of St. Thomas is that of the *magisterium* of the Church," and "It is not sufficient to regard Thomas as a model of study, for his teaching is in itself objectively true for all times. The Master cannot be separated from his teaching," and similar remarks, until he was interrupted by the Moderator, who was applauded for delivering the Fathers from this tirade.

The *relator,* Bishop Daem, then summed up. He said that most observations would be incorporated in the text and pleaded for acceptance. He proposed that the post-conciliar commission provided for in the text should draw up a fuller schema which would serve as a basis for action by episcopal conferences. The voting being favorable, the document was sent back to commission to be revised as the *relator* had requested.

At noon, on Thursday, November 19, 1964 (called "Black Thursday" because of the hubbub over the postponement of the vote on religious liberty), the Council, after the turmoil had somewhat died down, took up the last of the short texts to be considered, the *votum* or recommendations on the Sacrament of Marriage, so-called, because expressed in the form of a proposal by the Council of points to be considered in a forthcoming revision of the Code of Canon Law. The document had started out as a full treatment of all the sacraments, but had been gradually narrowed down to the present 11 propositions dealing with the sacrament of marriage from a strictly canonical and practical point of view.

The principal changes proposed by the *votum* were: 1) the suppression of the so-called minor impediments to marriage, e.g. consanguinity, etc.; 2) a less rigid canonical procedure for mixed marriages, in the spirit of the decree on Ecumenism, by distinguishing more clearly between different types of mixed marriages, by doing away with regulations which had the effect of seeming to penalize such marriages (nuptial mass, etc.), by recognizing as valid, though illicit, such marriages celebrated before a non-Catholic minister and by giving the bishop authority to grant dispensations in this matter, and by no longer requiring the non-Catholic partner to make the usual marriage promises (*cautiones*) to bring up any children as Catholics; and 3) a revision of the canonical form for marriage, which normally requires the marriage to be celebrated in the presence of a Catholic priest.

There were two main purposes behind the new proposals: to simplify marriage legislation so far as Catholics were concerned; and to remove any basis, to the extent that this was possible and permissible, for the charge of non-Catholics that the Church discriminated against baptized non-Catholics and treated them as second-class Christians by requiring them to participate in ceremonies and agree to promises which violated their consciences.

The text was introduced by Cardinal Masella, president of the conciliar Commission on the Discipline of the Sacraments, and by Bishop Schneider, of Bamberg, Germany, the official *relator,* who read the report of the Commission.

Most of the debate touched on Proposition 5, on Mixed Marriages, which, in translation, reads as follows:*

5. In order that canon law may show greater respect, and in a more opportune way, for the condition of persons, in accord-

* A French translation of Art. 5 appeared in *Le Monde,* November 13, 1964.

ance with the decrees on religious liberty and ecumenism, it is desirable above all to make a clear distinction between the regulations governing the marriage of a Catholic partner with a baptized non-Catholic, and the marriage of a Catholic partner with an unbaptized person. Consequently the following points are to be observed:

a) In all mixed marriages, when asking for a dispensation from the diriment impediment, the Catholic partner is to be seriously enjoined and must sincerely promise that he or she will see that all children will be baptized and brought up as Catholics, to the extent that he or she can (*in quantum poterit*).

With regard to the promise, which is to be made by the Catholic partner alone, the non-Catholic partner is to be informed about this at a suitable time and his or her consent obtained that he or she is not opposed to it.

The non-Catholic partner must also be informed about the ends and nature of marriage, and neither partner must have any reservations about this matter.

b) Mixed marriages must be contracted according to the canonical form, but if for grave reasons this is impossible, in order that a marriage involving a true matrimonial consent may not be lacking in validity, the ordinary shall have power to dispense from the canonical form.

c) Mixed marriages between two baptized persons shall no longer be celebrated in the sacristy but during mass. Also mixed marriages between a Catholic partner and an unbaptized partner may be celebrated in church during mass.

d) The excommunication required by present canon law against those who have contracted a marriage before a non-Catholic minister is abrogated.

All the speakers were favorable to the idea that existing marriage legislation needed modernization, and most of them approved of the proposals in the text. However, there was less enthusiasm for the latter in the concrete, among the American, Irish, British and Australian prelates than among their European confrères. Cardinal Ritter was the exception. He welcomed the document as a prudent measure, pointing particularly to its recommendations regarding the canonical

form, which avoided the extreme of abolishing all requirements and that of maintaining an inflexible attitude toward
the status quo. Archbishop Heenan of Westminster, while
disagreeing with the text on some matters, praised it as containing many excellent points and thanked the Commission
for its work, saying that it deserved to be "written in letters
of gold." He also added a word of praise for the work of the
periti, thus compensating for the rather disparaging remarks
with regard to them which he made in his speech on October
22. The archbishop seemed to have a knack for allowing his
enthusiasms to get out of hand, however. He went on to say
that he thought mixed marriages in the sacristy were more
like interments than marriages. Why should the organ not
be played on such occasions? "The chief difficulty about
mixed marriages concerns the religious upbringing of the
children," he said. "In our country, by far the majority of
mixed marriages take place with non-Catholic partners who
are only rarely found to be active members of any religious
community. For this reason the promises to bring up the children as Catholics rarely caused any difficulty, and so I think
it would be better to leave the promises by the partners as
the normal rule. When a mixed marriage takes place between a Catholic and a practicing Protestant, special rules
could be provided." His assumption that the requirement of
written pledges was "in no way against the conscience of a
non-Catholic," because "other Christian Churches do not
claim to be the one true Church, whereas Catholics do" did
not go down at all well with non-Catholic church leaders and
resulted in several sharp statements by the Archbishop of
Canterbury and other churchmen, who pointed out that it
was easy assumptions of this kind on the part of Catholic
prelates that were at the root of Catholic-Protestant differences about Catholic marriage legislation, which the *votum*
was intended to correct. Archbishop Heenan was also for
eliminating the saving clause, "to the extent that he or she
can," because it seemed to imply that the Catholic was not

bound by the promises if they became hard to fulfill; it was
tantamount to the Church's saying: "It is not necessary to
put up any fight for your children. For the sake of peace, go
ahead and let them abandon the Faith." He appeared more
liberal as regards ceremony, seeing no objection if the bride
and bridegroom wanted to go and receive a blessing in a non-
Catholic church after the Catholic marriage.

Cardinal Gilroy proposed that the whole matter of canonical form needed study and that it would be unwise to approve
what the schema recommended before this had been done.
He was opposed to granting the ordinary the authority to
dispense, as called for in 5b. "This cannot be done without
danger of scandal or indifferentism." In the name of Cardinal
Spellman, who had departed for New York, Bishop Fearns,
one of the auxiliary bishops of New York, read the cardinal's
speech. He also said that he was speaking in the name of
more than 100 American bishops. The intention of improving marriage legislation was declared to be "a cause for joy,"
but the cardinal warned against proposing changes that might
be beneficial for some countries, but would "cause serious
spiritual harm to our country," because of the special conditions obtaining in countries with a pluralistic religious
society. He demanded time for consultation with pastors before any approval was given to the present recommendations. The vague expression "grave reasons" might have the
effect of practically abolishing the form for mixed marriages
and eliminating any opportunity for spiritual guidance and
gaining assurances that the children would be brought up as
Catholics. If there were territories where such dispensations
were necessary, application could be made to the Holy See.
The text ignored the great accomplishment of the present
legislation regarding the education of children; it did not
provide for the solution of marriage problems in the fore-
seeable future; and it dangerously diminished the responsibility of pastors. Archbishop Krol was even more specific,

along the same lines. He demanded that the pre-nuptial written promises be preserved, with the ordinary being empowered to make dispensations in the case of non-Catholics "of deep religious convictions and strong church affiliations." With regard to dispensations from the canonical form for mixed marriages, he noted that "experience teaches that when the availability of a dispensation becomes known, the requests for such invitations increase." He also thought that "grave reasons" would be used to satisfy the whims of the partners and that the whole matter would become a scandal to the faithful.

A problem of concern to the French hierarchy because of the large number of nominal Catholics in France, but also found elsewhere, was raised by Bishop Renard of Versailles. It was whether to allow religious marriages in the case of two baptized persons who had no faith any longer, and who merely regarded the ceremony as a desirable formality not as a sacrament. Some bishops and pastors refused to allow such marriages to be celebrated because the partners did not have the proper dispositions; others were more tolerant, recalling the statements of the Popes about the natural right of marriage. The norms proposed by the present text did not cover this point. He suggested one solution might be to allow such persons to pronounce their vows before the pastor and witnesses without any religious ceremony.

The debate was ended on Friday, November 20, 1964 because of the lateness of the hour without any summation by the official *relator*. The Council was asked to vote on the following motion, proposed in accordance with an earlier recommendation of Cardinal Doepfner in the course of the debate: "Does it please the Fathers to send the propositions on the sacrament of marriage, together with the observations of the Fathers, to the Supreme Pontiff, so that he may take appropriate action in this regard?" By a vote of 1,592 to 426 the matter was left in the hands of the Holy Father, who is

expected to issue a Motu Proprio at a suitable time putting
into effect some, at least, of the recommendations without
waiting for the final revision of the Code of Canon Law. The
outcome was not entirely satisfactory to some of the bishops,
including the Americans, because it closed the door to any
further discussion of the matter in the Council. Motu Pro-
prios are not debated; they are accepted and obeyed.

Summary

November 11, 1964, Wednesday—120TH GENERAL CONGREGATION.
MASS: Archbishop Ferrand of Tours, France.
MODERATOR: Cardinal Suenens.
PRESENT: 2,109 Fathers.
ANNOUNCEMENTS: (by Moderator) invitation to visit exhibition of
  documents on history of councils in Vatican Archives; (by SG)
  end of discussion on Religious and preliminary vote tomorrow.
PENDING BUSINESS: Propositions on Religious.
SPEAKERS: 1. Cardinal de Barros Camara (Rio de Janeiro, Brazil).
  2. Cardinal Ruffini (Palermo, Sicily). 3. Cardinal Richaud
  (Bordeaux, France). 4. Cardinal Döpfner (Munich, Germany).
  5. Cardinal Landázuri Ricketts (Lima, Peru). 6. Cardinal
  Suenens (Malines-Brussels, Belgium). 7. Cardinal Bea (Curia).
  In the name of groups of Fathers: 8. Bishop Charue (Namur,
  Belgium). 9. Father Fernández (Master General of the Domini-
  cans). 10. Bishop Moors (Roermond, Holland). 11. Father
  Anastasio of the Holy Rosary (Superior General of Discalced
  Carmelites). 12. Bishop Sol (Coadjutor of Amboina, Indonesia).
  13. Archbishop Perantoni (Lanciano, Italy). 14. Archbishop
  Sartre (Cameroons). 15. Bishop Guilly (Georgetown, British
  Guiana). 16. Father Buckley (Superior General of Marists).
  17. Archbishop Athaide (Agra, India).

VOTE: Revised Schema on Ecumenism, Chap. II

	Total	*Placet*	*Non placet*	Invalid
Chap. II	2,109	2,021	85	3

November 12, 1964, Thursday—121ST GENERAL CONGREGATION.
MASS: Bishop Rancans, Auxiliary Bishop of Riga, Lettonia (exiled).
MODERATOR: Cardinal Suenens.
PRESENT: 2,042 Fathers.
ANNOUNCEMENTS: vote on Saturday on Chap. III of Ecumenism; vote on Saturday on individual propositions on Religious.
PENDING BUSINESS: Propositions on Religious.
SPEAKERS: (in name of groups of speakers) 1. Bishop Huyghe (Arras, France). 2. Father Hoffer (Superior General of Marianists). 3. Father Lalande (Superior General of Congregation of Holy Cross). 4. Bishop Carroll (Auxiliary of Sydney, Australia). 5. Archbishop Baraniak (Poznan, Poland). 6. Father Van Kerckhoven (Superior General of Missionaries of Sacred Heart). 7. Bishop Fiordelli (Prato, Italy). 8. Bishop Cekada (Skoplje, Yugoslavia).
NEW BUSINESS: Propositions on Priestly Formation.
SPEAKERS: *Relator:* Bishop Carraro (Verona, Italy). 9. Cardinal Bueno y Monreal (Seville, Spain). 10. Cardinal Meyer (Chicago, Ill.). 11. Bishop Drzazga (Auxiliary of Warsaw, Poland). 12. Archbishop Colombo (Milan, Italy).
STANDING VOTE on whether to close debate on Religious.

VOTE: Propositions on Religious, whether to proceed to vote or return it
to Commission
Relator: Bishop McShea (Allentown, Pa.).

	Total	*Placet*	*Non placet*	Invalid
Religious	2,042	1,155	882	5(3)

November 14, 1964, Saturday—122ND GENERAL CONGREGATION.
MASS: Archbishop Bukatko of Belgrade, Yugoslavia.
MODERATOR: Cardinal Agagianian.
PRESENT: 1,963 Fathers.
ANNOUNCEMENTS: possibility of general congregations in the afternoons of the coming week; distribution of brochure containing *modi* on Chaps. III–VIII of *De Ecclesia,* and voting on accept-

ance of *modi* next Tuesday and Wednesday; public session on
Nov. 21.

PENDING BUSINESS: Propositions on Priestly Formation.

SPEAKERS: 1. Cardinal de Barros Camara (Rio de Janeiro, Brazil).
2. Cardinal Ruffini (Palermo, Sicily). 3. Cardinal Léger (Montreal, Canada). 4. Cardinal Döpfner (Munich, Germany). 5.
Cardinal Suenens (Malines-Brussels, Belgium). 6. Archbishop
Staffa (Curia). 7. Bishop Fernández-Conde (Cordoba, Spain).
8. Bishop Sani (Den Pasar, Indonesia). 9. Archbishop Gopu
(Hyderabad, India). 10. Archbishop Jaeger (Paderborn, Germany). 11. Archbishop Botero Salazar (Medellín, Colombia).
12. Bishop Flores Martin (Barbastro, Spain). 13. Bishop Sauvage (Annecy, France).

VOTE: Revised text of Schema on Ecumenism, Chap. III

	Total	Placet	Non placet	Invalid
Chap. III	1,963	1,870	82	11(6)

VOTE: Propositions on Religious

	Total	Placet	Non placet	Placet iuxta modum	Invalid
Pref., Pr. 1-3	1,955	871	77	1,105	2
Prop. 4	1,960	1,049	64	845	2
Prop. 5-6	1,949	883	77	987	2
Prop. 7-10	1,950	907	66	975	2
Prop. 11-13	1,946	940	56	947	3
Prop. 14	1,844	1,676	65	103	–

November 16, 1964, Monday—123RD GENERAL CONGREGATION.

MASS: Bishop Valloppilly of Tellicherry, India.

MODERATOR: Cardinal Agagianian.

PRESENT: 2,122 Fathers.

ANNOUNCEMENTS: objections to votes and doubts about doctrine
relative to Chap. III of Ecumenism; authority of doctrine expressed in *De Ecclesia;* read "Explanatory Note" prefixed to
Chap. III of *De Ecclesia* (in the brochure containing the *modi*);
customary *quaesitum* omitted through error on p. 64 of *modi*
on Chap. III of *De Ecclesia;* Fathers wishing to imitate Pope's
act with regard to tiara, many give money offerings to

Secretary of State, as has already been done by cardinals and secretaries of the Council; preliminary vote tomorrow on Priestly Formation.

ᴘᴇɴᴅɪɴɢ ʙᴜsɪɴᴇss: Propositions on Priestly Formation.

ᴘᴇᴀᴋᴇʀs: 1. Cardinal Caggiano (Buenos Aires, Argentina). 2. Cardinal Bacci (Curia). 3. Bishop Komba (Auxiliary of Peramiho, Tanganyika). 4. Archbishop Hurley (Durban, South Africa). 5. Bishop Zorzi (Caxias, Brazil). 6. Bishop Schmitt (Metz, France). 7. Bishop Añoveros Ataún (Cadiz y Ceuta, Spain). 8. Bishop Pawlowski (Wroclawek, Poland). 9. Bishop Rivera Damas (Auxiliary of San Salvador, El Salvador). 10. Bishop Charue (Namur, Belgium). 11. Bishop Weber (Strasbourg, France). 12. Bishop Benavent Escuin (Coadjutor of Malaga, Spain).

ᴠᴏᴛᴇs: Propositions on Religious

	Total	Placet	Non placet	Placet iuxta modum	Invalid
Prop. 15-17	2,122	1,833	63	226	–
Prop. 18-19	2,117	1,936	50	131	–
Prop. 20	2,112	1,639	50	419	4

VI

The November Crisis;
Close of the Third Session

✠

As THE COUNCIL ENTERED its next to last week on November 9
the atmosphere of cautious optimism accompanying the de
bate on Schema 13 changed perceptibly to one of great un
certainty, if not downright gloom, as the evidence mounted
that almost all the texts destined to be proclaimed on the
final day, less than two weeks away, were in some kind of
trouble. Fortunately Ecumenism was in the hands of the
bishops and the voting would take place during the week
on the Secretariat's handling of the *modi* to each chapter
the last stage before a final (and largely formal) vote ap
proving the schema as a whole. The prospects were good
that this text would go through smoothly. But nothing else
seemed to be in such good shape.

It was known that the work of revising the two declara

ons, on Non-Christians and Religious Liberty, had been
ompleted by the Secretariat, but their present whereabouts
as something of a mystery. They were said to be variously
1 the hands of the Secretariat, of the Theological Commis-
on, about to go to the printer, or held up for unknown
easons. It was learned in the course of the week, however,
1at at a meeting of the Theological Commission on Mon-
ay, November 9, the Declaration on Religious Liberty had
een voted on; of the 28 members present, 12 voted *placet*,
non *placet*, and 9 *placet iuxta modum,* and 1 abstention.
ince the *iuxta modum* votes were considered positive, the
eclaration was carried and it was sent to the printer on
Vednesday. The Declaration on the Jews and Non-Chris-
ans was to be sent to the printer on Friday or Saturday, ac-
ording to word from a member of the Secretariat at the
ishops' press panel on Thursday. This reassuring news
emed to mean that both would be distributed and might
ossibly be voted on during the final week.

The schema on Divine Revelation, it was thought, would
robably not be ready in time for final voting and promulga-
on was therefore out of the question, because so much of
1e time of the Theological Commission had been taken up
ith work on the amendments to *De Ecclesia.* But this re-
ort turned out to be slightly erroneous. Revelation was
istributed to the Fathers shortly before the end of the Ses-
on, but there was not time for a vote. Likewise the revised
hema on the Pastoral Office of Bishops could hardly be
eadied, in view of the large number of *iuxta modum* votes
ast on the first two chapters, all of which had to be examined
nd considered. The prospects for the propositions on the
riental Churches were brighter. Final promulgation seemed
ossible, but the text was not yet ready.

The chief worry was over the fate of the remainder of
e Ecclesia (Chapters III–VIII), which was being held up
ecause of a mysterious disagreement over Chapter III—the
eart of the schema—on collegiality. The difficulty was said

to be not so much over the text itself, as over the terms c
an interpretation, or explanation, of collegiality which th
Pope was insisting on.

The voting on the three chapters of Ecumenism took plac
on November 10, 11 and 14. The chapters were all passe
with overwhelming majorities. By Saturday it was apparen
that there would be at least one document to proclaim on th
final day.

The Secretariat's firmness in rejecting most of the propose
amendments deserves to be noted. Since most of these wer
offered by the opposition, the action of the assembly in ap
proving the Secretariat's work amounted to a defeat for th
minority. Of the 217 *modi* proposed on Chapter I, only 1
were accepted by the Secretariat. Of the 59 *modi* propose
on Chapter II, only 5 were accepted. And of the 129 *mod*
proposed on Chapter III, only 11 were retained. Those ac
cepted related only to minor points. Had the amendment
offered by the minority been accepted, they would have ha
the effect of modifying the whole tenor of the document. Bu
the minority did not acknowledge defeat, as we shall see.

Would *De Ecclesia* fare as well? Would the Theologica
Commission prove as firm in rejecting the substantial change
to Chapter III which the minority had proposed and, if the
yielded to pressure, would the Council have the courage t
reject the Commission's handling of the *modi* and so bur
the Constitution on the Church for the Third Session, possi
bly causing a break-up of the Council itself?

Part of the answer came on Saturday, November 14, whe
the Fathers and *periti* were handed a fat booklet containin;
the *modi* to Chapters III–VIII of *De Ecclesia* together witl
the Commission's comments on each one. A hasty perusa
showed that the text of Chapter III had not been substanti
ally tampered with, though some changes had been intrc
duced and there was now prefixed to Chapter III an Explana
tory Note or *Nota Explicativa Praevia*, elucidating certai

expressions and defining the sense in which collegiality was to be understood.*

The Note was solemnly read in the council on Monday morning, November 16, by the Secretary General, Archbishop Felici, and printed copies of it along with certain other important remarks made by him at the same time (see below) were distributed to the Fathers. In his customary authoritarian vein, the archbishop admonished the Fathers "to study it carefully, because it is sometimes difficult to understand," referring to the highly technical and involved language of the Note. He made it clear that the votes on the following day were to be cast in the light of this authoritative interpretation. On Thursday, November 19, before the vote on *De Ecclesia* as a whole, he repeated this declaration, insisting that even though the Note was not to be found in the booklet containing the final, amended version of the schema, which the bishops had in their hands, it was nevertheless normative and "formed part of the official acts of the Council." The formal vote on the last day must also be governed by this interpretation.

Who was the author of the Note? By whose authority was it communicated to the Fathers? The Note was presented as if it came from the Theological Commission, but considering the circumstances in which it was made known, the fact that it was signed by Archbishop Felici and not by Cardinal Ottaviani (as would have been the case if it had really been issued under the authority of the Theological Commission), as well as the fact that the Secretary General failed to mention in whose name he was acting (he normally always stated whether his announcements were made on behalf of the Council Presidents or Moderators, if such were the case), it was obvious that the Note had come from the Pope himself and was being communicated to the Council on his authority, although he did not wish to acknowledge

* Text of Explanatory Note in Appendix, p. 347.

the fact openly, preferring to remain anonymous behind the vague curial phrase "superior authority." It would have been impossible for the Theological Commission to communicate a normative interpretation of this kind to the assembly, because it was merely one of several organs of the Council and was not "superior" with respect to the others. Moreover the Secretary General read the communication to the whole Council, the Presidents, Moderators and everybody, so that there could hardly be any doubt as to the document's provenance.

Why did Pope Paul prefer to act in this apparently paradoxical way? The reason can only be that he did not wish to appear to be intervening in the course of the Council directly, while at the same time it was made perfectly clear that that was precisely what he was doing. The Note was intended as a final effort on his part to win over the coterie of bishops and experts, belonging to the minority, who had resolutely and ceaselessly opposed the doctrine of collegiality ever since the Second Session. The opposition had crystallized then over the question of whether to put the famous Five propositions proposed by the Moderators to a vote. It had been insistently contended by the group, consisting of bishops from Latin countries, southern Italy, Spain, Brazil and Latin America, for the most part, as well as well known Roman theologians such as Father Bertrams, S.J. (Gregorian University) and curial officials like Archbishop Dino Staffa, Secretary of the Congregation of Seminaries, that the motion of the Moderators was illegal. When the vote finally was held anyway, on September 30, 1963, they contended that the results, so overwhelmingly favorable to the thesis of collegiality, were both invalid and contrary to sound doctrine. The doctrine of episcopal collegiality was, in their opinion, not only unhistorical but gravely injurious to the rights and prerogatives of the Roman pontiff as defined at Vatican Council I. Archbishop Staffa, in particular, spared no effort in making the objections of the group known to all and sundry through

Rome, July 25th 1964

Your Excellency,

I am presuming to send to Your Excellency a copy of a study which I have made in connection with the Council Schemata «De Ecclesia» and «De pastorali Episcoporum munere in Ecclesia».

I felt that it was most important to investigate the immediate source of episcopal jurisdiction, since the nature and foundation of episcopal collegiality depend on this. As Your Excellency will see, I have not merely collected opinions but have gone to the sources and, on studying these, it seems to me that they are irreconcilable with some of the fundamental propositions of the Schemata in question.

With all good wishes,

I remain,

Your Excellency's
devoted servant in Christ.

+ Dino Staffa

Letter with pamphlet opposing definition of collegiality, sent by Archbishop Dino Staffa of the Curia to the American bishops.

lectures, through booklets (mimeographed copies of a treatise
in English denouncing collegiality were distributed to all the
American bishops in Rome—see his covering letter, page 243—
at the start of the Third Session), through visits (on a visit to
the United States in the summer of 1964 he thought that he
had won a convert in Cardinal Cushing), and in every other
conceivable way.

Despite their repeated questioning of the vote of September 30, 1963, the Theological Commission took the results of
the vote into account. Subcommission No. 5 (consisting of
Archbishop Parente, Archbishop Florit, Bishop Schroeffer,
Bishop Henriquez Jimenez, and Bishop Heuschen, together
with a large number of *periti* including Bishop Colombo,
Father Rahner, Father Gagnebet, Father Ratzinger, Monsignor Thils, etc.) examined the interventions relating to
this point and drew up a revised text of Chapter III that
was approved by the Theological Commission as a whole on
March 6, 1964. Since doubts were still being raised about
the doctrine as expressed in the revised text, the Pope under-
took to examine Chapter III himself. On May 19, 1964, the
Secretary General transmitted the Pope's suggestions to the
Theological Commission in a letter with the request that the
Commission again examine Chapter III in their light. Since
the text had already been approved nearly unanimously by
the Commission, the Pope noted, the purpose of his suggestions was merely to eliminate any possible misunderstandings
and ambiguities.

The Commission then studied the Pope's suggestions and
adopted most of them at a meeting on June 5, 1964. From
then on Pope Paul spared no effort to win over the minority
to acceptance of the idea of collegiality. His statement, opening the Third Session on September 14, 1964, that the principal task of the Session was to formulate a doctrine of collegiality, was chiefly, though not exclusively, directed at them.
The permission granted to Bishop Franič, also a member of
the group, representing the minority on the Theological

Commission, to present a kind of "minority report" on September 21, 1964, was also part of the Pope's strategy, in the hope that an impression could be made on them by allowing the fullest possible expression for their views. So was the idea of having Archbishop Parente, the majority spokesman for collegiality, speak last and recommend acceptance of the doctrine as containing nothing contrary to sound teaching.

The tactics of this small group of opponents at the Third Session were principally two: 1) to prevent at all costs a vote on Chapter III, insisting instead that more time was needed for revision and seeing to it that in the course of the revision the dangerous doctrine of collegiality was watered down to an innocuous statement on which all could agree; 2) when this failed and it became apparent how large a majority favored collegiality as a result of the vote on September 30, 1964, they began to urge a revision of at least certain phrases or passages that would allow greater latitude in accepting or rejecting the doctrine, in spite of the fact that the Council had already decided affirmatively on the question. They claimed that collegiality was a vague notion not yet ready for definition; that it was not solidly based on Scripture, Tradition or history; and that dire consequences could be expected to follow if a doctrine were proclaimed that was opposed to Vatican Council I—the Church would have to admit that it had been wrong for centuries, the bishops would not stop until they had completely rejected the authority of the Roman pontiff, and other extravagances of this sort.

The majority committed the mistake of limiting the number of their *modi* to Chapter III, on September 30, with a view to facilitating the work of the Theological Commission and not holding up the document any longer than was necessary. They agreed to have their suggestions submitted by cardinals, patriarchs and prominent bishops in order to lend them greater weight. Most of their modifications related to removing the excessive emphasis on the papal primacy and eliminating certain ambiguities (for example, the exact

status of councils like the Council of Constance that had
removed three Popes in order to elect a legitimate Pope,
and the validity of the acts performed by the present Orthodox clergy). They received an assurance that their wishes
would be met, at least in principle. The minority, for its part,
submitted all the *modi* that they could, each member submitting at least one. (Many of the recommendations over-
lapped and were therefore counted as a single recommendation.) The result was that the majority seemed to have
offered relatively few amendments, whereas the minority
loomed disproportionately large because of numbers.

Of the 242 amendments to Chapter III recorded by the
Commission, 31 were accepted for inclusion in the text, and
of these 10 related to collegiality. Among this group there
were none that altered the nature of collegiality in any essential way, but there were some that further strengthened the
already heavy emphasis on the Pope's primacy. However,
while the majority received no satisfaction on its demands
for improving the text at all, the minority were awarded, in
addition to a few slight alterations in the text, the bonus of
the Explanatory Note.

The abstemious and overly cautious attitude of the majority seemed to have proved once again the futility, in Rome,
of relying on good dispositions or vague assurances and not
taking appropriate massive action at the proper time.

When it became apparent to the minority—through an
extraordinary indulgence on the Pope's part they were kept
abreast of the examination of the *modi* at all stages, to eliminate any possibility of a charge that anything had been done
behind their backs—that the Commission would not accept
their most important requests, they literally besieged the
Pope with entreaties that he act on his own authority to see
that they received satisfaction. The Pope is even said to have
recommended to the Theological Commission not to be too
strict in its interpretation of the rules and reconsider amendments relating to points already approved by the Council, so

that its reason for having rejected the amendments could be stated fully in its report.

The result of so many entreaties was that the Pope ordered the Theological Commission to prepare the Explanatory Note. There can be no doubt that this was "requested, willed, revised, reviewed and approved" by the Pope himself, as Father G. Caprile, S.J., puts it.* It also seems clear that the Theological Commission objected to the suggestion for a Note on principle, because such a document would tend to cast doubt on the integrity of the doctrine expressed in the text rather than throw light on it, but they eventually bowed to pressure. Two mysterious plenary meetings of the Commission toward the first of November, from which all the *periti* were excluded, may have had something to do with the controversy. In any case, Father Caprile's assurance that relations between the Pope and the Commission were always conducted on an absolutely serene level, far removed from any bickering or haggling, is not very convincing in the light of the numerous "comings and goings" between the Fourth Floor and the Commission that were observed about this time. However that may be, on November 10, 1964, Cardinal Cicognani wrote a letter to Cardinal Ottaviani— was this done only after the Theological Commission had balked at the suggestion of a Note?—informing the head of the Theological Commission that because the Pope was obliged to make his own and promulgate the Constitution on the Church, he wanted an Explanatory Note added to it dealing with the meaning and purport of the amendments. The Commission was to work out an explanation in such a way as to relieve the doubts of the minority and achieve a unanimous and sincere acceptance of the schema. He particularly asked the point to be made that the collegiality of the bishops depended on the *consent* of the Roman pontiff for its exercise. Enclosed with the letter was a list of the

* *L'Osservatore Romano,* February 20, 1965 and *La Civiltà Cattolica,* March 1, 1965.

points still contested by the minority together with a memo-
randum from Father Bertrams, S.J., on the difficulties in
question. The Note was to be drafted in accordance with the
written and oral communications of the Fathers and the
suggestions offered at different times by the Pope himself.

The Note deals with four points:

1. The term "college" as used in the text, is not to be
understood in a strictly juridical sense as implying a body of
equals, who delegate their powers to a president (= Roman
law meaning of *collegium*). It is used in a looser, Christian,
sui generis sense and that is why other terms such as "stable
body," "body," and "order" are also employed.

2. An important distinction is made between the *powers*
which a bishop receives by the sacrament of consecration
(of teaching, sanctifying and governing) and the *exercise* of
these powers, the latter being by its nature a juridical determination. Consecration makes a bishop a bishop, but he
can exercise authority in the Church only "according to
norms approved by the supreme authority" and in accordance with the age-old requirements for "hierarchical communion with the head and members of the Church," as the
Constitution states. The use of the term "hierarchical *communion*," the latter word especially, was an important concession to Eastern theology and also to Western theologians
of collegiality. However, the Note adds nothing to what the
text of the Constitution already states on this whole point.

3. Some had refused to acknowledge that the episcopal
college had "full" authority over the Church. But this would
be tantamount to denying the Pope's plenitude of power, because the college cannot exist without him since he is *always
its head*. As the Note put it: "This must be admitted so that
the full power of the Roman pontiff will not be placed in
contention." The term "college" must always be understood
as meaning the bishops *with* the Pope, never without him.
However, the Pope's headship of the college does not pre-
clude acting on his own, without every single act of his

being strictly collegial in character, or as the Note puts it: "whether personally or collegially."

4. The episcopal college always exists, but it does not always act in a strictly collegial manner. In fact, it acts in such a manner only occasionally or at intervals, and always with the consent of its head, who is not outside but forms part of the episcopal collegial body. If the bishops acted independently of the Pope, they would not be acting as a college.

A final paragraph, added at the end, introduced simply by the words *Nota Bene*, declared that it was not the intention of the commission to go into the question of the liceity and validity of the power "which is in fact exercised by the separated Eastern brethren." This was one of the points that the majority wanted clarified. By stating that "hierarchical communion" with the head of the Church was necessary for the validity of episcopal acts, the text of the Constitution leaves the door open to the contention that Orthodox orders and sacraments may be invalid—a thesis maintained by a few recent Catholic theologians—but this of course would contradict the decree on Ecumenism calling for a limited amount of intercommunion and statements by Pope Paul clearly recognizing the legitimacy of the Orthodox hierarchy and the validity of their sacramental acts. By leaving the door open, the Note fails to remove this embarrassing ambiguity, and in fact draws attention to it.

One of the cardinals belonging to the minority, it seems, had objected to the way in which the September 30 vote on Chapter III had been conducted, by dividing the text into two parts and voting on each part separately. He maintained that this was contrary to the rules in that it served to limit the number of *modi* which could be submitted on the chapter as a whole, thus compelling those who submitted their *modi* to confine them to particular parts. As things turned out, however, the minority came out better on the *modi* than the majority, by being so careful. In the name of the moderators and presidents, Archbishop Felici declared that "these difficulties have been most carefully examined by the competent authority and they are certain that the rules of the Council have been followed scrupulously."

A second objection related to doubts raised about the exact theological significance of the Constitution on the Church. The reply of the Theological Commission was that only those matters could be regarded as being formally defined *de fide,* or infallibly in the most solemn way, which were expressly declared to be so defined; all other doctrinal statements were to be "received and embraced by each and all of the faithful as the doctrine of the supreme magisterium of the Church." Since neither the Constitution as a whole nor Chapter III on collegiality were intended as solemn definitions in the ultimate sense of the term, unlike the definition of the papal primacy and infallibility by Vatican Council I in 1870, the present text was intended as a solemn statement but not an infallible pronouncement or *de fide* definition.

After receiving all these assurances and explanations, and weighing their consciences, the Fathers voted on the Commission's handling of the *modi* to Chapters III–VIII of *De Ecclesia* on November 17 and 18. On the crucial Chapter III there were only 46 *non placets;* on the other chapters much fewer. It was apparent then that the minority opposition to collegiality had faded away. Word had been received, before the vote, from the leaders of that group (and from the Pope himself, it is said) that the text was now satisfactory when interpreted in the light of the Explanatory Note. When the Constitution on the Church was voted as a whole on Thursday, the opposition had dwindled to 10, and in the final vote on Saturday, November 21, it was only 5. Some of the opposing votes in these ballots unquestionably came from bishops displeased with the Explanatory Note, but the number was almost negligible even so.*

* If it is true that the doctrine of collegiality was not altered in any essential way by either the Explanatory Note or the last-minute changes in the text, then there was a real capitulation on the part of its opponents. One

It may be asked, why did the majority give in so easily if it really thought that the doctrine of collegiality had been seriously compromised by additions to the text and the obscurely worded Note? There was much soul-searching over the weekend as to what course of action to follow. In the end the bishops and experts decided that rather than risk having no Constitution at all, it was better to put up with an imperfect text representing years of hard labor and not really substantially altered in any of its parts. They found themselves caught in the same dilemma which had confronted the Council before, and would again face it in a day or two, namely whether to reject a series of emendations offered *en bloc* because a few were regarded as unsatisfactory, or approve the lot which was held to be satisfactory as a whole. In voting on Chapter I of the schema on the Pastoral Office of Bishops on November 4, the bishops had swamped the commission with *modi* because of their displeasure over the way in which collegiality seemed to be downgraded, as compared to its treatment in *De Ecclesia*, and they "rejected" Chapter II of the same schema the following day because of dissatisfaction over other emendations, but the circumstances were different. They were voting then *iuxta modum*, at a time when revision was still possible. Here the choice was merely *placet* or *non placet* and the consequences of rejection

---

of them, the Brazilian Archbishop de Proença-Sigaud, in a circular distributed on November 2, declared categorically: "Collegiality has no basis either in the Bible, in tradition, or in the history of the Church . . . It would give rise to a lack of discipline in the Church, whether with respect to the bishops and the Pope, or priests and bishops . . . We have an example of the lack of obedience that would inevitably follow in the recent letter of the 17 cardinals to the Pope regarding the declaration on religious liberty. Bishops would be subjected to episcopal conferences, that is a collective authority, the worst kind there is . . ." In a circular distributed the day of the fateful vote, on November 17, the same bishop wrote: "The difficulties which we had regarding the doctrine of Chapter III have been dissipated by the Explanatory Note [and the announcements of Archbishop Felici] and the anxiety of our consciences has now been laid to rest . . . The Fathers of our group will vote *placet* and we suggest that all others do likewise in order to realize a moral unanimity which will greatly please the Holy Father." ICI, December 1, 1964, pp. 11–12.

were incalculable. What is astounding is not so much the fact that the bishops accepted an imperfect text, as the decision of the authorities to require them to vote *en bloc* on such a large number of controversial emendations, at such a late date. Again this seems to have been but another instance of the wishes of the majority being rather thoughtlessly sacrificed to the need for conciliating the minority.

The dwindling of the opposition to collegiality from less than 300 to something like half of the 46 votes recorded on November 17 was the tangible reward which the Pope reaped for repeated efforts on his part for over a year to reduce the opposition to the vanishing point,* and his much discussed remark on November 21, 1964 declaring that "nothing in traditional doctrine is really changed," was probably intended more as a final gesture to this same minority than as a blanket statement rejecting the notion of doctrinal change as such, for the decrees themselves are evidence that there has been much change.

The question may well be raised, however, whether it was really worth all the trouble to achieve a quasi-unanimity on this point, particularly when the doctrine of collegiality, as finally defined by the Council, was expressly declared to be something less than infallible? And whether the amount of time involved in producing this quasi-unanimity could not have been spent on expediting the work of the Second and Third Sessions? And finally, whether it is really such a good idea, after all, to achieve quasi-unanimity, if this has to be done at too high a cost, through the promulgation of a needlessly unbalanced and disfigured document accompanied by a tortuous, ambiguous, over-subtle explanation of an explanation? In his extreme anxiety to conciliate an unimportant minority, Pope Paul seems to have forgotten that he might be doing less than justice to the majority.**

---

* The Pope sent a letter to Cardinal Ottaviani on November 13, 1964, thanking him for the part played by the Theological Commission in the preparation of the Constitution on the Church.

** Père R. Rouquette, in *Études*, Jan. 1965, p. 116.

What consoles the majority and undoubtedly caused many of them to vote favorably on the Constitution is that, despite a disfiguring overemphasis on the Pope's primacy, introduced to satisfy the qualms of the minority, and some other imperfections, the Constitution on the Church still appears to safeguard an essential point by repudiating the theory, widely held by Catholic theologians and canonists, that all jurisdiction in the Church comes from the Pope as from its "source," a doctrine which, if pressed to extremes would make of the bishops merely the Pope's vicars and rule out any effective collegiality. This doctrine has been the chief weapon in the arsenal of those who have exalted the authority of the Pope in the past at the expense of the collegiality of the bishops. The new text expressly declares that bishops are not "to be regarded as vicars of the Roman pontiffs," and both the Constitution and the Explanatory Note (seem to) speak only of a regulation of the exercise of episcopal jurisdiction by the Pope, not of the Pope as being the "source" of that jurisdiction. References are made to the Pope as the "visible source and foundation of unity and faith and communion," but this is not the same thing as saying that he is the source of episcopal jurisdiction. To put it simply, the bishops possess, through their consecration, all the powers needed for the exercise of their office, but they may not exercise these powers without leave from the Pope (= *potestas expedita*). The distinction between episcopal *munera* and *potestates,* which the Note seeks to develop (apparently an idea of Father Bertrams'), does not seem to have any real ontological basis, any more than the well known distinction between "order" and "jurisdiction," which Archbishop Parente declared, on the Council floor and more recently in an article in *L'Osservatore Romano* (December 19, 1964), was not ancient at all, but a distinction introduced "through the excessive influence of law on theology, which gradually caused the power of jurisdiction to be torn from the power of order, and the thesis to be maintained that the former power came to a bishop by means of an extrinsic grant on the part of the Pope, whereas

the latter power came to him from his consecration." Parente
continued: "The Council has now returned to a more primitive conception and asserts that the bishop receives, by his
consecration, not only the power of order, but also, at least
radically, that of jurisdiction which, however, by its very
nature cannot be exercised by any organ in the Church except in communion with the hierarchy and especially with
the Pope, who is empowered to regulate the functioning of
the organ for the good of the Church."

On Tuesday of the last week, the long awaited Declaration
on Religious Liberty made its appearance and it was announced that there would be a vote Thursday, first a ballot
by *placet* or *non placet* on the individual parts, this to be
followed by a ballot on the text as a whole at which time
iuxta modum votes could be cast. The following day Wednesday, the Declaration on Jews and Non-Christians was also
handed out, and it was announced that it would be voted on
Friday according to the same pattern.

The appearance of these two key texts and the information
that they would in fact be voted on before the end of the Session shifted attention away from the uneasiness felt by many
with regard to the fate of collegiality.

Consequently, when Archbishop Felici announced toward
the very end of the meeting on Wednesday, that the Council
Presidents and Moderators had decided to heed a petition
submitted to them requesting more time for consideration
of the Declaration on Religious Liberty before voting on it,
by allowing a preliminary vote on Thursday (*placet* or *non
placet*) on whether to proceed at once to the balloting already
scheduled, there was some consternation, but the news was
not altogether alarming because the majority were certain
of enough votes to overcome this hurdle. The Presidents and
Moderators had made this decision, Archbishop Felici explained, because the issue raised by the petition was so serious that they wanted the Fathers to decide it for themselves.

The petition, which he also read, appealed to Art. 30 par. 2 of the rules which specified that adequate time must be allowed for considering the texts of schemata, and Art. 35 which allowed an "examination" of amended texts before they were voted. The new text of the Declaration on Religious Liberty had been so altered that it was virtually a new document, they claimed, and so should be handled in accordance with these provisions of the rules.* The petition was signed by about 200 prelates.

A word must be said about the revised Declaration on which the Fathers were being asked to vote. In the judgment of competent persons it was not the best of the many forms through which the document had gone since its presentation as one of the chapters of the decree on Ecumenism in November 1963. As revised by the Secretariat after the September debate, in the light of suggestions made by the Mixed Commission which the Pope ordered to examine it in his letter of October 16 as well as by the Theological Commission, it made important concessions to the minority by noting the existence of a universal desire for religious liberty but without attempting to justify it theologically; by stressing, in an awkward way, the connection between the famous *Syllabus Errorum* of Pio Nono's days and the present text; and by attempting to justify a special claim to religious liberty on the part of the Catholic Church because of its sole possession of the truth. In an informative article in *America* (January 9, 1965), Father John Courtney Murray, S.J., one of the drafters, indicated that he was not unhappy about the fate of the text, and he hoped that, as a result of the delay, a better text might be produced for the Fourth Session. He especially hoped the new text would acknowledge more freely the "infringements

* Art. 30 par. 2: "The schemata of decrees and canons, as well as all texts to be approved, must be distributed to the Fathers in such a way as to permit them adequate time to consider them, for their judgments and decide on their vote." Art. 35: "The general congregation, after hearing the report of the *relator*, shall examine the parts of every amended text one by one and then approve them or not."

of religious liberty by the Church in the past," according to a statement made at Union Theological Seminary (February 2, 1965).

Neither the minority nor the majority, therefore, were satisfied with it. But this was not really the primary issue. The minority were determined, as in the case of collegiality, to prevent the document from coming to a vote at all, if they possibly could, on the grounds that it was dangerous for the Church to acknowledge the existence of religious liberty in any sense except that of bare "toleration." The majority were anxious for a vote, both in order to facilitate the work of further revision by allowing the Fathers to indicate their minds with regard to different points, and also because of the vital ecumenical implications of a vote. By persistently refusing to vote on religious liberty, the Council was creating the impression that it was somehow insincere with regard to the principles it claimed to be advocating in the decree on Ecumenism.

In order to get a vote, the Secretariat for Unity worked out a wording designed to attract as many positive votes as possible, from the opposition, with the idea of restoring the watered-down parts to full strength when the *modi* were considered in revision. To forestall action on the part of the opposition, it was deliberately decided to keep the text under cover until the last possible minute. Unfortunately this little maneuvre failed. The opposition got word of what was being done. At a meeting Monday evening, November 16, consisting mainly of Italian and Spanish bishops (of the 80 Spanish prelates present only 25 signed, as was later disclosed by one of the Spanish bishops), the petition was drawn up and signed which Archbishop Felici read in the assembly on Wednesday. There were about 200 signatures. One of the leading instigators of this protest, as of other moves by the minority, was the Secretary of the Congregation of Seminaries, Archbishop Dino Staffa.

An air of anxiety and uncertainty hung over the assembly

as it resumed its labors on the morning of "Black Thursday." There was not only the disquieting announcement about a preliminary vote on Religious Liberty but, strangely, the lack of any word about when the decree on Ecumenism would be presented for a final vote, necessary before promulgation. Things were obviously not going as smoothly as could be expected, yet time was running out: only one more business session remained. The successful vote approving the Constitution on the Church as a whole brought forth cheers, which served to relieve the tension, but the Secretary General's disappointing information about the decree on Ecumenism caused a resurgence of fears (see below). It was about ten minutes past eleven, while the Council was part way through its discussion of the propositions on Christian Education and was beginning to grow restless over when the promised vote on Religious Liberty would take place, that Archbishop Staffa was seen at the Secretary General's side. The latter motioned him to Cardinal Tisserant, who as president of the board of Council Presidents was sitting at the middle of their table directly behind the four Moderators. Staffa and the cardinal exchanged words briefly, after which Tisserant was seen hastily consulting with the other presidents on either side of him. Cardinal Meyer, who was sitting at one end of the table, Cardinal Alfrink and Cardinal Frings, apparently either did not hear what Cardinal Tisserant was saying or did not grasp its meaning. Suddenly Tisserant rose, stopped the proceedings, and announced: "Several Fathers are of the opinion that not enough time has been allowed for an examination of the text on Religious Liberty, which appears to be an essentially new document. Therefore it has seemed best to the Council Presidents, in conformity with the rules, not to proceed to a vote as announced. After the *relatio* on the declaration by Bishop de Smedt, there will be no vote. The Fathers can then examine the document at their leisure and send their observations to the Secretariat by January 31, 1965."

His words were at first greeted by a feeble burst of applause from the minority bishops, but this was at once drowned out by a wave of grumbling, protests, and commotion which spread throughout the hall. One would have to go back to one of the early church Councils, that of Trent, for example, when an enraged bishop pulled another's beard, to find a precedent for the scene of consternation, outrage, and disarray that took place on this memorable morning. The bishops felt cheated, betrayed, insulted, and humiliated. One bishop, not a progressive, said afterward: "We were treated like children!" By what authority had Cardinal Tisserant made his announcement? The Fathers asked. How can *they*—meaning either the secretariat or the Pope—treat the Council in this way! The Council was transformed into a beehive, as bishops swarmed from their places. Two of the four Moderators and seven of the ten Presidents got up from their seats and joined groups milling around the confession of St. Peter's. Nobody was paying the slightest attention to the remaining speakers on Christian Education when finally a semblance of order was restored and the debate went on. The rest of the morning was completely dominated by the agitation produced by Tisserant's thunderbolt.

Cardinal Meyer, normally a calm and dignified figure, turned in consternation to the colleague sitting next to him to inquire whether the postponement of the vote had been discussed with the other presidents, then got up from his chair and went around to the front to argue and remonstrate with Tisserant. The only reply he got was that the decision had been made and there could be no change.

The occasion was a rude awakening for the majority of the Council Fathers, and especially for the American bishops. Though they should have been on their guard against last-minute moves by the minority, they were too trusting and innocently confident that all would go well. It seemed inconceivable when the authorities had announced a vote that they would reverse what they had decided. In the spring of 1964

Cardinal Cushing had stated that if the Council did not make a pronouncement on religious liberty, the ecumenical movement would collapse. In April Pope Paul himself, in an address to representatives of the United Nations, had declared: "There is every reason to expect the promulgation of a text on this matter, which will have great consequences." Just before the fatal day, Cardinal Cushing had wired the American bishops to bring home the religious liberty declaration with them. There can hardly be any doubt that the American attitude toward the religious liberty question as a whole was somewhat oversimplified and even naive. As Cardinal Ritter, one of the leading supporters of the declaration, said later: "If anyone was at fault, we were, for being too trustful . . . We had been too sure of a vote—which we would have won by a big majority." The impression was sometimes given that achievement of a vote would mean promulgation of the document.

One report had it afterward that the move on Staffa's part, and possibly also the decision of Tisserant, were not as spontaneous as they seemed. Word about what was being planned is said to have reached the ears of certain American prelates connected with various organs of the Council, but they neglected to forewarn their colleagues in the hierarchy, so that it came as a complete surprise to the majority. If the Americans were faulty in not being sufficiently vigilant, they made up for this defect by their reaction, which was immediate, violent, spontaneous and, for once, instinctively well organized. When Cardinal Meyer and the other presidents and moderators left their places and pandemonium broke loose on the council floor, the Pope, who was watching the scene on his closed circuit TV, telephoned Archbishop Felici and ordered him to come to his apartment at once. With the forceful, restraining figure of the domineering Secretary General gone from the hall, the pent-up emotions of the bishops were given free play. Muttering "This man is hopeless," Cardinal Meyer stalked away from Tisserant and joined a group of prelates and *periti* gathering beside the tribune on the left side of the nave. Somebody, either Bishop Francis Reh, recently appointed rector of the American College, or one of the *periti*, said, "Let's not stand here talking—who's got some paper?" With the help of several bishops and other *periti*, the following petition to Pope Paul was written out by hand, in Latin:

Your Holiness:

With reverence but urgently, very urgently, most urgently [*instanter, instantius, instantissime*], we request that a vote on the declaration on religious liberty be taken before the end of this session of the Council, lest the confidence of the world, both Christian and non-Christian, be lost.

Additional copies, also handwritten, were circulated and signatures collected by bishops who moved up and down the banked tiers of seats. When the canvassing was completed, some 500 signatures had been collected, no small feat considering the limited time in which it had to be done. The session was due to end in only a little over an hour.* While the copies were still being handed around, Bishop de Smedt, of Bruges, rose to give his *relatio* on Religious Liberty. The Fathers listened to him with almost compulsive attention, applauding vigorously from time to time—one line was punctuated by four outbursts of applause. Then when he had concluded, rhythmic applause rose from the seats, the longest and most sustained applause accorded any speech at the Council, which the Moderator was powerless to stop. Some of the bishops stood up in order to clap their hands more freely. Thwarted of a formal vote, the bishops took their revenge by voting in this way, if not for the text of the declaration, then for the principle of religious liberty. The Pope must allow a vote; the world would never believe that the declaration had again been postponed because of lack of time.

* Fr. G. Caprile, S.J., says there were only 441 signatures (*La Civiltà Cattolica*, March 1, 1965), which is probably correct, so far as the document presented to the Pope is concerned, but during the afternoon additional signatures were collected totalling well over a thousand.

At the end of the morning's session, Cardinal Meyer and Ritter, joined by Cardinal Léger of Montreal because of his knowledge of the Vatican layout and experience in dealing with its functionaries, left the Council hall to carry the petition to the Pope. On their way up to the papal apartment they were met by Archbishop Felici on his way down. Attendants protested that it would be impossible for them to see the Pope, but they insisted and were finally admitted to his presence. He received them kindly and tried to palliate their anger, informing them that, according to a ruling of Cardinal Roberti, the Council's legal expert, Cardinal Tisserant's decision had been made according to the rules. The Pope said that it was not his policy to interfere in the Council's actions so he could not, under the circumstances, force a vote as they had requested. He ended by giving them a guarantee—repeated publicly in his address two day later— that the Declaration on Religious Liberty would be the first order of business in the Fourth and final Session in 1965.

Later in the afternoon, the cardinals gathered in the Pope's study for a "Little Conclave." This meeting had been arranged the previous day and was therefore not directly concerned with the disturbing events of the morning. The Pope wished to see the cardinals and have a few words with them before many of them left Rome. The atmosphere of the gathering is said to have been awkward. Cardinal Roberti gave a report on his study of the reorganization of the Curia, which the Pope had ordered a year ago. Cardinal Frings, it seems, brought up the subject of the morning's postponed vote and begged His Holiness, in the name of more than one thousand Fathers, to allow a vote before the end of the session. Cardinal Suenens commented that while the decision to put off the vote may have had a basis in the rules, the psychological effect was deplorable. Two of the American cardinals and one German cardinal intimated that if any attempt were made to put off the vote on the Declaration on the Jews and Non-Christians scheduled for the final day, they would have no alterna-

tive but to absent themselves from the closing session in protest. No doubt they had in mind the action of the sizeable
group at Vatican Council I in 1870 that left Rome rather
than attend the final public session proclaiming papal infallibility.

The contention of the Pope and the minority that Cardinal
Tisserant's decision was taken in accordance with the rules,
and therefore the Pope could do nothing about it without
infringing those rules, does not stand up under examination,* because the articles to which the minority appealed
(Art. 30 par. 2 and Art. 35)** are vaguely worded and not
conclusive. A decision should have been based on the *procedure* of the Council in submitting texts to a vote rather
than upon the ambiguously worded rules. Instead of basing
themselves on the letter of the law, the minority would have
done better to appeal to the "spirit" of the rules. The Declaration on Religious Liberty had not followed the normal course
of other conciliar texts. It was not voted on when the rest
of the schema on Ecumenism (of which it had originally
formed a chapter) had been voted in 1963. It was presented
in September 1964 as an appendix of that schema, but no
vote had followed the discussion on the floor, and finally it
appeared at the end of the Third Session as a separate
"Schema of the Declaration on Religious Liberty," being
offered for a first vote. However, the Secretariat for Unity
acted as if it had gone through the earlier stages through
which texts passed and was being presented for a vote as
though it had reached the stage before a final vote, whereas
in reality it had only reached a midway stage, two places
removed from the final vote. The minority should have
appealed to the procedure adopted for handling the *propositions* and called for a preliminary vote, as announced,
correctly, on Wednesday. This was the procedure followed

* See the illuminating study of this question by Père Rouquette, S.J., in
Études, January 1965, p. 111 ff.
** See p. 255.

for the Declaration on the Jews and Non-Christians, and the
text on Religious Liberty was exactly parallel. The argument
that there was not enough time to consider the text was not
convincing, because the interval between Tuesday and Thursday was adequate to allow an opinion to be formed with regard to a preliminary vote. The truth of the matter is that the
minority, knowing that it would be hopelessly outvoted in
any kind of a vote, appealed to Article 30.2 and counted upon
the Pope's scrupulosity about allowing the opposition every
benefit of a doubt to win their point. It was a gamble, but it
worked. The question as to whether Cardinal Tisserant was
privy to the minority's plan must be left unanswered.

The Pope's decision regarding the petition for a vote submitted by the three cardinals was not known until Friday.
There had been hope that he would accede to the wishes of
such a large number of Fathers. Therefore the news was all
the more shattering when Archbishop Felici gave the floor to
Cardinal Tisserant, who rose and read from a piece of paper:

Many Fathers were deeply disappointed by the announcement
that the vote on Religious Liberty was to be postponed and
petitioned the Holy Father that a vote be taken before the end
of this Session. In the name of the Supreme Pontiff, I wish to
make the following announcement: The request that voting be
delayed was granted because according to the *Ordo* (Rules) of
the Council it had to be granted out of respect for the freedom
of the Fathers in their desire to examine fully and in accordance
with the *Ordo* a document of such great importance. That is
why the schema of the Declaration on Religious Liberty will be
treated in the next Session and, if possible, before any other
matters.

His words were succeeded by a stunned silence for a moment, followed by a light scattering of applause. The Council then went on with its work.

Before the incident of the postponed vote, on Thursday,
the Council had also received a jolt over the decree on Ecumenism. Archbishop Felici announced that the printing of

the final text was not yet completed. This would be done during the coming night. The Fathers, therefore, would not have a chance to look it over before casting their ballots tomorrow. The reason for the delay was that some last-minute changes "had been made to make the text more clear. These changes have been made on higher authority. You will shortly receive a mimeographed copy of the changes. They could not be printed because there was not enough time. I will now read them to you." He then proceeded to read, from a sheet in his hand, the 19 last-minute changes ordered in the text of *De Oecumenismo* by the Pope. The emendations were sent to Cardinal Bea as "suggestions," but in view of the lateness of the hour—it is said that they were communicated the previous evening when it was no longer possible to discuss them in a full meeting of the Secretariat and the final decision as to whether to accept or reject them had to be made by the cardinal with some of his aides—there can be little doubt that the papal suggestions were the equivalent of an "order." To have refused them would have jeopardized the whole decree. There were actually 40 suggestions or emendations proposed by the Pope, of which the Secretariat chose to accept 19, and this proved to be acceptable to His Holiness.

Where did the emendations come from? Father Caprile, S.J. ,an editor of the Jesuit periodical *La Civiltà Cattolica,** seems to have established that some or all of them came from the same minority which opposed the decree on Ecumenism earlier in the session, for by comparing the *modi* rejected by the Secretariat with the 19 emendations, he has determined that 8 of them, at least, are identical. In other words, when the opposition failed to persuade the Secretariat to adopt its recommendations, which would have had the effect of substantially altering the nature of the text, they appealed directly to the Pope, who endeavored to give these opponents some kind of last-minute satisfaction in the way that he did.

* *La Civiltà Cattolica,* March 1, 1965.

It must be said in the Pope's favor, if Father Caprile's analysis and deductions are correct, that the most ruinous changes desired by the minority were apparently screened out by the Pope and not forwarded to the Secretariat. Those suggested, and the ones accepted, were all of a relatively minor nature, mostly verbal corrections designed to change the emphasis slightly, without altering the fundamental sense. Unfortunately all the Pope's suggestions, intended merely to effect "a greater clarity in the text," were minimistic in tendency, toning down or qualifying some more direct statement in the original text. Quite a few of them had to do with the introduction of such qualifying adverbs as *fere, etiam, frequentius, non raro,* etc.* While not altering the text substantially, in the opinion of experts, the fact that they had a definite anti-Protestant slant was gravely offensive to the Protestant Observers, who were perhaps more aggrieved by the arbitrary, unconventional way in which they were "foisted" on the assembly at the last minute, than by their theological implications. It is almost incredible that Pope Paul, if he really was aware of the above tendency, or thought at all about the bad impression that they might make on Protestants, would have consciously suggested to the Secretariat that these

AMENDED TEXT AFTER 19 EMENDATIONS	*Modi* INSPIRING EMENDATIONS
1. quae Ecclesiae *catholicae* concredita est	dicatur quae *uni Ecclesiae* Christi concredita est
2. Afflante Spiritus Sancti *gratia*	dicatur afflante quidem Sancti Spiritus *gratia*
3. totius Ecclesiae *facultatem* habere	vox *officium* expungatur
4. formulae *non raro* potius inter se compleri	inseratur *saepe saepius* in sententiam: variae illae theologicae formulae . . . potius inter se compleri
5. Spiritum Sanctum *invocantes*	verba Spiritu Sancto *movente,* deleantur
6. Deum *inquirunt*	loco *inveniunt,* dicatur quaerunt
7, 8. *genuinam atque integram* substantiam	deleatur verbum *plenam;* loco *plenam* dicatur veram

*Fr. Caprile's list of the 8 instances where *modi* seem to correspond to corrections is as follows. The last item counts as two:

emendations be taken seriously. Why was so much placed in jeopardy for so very little?*

The next morning, Friday, at the opening of the final busi ness day of the session, observers were fascinated by the dif ference in the officials' behavior. When an emissary of the curial minority approached Secretary General Felici with a petition requesting a postponement, "for further study," of the vote on Cardinal Bea's declaration on non-Christian Re ligions, Felici was seen to draw back as if from something unclean. He quickly motioned the unlucky messenger toward Cardinal Tisserant, who dropped the petition on the Presi dents' table as if it were a hot potato, and that was that. The Council then proceeded to vote on the latest wording of the text of this declaration, which had gone through many haz ardous revisions since it was drawn up in 1962 by the Sec retariat for Christian Unity. In order to nullify the allegation made by Arab countries that the document was intended to be political and not religious, Cardinal Bea's new draft, exon erating the Jewish people from the ancient charge of deicide had been incorporated into a larger context, dealing with other non-Christian religions. The declaration now received the following vote from the Fathers: 1,651 *placet*, 242 *place iuxta modum,* and 99 *non placet*. This vote represented a vin dication of the years of work done by Cardinal Bea and his associates. As the elderly and kindly prelate described the long and tortuous history of the text, whose form now ap peared to be finally settled and which would be ready for final voting and promulgation in 1965, he seemed to personify all

* The Vatican presses printing the text of the degree on Ecumenism Thursday evening, were suddenly stopped about 9 P.M. Several members of Bea's Secretariat made a hasty appearance, after which the printing was re sumed. There was apparently some uncertainty whether the decree would be promulgated on Saturday: the title-page did not bear the customary words "For submission at the public session on November 21." Some German bishops, it seems, tried to have the decree held over till the Fourth Session in the hope that it could be purified of its disfigurements.

hat was best in the Council—an image of a dedicated prelate
who had learned through rebuffs and reverses how to find his
way successfully through the mazes of determined and in-
genious opposition. At the end, he was warmly applauded.

Final approval of the decree on Ecumenism was another
bonus for the Secretariat on Friday. There were only 64 *non
placets* (reduced to 11 in the formal vote on Saturday), an
insignificant number. Some were certainly cast by bishops displeased over the 19 amendments. The Council also gave approval to the schema on the Oriental Churches by a comfort-
able margin. Characteristically, or perhaps prophetically,
the lights in St. Peter's went out momentarily, about an hour
before the end of Friday's session, owing to a power failure.

Pope Paul was carried into the basilica on Saturday morning, November 21, for the closing public session, through
tiers of stony-faced bishops in white mitres and copes. There
was no applause. He himself looked glum and tense. The
strained feelings between the bishops and their head which
the events of the last few days had produced were mirrored
in the lack of warmth which pervaded the ceremony. Whereas
one might have expected that there would be joy over the
final promulgation of the Constitution on the Church and
the decree on Ecumenism, both milestones on the road to
aggiornamento, the applause accompanying their proclamation was somewhat perfunctory and came mostly from the
throngs of visitors, monks, nuns and tourists crowded in the
transepts. The bishops were restrained in their clapping, or
preferred not to manifest any emotion at all.

A final disappointment awaited the bishops and particularly the Protestant observer-delegates. Everyone knew that
the Pope intended to confer the title of "Mother of the
Church" on Mary, for he had announced that he would do
so at an audience on Wednesday, and intimated earlier in the
session that this was his intention. What shocked his theologically perceptive hearers was his response to the highly
articulate minority of Italian, Spanish, Indonesian and Polish

mariological zealots clamoring for the definition of a new
Marian dogma. While the Pope was not prepared to go quite
this far, his speech—fully half his address was taken up with
Marian theology—was an indirect rebuke to the Theological
Commission for having refused Mary the title which he now
gave her. The Commission, in commenting on the *modi* to
Chapter VIII of the Constitution on the Church, dealing
with Mary, stated its reasons for not acquiescing in the per
sistent demand of this group that a new title be added to
those traditionally accorded Mary: "The phrase *mater ec
clesiae* is sometimes found in ecclesiastical writers, but very
rarely, and it cannot be said to be traditional. Moreover, it
is generally accompanied by such titles as 'daughter' and
'sister' of the Church. It is evident therefore that it is being
used in a comparative sense. From the ecumenical point of
view, the title can certainly not be recommended, although
it can be admitted theologically. The Commission therefore
deemed it sufficient to express the idea in equivalent terms.'
In effect, this sober, carefully worded, balanced, ecumenically
inspired, collegially-expressed reasoning of the Commission
was a rebuke to all who would keep mariology as an un
necessary bone of contention hindering the ecumenical move
ment. Without denying any essential element of the Church'
teaching on Mary, it attempts to recommend this teaching in
a persuasive, biblically-inspired way. After the Council had
gone to so much trouble to achieve a balanced theologica
statement of an issue disputed among Catholics themselves, i
certainly showed poor judgment to appear to be undercutting
that statement and reverse a decision of the Council. The
Pope's own carefully phrased explanation of the term was
typically, drowned out by the applause from the gallery ac
companying the pronouncement. Another case of sacrificing
the interests of the whole to the desires of a persistent, well
organized minority, which can count on support in high
places.

The first part of the Pope's speech was a commentary on
De Ecclesia. The decrees on Ecumenism and the Oriental

Churches were virtually ignored. It is known that he worked
n the text of the speech until the last minute, because trans-
itions were not ready for newsmen Saturday morning in
accordance with custom. His remarks were typically Pauline.
Nothing really new was said. There were the same vague
references to post-conciliar commissions and the projected reform of the Curia, to which his hearers had grown accus-
tomed, but no details were revealed. The only sign that the
unprecedented events of the last few days had made some
kind of an impression on him came when he insisted, "We
do not fear that our authority will be lessened or hampered
while we acknowledge and extol yours; but rather we feel
strong because of the tie that draws us together," and when
he was careful to explain that "It was of the highest importance that this recognition of the prerogatives of the office of
the supreme pontiff should be stated explicitly at this time
when the question of episcopal authority in the Church was
to be dealt with, in order that this authority would not be in
contrast with the power of the Pope, but should stand out in
full harmony with the Vicar of Christ as head of the apostolic
body." This last passage, virtually a quotation from the Explanatory Note, is probably the key to his whole attitude.

Noteworthy, perhaps, was his reference to "the *monarchi-
al and hierarchical* character of the Church." The second
adjective may possibly have been a mere slip for "collegial,"
which seems called for by the context, but it also could have
been his intention to stress the lines of authority in this subtle
way.

After the ceremonies, the grim-faced Pope was carried out
of the basilica through the same tiers of stony-faced, unresponsive bishops, whose lack of enthusiasm was the dominant note of the proceedings. The contrast with the closing
of the First Session under Pope John could not have been
more marked.

Yet the conclusion would be unwarranted that the results
of the Third Session were wholly negative. The Constitution

on the Church and the Decree on Ecumenism, taken to
gether with the Constitution on the Sacred Liturgy, pro
claimed in 1963, represent essential segments of *aggiorn*
mento, for which Vatican II was summoned, and they mu:
be regarded as the Council's real and substantial achieve
ments so far. They are revolutionary documents that bea
the seeds of potentially great consequences. Opinion abou
the decree on the Oriental Churches is mixed, but then :
only purports to be a temporary laying down of norms "i
view of the present situation, till such time as the Catholi
Church and the separated Eastern Churches come togethe
in complete unity." The reaction of one Orthodox arcl
bishop active in the ecumenical movement was: "It coul
have been worse." The debate on this document reveale
that the Eastern-Rite Catholics in communion with Rom
were divided among themselves about a number of impor
tant points, so that the final text, a compromise, probabl
represents the best that could be achieved under the circum
stances.

Cardinal Bea lost no time in providing the decree on Ect
menism with an official commentary in the two Decembe
issues of the Jesuit periodical, *La Civiltà Cattolica,* whic
was widely translated into all languages. He stressed particu
larly the positive, and even revolutionary, implications of th
principle that baptism joins all Christians in a communion c
kind of unity, with each other, however imperfect, whic
needs to be deepened and strengthened; and the desirabilit
of putting the principles now defined into practice, in cor
crete ways, so that the momentum gained would not be los
Practicing what he preached, the 83-year-old cardinal ac
cepted an invitation to visit the seat of the World Counci
of Churches in Geneva (February 19, 1965), the citadel c
Calvinism, sharing the platform in the Hall of the Reforma
tion with the 84-year-old president emeritus of the Protestan
Federation of France, Pastor Marc Boegner. Both spoke c
the contrasts as well as the similarities between the Reforme

nd Catholic traditions and expressed the hope that fraternal
ooperation "based on love" would eventually lead to or-
anic unity. The cardinal announced officially that the Vati-
an had accepted the suggestion to enter into dogmatic dis-
ussions with the WCC, proposed at a recent meeting in
.frica of that body. An ancillary purpose of the cardinal's
isit was to help remove any lingering Protestant malaise
ver the final days of the Third Session. There are other
gns that while the Protestants and Orthodox were undoubt-
dly dismayed and perplexed by what they witnessed, they
ere not thrown off balance and have no intention of in-
errupting contacts so full of promise, because of momentary
etbacks and inconsistencies. While operational tactics may
ave to be changed to suit different conditions, as the Ortho-
ox seem to have done at Rhodes under prodding from the
.ussian delegation, the ultimate goal remains the same,
:hristian reunion. As Dr. Douglas Horton, one of the Ob-
erver-Delegates put it, reunion is "the only hope for a united
orld," but we must not expect "the millennium to be de-
vered with the morning milk." He also advised against
bandoning "our Catholic friends" because of trouble with
ie Fourth Floor of the Vatican.

While the conciliar commissions labor to revise their texts
a the light of the debates to have them ready for the Fourth
:ssion expected in the fall of 1965, attention has shifted
vay from the accomplishments of the Council to the char-
:ter of the man who is Pope. Even the most casual observer
 aware that something went wrong and that all is not well
ith the Council. It would be incorrect to concur in the
adgment of the popular Italian weekly, *L'Espresso,* that in
oite of Pope Paul's jet-flight pilgrimages, the crowds that
:eet him with garlands of flowers, and his contacts with the
oor, "he is not a popular Pope" after a year and a half in
lice, yet there can be little doubt that he has suffered a
.ther marked loss of prestige and affection in contrast to
is predecessor, particularly in Western Europe and the

United States. It could hardly be otherwise, given his high
intellectual, lonely, aloof nature, which does not attempt t
evoke deep sympathy. It is said that, as Monsignor Montin
he used to criticize Pope Pius XII for not going out of th
Vatican more often and coming into contact with differen
types of people as a pastor should; yet when he himself ap
pears the feeling of *rapport* is not quite complete. He seem
incapable of inspiring either the warmth of John XXIII o
the awe of Pius XII. Paul is known to be an extremely chari
table and kindly person and frequently acts on these im
pulses, but he has no Monsignor Capovilla to draw attentio
to these acts, so the world generally knows nothing abou
them. Like a true intellectual, he is capable of a real inspira
tion—that is the only word for the pilgrimage to Jerusalen
and the flight to India—but he fails to reap the fullest reward
from these unprecedented acts because a stiffness of manne
and an excessive scrupulosity about questions of protocc
and prestige seem to rob them of much of their spontaneit
   He makes all the right gestures, for the right reasons an
with utter sincerity, but some aspect is often not quite righ
For example, various movements have been afoot at th
Council to promote more respect for the ideal of povert
which the Church proclaims but does little to realize i
practice in so far as its outward structure and ceremonies ar
concerned. The Pope's gesture in laying his tiara on the alta
of St. Peter's as a symbolic gift to the poor (November 1
1964) was widely hailed as a significant step in the right direc
tion, yet the feeling persists that its subsequent presentatio
to Cardinal Spellman as a gift for the American people wa
somehow an awkward and unsatisfying way to "dispose" of i
His act naturally raised the question whether the bishop
ought not to participate by despoiling themselves of some c
their finery and trappings—for example, it was suggested tha
a basket be passed in St. Peter's to collect the episcopal rings-
but all movements along this line have been firmly di
couraged. Those prelates who in the very First Session calle

for a simplification of episcopal dress are still waiting for
their pleas to be answered. If the recent consistory provides
any clue to Paul's mind on the subject of ceremonial, those
who are panting for drastic and far-reaching reforms are not
likely to be pleased by what is in store. In spite of much
heralded reports that the costume of the cardinals would be
simplified, no changes were apparent. As for the rites themselves, said to have been worked out by the Pope and Cardinal Dante jointly, only the most practiced eye would have
discerned the nuances, for example, the cardinal patriarchs
were embraced whereas the other cardinals knelt to kiss the
Pope's ring when receiving the insignia of their new rank,
while the *galero* or large-brimmed hat, symbolic of the cardinalate, was no longer held over their heads but merely dis-
patched to their residences. His Holiness apparently agreed
with a recent editorial in the London *Times,* which declared
that "the British, who . . . are firm believers in pomp and
colour on great occasions, expect a little pomp from Rome"
and warned against "too much drabness of display."

The Pope is a man obviously torn by doubts, tormented
by scruples, haunted by thoughts of perfection, and above all
dominated by an exaggerated concern—some call it an ob-
session—about the prestige of his office as Pope. His remarks
on this score at times display an almost messianic fervor, a
note missing in the more sedate utterances of his predecessors.
His innumerable statements on the subject are made on almost every occasion, from casual week-day audiences or Sunday sermons from the window of his apartment to the most
solemn gatherings, in season and out of season. It is as if he
were tortured by the thought that the world might forget
who the Pope really is, at a time when the world has never
known better. Since it is part of the strategy of the minority
to accuse the majority of disloyalty toward the Holy Father,
Paul's constant harping has inevitably caused the majority
to think that he perhaps does share these misgivings, at least
to a certain extent. It has been noticed by students of Paul's

remarks that while he shows an openmindedness about almost any other subject, on the single theme of the papacy his mind remains strangely closed to analysis. He refuses to admit any distinction here between what is essential and what has been added through the centuries, as modern theologians like Karl Rahner and Yves Congar do. Everything must be retained no matter how incongruous, transfigured, modernized, simplified but no peripheral attributes are to be surrendered. This naturally shocks and alienates the Orthodox, who feel that some agreement might be reached on the basis of the role and function of the papacy in the ancient Church, but they have no wish to saddle themselves with the extravagant claims of medieval theorists. A classic example of the Pauline style in this connection appeared in the passage in his encyclical *Ecclesiam suam* in which he said that it pained him to think that the Orthodox regarded the Pope's "primacy of honor and jurisdiction" as a stumbling-block to reunion. What pains the Orthodox—this passage in particular—is the thought that the Pope should appear to be so naïve as to assume that they ever wanted the Catholic Church "to be without the Pope." Paul's whole attitude is somewhat mystifying because it seems to contradict a sound piece of advice he gave in this same encyclical, namely when dealing with the "separated brethren" not to stress differences, but the "things we have in common."

His approach to the problem of reform is typically Roman. Nothing is ever to be repudiated outright. His fondness for gradualism—also called the policy of two steps forward and one step backward—is what causes nightmares to those who are counting on Paul to carry through a promised reform of the Curia and realize the aspirations of the Council with respect to collegiality by setting up an episcopal "senate."

Pope Paul has been called the Pope of "buts," because he never seems to make a positive statement without qualify-

ing it in some way. This is his greatest difference from John
XXIII. This typical failing of the intellectual mind is probably related to another trait of Paul's: he has a horror of a
void, he cannot bear the thought that minority and majority
should remain permanently unreconciled. Appreciating the
merits of both sides so well, he finds all bitter-end resistance
unthinkable and abhorrent. Some formula can surely be
worked out that will be capable of reconciling opposites,
according to the motto *non vincere, ma convincere*. Observers find it difficult to understand why the Pope has expended
so much time and effort on attempting to persuade a minority
to accept compromises to the extent of seeming at times to
be almost completely under the thumb of this group of conservative bishops, prelates and theologians, some of whom
belong to his immediate entourage and are therefore in an
excellent position to press their views on the Pope. The
answer appears to be, partly because he is confident that they
can be won over, and partly because he shares certain of their
misgivings, particularly with regard to a lack of respect for
the papal prerogatives being shown by the majority, but also
undoubtedly because of an *esprit de corps* which he shares
with many of the minority dating from his own days in the
Curia.

That Pope Paul has been affected by the wave of adverse
criticism that swept the world press following the close of the
Third Session is clear from his remarks to journalists on
January 24, 1965 when he deplored "a certain low level of
tone" reached by the press in reporting the events of the
session and accounts which were "sometimes completely
fantastic and not corresponding to the truth at all," as well
as by an unusually detailed defense of the Pope's motives and
actions against unjust insinuations by one of the Jesuit editors of *La Civiltà Cattolica* (March 1, 1965), excerpted *in
advance* in the February 20, 1965 issue of the official Vatican
newspaper, *L'Osservatore Romano*. The somewhat over-

drawn portrayal of the Pope's lofty motives as an "honest broker" striving only to reconcile opposing factions and offering suggestions with a view merely to "clarifying the meaning" of conciliar texts, perhaps reflects, to some extent, Pope Paul's own view of his role. The reader is assured that the Pope had acted only to "overcome all difficulties, calming the atmosphere, assuring a genuine support and an almost unanimous approval for the Constitution on the Church."—This admission of the need for the Pope's frequent intervention only tends to confirm the story as told here. But the hand of the Secretary General is unmistakably evident in the last paragraph of Father Caprile's article. It concludes by assuring us that when the full record is published, the various maneuvers, accusations and plots laid at the door of the Secretary General will be found to be without basis. It will then be apparent "how prudently and how wisely he acted to handle situations which otherwise could have proved fatal to the success of the Council."

This deduction becomes a certainty, when we compare Caprile's account with the interview Archbishop Felici gave toward the end of November, shortly after the end of the Third Session (reported in *L'Osservatore Romano*, November 29, 1964), in which he accused newsmen who reported the Council of being "parasites and fungi" growing at the feet of "robust and healthy trees," meaning himself and the conservative bishops. Such voices, he said, "promoting confusion, insubordination and error," had to be tolerated as a "necessary evil" and allowed to grow until the end of the Council, according to the Gospel adage, "Let both grow until the harvest." As an old Irish Vatican hand put it, "The very fact that he acknowledges this criticism in public would be sufficient to have him convicted in an Italian court of law, where the party is guilty until he can prove his innocence." It is typical of the worst type of curial mind that it never presumes to ask what wrongs were committed that gave rise to such widespread indignation and criticism. To do so would be to violate a cardinal rule of the Curia: never acknowledge faults, at least publicly. It is this arrogance and impervious-ness of certain officials of the Curia, their disdainful and careerist outlook, that has brought the whole body into dis-repute and focused attention on the Pope's plans for the re-form of the Curia as the key to his intentions with regard to *aggiornamento* as a whole.

In January 1965, at the Pope's order, a letter was sent by Cardinal Cicognani to all the heads of curial offices remind-ing them of the widespread criticisms levelled against the Curia, and of the Pope's own admissions in this regard. They were told to "show docility to the reforms which will be decreed in the future," presumably meaning the near future, though not necessarily before the Fourth Session. They were also advised to refrain from engaging in controversy with the bishops over the work of the Council, because experience had shown that "this kind of indiscretion" in the past had done more harm to the Curia than good. One has only to recall the remark attributed to Monsignor Romeo, a staunch critic of Cardinal Bea and the Biblical Institute, characterizing the Council bishops as "Two thousand good-for-nothings, many of whom in spite of the pectoral crosses around their necks, don't believe in the Blessed Trinity or the Virgin birth." The monsignor indignantly denied the charge in a letter to the Vatican newspaper.* Whether the words are apocryphal or not, they can be taken as typifying an attitude that has been all too common, as the debates on the floor of the Coun-cil prove. Diocesan bishops would not have complained about the Curia without cause, nor would Cardinal Cicog-nani have written his letter at the behest of the Pope, unless there was good reason to believe that the proposed reform of the Curia would meet with some rather stiff resistance on the part of those about to be reformed. As a curious example of what is probably in store during the post-conciliar period unless lines of authority are strictly enforced, we have the odd

* *L'Osservatore Romano,* October 21, 1964.

spectacle of two Roman organs issuing wholly contradictory orders recently: the post-conciliar Consilium for Liturgical Renewal authorized the Jesuit Biblical Institute to concelebrate freely, whereas the conservative Congregation of Rites restricted the Jesuit Gregorian University to concelebration one day a year.

The whole course of Vatican Council II to date clearly points to the urgent necessity for establishing some form of episcopal group as quickly as possible, in Rome, to collaborate with the Pope in the business of governing the Church, in a purely advisory capacity. The "burden of office" to which Pope Paul has referred rather frequently of late might become less burdensome if representatives of the episcopal order were on hand to offer advice and by their participation in papal decisions lend the weight of their presence, experience and prestige toward making those decisions seem less arbitrary, less partisan, more balanced, and more universally welcomed, than they are at present. Tension is probably inevitable between the earthly head of the Church and the rest of the bishops, because of the special divinely-ordered constitution of the Church, with the supreme power being shared by a college consisting of the bishops *with* the Pope. History amply demonstrates that this has been true in the past. While there can be no assurance of ultimately perfect agreement, human nature being what it is, that "harmony" which, as the Constitution on the Church says, ought to prevail between the two could probably be achieved in no better way than by the establishment in the near future of a really effective "senate." This is now widely regarded as almost a certainty.

Pope Paul's decision to travel to India for a "brief and simple visit limited to one stop-over" came as a genuine surprise to the majority of the Council Fathers present in St. Peter's on October 18, the mid-point of the Third Session. This day was also the occasion of the canonization ceremony of the 22 Uganda martyrs. The Pope had confided his decision to visit India to tall, handsome Cardinal Valerian Gracias of Bombay in late September, saying, "If it pleases the Lord, I will come to India. And I come." But the pontiff made it clear that he himself would divulge the news on the occasion of the canonization, and that the journey would be confined to a strictly spiritual objective—honoring Christ at the international Eucharistic Congress in Bombay from November 28 to December 6, and visiting the poor without distinction of caste or creed.

In declaring that the Uganda martyrs had been put to death for their religious beliefs by a tribal chieftain in the village of Namugongo in 1886, the Pope also cited the 12 Anglican natives who were martyred at the same time. He also pointed out a crucial distinction between evangelization and colonization:

Whereas evangelization implants the Christian religion as a new vitality that releases the spiritual powers and the latent talents of the local population and so sets people free . . . colonization, based on purely utilitarian and material motives, pursues of the native populace.

Alluding to the fact that this was the second time he had occasion to announce a journey abroad while presiding at a function in St. Peter's (he first announced his trip to the Holy Land in January, 1964), Pope Paul admitted that the journey was unusual but was part of the papal apostolic ministry in modern times: "The Pope is becoming a pilgrim, you will say. Yes, the Pope is a pilgrim, which means a witness, a shepherd, an apostle on the move . . ."

Reaction to the papal decision was uniformly favorable among the Council Fathers and the world press. Resentment was expressed by two sources—religious fanatics among the Hindus, and Catholic Portugal. The Portuguese Foreign Minister, Alberto Franco Noguiera, recalled India's sequestration of three Portuguese colonial enclaves a few years ago and announced that Pope Paul's visit was a gratuitous offense "committed by Catholicism's chief in relation to a Catholic nation. . . . Henceforth we must maintain the deepest silence, wounded and with dignity." It is curious reasoning that would have deprived the Catholics of India of seeing the Holy Father on a religious occasion, because of a political conflict in which the Pope had no part whatsoever.

The pilgrimage to India proved to be successful beyond all expectations, perhaps because Indians are people of deep spiritual motivation. It was an example of Pauline inspiration when the Pope, in the prayer which he composed and read to the crowds, quoted from the Upanishads. The people sensed his profound humility and sincerity and called him *"bada guru,"* or "great holy man." Oddly enough, it was a pro-Communist weekly, *Blitz,* that carried the most memorable description of Paul's visit: "We have seen Eisenhower, Khrushchev, Chou, the Shah of Persia and the Queen of England, Nasser, Tito, Sukarno and others ride in glory through our capital during the mighty Nehru epoch but this humble pilgrim of God and Vicar of Christ got a reception that surpassed them all."

Summary

November 17, 1964, Tuesday—124TH GENERAL CONGREGATION.
MASS: Archbishop Gori, Latin Patriarch of Jerusalem.
MODERATOR: Cardinal Lercaro.
PRESENT: 2,146 Fathers.

ANNOUNCEMENTS: distribution of text of announcements made yesterday; distribution of revised text of Religious Liberty, vote on Thursday; voting cannot be done by proxy in public sessions or otherwise.

PENDING BUSINESS: Propositions on Priestly Training.

SPEAKERS: (in name of at least 70 Fathers) 1. Archbishop Garrone (Toulouse, France). 2. Bishop Mendez Arceo (Cuernavaca, Mexico). 3. Bishop Reuss (Auxiliary of Mainz, Germany). *Relator:* Bishop Carraro (Verona, Italy). Parish Priest: Don Luis Marcos (Madrid).

NEW BUSINESS: Declaration on Christian Education.

SPEAKERS: *Relator:* Bishop Daem (Antwerp, Belgium). 4. Cardinal Spellman (New York, N.Y.). 5. Cardinal Ritter (St. Louis, Missouri). 6. Bishop Elchinger (Coadjutor of Strasbourg, France). 7 Archbishop Gouyon (Rennes, France). 8. Archbishop Cody (New Orleans, Louisiana).

VOTES: handling of *modi* for Chaps. III–V of *De Ecclesia.*

	Total	Placet	Non placet	Invalid
Chap. III	2,146	2,099	46	1(1)
Chap. IV	2,144	2,135	8	1
Chap. V	2,146	2,142	4	–

VOTES: Propositions on Priestly Formation, whether to proceed to voting, and propositions voted individually

	Total	Placet	Non placet	Placet iuxta modum
Preliminary vote	2,117	2,076	41	–
Preface & Prop. 1	1,830	1,707	3	120
Prop. 2-3	1,880	1,721	10	149
Prop. 4-7	1,966	1,808	4	154

November 18, 1964, Wednesday—125TH GENERAL CONGREGATION.

MASS: Patriarch Ignace Pierre XVI Batanian, Armenian Patriarch of Cilicia, in Armenian rite, in presence of Pope Paul VI.

MODERATOR: Cardinal Lercaro.

PRESENT: 2,131 Fathers.

ANNOUNCEMENTS: distribution of Declaration on Relationship of Church with Non-Christians, vote on Friday; proposal to defer vote on Religious Liberty to allow more time for study will be voted on tomorrow, by decision of Council Presidency and Moderators; final vote tomorrow on whole Constitution on the Church; tomorrow vote on Christian Education.

PENDING BUSINESS: Declaration on Christian Education.

SPEAKERS: (in name of at least 70 Fathers) 1. Cardinal Léger (Montreal, Canada). 2. Bishop Malone (Auxiliary of Youngstown, Ohio). 3. Bishop Rivera Damas (Auxiliary of San Salvador, El Salvador). 4. Bishop Olu Nwaezeapu (Warri, Nigeria). 5. Bishop Henriquez Jimenez (Auxiliary of Caracas, Venezuela). 6. Archbishop Beck (Liverpool, England). 7. Bishop Schneiders (Makassar, Indonesia). 8. Bishop Hoa Nguyen-van-Hien (Dalat, Vietnam). 9. Archbishop Muñoz-Vega (Coadjutor of Quito, Ecuador).

VOTES: handling of *modi* on Chaps. VI–VIII of *De Ecclesia*

	Total	*Placet*	*Non placet*	Invalid
Chap. VI	2,131	2,114	12	5(4)
Chap. VII	2,131	2,127	4	–
Chap. VIII	2,120	2,096	23	1

VOTES: Propositions on Priestly Formation

	Total	*Placet*	*Non placet*	*Placet iuxta modum*	Invalid
Prop. 8-12	1,996	1,773	10	213	–
Prop. 13-15	1,943	1,618	5	319	1
Prop. 16-18	1,960	1,644	8	307	1
Prop. 19-22	1,945	1,845	6	93	1

November 19, 1964, Thursday—126TH GENERAL CONGREGATION.
MASS: Bishop Ijjas, Apostolic Administrator of Csanad, Hungary.
MODERATOR: Cardinal Döpfner.
PRESENT: 2,145 Fathers.
ANNOUNCEMENTS: the "Explanatory Note" read on Nov. 16 should be considered part of the Acts of the Council; final vote to-

morrow on decree on Ecumenism, distribution of mimeographed sheet listing 19 additional *modi* or changes in text
suggested by "higher authority" (Pope) and accepted by
Secretariat for Unity; distribution of *modi* and amended text
of propositions on Oriental Churches, vote tomorrow; (by
Cardinal Tisserant, in name of Cardinal Presidents) there will
be no vote today on Religious Liberty, after reading of *relatio,*
as "many Fathers" have requested more time for study.

PENDING BUSINESS: Declaration on Christian Education.

SPEAKERS: 1. Bishop Pohlschneider (Aachen, Germany). 2. Bishop
Okoye (Port Harcourt, Nigeria). 3. Archbishop Abed (Tripoli,
Lebanon). 4. Bishop Nwedo (Umuahia, Nigeria). (in name of
at least 70 Fathers): 5. Father Fernández (Master General of
Dominicans). 6. Bishop Bejze (Auxiliary of Lodz, Poland).
7. Bishop Van Waeyenbergh (Auxiliary of Malines-Brussels,
Belgium). *Relator:* Bishop Daem (Antwerp, Belgium).

NEW BUSINESS: Votum on Matrimony. *Relatores:* Cardinal Masella
and Archbishop Schneider (Bamburg, Germany).

SPEAKERS: 8. Cardinal Gilroy (Sydney, Australia).

VOTE: final vote on *De Ecclesia*

	Total	Placet	Non placet	Invalid
De Ecclesia as whole	2,145	2,134	10	1

VOTES: Declaration on Christian Education: preliminary vote, and vote on individual propositions

	Total	Placet	Non placet	Placet iuxta modum	Invalid
Preliminary vote	1,879	1,457	419	–	3
Pref., Prop. 1-3	1,891	1,592	157	140	2
Prop. 4-6	1,906	1,465	159	280	2
Prop. 7-8	1,891	1,592	155	141	3
Prop. 9-11	1,873	1,588	173	110	2

VOTE: cancelled vote on Religious Liberty. *Relator:* Bishop De Smedt
(Bruges, Belgium).

November 20, 1964, Friday—127TH GENERAL CONGREGATION.
MASS: Archbishop Heenan of Westminster, England.
MODERATOR: Cardinal Döpfner.
PRESENT: 2,129 Fathers.
ANNOUNCEMENTS: (by Cardinal Tisserant) many Fathers disappointed by postponement of vote yesterday on Religious Liberty, in accordance with the Rules, and while Holy Father has declined to intervene on basis of new petition for a vote, the text on Religious Liberty will have priority in agenda for the Fourth Session; (by SG); distribution of revised schema on Divine Revelation and revised schema on Priestly Life and Ministry, to be voted at next session; text of decree on Pastoral Office of Bishops not quite ready, to be voted at next session; observations on these texts, as well as Religious Liberty, to be sent in by Jan. 31, 1965; observations on *votum* on Matrimony should be sent in by end of November.
PENDING BUSINESS: *Votum* on Matrimony.
SPEAKERS: 1. Cardinal Ruffini (Palermo, Sicily). 2. Cardinal Bueno y Monreal (Seville, Spain). 3. Cardinal Döpfner (Munich, Germany). 4. Cardinal Ritter (St. Louis, Missouri). 5. Bishop Fearns (Auxiliary of New York, speaking for Cardinal Spellman). 6. Archbishop Krol (Philadelphia, Pa.). 7. Bishop Renard (Versailles, France). 8. Bishop Charrière (Lausanne, Switzerland). 9. Bishop Taguchi Yoshigoro (Osaka, Japan). 10. Archbishop Heenan (Westminster, England). 11. Bishop Moors (Roermond, Holland). 12. Archbishop Conway (Armagh, Ireland). 13. Archbishop Djajasepoetra (Djakarta, Indonesia).

VOTE: final vote on decree on Ecumenism

	Total	*Placet*	*Non placet*	Invalid
Ecumenism	2,129	2,054	64	11(6)

VOTES: Decree on Oriental Churches

	Total	*Placet*	*Non placet*	Invalid
Art. 2-4	2,129	1,841	283	5(1)
Handling of *modi*	2,115	1,923	188	4
Text as whole	2,104	1,964	135	5(1)

VOTES: Declaration on Relationship of Church with Non-Christians
Relator: Cardinal Bea.

	Total	Placet	Non placet	Placet iuxta modum	Invalid
Pref., Art.					
1-3	1,987	1,838	136	–	13(4)
Art. 4-5	1,969	1,770	185	–	14(7)
Declaration as whole	1,996	1,651	99	242	4

VOTE: Whether *votum* on Matrimony should be transmitted to Holy Father for appropriate action

	Total	Placet	Non placet	Invalid
Votum on Matrimony	2,024	1,592	427	5(2)

November 21, 1964, Saturday—SOLEMN CLOSING PUBLIC SESSION.
MASS: concelebrated by Pope Paul VI with 24 Council bishops.
PRESENT: 2,156 Fathers.

VOTING AND PROMULGATION OF DECREES

	Total	Placet	Non placet
Constitution on the Church	2,156	2,151	5
Decree on Oriental Churches	2,149	2,110	39
Decree on Ecumenism	2,148	2,137	11

ANNOUNCEMENT: (by SG) relaxation of norms for eucharistic fast.
SPEAKER: Address by Pope Paul VI closing the Third Session.

Opening Address of Pope Paul VI

SEPTEMBER 14, 1964

✠

Under the sign of the holy cross, in whose honor we have con-celebrated holy mass, we open today the third session of the second Ecumenical Vatican Council.

The church is present here. We are the church. We are the church as members of the mystical body of Christ, for God has granted us the inestimable favor of being baptized, or being believers united by love and constituting the consecrated and visible people of God. We are the church since we are ministers of the church herself, priests invested with a special character received at our sacramental ordination.

On us is conferred marvelous and tremendous powers, making of us a hierarchy entrusted with functions meant to perpetuate Christ.

We are the church, finally, because as teachers of the faith, pastors of souls, stewards of the mysteries of God (I Corinthians, iv, 1), we represent here the entire church, not as delegates or deputies of the faithful towards whom our ministry is directed, but as fathers and brothers who personify the communities entrusted to the care of each one of us, and as a plenary assembly legitimately convoked by the Holy Father.

The Pope has called the Council into session in his capacity, which links him with all of you, as your brother, the Bishop of historic Rome, and as the humble but authentic successor of the apostle Peter—before whose tomb we are devoutly gathered—and therefore as the unworthy but true head of the Catholic Church and Vicar of Christ, servant of the servants of God.

Recapitulating in our persons and in our functions the universal church, we proclaim this Council ecumenical: here is the exercise of unity, here the exercise of that universality by which the church gives evidence of her prodigious vitality, her marvelous capacity to make men brothers and to welcome within her embrace the most diverse civilizations and languages, the most varied expressions of national, social and cultural genius, harmonizing all in the felicitous union, yet always respecting legitimate variety and complexity.

Here is the exercise of the holiness of the church because here she calls on the mercy of God, for the weaknesses and deficiencies of the sinners that we are, and because here as nowhere else do we become aware of the power granted to our ministry to draw from the "unfathomable riches of Christ" (Ephesians, iii, 8) the treasures of salvation and sanctification for all men; here we realize that this ministry of ours has no other purpose than to "prepare for the Lord a perfect people." (Luke, i, 17); there, finally, is made manifest the apostolicity of the church, a prerogative which is a marvel even to us, to us who have experienced our own weakness and who know how history bears witness to the frailty of even the most powerful of human institutions and at the same time we know with what continuity and fidelity the mandate of Christ has been transmitted from the apostles to our lowly and ever-astonished persons; we know how inexplicably and how triumphantly the church has endured throughout the ages, this church which is ever living and always capable of finding in herself the irrepressible spirit of youth.

At this point we can repeat with Tertullian: "It is the whole Christian world which is here represented and which we venerate. And see how good it is that from all sides men are gathered because of faith in Christ. See how good and happy it is for brothers to dwell together." (De Ieiuniis).

Now if the church is heard, here also is the spirit, the advocate, whom Christ promised to his apostles for the building of the church: "I will ask the Father and He will give you another advocate to dwell with you forever, the spirit of truth whom the world cannot receive, because it neither sees him nor knows him. But you shall know him, because he will dwell with you, and be in you." (John, xiv, 16–17).

For there are, as we know, two factors which Christ has promised and arranged in different ways to continue His mission, to extend in time and on earth the kingdom He founded and to make of redeemed mankind His church, His mystical body, His fulness, in expectation of His definitive and triumphant return at the end of time: these two factors are the apostolate and the spirit.

The apostolate is the external and objective factor, it forms the material body, so to speak, of the church and is the source of her visible and social structures. The holy spirit is the internal factor who acts within each person, as well as on the whole community, animating, vivifying, sanctifying.

These two agents, the apostolate which is entrusted to the sacred hierarchy, and the spirit of Jesus, which uses the hierarchy as its ordinary instrument in the ministry of the word and the sacraments, cooperate with one another.

Pentecost shows them wonderfully linked at the beginning of the great work of Jesus, who although invisible remains ever present in His apostles and their successors, "whom He set over His church as His shepherds and vicars" (Preface of Apostles). These two agents, differently yet harmoniously, bear equal witness to Christ the Lord in a combination that confers on apostolic activity its supernatural force (I Peter, i, 12).

May we believe that this salvific plan, by which the redemption of Christ reaches and is fulfilled in us, is even now in action? Yes, my brethren, we must believe, indeed, that this plan is continued and actuated by our means, in virtue of a power and sufficiency that comes from God, "who has made us fit ministers of the new covenant, not of the letter but of the spirit . . . which gives life" (II Corinthians, iii, 6).

To doubt this would be an insult to Christ's faithfulness to His promises, a betrayal of our apostolic mandate, a depriving of the church of her certainty, which the divine word has guaranteed and history has confirmed, and of her indefectibility.

The spirit is here. Not yet to confirm with sacramental grace the work which all of us, united in the Council, are bringing to completion, but rather to illuminate and guide our labors to the benefit of the church and all mankind. The spirit is here. We call upon Him, wait for Him, follow Him. The spirit is here.

Let us reflect on this doctrine and this present reality so that, above all, we may realize once more and in the fullest and sublimest degree possible our communion with the living Christ: it is the spirit who joins us to Him.

Let us reflect on this truth also so that we may put ourselves before Him in trepidation, fully at His disposal, that we may become aware of the humiliating emptiness of our misery and the crying need we have of His halo and mercy, that we may hear as if spoken in the secret recesses of our soul the words of the apostle: "Discharging this ministry in accordance with the mercy shown us, we do not lose heart" (II Corinthians, iv, 1).

The Council is for us a moment of deep interior docility, a moment of complete and filial adherence to the word of the Lord, a moment of

fervent, earnest invocation and of love, a moment of spiritual exalta-
tion. To this unique occasion the poetic words of St. Ambrose apply
with a special aptness: "Let us drink in joy the sober inebriation of the
spirit" (hymn at lauds). Such for us should be this blessed time of
Council.

And finally we have this to say: The hour has sounded in history
when the church, which expresses herself in us and from us receives
structure and life, must say of herself what Christ intended and willed
her to be, and what the age-long meditation of the fathers, pontiffs and
doctors in their wisdom has explored with piety and fidelity.

The church must give a definition of herself and bring out from her
true consciousness the doctrine which the Holy Spirit teaches her,
according to the Lord's promise "But the Paraclete, the Holy Spirit,
whom the Father will send in my name, He will teach you all things
and bring to your mind whatever I have said to you" (John xiv 26).
"The Spirit Himself bears witness to our spirit that we are the sons
of God" (Romans, i, 16).

Thus must be completed the doctrines, the council was preparing to
enunciate, but which external obstacles prevented it from defining, except in its first part dealing with the head of the church, the Roman
Pontiff, and his sovereign prerogatives regarding primacy of jurisdiction
and infallibility of teaching, which Christ was pleased to bestow upon
the Apostle Peter. His visible vicar on earth, and upon those who succeed him in so sublime and tremendous an office.

The discussion on this doctrine remains to be completed, so as to
explain the mind of Christ on the whole of His church and especially
on the nature and function of the successors of the apostles, that is of
the episcopate, with which dignity and office the greater part of you,
venerable fathers, and we ourselves, most reverend brothers, are by
God's good pleasure invested.

The Council has many other important subjects to treat of, but this
one seems to us to be the weightiest and most delicate. The Council's
deliberations on this subject will certainly be what distinguishes this
solemn and historic synod in the memory of future ages.

It must undertake a number of difficult theological discussions, it must
determine the nature and mission of the pastors of the church, it must
discuss, and with the favor of the Holy Spirit, decide the constitutional
prerogatives of the episcopate, it must delineate the relations between
the episcopate and the Holy See, it must show how homogeneous is the
constitutional idea of the church under its differing Eastern and
Western expressions, it must make clear for the faithful of the Catholic
Church and also for the separated brethren the true notion of the
hierarchical organs which "the Holy Spirit has appointed as bishops to
rule the church of God" (Acts xx, 28), with unquestionably valid authority in the humble and patient service of the brethren, as becomes
pastors, ministers, that is, of faith and charity.

These thoughts are all the more important for us, and certainly for you, venerable brothers, because of the fact that this third session of the Ecumenical Council has chosen from among its many concerns this central objective: to investigate and clarify the doctrine of the nature of the church, thus resuming and integrating the work done in the first two sessions, and making this solemn synod the logical continuation of the first Vatican Council.

At this point the church wants to study itself, or rather probe into the mind of Christ, its divine founder: just what and how much to say in order to honor His wisdom and charity and, by restoring to Him the full practice of its faith and fidelity, to render itself an even more fit instrument in the work of salvation for which it was founded.

But in case anyone should think that in doing this the church is closing in on itself in an attitude of complacency, forgetting on the one hand Christ, from whom it receives everything and to whom it owes everything, or on the other hand humanity, to whose service it is committed; it places itself between Him and the world, not satisfied with itself, not as a forbidding barrier, not as an end in itself, but deeply concerned to be completely the Church of Christ, in Christ, for Christ, as well as completely the church of men, among men, for men; humble and yet glorious, the church of the Savior and yet reaching out to all men, preserving and yet diffusing the truth and the grace of the supernatural life.

In our time, which seems to be blessed in a special way, this seems to be all the more true and important, for today the inquiry concerning the church will have a point of great interest for us, and especially for you, namely the hierarchic structure of the church itself, and consequently the origin, nature, function and power of the episcopate, which is a major part of the hierarchy, in which with us "the Holy Spirit has made you bishop to keep watch over God's church" (Acts xx, 28).

And so we have in mind to tune in with a plan of divine providence in celebrating this historic moment by giving to you, our venerated and beloved brothers in the episcopate, the honor which our Lord desired to be shown to the apostles together with Peter.

The fathers of the first Vatican Council defined and proclaimed the truly unique and supreme powers conferred by Christ on Peter and handed on to his successors. This recognition has appeared to some as having limited the authority of bishops, the successors of the apostles, and as having rendered superfluous and prevented the convocation of a subsequent Ecumenical Council, which, however, according to canon law has supreme authority over the entire church.

The present ecumenical synod is certainly going to confirm the doctrine of the previous one regarding the prerogatives of the Roman Pontiff. But it will also have as its principal objective the task of describing and honoring the prerogatives of the episcopate.

Let every one understand that the convocation of this Council has been a free and spontaneous act on the part of our venerated predecessor, of happy memory John XXIII, an act which we have readily confirmed knowing full well that the theme of this sovereign and sacred assembly would deal with the episcopate. It could not have been otherwise taking into consideration not only the proper interconnection of the doctrines concerned but also because of a sincere determination to proclaim the glory, the mission, the merits and the friendship of our brothers entrusted with the work of instructing, sanctifying and governing the church of God.

Let us repeat as our own those well-known words which our distant and saintly predecessor of immortal memory, Gregory the Great, wrote to Eulogius, Bishop of Alexandria: "My honor is the honor of the universal church. My honor is the strength of my brothers. I am thus truly honored when the honor due to each and every one of them is not denied to them."

The integrity of Catholic truth now calls for a clarification consonant with the doctrine of papacy which will place in its splendid light the role and mandate of the episcopate. In its work of tracing the outlines of such a role and such mandate, the Council will be anxious about nothing except interpreting the thought of Jesus Christ at its true source and genuine origin.

We have already had the pleasure of recognizing in the bishops our true brothers, addressing them, as the Apostle Peter did, as "elders," and gladly claiming for ourselves the equivalent title of "fellow elder" (I Peter, v, 1). We have had the pleasure of addressing to them the words of the Apostle Paul: "my partners in tribulations and consolations" (II Corinthians, v, 7). We have been anxious to reassure them of those religious convictions that characterize our relations with them: esteem, affection, solidarity.

We are bound by our duty to recognize them as the teachers, rulers, and sanctifiers of the Christian people, the "stewards of the mysteries of God" (I Corinthians, iii, v, 1), the witnesses to the Gospel, the ministers of the New Testament and, in a certain sense, the very reflection of the glory of the Lord (II Corinthians, iii, 6–18).

As successors of Peter and, therefore, as possessors of full power over the entire church, we have the duty of heading the body of the episcopate, although we are surely unworthy of this dignity. It is not our intention to deprive you of the authority which belongs to you. On the contrary, we are among the first to respect that sacred authority. If our apostolic duty obliges us to impose restrictions, to define terminology, to prescribe modes of action, to regulate the methods which concern the exercise of episcopal authority, you realize that this is done for the good of the entire church, for the unity of that church which has proportionately greater need of centralized leadership as its worldwide extension becomes more complete, as more serious dangers and more pressing needs threaten the Christian people in the varying circumstances of history, and we may add as more rapid means of communication become operative in modern times.

No one should regard as a device formulated by pride such centralization, which will surely be always tempered and balanced by an alert and timely delegation both of authority and facilities for local pastors.

We assure you, our brothers in the episcopate, that this centralization is rather a service and a manifestation of the unifying and hierarchical spirit of the church. It is the glory, the power, the beauty which Christ promised to His church and which He gradually grants to it as the ages run their course.

Apropos of this topic, we can recall the words which Pius XII, of happy memory, addressed to a certain group of bishops: "This union and this timely communication with the Holy See arises, not from a kind of longing to achieve centralization and homogeneity, but rather from the divine law itself and from a truly fundamental principle affecting the very essence of the church of Christ."

Such centralization strengthens rather than weakens the authority of bishops, whether that authority be considered in the individual bishop or in the collegiality of the bishops.

Oh, how deeply we admire, how staunchly we support the rights and duties proper to the sacred hierarchy, which is the very instrument, born of the charity of Christ, and fashioned by Him to complete, to communicate, and to safeguard the integral and fruitful transmission of the treasures of faith, of example, of precepts, and of favors bequeathed by Christ to His church.

The hierarchy is the mother of the community of the faithful, it is the architect of its visible framework, it is the public representative which wins for the church the titles of mother and teacher, it is the bearer of the riches of the sacraments, the conductor of the symphony of prayer, the inspiration of works of charity.

Placed at the head of this sacred institution, how could we fail to devote to it our solicitude, our trust, our support? How could we fail to defend it? What duty presses upon us with greater frequency, with graver consequence or with deeper satisfaction than that of safeguarding the independence, the freedom, the dignity of the sacred hierarchy throughout the world?

Is it not true that this exhausting task has been the very fabric of which has been woven the tapestry of the history of the papacy, especially in these years of political upheavals?

Let us add one further thought to this tribute to the episcopate—in order to show how much its intrinsic nobility and its effective charity are enhanced by the harmonious unity which must bind it in close union with the apostolic see, and how much the apostolic see needs you, venerable brothers.

For your part, dispersed as you are all over the world, if you are to give shape and substance to the true catholicity of the church, you have the need of a center, a principle of unity in faith and communion, a unifying power, such as, in fact, you find in this chair of Peter.

Similarly, we need to have you always nearby, to give more fully to the countenance of the apostolic see its beauty, its human and historic reality, even to give harmony to its faith, to be an example in the fulfillment of its duties, and a consolation in its times of stress.

So that, whilst we look forward to the clearer definition which the Council's deliberations will give to the doctrine of the episcopacy, we here and now pay you honor, pledge to you our affection as brother and father, and ask of you cooperation and support; may the communion, which binds together the Catholic hierarchy in living faith and charity, emerge from this Council deeper, stronger and more holy. It will be to the glory of Christ, the peace of the church and the light of the world.

There is much more we would like to say on this question and on many others of the first importance which have been brought up for the attention of the Council, but we do not wish to tax your patience.

However, we cannot forgo the pleasure of sending a special greeting at this moment from this Holy See to the various dioceses and parishes whom you represent here. And first of all to our beloved and esteemed priests who labor so unselfishly in collaboration with their bishops. And to religious, striving for every perfection that will make them like Christ and serviceable to their fellow men. To the Catholic laity, working with the hierarchy for the good of the church and for the good of society. To the poor, the persecuted and the suffering. And especially to those whom the lack of freedom still prevents from coming to this Council.

We wish, also, to welcome the auditors here present: their high ideals and outstanding merits are no secret to us. And we are delighted to welcome among the auditors our beloved daughters in Christ, the first women in history to participate in a conciliar assembly. The auditors—both men and women—will not be slow to realize that behind this welcome of ours lies our fatherly love for all groups who make up the people of God, our desire to give to the Christian community an ever-increasing sense of harmony, collaboration and charity.

And now we turn to you, the observers, with reverence and esteem, for you have once more accepted our invitation to attend the Council. We welcome and thank you, we wish to assure you once more of our purpose and hope to be able one day to remove every obstacle, every misunderstanding, every hesitancy that still prevents us from feeling fully of one heart and one soul in Christ, in His church (Acts, iv, 32).

For our part, we shall do all that the possibilities allow to this end. We are fully aware that the restoration of this unity is something of no small moment, and we shall give it all the attention and the time that it calls for.

It is something new, in contrast with the long, sad history which led up to the various separations, and we shall wait patiently for the conditions to ripen that will make possible a positive and friendly solution.

It is something, too, of deepest significance, having its roots in the mysterious counsels of God, and we shall strive, in humility and faith, to dispose ourselves to deserve so great a grace. We recall the words of the Apostle Paul, who brought the gift of the Gospel to all nations, seeking to become all things to all men (I Corinthians, ix, 22). Such an adaptability as we might today be tempted to call pluralism in practice; at the same time we recall how the same apostle has exhorted us to preserve the unity of the spirit in the bond of peace because there is only one Lord, one faith, one baptism, one God and father of all (Ephesians, iv, 2, 5–6).

We shall therefore strive, in loyalty to the unity of Christ's church, to understand better and to welcome all that is genuine and admissible in the different Christian denominations that are distinct from us, and at the same time we beg of them to try to understand the Catholic faith and life better and, when we invite them to enter into the fullness of truth and charity which, as an unmerited blessing but a formidable responsibility, Christ has charged us to preserve, we beg them not to take it in bad part, but as being prompted by respect and brotherly love.

For that fullness of truth and charity will be made the more manifest when all those who profess the name of Christ are reassembled into one.

Meanwhile, through you, our reverend and esteemed guests and observers in this Council, we wish to send our cordial greetings to the various Christian communities which you represent. May our respectful regard reach those too which are not represented here.

We gather together in our prayer and our affections all those members who are still parted from the full spiritual and visible wholeness of the mystical body of Christ, and in this yearning of our love and concern, our sorrow grows, our hopes increase.

Oh, churches that are so far and yet so close to us. Churches for whom our heart is filled with longing. Churches, the nostalgia of our sleepless nights. Churches of our tears and of our desire to do you honor by our embrace in the sincere love of Christ, oh may you hear, sounding from this keystone of unity, the tomb of Peter, apostle and martyr, and from this Ecumenical Council of brotherhood and peace, the loving cry we send you.

Maybe great distances separate us yet, maybe it will be long before our full and effective meeting can be realized, but know for sure that already we hold you in our heart. May the God of mercies support this our deeply felt yearning and hope.

And finally may our thoughts go out to the world about us, with its own interests, with its indifference too, perhaps even its hostility: We renew the greeting which we addressed to it from Bethlehem with our resolute purpose of placing the church at the service of its spiritual salvation and of its social prosperity, to bring it peace and true happiness.

We invite you all now, venerable brothers, to call upon the Holy Spirit together, as we make ready to inaugurate the third session of this second Council of the Vatican, and in the name of the Lord, with trust in the help of Mary most holy and of the holy apostles Peter and Paul, we bestow upon you all our apostolic blessing.

Constitution on the Church

PROMULGATED NOVEMBER 21, 1964

✠

1. Christ is the Light of nations. Because this is so, this Sacred Synod gathered together in the Holy Spirit eagerly desires, by proclaiming the Gospel to every creature, to bring the light of Christ to all men, a light brightly visible on the countenance of the Church. Since the Church is in Christ like a Sacrament or as a sign and instrument both of a very closely knit union with God and of the unity of the whole human race, it desires now to unfold more fully to the faithful of the Church and to the whole world its own inner nature and universal mission. This it intends to do following faithfully the teaching of previous Councils. The present day conditions of the world add greater urgency to this work of the Church so that all men, joined more closely today by various social, technical and cultural ties, might also attain fuller unity in Christ.

CHAPTER I
The Mystery of the Church

2. The Eternal Father, by a free and hidden plan of His own wisdom and goodness, created the whole world. His plan was to raise men to a

participation of the divine life. Fallen in Adam, men were not left to themselves by God the Father, but they are ceaselessly offered helps to salvation, in view of Christ, the Redeemer "who is the image of the invisible God, the firstborn of every creature." All the elect, before time began, the Father "foreknew and predestined to become conformed to the image of His Son, that he should be the firstborn among many brethren." He planned to assemble in the holy Church all those who would believe in Christ. Already from the beginning of the world the foreshadowing of the Church took place. It was prepared in a remarkable way throughout the history of the people of Israel and by means of the Old Covenant. In the present era of time the Church was constituted and, by the outpouring of the Spirit, was made manifest. At the end of time it will gloriously achieve completion, when, as is read in the Fathers, all the just, from Adam and "from Abel, the just one, to the last of the elect," will be gathered together with the Father in the universal Church.

3. The Son, therefore, came sent by the Father. It was in Him, before the foundation of the world, that the Father chose us and predestined us to become adopted sons, for in Him it pleased the Father to re-establish all things. To carry out the will of the Father Christ inaugurated the Kingdom of heaven on earth and revealed to us the mystery of that kingdom. By His obedience He brought about redemption. The Church, or, in other words, the kingdom of Christ now present in mystery, grows visibly through the power of God in the world. This inauguration and this growth are both symbolized by the Blood and Water which flowed from the open side of the crucified Jesus, and are foretold in the words of the Lord referring to His death on the Cross: "And I, if I be lifted up from the earth, will draw all things to myself." As often as the sacrifice of the cross in which Christ our Passover was sacrificed is celebrated on an altar, the work of our redemption is carried on, and, in the Sacrament of the Eucharistic bread, the unity of all believers who form one body in Christ is both expressed and brought about. All men are called to this union with Christ, who is the light of the world, from whom we go forth, through whom we live, and toward whom our whole life strains.

4. When the work which the Father gave the Son to do on earth was accomplished, the Holy Spirit was sent on the day of Pentecost in order that He might continually sanctify the Church, and thus, all those who believe would have access through Christ in one Spirit to the Father. He is the Spirit of Life, a fountain of water springing up to life eternal. To men, dead in sin, the Father gives life through Him, until, in Christ, He brings to life their mortal bodies. The Spirit dwells in the Church and in the hearts of the faithful, as in a temple. In them He prays on their behalf and bears witness to the fact that they are adopted sons. The Church, which the Spirit guides in the way of all truth and which

He unified in communion and in works of ministry, He both equips and directs with hierarchical and charismatic gifts and adorns with His fruits. By the power of the Gospel He makes the Church keep the freshness of youth. Uninterrupted, He renews it and leads it to perfect union with its Spouse. The Spirit and the Bride both say to Jesus, the Lord, "Come!"

Thus, the Church has been seen as "a people made one with the unity of the Father, the Son and the Holy Spirit."

5. The Mystery of the holy Church to manifest is its very foundation for the Lord Jesus set it on its course by preaching the Good News, that is, the coming of the Kingdom of God, which, for centuries, had been promised in the Scriptures: "The time is fulfilled, and the kingdom of God is at hand." In the word, in the world, and in the presence of Christ, this kingdom was clearly open to the view of men. The *Word* of the Lord may be compared to a seed which is sown in a field; those who hear the Word with faith and become part of the little flock of Christ, have received the Kingdom itself. Then, by its own power the seed sprouts and grows until harvest time. The *Miracles* of Jesus also confirm that the Kingdom has already arrived on earth: "If I cast out devils by the finger of God, then the kingdom of God has come upon you." Before all things, however, the Kingdom is clearly visible in the very *Person* of Christ, of the Son of God and of the Son of Man, who came "to serve and to give His life as a ransom for many."

When Jesus, who had undergone the death of the cross, had risen, He appeared as the one constituted as Lord, Christ and eternal Priest, and He poured out on His disciples the Spirit promised by the Father. From this source the Church, equipped with the gifts of its founder and faithfully guarding His precepts of charity, humility and self-sacrifice, receives the mission to proclaim and to spread among all peoples the Kingdom of Christ and of God and to be, on earth, the initial budding forth of that kingdom. While it slowly grows, the Church strains toward the completed Kingdom and, with all its strength, hopes and desires to be united in glory with its King.

6. In the Old Testament the revelation of the Kingdom is often conveyed by means of metaphors. In the same way the inner nature of the Church is now made known to us in different images. Taken either from tending sheep or cultivating the land, from building or even from family life and from husband and wife, the images receive preparatory shaping in the books of the Prophets.

The Church is a SHEEPFOLD whose one necessary door is Christ. It is a flock of which God Himself foretold He would be the shepherd, and whose sheep, although tended by human shepherds, are nevertheless ceaselessly led and nourished by Christ Himself, the Good Shepherd and the Prince of the shepherds, who gave His life for the sheep.

The Church is a piece of land to be cultivated, the TILLAGE of God.

On that land the ancient olive tree grows whose holy roots were the
Prophets and in which the reconciliation of Jews and Gentiles has been
brought about and will be brought about. That land, like a choice vine-
yard, has been planted by the heavenly Cultivator. The true vine is
Christ who gives life and the power to bear abundant fruit to the
branches, that is, to us, who through the Church remain in Christ without whom we can do nothing.

Often the Church has also been called the BUILDING of God. The Lord
Himself compared Himself to the stone which the builders rejected, but
which was made into the cornerstone. On this foundation the Church
is built by the apostles, and from it the Church receives durability and
consolidation. This edifice has many names to describe it: the house of
God in which dwells His FAMILY; the household of God in the Spirit;
the dwelling place of God among men; and, especially, the holy TEMPLE.
This Temple, symbolized in places of worship built out of stone, is
praised by the Holy Fathers and, not without reason, is compared in
the liturgy to the Holy City, the New Jerusalem. As living stones we
here on earth are built into it. Prepared like a bride adorned for her
husband, John contemplates this holy city coming down out of heaven
from God when the world is made anew.

The Church, further, "that Jerusalem which is above" is also called
"our mother." It is described as the spotless SPOUSE of the spotless Lamb,
whom Christ "loved and for whom He delivered Himself up that He
might sanctify her," and whom He unceasingly "nourishes and cherishes," and once purified, He willed to be cleansed and joined to Himself, subject to Him in love and fidelity, and whom, finally, He filled
with heavenly gifts for all eternity, in order that we may know the love
of God and of Christ for us, a love which surpasses all knowledge. The
Church, while on earth it journeys in a foreign land away from the
Lord, is like an exile. It seeks and experiences those things which are
above, where Christ is seated at the right-hand of God, where the life
of the Church is hidden with Christ in God until it appears in glory
with its Spouse.

7. In the human nature united to Himself the Son of God, by over-
coming death through His own death and resurrection, redeemed man
and remolded him into a new creation. By communicating His Spirit,
Christ made His brothers, called together from all nations, mystically the
components of His own Body.

In that Body the life of Christ is poured into the believers who,
through the Sacraments, are united in a hidden and real way to Christ
who suffered and was glorified. Through Baptism we are formed in the
likeness of Christ: "For in one Spirit we were all baptized into one
body." In this sacred rite a oneness with Christ's death and resurrection
is both symbolized and brought about. "For we were buried with Him
by means of Baptism into death"; and if "we have been united with
Him in the likeness of His death, we shall be so in the likeness of His

resurrection also." Really partaking of the body of the Lord in the breaking of the Eucharistic bread, we are taken up into communion with Him and with one another. "Because the bread is one, we though many, are one body, all of us who partake of the one bread." In this way all of us are made members of His Body, "but severally members one of another."

As all the members of the human body, though they are many, form one body, so also are the faithful in Christ. Also, in the building up of Christ's body various members and functions have their part to play. There is only one Spirit who, according to His own richness and the needs of the ministries, gives His different gifts for the welfare of the Church. What has a special place among these gifts is the grace of the apostles to whose authority the Spirit Himself subjected even those who were endowed with charisms. Giving the body unity through Himself and through His power and inner joining of the members, this same Spirit produces and urges love among the believers. From all this it follows that if one member endures anything, all the members co-endure it, and if one member is honored, all the members together rejoice.

The Head of this Body is Christ. He is the image of the invisible God and in Him all things came into being. He is before all creatures and in Him all things hold together. He is the head of the Body which is the Church. He is the beginning, the first-born from the dead, that in all things He might have the first place.

By the greatness of His power He rules the things in heaven and the things on earth, and with His all-surpassing perfection and way of acting He fills the whole body with the riches of His glory.

All the members ought to be molded in the likeness of Him, until Christ be formed in them. For this reason we, who have been made to conform with Him, who have died with Him and risen with Him, are taken up into the mysteries of His life, until we will reign together with Him. On earth, still as pilgrims in a strange land, tracing in trial and in oppression the paths He trod, we are made one with His sufferings like the body is one with the Head, suffering with Him, that with Him we may be glorified.

From Him "the whole body, supplied and built up by joints and ligaments, attains a growth that is of God." He continually distributes in His body, that is, in the Church, gifts of ministries in which, by His own power, we serve each other unto salvation so that, carrying out the truth in love, we might through all things grow unto Him who is our Head.

In order that we might be unceasingly renewed in Him, He has shared with us His Spirit who, existing as one and the same being in the Head and in the members, gives life to, unifies and moves through the whole body. This He does in such a way that His work could be compared by the holy Fathers with the function the principle of life, that is, the soul, fulfills in the human body.

Christ loves the Church as His bride, having become the model of a man loving his wife as his body; the Church, indeed, is subject to its Head. "Because in Him dwells all the fulness of the Godhead bodily," He fills the Church, which is His body and the fulness, with His divine gifts so that it may expand and reach all the fulness of God.

8. Christ, the one Mediator, established and ceaselessly sustains here on earth His holy Church, the community of faith, hope and charity as an entity with visible delineation through which He communicated truth and grace to all. But, the society structured with hierarchical organs and the Mystical Body of Christ, are not to be considered as two realities, nor are the visible assembly and the spiritual community, nor the earthly Church and the Church enriched with heavenly things; rather they form one complex reality which coalesces from a divine and a human element. For this reason, by no weak analogy, it is compared to the mystery of the incarnate Word. As the assumed nature insepara- bly united to Him, serves the divine word as a living organ of salvation, so, in a similar way, does the visible social structure of the Church serve the Spirit of Christ, who vivifies it, in the building up of the body.

This is the one Church of Christ which in the Symbol of Faith is professed as one, holy, catholic and apostolic, which our Saviour after His Resurrection, commissioned Peter to shepherd, and him and the other apostles to extend and direct with authority, which He erected for all ages as "the pillar and mainstay of the truth." This Church constituted and organized in the world as a society, subsists in the Catholic Church, which is governed by the successor of Peter and by the bishops in his communion, although many elements of sanctification and of truth are found outside of its visible structure. These elements, as gifts belonging to the Church of Christ are forces impelling toward catholic unity.

Just as Christ carried out the work of redemption in poverty and oppression, so the Church is called to follow the same route that it might communicate the fruits of salvation to men. Christ Jesus, "though He was by nature God . . . emptied Himself, taking the nature of a slave," and "being rich, became poor" for our sakes. Thus, the Church, although it needs human resources to carry out its mission, is not set up to seek earthly glory, but to proclaim, even by its own example, humil- ity and self-sacrifice. Christ was sent by the Father "to bring good news to the poor, to heal the contrite of heart" "to seek and to save what was lost." Similarly, the Church encompasses with love all those who are poor and who suffer the image of its poor and suffering Founder. It does all it can to relieve their need and in them it strives to serve Christ. While Christ, holy, innocent and undefiled knew nothing of sin, but came to expiate only the sins of the people, the Church, embracing in its bosom sinners, at the same time holy and always in need of being purified, follows the endless way of penance and renewal. The Church, "like a stranger in a foreign land, presses forward amid the persecutions of the world and the consolations of God," announcing the cross and death of the Lord until He comes. By the power of the risen Lord it is given strength that it might, in patience and in love, overcome its sorrows and its challenges, both within itself and from without, and that it might reveal to the world, faithfully though darkly, the mystery of its Lord until, in the end, it will be manifested in full light.

CHAPTER II
On the People of God

9. At all times and in every race God has given welcome to whosoever fears Him and does what is right (cfr. Acts 10, 35). God, however, does not make men holy and save them merely as individuals, without bond or link between one another. Rather has it pleased Him to bring men together as one people, a people which acknowledges Him in truth and serves Him in holiness. He therefore chose the race of Israel as a people unto Himself. With it He set up a covenant. Step by step He taught and prepared this people, making known in its history both Himself and the decree of His will and making it holy unto Himself. All these things, however, were done by way of preparation and as a figure of that new and perfect covenant, which was to be ratified in Christ, and of that fuller revelation which was to be given through the Word of God Himself made flesh. "Behold the days shall come, saith the Lord, and I will make a new covenant with the House of Israel, and with the house of Judah . . . I will give my law in their bowels, and I will write it in their heart, and I will be their God, and they shall be my people . . . For all of them shall know Me, from the least of them even to the greatest, saith the Lord" (Jer. 31, 34). Christ instituted this new covenant, the new testament, that is to say, in His Blood (cfr. I Cor. XI, 25), calling together a people made up of Jew and gentile, making them one, not according to the flesh but in the Spirit. This was to be the new People of God. For those who believe in Christ, who are reborn not from a perishable seed but from an imperishable through the word of the living God (cfr. I Pet. 1, 23), not from the flesh but from water and the Holy Spirit (cfr. Jo. III, 5–6), are finally established as "a chosen race, a royal priesthood, a holy nation, a purchased people . . . you who in times past were not a people, but are now the people of God" (I Pet. II, 9–10).

That messianic people has Christ for its head, "Who was delivered up for ours sins, and rose again for our justification" (Rom. IV, 25), and now, having won a name which is above all names, reigns in glory in heaven. The state of this people is that of the dignity and freedom of the sons of God, in whose hearts the Holy Spirit dwells as in His temple. Its law is the new commandment to love as Christ loved us. Its end is the kingdom of God, which has been begun by God Himself on earth, and which is to be further extended until it is brought to perfection by Him at the end of time, when Christ, our life (cfr. Col. III,

4), shall appear, and "creation itself will be delivered from its slavery
to corruption into the freedom of the glory of the sons of God" (Rom
VIII, 21). So it is that messianic people, although it does not actually
include all men, and at times may look like a small flock, is nonetheless
a lasting and sure seed of unity, hope and salvation for the whole human race. Established by Christ as a communion of life, charity and
truth, it is also used by Him as an instrument for the redemption of all,
and is sent forth into the whole world as the light of the world and the
salt of the earth (cf. Mt. V, 13–16).

Israel according to the flesh, which wandered as an exile in the desert,
was already called the Church of God (cfr. Num. XX, 4; Deut. XXIII
1 sq). So likewise the new Israel which while living in this present age
goes in search of a future and abiding city (cf. Heb. XIII, 14), is called
the Church of Christ. For He has bought it for Himself with His blood
(cf. Acts XX, 28), has filled it with His Spirit and provided it with
those means which befit it as a visible and social union. God gathered
together as one all those who in faith look upon Jesus as the author
of salvation and the source of unity and peace, and established them
as the Church, that for each and all it may be the visible Sacrament of
this saving unity. While it transcends all limits of time and confines of
race, the Church is destined to extend to all regions of the earth and
so enters into the history of mankind. Moving forward through trial
and tribulation, the Church is strengthened by the power of God's
grace, which was promised to her by the Lord, so that in the weakness
of the flesh she may not waver from perfect fidelity, but remain a bride
worthy of her Lord, and moved by the Holy Spirit may never cease to
renew herself, until through the Cross she arrives at the light which
knows no setting.

10. Christ the Lord, High Priest taken from among men (Heb. V,
1–5), made the new people, "a kingdom and priests to God the Father"
(Apoc. I, 6; V, 9–10). The baptized, by regeneration and the anointing
of the Holy Spirit, are consecrated as a spiritual house and a holy
priesthood, in order that through all those works which are those of the
Christian man they may offer spiritual sacrifices and proclaim the power
of Him who has called them out of darkness into His marvelous light
(cf. I Pet. II, 4–10). Therefore all the disciples of Christ, persevering in
prayer and praising God (cf. Acts II, 42, 47), should present themselves
as a living sacrifice, holy and pleasing to God (cf. Rom. XII, 1). Everywhere on earth they must bear witness to Christ and give an answer to
those who seek an account of that hope of eternal life which is in them
(cf. I Pet. III, 15).

Though they differ from one another in essence and not only in
degree, the common priesthood of the faithful and the ministerial or
hierarchical priesthood are nonetheless interrelated: each of them in its
own special way is a participation in the one priesthood of Christ. The
ministerial priest, by the sacred power he enjoys, teaches and rules the

priestly peoples; acting in the person of Christ, he makes present the eucharistic sacrifice, and offers it to God in the name of all the people. But the faithful, in virtue of their royal priesthood, join in the offering of the Eucharist. They likewise exercise that priesthood in receiving the sacraments, in prayer and thanksgiving, in the witness of a holy life, and by self-denial and active charity.

11. It is through the sacraments and the exercise of the virtues that the sacred nature and organic structure of the priestly community is brought into operation. Incorporated in the Church through baptism, the faithful are consecrated by the baptismal character to the worship of the Christian religion; reborn as sons of God they must confess before men the faith which they have received from God through the Church (4). More perfectly bound to the Church by the sacrament of Confirmation, the Holy Spirit endows them with special strength so that they are more strictly obliged to spread and defend the faith, both by word and by deed, as true witnesses of Christ (5). Taking part in the eucharistic sacrifice, which is the fount and apex of the whole Christian life, they offer the Divine Victim to God, and offer themselves along with It. Thus both by reason of the offering and through Holy Communion all act their dual part in this liturgical service not indeed, all in the same way but each in that way which is proper to himself. Strengthened at the holy table by the Body of Christ, they then manifest in a concrete way that unity of the people of God which is suitably signified and wondrously brought about by this most holy sacrament.

Those who approach the sacrament of Penance obtain pardon from the mercy of God for the offense committed against Him and are at the same time reconciled with the Church, which they have wounded by their sins, and which by charity, example, and prayer seeks their conversion. By the sacred anointing of the sick and the prayer of her priests the whole Church commends the sick to the suffering and glorified Lord asking that He may lighten their suffering and save them (cf. Jas. 5, 15–16); she exhorts them, moreover, to contribute to the welfare of the whole people of God by associating themselves freely with the passion and death of Christ (cf. Rom. 8, 17; Col. 1, 24; II Tim. 2, 11–12; I Pet. 4, 13). Those of the faithful who are consecrated by Holy Orders are appointed to feed the Church in Christ's name with the word and the grace of God. Finally, Christian spouses, in virtue of the sacrament of matrimony, whereby they signify and partake of the mystery of that unity and fruitful love which exists between Christ and his Church (cf. Eph. 5, 32), help each other to attain to holiness in their married life and in the rearing and education of their children. By reason of their state and rank in life they have their own special gift among the people of God (cf. 1 Cor. 7, 7). From the wedlock of Christians there comes the family, in which new citizens of human society are born, who by the grace of the Holy Spirit received in baptism are made children of God, thus perpetuating the people of God through the centuries.

The family is, so to speak, the domestic Church. In it parents should, by their word and example, be the first preachers of the faith to their children; they should encourage them in the vocation which is proper to each of them, fostering with special care vocation to a sacred state.

Fortified by so many and such powerful means of salvation, all the faithful, whatever their condition or state, are called by the Lord, each in his own way, to that perfect holiness whereby the Father Himself is perfect.

12. The holy people of God shares also in Christ's prophetic office; it spreads abroad a living witness to Him, especially by means of a life of faith and charity and by offering to God a sacrifice of praise, the tribute of lips which give praise to His name (cf. Heb. 13, 15). The entire body of the faithful, anointed as they are by the Holy One (cf. 1 Jn. 2, 20, 27), cannot err in matters of belief. They manifest this special property by means of the whole peoples' supernatural discernment in matters of faith when "from the bishops down to the last of the lay faithful" (8) they show universal agreement in matters of faith and morals. That discernment in matters of faith is aroused and sustained by the Spirit of truth. It is exercised under the guidance of the sacred teaching authority, in faithful and respectful obedience to which the people of God accepts that which is not just the word of men but truly the word of God (cf. 1 Thess. 2, 13). Through it, the people of God adheres unwaveringly to the faith given once and for all to the saints (cf. Jud. 2), penetrates it more deeply with right thinking, and applies it more fully in its life.

It is not only through the sacraments and the ministries of the Church that the Holy Spirit sanctifies and leads the people of God and enriches it with virtues, but, "allotting his gifts to everyone according as He wills" (1 Cor. 13, 11), He distributes special graces among the faithful of every rank. By these gifts He makes them fit and ready to undertake the various tasks and offices which contribute toward the renewal and building up of the Church, according to the words of the Apostle: "The manifestation of the Spirit is given to everyone for profit" (I Cor. 12, 7). These charisms, whether they be the more outstanding or the more simple and widely diffused, are to be received with thanksgiving and consolation for they are perfectly suited to and useful for the needs of the Church. Extraordinary gifts are not to be sought after, nor are the fruits of apostolic labor to be presumptuously expected from their use; but judgment as to their genuinity and proper use belongs to those who are appointed leaders in the Church, to whose special competence it belongs not indeed to extinguish the Spirit, but to test all things and hold fast to that which is good (cf. 1 Thess. 5, 12, 19, 21).

13. All men are called to belong to the new people of God. Wherefore this people, while remaining one and only one, is to be spread through-

out the whole world and must exist in all ages, so that the decree of God's will may be fulfilled. In the beginning God made human nature one and decreed that all His children, scattered as they were, would finally be gathered together as one (cf. Jo. 11, 52). It was for this purpose that God sent His Son, whom He appointed heir of all things (cf. Heb. 1, 2), that He might be teacher, king and priest of all, the head of the new and universal people of the sons of God. For this too God sent the Spirit of His Son as Lord and Life-giver. He it is who brings together the whole Church and each and every one of those who believe, and who is the well-spring of their unity in the teaching of the apostles and in fellowship, in the breaking of bread and in prayers (cf. Acts 2, 42).

It follows that though there are many nations there is but one people of God, which takes its citizens from every race, making them citizens of a kingdom which is of a heavenly rather than of an earthly nature. All the faithful, scattered though they be throughout the world, are in communion with each other in the Holy Spirit, so that "he who occupies the see of Rome knows those afar as his members" (9). Since the kingdom of Christ is not of this world (cf. Jo. 18, 36) the Church or people of God in establishing that kingdom takes nothing away from the temporal welfare of any people. Rather does it foster and take to itself, insofar as they are good, the ability, riches and customs in which the genius of each people expresses itself. Taking them to itself it purifies, strengthens, elevates and consecrates them. The Church in this is mindful that she must work with and for that King to whom the nations were given for an inheritance (Ps. 71, 10; Is. 9, 4–7; Apoc. 21, 24). This characteristic of universality which adorns the people of God is a gift from the Lord himself. By reason of it, the Catholic Church strives constantly and with due effect to bring all humanity and all its possessions back to its source in Christ, with Him as its head and united in His Spirit.

In virtue of this catholicity each individual part contributes through its special gifts to the good of the other parts and of the whole Church. Through the common sharing of gifts and through the common effort to attain fulness in unity, the whole and each of the parts receive increase. Not only, then, is the people of God made up of different peoples but in its inner structure also it is composed of various ranks. This diversity among its members arises either by reason of their duties, as is the case with those who exercise the sacred ministry for the good of their brethren, or by reason of their condition and state of life, as is the case with those many who enter the religious state and, tending toward holiness by a narrower path, stimulate their brethren by their example. Moreover, within the Church particular Churches hold a rightful place; these Churches retain their own traditions, without in any way opposing the primacy of the Chair of Peter, which presides over the whole assembly of charity and protects legitimate differences, while at the same time assuring that such differences do not hinder unity but rather contribute toward it. Between all the parts of the Church there remains a bond of close communion whereby they share spiritual riches, apostolic workers and temporal resources. For the members of the people of God are called to share these goods in common, and of each of the Churches the words of the apostle hold good: "According to the gift that each has received, administer it to one another as good stewards of the manifold grace of God" (I Pet. 4, 10).

All men are called to be part of this Catholic unity of the people of God which in promoting universal peace presages it. And there belong to or are related to it in various ways, the Catholic faithful, all who believe in Christ, and indeed the whole of mankind, for all men are called by the grace of God to salvation.

14. This Sacred Council wishes to turn its attention firstly to the Catholic faithful. Basing itself upon Sacred Scripture and Tradition, it teaches that the Church, now sojourning on earth as an exile, is necessary for salvation. Christ, present to us in His Body, which is the Church, is the one Mediator and the unique way of salvation. In explicit terms He Himself affirmed the necessity of faith and baptism (cf. Mc. 16, 16; Jo. 3, 5) and thereby affirmed also the necessity of the Church, for through baptism as through a door men enter the Church. Whosoever, therefore, knowing that the Catholic Church was made necessary by Christ, would refuse to enter it or to remain in it, could not be saved.

They are fully incorporated in the society of the Church who, possessing the Spirit of Christ, accept her entire system and all the means of salvation given to her, and are united with her as part of her visible bodily structure and through her with Christ, who rules her through the Supreme Pontiff and the bishops. The bonds which bind men to the Church in a visible way are profession of faith, the sacraments and ecclesiastical government and communion. He is not saved, however, who, though part of the body of the Church, does not persevere in charity. He remains indeed in the bosom of the Church, but, as it were, only in a "bodily" manner and not "in his heart." All the Church's children should remember that their exalted status is to be attributed not to their own merits but to the special grace of Christ. If they fail moreover to respond to that grace in thought, word and deed, not only shall they not be saved but they will be the more severely judged.

Catechumens who, moved by the Holy Spirit, seek with explicit intention to be incorporated into the Church are by that very intention joined with her. With love and solicitude Mother Church already embraces them as her own.

15. The Church recognizes that in many ways she is linked with those who, being baptized, are honored with the name of Christian, though they do not profess the faith in its entirety or do not preserve unity of communion with the successor of Peter. For there are many who honor Sacred Scripture taking it as a norm of belief and a pattern

of life, and who show a true apostolic zeal. They lovingly believe in God the Father Almighty and in Christ, the son of God and Saviour. They are consecrated by baptism, in which they are united with Christ. They also recognize and accept other sacraments within their own Churches or ecclesiastical communities. Many of them rejoice in the episcopate, celebrate the Holy Eucharist and cultivate devotion toward the Virgin Mother of God. They also share with us in prayer and other spiritual benefits. Likewise we can say that in some real way they are joined with us in the Holy Spirit, for to them too He gives His gifts and graces whereby He is operative among them with His sanctifying power. Some indeed He has strengthened to the extent of the shedding of their blood. In all of Christ's disciples the Spirit arouses the desire to be peacefully united, in the manner determined by Christ, as one flock under one shepherd, and He prompts them to pursue this end. Mother Church never ceases to pray, hope and work that this may come about. She exhorts her children to purification and renewal so that the sign of Christ may shine more brightly over the face of the earth.

16. Finally, those who have not yet received the Gospel are related in various ways to the people of God. In the first place we must recall the people to whom the testament and the promises were given and from whom Christ was born according to the flesh (cf. Rom. 9, 4–5). On account of their fathers this people remains most dear to God, for God does not repent of the gifts He makes nor of the calls He issues (cf. Rom. 11, 28–29). But the plan of salvation also includes those who acknowledge the Creator. In the first place amongst these there are the Musulmans, who professing to hold the faith of Abraham, along with us adore the one and merciful God, who on the last day will judge mankind. Nor is God far distant from those who in shadows and images seek the unknown God, for it is He who gives to all men life and breath and all things (cf. Acts 17, 25–28), and as Saviour wills that all men be saved (cf. I Tim. 2, 4). Those also can attain to salvation who through no fault of their own do not know the Gospel of Christ of His Church, yet sincerely seek God and moved by grace strive by their deeds to do His will as it is known to them through the dictates of conscience. Nor does Divine Providence deny the helps necessary for salvation to those who, without blame on their part, have not yet arrived at an explicit knowledge of God and with His grace strive to live a good life. Whatever good or truth is found amongst them is looked upon by the Church as a preparation for the Gospel. She knows that it is given by Him who enlightens all men so that they may finally have life. But often men, deceived by the Evil One, have become fantastic in their notions and have exchanged the truth of God for a lie, serving the creature rather than the Creator. Or some there are who, living and dying in this world without God, are left finally in a state of hopelessness. Wherefore to promote the glory of God and procure the salvation of all the aforementioned, and mindful of the command of the Lord, "Preach the Gospel

to every creature" (Mk. 16, 16), the Church fosters the mission with care and attention.

17. As the Son was sent by the Father (cf. Jo. 20, 21), so He too sent the Apostles, saying: "Go, therefore, make disciples of all nations, baptizing them in the name of the Father and of the Son and of the Holy Spirit, teaching them to observe all things whatsoever I have commanded you. And behold I am with you all days even to the consummation of the world" (Mt. 21, 18–20). The Church has received this solemn mandate of Christ to proclaim the saving truth from the apostles and must carry it out to the very ends of the earth (cf. Acts 1, 8). Wherefore she makes the words of the Apostle her own: "Woe to me, if I do not preach the Gospel" (I Cor. 9, 16), and continues unceasingly to send heralds of the Gospel until such time as the infant churches are fully established and can themselves continue the work of evangelizing. For the Church is compelled by the Holy Spirit to do her part that God's plan may be fully realized, whereby He has constituted Christ as the source of salvation for the whole world. By the proclamation of the Gospel she prepares her hearers to receive and profess the faith. She gives them the dispositions necessary for baptism, snatches them from the slavery of error and of idols and incorporates them in Christ so that through charity they may grow up into full maturity in Christ. Through her work, whatever good is in the minds and hearts of men, whatever good lies latent in the religious practices and cultures of diverse peoples, is not only saved from destruction but is also cleansed, raised up and perfected unto the glory of God, the confusion of the devil and the happiness of man. The obligation of spreading the faith is imposed on every disciple of Christ, according to his state. Although, however, all the faithful can baptize, the priest alone can complete the building up of the Body in the eucharistic sacrifice. Thus are fulfilled the words of God, spoken through His prophet: "From the rising of the sun until the going down thereof my name is great among the gentiles, and in every place a clean oblation is sacrificed and offered up in my name" (Mal. 1, 11). In this way the Church both prays and labors in order that the entire world may become the People of God, the Body of the Lord and the Temple of the Holy Spirit, and that in Christ, the Head of all, all honor and glory may be rendered to the Creator and Father of the Universe.

CHAPTER III
The Hierarchical Structure of the Church: The Episcopate

18. For the nurturing and constant growth of the People of God, Christ the Lord instituted in His Church a variety of ministries, which work for the good of the whole body. For those ministers, who are endowed with sacred power, serve their brethren, so that all who are of the People of God, and therefore enjoy a true Christian dignity, work-

ing toward a common goal freely and in an orderly way, may arrive at salvation.

This Sacred Council, following closely in the footsteps of the First Vatican Council, with that Council teaches and declares that Jesus Christ, the eternal Shepherd, established His holy Church, having sent forth the apostles as He himself had been sent by the Father (Jn. 20, 21); and He willed that their successors, namely the bishops, should be shepherds in His Church even to the consummation of the world. And in order that the episcopate itself might be one and undivided, He placed Blessed Peter over the other apostles, and instituted in him a permanent and visible source and foundation of unity of faith and communion. And all this teaching about the institution, the perpetuity, the meaning and reason for the sacred primacy of the Roman Pontiff and of his infallible magisterium, this sacred council again proposes to be firmly believed by all the faithful. Continuing in that same undertaking, this council is resolved to declare and proclaim before all men the doctrine concerning bishops, the successors of the apostles, who together with the successor of Peter, the Vicar of Christ, the visible Head of the whole Church, govern the house of the living God.

19. The Lord Jesus, after praying to the Father, calling to Himself those whom He desired, appointed 12 to be with Him, and whom He would send to preach the Kingdom of God (Mk. 3, 13–19; Mt. 10, 1–42); and these apostles (Lk. 6, 13) He formed after the manner of a college or a stable group, over which He placed Peter chosen from among them. He sent them first to the children of Israel and then to all nations (Rom. 1, 16), so that as sharers in His power they might make all peoples His disciples, and sanctify and govern them (Mt. 26, 16–20; Mk. 16, 15; Lk. 24, 45–48; Jn. 20, 21–23), and thus spread His Church, and by ministering to it under the guidance of the Lord, direct it all days even to the consummation of the world (Mt. 28, 20). And in this mission they were fully confirmed on the day of Pentecost (Acts 2, 1–26) in accordance with the Lord's promise: "You shall receive power when the Holy Spirit comes upon you, and you shall be witnesses for me in Jerusalem, and in all Judea and in Samaria, and even to the very ends of the earth" (Acts 1, 8). And the apostles, by preaching the Gospel everywhere (Mk. 16, 20), and it being accepted by their hearers under the influence of the Holy Spirit, gather together the universal Church, which the Lord established on the Apostles and built upon blessed Peter, their chief, Christ Jesus Himself being the supreme cornerstone (Apoc. 21, 14; Mt. 16, 18; Eph. 2, 20).

20. That divine mission, entrusted by Christ to the apostles, will last until the end of the world (Mt. 28, 20), since the Gospel they are to teach is for all time the source of all life for the Church. And for this reason the apostles, appointed as rulers in this society, took care to appoint successors.

For they not only had helpers in their ministry, but also, in order that the mission assigned to them might continue after their death, they passed on to their immediate cooperators, as it were, in the form of a testament, the duty of confirming and finishing the work begun by themselves, recommending to them that they attend to the whole flock in which the Holy Spirit placed them to shepherd the Church of God (Acts 20, 28). They therefore appointed such men, and gave them the order that, when they should have died, other approved men would take up their ministry. Among those various ministries which, according to tradition, were exercised in the Church from the earliest times, the chief place belongs to the office of those who, appointed to the episcopate, by a succession running from the beginning, are passers-on of the apostolic seed. Thus, as St. Irenaeus testifies, through those who were appointed bishops by the apostle, and through their successors down to our own time, the apostolic tradition is manifested and preserved.

Bishops, therefore, with their helpers, the priests and deacons, have taken up the service of the community, presiding in place of God over the flock, whose shepherds they are, as teachers for doctrine, priests for sacred worship, and ministers for governing. And just as the office granted individually to Peter, the first among the Apostles, is permanent and is to be transmitted to his successors, so also the Apostles' office of nurturing the Church is permanent, and is to be exercised without interruption by the sacred order of bishops. Therefore, the sacred council teaches that bishops by divine institution have succeeded to the place of the apostles, as shepherds of the Church, and he who hears them, hears Christ, and he who rejects them, rejects Christ and Him who sent Christ (cf. Lk. 10, 16).

21. In the bishops, therefore, for whom priests are assistants, Our Lord Jesus Christ, the Supreme High Priest, is present in the midst of those who believe. For sitting at the right hand of God the Father, He is not absent from the gathering of His high priests, but above all through their excellent service He is preaching the word of God to all nations, and constantly administering the sacraments of faith to those who believe; by their paternal functioning He incorporates new members in His body by a heavenly regeneration, and finally by their wisdom and prudence He directs and guides the People of the New Testament in their pilgrimage toward eternal happiness. These pastors, chosen to shepherd the Lord's flock of the elect, are servants of Christ and stewards of the mysteries of God (cf. I Cor. 4, 1), to whom has been assigned the bearing of witness to the Gospel of the grace of God (cf. Rom. 15, 16; Acts 20, 24), and the ministration of the Spirit and of justice in glory (cf. II Cor. 3, 8–9).

For the discharging of such great duties, the apostles were enriched by Christ with a special outpouring of the Holy Spirit coming upon them (cf. Acts 1, 8; 2, 4; Jn. 20, 23), and they passed on this spiritual gift to their helpers by the imposition of hands (cf. I Tim. 4, 14; II Tim. 1,

6–7), and it has been transmitted down to us in episcopal consecration. And the sacred council teaches that by episcopal consecration the fulness of the sacrament of Orders is conferred, that fulness of power, namely, which both in the Church's liturgical practice and in the language of the Fathers of the Church is called the high priesthood, the supreme power of the sacred ministry. But episcopal consecration, together with the office of sanctifying, also confers the office of teaching and of governing, which, however, of its very nature, can be exercised only in hierarchical communion with the head and the members of the college. For from the tradition, which is expressed especially in liturgical rites and in the practice of both the Church of the East and of the West, it is clear that, by means of the imposition of hands and the words of consecration, the grace of the Holy Spirit is so conferred, and the sacred character so impressed, that bishops in an eminent and visible way sustain the roles of Christ Himself as Teacher, Shepherd and High Priest, and that they act in His person. Therefore it pertains to the bishops to admit newly elected members into the episcopal body by means of the sacrament of Orders.

22. Just as in the Gospel, the Lord so disposing, St. Peter and the other apostles constitute one apostolic college, so in a similar way the Roman Pontiff, the successor of Peter, and the bishops, the successors of the apostles, are joined together. Indeed, the very ancient practice whereby bishops duly established in all parts of the world were in communion with one another and with the Bishop of Rome in a bond of unity, charity and peace, and also the councils assembled together, in which more profound matters, after prudent deliberation on the opinion of the many, were settled in common, both of these factors are already an indication of the collegiate character and aspect of the episcopal order; and the ecumenical councils held in the course of centuries are also manifest proof of that same character. And it is intimated also in the practice, introduced in ancient times, of summoning several bishops to take part in the elevation of the newly elected to the ministry of the high priesthood. Hence, one is constituted a member of the episcopal body in virtue of sacramental consecration and hierarchical communion with the head and members of the body.

But the college or body of bishops has no authority unless it is understood together with the Roman pontiff, the successor of Peter as its head. The pope's power of primacy over all, both pastors and faithful, remains whole and intact. In virtue of his office, that is as Vicar of Christ and pastor of the whole Church, the Roman pontiff has full, supreme and universal power over the Church. And he is always free to exercise this power. The order of bishops, which succeeds to the college of apostles and gives this apostolic body continued existence, is also the subject of supreme and full power over the universal Church, provided we understand this body together with its head the Roman pontiff. For Our Lord placed Simon alone as the rock and the bearer of the keys of the Church (Mt. 16, 18–19) and made him shepherd of the whole flock (Jn. 21, 15); it is evident, however, that the power of binding and loosing, which was given to Peter (Mt. 16, 19), was granted also to the college of apostles, joined with their head (Mt. 18, 18). This college insofar as it is composed of many, expresses the variety and universality of the People of God, but insofar as it is assembled under one head, it expresses the unity of the flock of Christ. In it, the bishops, faithfully recognizing the primacy and pre-eminence of their head, exercise their own authority for the good of their own faithful, and indeed of the whole Church, which this college enjoys, is exercised in a solemn way in an ecumenical council. A council is never ecumenical unless it is confirmed or at least accepted as such by the successor of Peter; and it is a prerogative of the Roman pontiff to convoke these councils, to preside over them and to confirm them. This same collegiate power can be exercised together with the pope by the bishops living in all parts of the world, provided that the head of the college calls them to collegiate action, or at least approves of or freely accepts the united action of the scattered bishops, so that it is thereby made a collegiate act.

23. This collegial union is apparent also in the mutual relations of the individual bishops with particular churches and with the universal Church. The Roman pontiff, as the successor of Peter, is the perpetual and visible principle and foundation of unity of both the bishops and of the faithful. The individual bishops, however, are the visible principle and foundation of unity in their particular churches, fashioned after the model of the universal Church, in and from which churches comes into being the one and only Catholic Church. For this reason the individual bishops represent each his own church, but all of them together and with the Pope represent the entire Church in the bond of peace, love and unity.

The individual bishops, who are placed in charge of particular churches, exercise their pastoral government over the portion of the People of God committed to their care, and not over other churches nor over the universal Church. But each of them, as a member of the espiscopal college and legitimate successor of the apostles, is obliged by Christ's institution and command to be solicitous for the whole Church, and this solicitude, though it is not exercised by an act of jurisdiction, contributes greatly to the advantage of the universal Church. For it is the duty of all bishops to promote and to safeguard the unity of faith and the discipline common to the whole Church, to instruct the faithful in love for the whole mystical body of Christ, especially for its poor and sorrowing members and for those who are suffering persecution for justice's sake (Mt. 1, 10), and finally to promote every activity that is of interest to the whole Church, especially that the faith may take increase and the light of full truth appear to all men. And this also is important, that by governing well their own church as a portion of the universal

Church, they themselves are effectively contributing to the welfare of the whole Mystical Body, which is also the body of the churches.

The task of proclaiming the Gospel everywhere on earth pertains to the body of pastors, to all of whom in common Christ gave His command, thereby imposing upon them a common duty, as Pope Celestine in his time recommended to the Fathers of the Council of Ephesus. From this it follows that the individual bishops, insofar as their own discharge of their duty permits, are obliged to enter into a community of work among themselves and with the successor of Peter, upon whom was imposed in a special way the great duty of spreading the Christian name. With all their energy, therefore, they must supply to the missions both workers for the harvest and also spiritual and material aid, both directly and on their own account, as well as by arousing the ardent cooperation of the faithful. And finally, the bishops, in a universal fellowship of charity, should gladly extend their fraternal aid to other churches, especially to neighboring and more needy dioceses in accordance with the venerable example of antiquity.

By divine Providence it has come about that various churches, established in various places by the apostles and their successors, have in the course of time coalesced into several groups, organically united, which, preserving the unity of faith and the unique divine constitution of the universal Church, enjoy their own discipline, their own liturgical usage, and their own theological and spiritual heritage. Some of these churches, notably the ancient patriarchal churches, as parent-stocks of the Faith, so to speak, have begotten others as daughter churches, with which they are connected down to our own time by a close bond of charity in their rights and duties. This variety of local churches with one common aspiration is splendid evidence of the catholicity of the undivided Church. In like manner the episcopal bodies of today are in a position to render a manifold and fruitful assistance, so that this collegiate feeling may be put into practical application.

24. Bishops, as successors of the apostles, receive from the Lord, to whom was given all power in heaven and on earth, the mission to teach all nations and to preach the Gospel to every creature, so that all men may attain to salvation by faith, baptism and the fulfilment of the commandments (cf. Mt. 28, 18; Mk. 16, 15–16; Acts 26, 17 sq.). To fulfill this mission, Christ the Lord promised the Holy Spirit to the Apostles, and on Pentecost day sent the Spirit from heaven, by whose power they would be witnesses to Him before the nations and peoples and kings even to the ends of the earth (Acts 1, 8; 2, 1 ff; 9, 15). And that duty, which the Lord committed to the Shepherds of His people, is a true service, which in sacred literature is significantly called "diakonia" or ministry (Acts 1, 17, 25; 21, 10; Rom. 11, 13; I Tim. 1, 12).

The canonical mission of bishops can come about by legitimate customs that have not been revoked by the supreme and universal authority of the Church, or by laws made or recognized by that same authority, or directly through the successor of Peter himself; and if the latter refuses or denies apostolic communion, such bishops cannot assume any office.

25. Among the principal duties of bishops the preaching of the Gospel occupies an eminent place. For bishops are preachers of the faith, who lead new disciples to Christ, and they are authentic teachers, that is, teachers endowed with the authority of Christ, who preach to the people committed to them the faith they must believe and put into practice, and by the light of the Holy Spirit illustrate that faith. They bring forth from the treasury of Revelation new things and old (Mt. 13, 52), making it bear fruit and vigilantly warding off any errors that threaten their flock (II Tim. 4, 1–4). Bishops, teaching in communion with the Roman pontiff, are to be respected by all as witnesses to divine and Catholic truth. In matters of faith and morals, the bishops speak in the name of Christ and the faithful are to accept their teaching and adhere to it with a religious assent. This religious submission of mind and will must be shown in a special way to the authentic magisterium of the Roman pontiff, even when he is not speaking *ex cathedra;* that is, it must be shown in such a way that his supreme magisterium is acknowledged with reverence, the judgments made by him are sincerely adhered to, according to his manifest mind and will. His mind and will in the matter may be known either from the character of the documents, from his frequent repetition of the same doctrine, or from his manner of speaking.

Although the individual bishops do not enjoy the prerogative of infallibility, they nevertheless proclaim Christ's doctrine infallibly whenever, even though dispersed through the world, but still maintaining the bond of communion among themselves and with the successor of Peter, and authentically teaching matters of faith and morals, they are in agreement on one position as definitively to be held. This is even more clearly verified when, gathered together in an ecumenical council, they are teachers and judges of faith and morals for the universal Church, whose definitions must be adhered to with the submission of faith.

And this infallibility with which the Divine Redeemer willed His Church to be endowed in defining doctrine of faith and morals, extends as far as the deposit of Revelation extends, which must be religiously guarded and faithfully expounded. And this is the infallibility which the Roman pontiff, the head of the college of bishops, enjoys in virtue of his office, when, as the supreme shepherd and teacher of all the faithful, who confirms his brethren in their faith (cf. Lk. 22, 32), by a definitive act he proclaims a doctrine of faith or morals. And therefore his definitions, of themselves, and not from the consent of the Church, are justly styled irreformable, since they are pronounced with the assistance of the Holy Spirit, promised to him in blessed Peter, and therefore they need no approval of others, nor do they allow an appeal to any other judgment. For then the Roman pontiff is not pronouncing judgment as a private person, but as the supreme teacher of the universal Church, in whom the charism of infallibility of the Church itself is individually present, he is expounding or defending a doctrine of Catholic faith. The infallibility promised to the Church resides also in the Body of Bishops, when that body exercises the supreme magisterium with the successor of Peter. To these definitions the assent of the Church can never be wanting, on account of the activity of that same Holy Spirit, by which the whole flock of Christ is preserved and progresses in unity of faith.

But when either the Roman pontiff or the Body of Bishops together with him defines a judgment, they pronounce it in accordance with Revelation itself, which all are obliged to abide by and be in conformity with, that is, the Revelation which as written or orally handed down is transmitted in its entirety through the legitimate succession of bishops and especially in care of the Roman pontiff himself, and which under the guiding light of the Spirit of truth is religiously preserved and faithfully expounded in the Church. The Roman pontiff and the bishops, in view of their office and the importance of the matter, by fitting means diligently strive to inquire properly into that revelation and to give apt expression to its contents; but a new public revelation they do not accept as pertaining to the divine deposit of faith.

26. A bishop marked with the fulness of the sacrament of Orders, is "the steward of the grace of the supreme priesthood," especially in the Eucharist, which he offers or causes to be offered, and by which the Church continually lives and grows. This Church of Christ is truly present in all legitimate local congregations of the faithful which, united with their pastors, are themselves called churches in the New Testament. For in their locality these are the new People called by God, in the Holy Spirit and in much fulness (cf. I Thess. 1, 5). In them the faithful are gathered together by the preaching of the Gospel of Christ, and the mystery of the Lord's Supper is celebrated, that by the food and blood of the Lord's body the whole brotherhood may be joined together. In any community of the altar, under the sacred ministry of the bishop, there is exhibited a symbol of that charity and "unity of the mystical Body, without which there can be no salvation." In these communities, though frequently small and poor, or living in the Diaspora, Christ is present, and in virtue of His presence there is brought together one, holy, catholic and apostolic Church. For "the partaking of the body and blood of Christ does nothing other than make us be transformed into that which we consume" (St. Leo Gt: Serm. 63, 7).

Every legitimate celebration of the Eucharist is regulated by the bishop, to whom is committed the office of offering the worship of Christian religion to the Divine Majesty and of administering it in accordance with the Lord's commandments and the Church's laws, as further defined by his particular judgment for his diocese.

Bishops thus, by praying and laboring for the people, make out-pourings in many ways and in great abundance from the fulness of Christ's holiness. By the ministry of the word they communicate God's power to those who believe unto salvation (cf. Rom. 1, 16), and through the sacraments, the regular and fruitful distribution of which they regulate by their authority, they sanctify the faithful. They direct the conferring of baptism, by which a sharing in the kingly priesthood of Christ is granted. They are the original ministers of confirmation, dis-pensers of sacred Orders and the moderators of penitential discipline, and they earnestly exhort and instruct their people to carry out with faith and reverence their part in the liturgy and especially in the holy sacrifice of the Mass. And lastly, by the example of their way of life they must be an influence for good to those over whom they preside, refraining from all evil and, as far as they are able with God's help, exchanging evil for good, so that together with the flock committed to their care they may arrive at eternal life.

Bishops, as vicars and ambassadors of Christ, govern the particular churches entrusted to them by their counsel, exhortations, example, and even by their authority and sacred power, which indeed they use only for the edification of their flock in truth and holiness, remembering that he who is greater should become as the lesser and he who is the chief become as the servant (cf. Lk. 22, 26–27). This power, which they personally exercise in Christ's name, is proper, ordinary and immediate, although its exercise is ultimately regulated by the supreme authority of the Church, and can be circumscribed by certain limits, for the advantage of the Church or of the faithful. In virtue of this power, bishops have the sacred right and the duty before the Lord to make laws for their subjects, to pass judgment on them and to moderate everything pertaining to the ordering of worship and the apostolate.

The pastoral office or the habitual and daily care of their sheep is entrusted to them completely; nor are they to be regarded as vicars of the Roman pontiffs, for they exercise an authority that is proper to them, and are quite correctly called "prelates," heads of the people whom they govern. Their power, therefore, is not destroyed by the supreme and universal power, but on the contrary it is affirmed, strengthened and vindicated by it, since the Holy Spirit unfailingly preserves the form of government established by Christ the Lord in His Church.

A bishop, since he is sent by the Father to govern his family, must keep before his eyes the example of the Good Shepherd, who came not to be ministered unto but to minister (Mt. 20, 28; Mk. 10, 45), and to lay down his life for his sheep (Jn. 10, 11). Being taken from among men, and himself beset with weakness, he is able to have compassion on the ignorant and erring (Heb. 5, 1–2). Let him not refuse to listen to his subjects, whom he cherishes as his true sons and exhorts to cooperate readily with him. As having one day to render an account for their souls, he takes care of them by his prayer, preaching, and all the works of charity, and not only of them but also of those who are not yet of the one flock, who also are commended to him in the Lord. Since, like Paul the Apostle, he is debtor to all men, let him be ready to preach the Gospel to all, and to urge his faithful to apostolic and missionary activity. But the faithful must cling to their bishop, as the Church does to Christ, and Jesus Christ to the Father, so that all may be of one mind through unity, and abound to the glory of God (2 Cor. 4, 15).

27. Christ, whom the Father has sanctified and sent into the world, has through His apostles, made their successors the bishops partakers of His consecration and His mission. They have legitimately handed on to different individuals in the Church various degrees of participation in this ministry. Thus the divinely established ecclesiastical ministry is exercised on different levels by those who from antiquity have been called bishops, priests and deacons. Priests, although they do not possess the highest degree of the priesthood, and although they are dependent on the bishops in the exercise of their power, nevertheless they are united with the bishops in sacerdotal dignity. By the power of the sacrament of Orders, in the image of Christ the eternal high Priest, they are consecrated to preach the Gospel and shepherd the faithful and to celebrate divine worship, so that they are true priests of the New Testament. Partakers of the function of Christ the sole Mediator, on their level of ministry, they announce the divine word to all. They exercise this function of Christ especially in the Eucharist liturgy or synaxis wherein, acting in the person of Christ and proclaiming His mystery, they join the offerings of the faithful to the sacrifice of their Head and, until the coming of the Lord, they represent and apply in the sacrifice of the Mass the one sacrifice of the New Testament, namely the sacrifice of Christ offering Himself once and for all to His Father as a spotless victim. For the sick and sinners among the faithful, they exercise the ministry of alleviation and reconciliation and they present the needs and the prayers of the faithful to God the Father (Heb. 5, 1–4). Exercising within the limits of their authority the function of Christ as Shepherd and Head, they gather together God's family as a brotherhood all of one mind, and lead them in the Spirit, through Christ, to God the Father. In the midst of the flock they adore Him in spirit and in truth (Jo. 4, 24). Finally, they labor in word and doctrine, believing what they have believed, and putting in practice in their own lives what they have taught.

28. Priests, prudent cooperators with the episcopal order, its aid and instrument, called to serve the people of God, constitute one priesthood with their bishop although bound by a diversity of duties. Associated with their bishop in a spirit of trust and generosity, they make him present in a certain sense in the individual local congregations, and take upon themselves, as far as they are able, his duties and the burden of

his care, and discharge them with a daily interest. And as they sanctify and govern under the bishop's authority, that part of the Lord's flock entrusted to them, they make the universal Church visible in their own locality and bring an efficacious assistance to the building up of the whole body of Christ (Eph. 4, 12). Intent always upon the welfare of God's children, they must strive to lend their effort to the pastoral work of the whole diocese, and even of the entire Church. On account of this sharing in their priesthood and mission, let priests sincerely look upon the bishop as their father and reverently obey him. And let the bishop regard his priests as his co-workers and as sons and friends, just as Christ called His disciples now not servants but friends (Jn. 15, 15). All priests, both diocesan and religious, by reason of Orders and ministry, fit into this body of bishops and priests, and serve the good of the whole Church according to their vocation and the grace given to them.

In virtue of their common sacred ordination and mission, all priests are bound together in intimate brotherhood, which naturally and freely manifests itself in mutual aid, spiritual as well as material, pastoral as well as personal, in their meetings and in communion of life, of labor and charity.

Let them, as fathers in Christ, take care of the faithful whom they have begotten by baptism and their teaching (1 Cor. 4, 15; 1 Pet. 1, 23). Becoming from the heart a pattern of the flock (1 Pet. 5, 3), let them so lead and serve their local community that it may worthily be called by that name, by which the one and entire people of God is signed, namely, the Church of God (1 Cor. 1, 2; 2 Cor. 1, 1). Let them remember that by their daily life and interests they are showing the face of a truly sacerdotal and pastoral ministry to the faithful and the infidel, to Catholics and non-Catholics, and that to all they bear witness to the truth and life, and as good shepherds go after those also (Lk. 15, 4–7), who though baptized in the Catholic Church have fallen away from the use of the sacraments, or even from the faith.

Because the human race today is joining more and more into a civic, economic and social unity, it is that much the more necessary that priests, by combined effort and aid, under the leadership of the bishops and the Supreme Pontiff, wipe out every kind of separateness, so that the whole human race may be brought into the unity of the family of God.

29. At a lower level of the hierarchy are deacons, upon whom hands are imposed "not unto the priesthood, but unto a ministry of service." For strengthened by sacramental grace, in communion with the bishop and his group of priests they serve in the diaconate of the liturgy, of the word, and of charity to the people of God. It is the duty of the deacon, according as it shall have been assigned to him by competent authority, to administer baptism solemnly, to be custodian and dispenser of the Eucharist, to assist at and bless marriages in the name of the

Church, to bring Viaticum to the dying, to read the Sacred Scripture to the faithful, to administer sacramentals, to officiate at funeral and burial services. Dedicated to duties of charity and of administration, let deacons be mindful of the admonition of Blessed Polycarp: "Be merciful, diligent, walking according to the truth of the Lord, who became the servant of all."

Since these duties, so very necessary to the life of the Church, can be fulfilled only with difficulty in many regions in accordance with the discipline of the Latin Church as it exists today, the diaconate can in the future be restored as a proper and permanent rank of the hierarchy. It pertains to the competent territorial bodies of bishops, of one kind or another, with the approval of the Supreme Pontiff, to decide whether and where it is opportune for such deacons to be established for the care of souls. With the consent of the Roman Pontiff, this diaconate can, in the future, be conferred upon men of more mature age, even upon those living in the married state. It may also be conferred upon suitable young men, for whom the law of celibacy must remain intact.

CHAPTER IV
The Laity

30. Having set forth the functions of the hierarchy, the Sacred Council gladly turns its attention to the state of those faithful called the laity. Everything that has been said above concerning the People of God is intended for the laity, religious and clergy alike. But there are certain things which pertain in a special way to the laity, both men and women, by reason of their condition and mission. Due to the special circumstances of our time the foundations of this doctrine must be more thoroughly examined. For their pastors know how much the laity contribute to the welfare of the entire Church. They also know that they were not ordained by Christ to take upon themselves alone the entire salvific mission of the Church toward the world. On the contrary they understand that it is their noble duty to shepherd the faithful and to recognize their ministries and charisms, so that all according to their proper roles may cooperate in this common undertaking with one mind. For we must all "practice the truth in love, and so grow up in all things in Him who is head, Christ. For from Him the whole body, being closely joined and knit together through every joint of the system, according to the functioning in due measure of each single part, derives its increase to the building up of itself in love" (Eph. 4:15–16).

31. The term laity is here understood to mean all the faithful except those in holy orders and those in the state of religious life specially approved by the Church. These faithful are by baptism made one body with Christ and are constituted among the People of God; they are in their own way made sharers in the priestly, prophetical and kingly

functions of Christ; and they carry out for their own part the missions of the whole Christian people in the Church and in the world.

What specifically characterizes the laity is their secular nature. It is true that those in holy orders can at times be engaged in secular activities, and even have a secular profession. But they are by reason of their particular vocation especially and professedly ordained to the sacred ministry. Similarly, by their state in life, religious give splendid and striking testimony that the world cannot be transformed and offered to God without the spirit of the beatitudes. But the laity, by their very vocation, seek the kingdom of God by engaging in temporal affairs and by ordering them according to the plan of God. They live in the world, that is, in each and in all of the secular professions and occupations. They live in the ordinary circumstances of family and social life, from which the very web of their existence is woven. They are called there by God that by exercising their proper function and led by the spirit of the Gospel they may work for the sanctification of the world from within as a leaven. In this way they may make Christ known to others, especially by the testimony of a life resplendent in faith, hope and charity. Therefore, since they are tightly bound up in all types of temporal affairs it is their special task to order and to throw light upon these affairs in such a way that they may come into being and then continually increase according to Christ to the praise of the Creator and the Redeemer.

32. By divine institution Holy Church is ordered and governed with a wonderful diversity. "For just as in one body we have many members, yet all the members have not the same function, so we, the many are one body in Christ, but severally members one of another" (Rom. 12: 4-5). Therefore, the chosen People of God is one: "one Lord, one faith, one baptism" (Eph. 4:5); sharing a common dignity as members from their regeneration in Christ; having the same filial grace and the same vocation to perfection; possessing in common one salvation, one hope and one undivided charity. There is, therefore, in Christ and in the Church no inequality on the basis of race or nationality, social condition or sex, because "there is neither Jew nor Greek: there is neither bond nor free: there is neither male nor female. For you are all 'one' in Christ Jesus" (Gal. 3:28; cf. Col. 3:11).

If therefore in the Church everyone does not proceed by the same path, nevertheless all are called to sanctity and have received an equal privilege of faith through the justice of God (cf. 2 Pt. 1:1). And if by the will of Christ some are made teachers, pastors and dispensers of mysteries on behalf of others, yet all share a true equality with regard to the dignity and to the activity common to all the faithful for the building up of the Body of Christ. For the distinction which the Lord made between sacred ministers and the rest of the People of God bears within it a certain union, since pastors and the other faithful are bound to each other by a mutual need. Pastors of the Church, following the example of the Lord, should minister to one another and to the other faithful. These in their turn should enthusiastically lend their joint assistance to their pastors and teachers. Thus in their diversity all bear witness to the wonderful unity in the Body of Christ. This very diversity of graces, ministries and works gathers the children of God into one, because "all these things are the work of one and the same Spirit" (1 Cor. 12:11).

Therefore, from divine choice the laity have Christ for their brother, who though He is the Lord of all, came not to be served but to serve (cf. Mt. 20:28). They also have for their brothers those in the sacred ministry who by teaching, by sanctifying and by ruling with the authority of Christ may be fulfilled by all. St. Augustine puts this very beautifully when he says: "What I am for you terrifies me; what I am with you consoles me. For you I am a bishop; but with you I am a Christian. The former is a duty; the latter a grace. The former is a danger; the latter, salvation."

33. The laity are gathered together in the People of God and make up the Body of Christ under one head. Whoever they are they are called upon, as living members, to expend all their energy for the growth of the Church and its continuous sanctification, since this very energy is a gift of the Creator and a blessing of the Redeemer.

The lay apostolate, however, is a participation in the salvific mission of the Church itself. Through their Baptism and Confirmation all are commissioned to that apostolate by the Lord Himself. However, by the Sacraments, especially Holy Eucharist, that charity toward God and man which is the soul of the apostolate is communicated and nourished. Now the laity are called in a special way to make the Church present and operative in those places and circumstances where only through them can it become the salt of the earth. Thus every layman, in virtue of the very gifts bestowed upon him, is at the same time a witness and a living instrument of the mission of the Church itself "according to the measure of Christ's bestowal" (Eph. 4:7).

Besides this apostolate which certainly pertains to all Christians, the laity can also be called in various ways to a more direct form of co-operation in the apostolate of the Hierarchy. This was the way certain men and women assisted Paul the Apostle in the Gospel, laboring much in the Lord (cf. Phil. 4:3; Rom. 16:3 ff). Further, they have the capacity to assume from the Hierarchy certain ecclesiastical functions, which are to be performed for a spiritual purpose.

Upon all the laity, therefore, rests the noble duty of working to extend the divine plan of salvation to all men of each epoch and in every land. Consequently, may every opportunity be given them so that, according to their abilities and the needs of the times, they may zealously participate in the saving work of the Church.

34. The supreme and eternal Priest, Christ Jesus, since He wills to continue His witness and service also through the laity, vivifies them

in this Spirit and increasingly urges them on to every good and perfect work.

For besides intimately linking them to His life and His mission, He also gives them a sharing in His priestly function of offering spiritual worship for the glory of God and the salvation of men. For this reason the laity, dedicated to Christ and anointed by the Holy Spirit, are marvelously called and wonderfully prepared so that ever more abundant fruits of the Spirit may be produced in them. For all their works, prayers and apostolic endeavors, their ordinary married and family life, their daily occupations, their physical and mental relaxation, if carried out in the Spirit, and even the hardships of life, if patiently borne— all these become "spiritual sacrifices acceptable to God through Jesus Christ" (1 Pet. 2:5). Together with the offering of the Lord's body, they are most fittingly offered in the celebration of the Eucharist. Thus, as those everywhere who adore in holy activity, the laity consecrate the world itself to God.

35. Christ the great Prophet, who proclaimed the Kingdom of His Father both by the testimony of His life and the power of His words, continually fulfills His prophetic office until the complete manifestation of glory. He does this not only through the hierarchy who teach in His name and with His authority, but also through the laity whom He made His witnesses and to whom He gave an understanding of the faith (sensu fidei) and an attractiveness in speech (cf. Acts, ii, 17–18; Apocalypse, 10) so that the power of the Gospel might shine forth in their daily social and family life. They conduct themselves as children of the promise, and thus strong in faith and in hope they make the most of the present (cf. Ephesians, v, 16; Colossians, iv, 5), and with patience await the glory that is to come (cf. Romans, viii, 25). Let them not, then, hide this hope in the depths of their hearts, but even in the program of their secular life let them express it by a continual conversion and by wrestling "against the world rulers of this darkness, against the spiritual forces of wickedness" (Ephesians, vi, 12).

Just as the sacraments of the new law, by which the life and the apostolate of the faithful are nourished, prefigure a new heaven and a new earth (cf. Apocalypse, xxi, 1), so too the laity go forth as powerful proclaimers of a faith in things to be hoped for (cf. Hebrews, xi, 1), when they courageously join to their profession of faith a life springing from faith. This evangelization, that is this announcing of Christ by a living testimony as well as by the spoken word, takes on a specific quality and a special force in that it is carried out in the ordinary surroundings of the world.

In connection with the prophetic function, that state of life which is sanctified by a special sacrament is obviously of great importance, namely, married and family life. For where Christianity pervades the entire mode of family life, and gradually transforms it, one will find there both the practice and an excellent school of the lay apostolate.

In such a home husbands and wives find their proper vocation in being witnesses of the faith and love of Christ to one another and to their children. The Christian family loudly proclaims both the present virtues of the kingdom of God and the hope of a blessed life to come. Thus, by its example and its witness, it accuses the world of sin and enlightens those who seek the truth.

Consequently, even when preoccupied with temporal cares, the laity can and must perform a work of great value for the evangelization of the world. For even if some of them have to fulfill their religious duties on their own, when there are no sacred ministers, or in times of persecution; and even if many of them devote all their energies to apostolic work; still it remains for each one of them to cooperate in the external spread and the dynamic growth of the kingdom of Christ in the world. Therefore, let the laity devotedly strive to acquire a more profound grasp of revealed truth, and let them insistently beg of God the gift of wisdom.

36. Christ, becoming obedient even unto death and because of this exalted by the Father (cf. Philippians, ii, 8–9), entered into the glory of this kingdom. To Him all things are made subject until He subjects Himself and all created things to the Father, that God may be all in all (cf. I Corinthians, xv, 27–28). Now Christ had communicated this royal power to His disciples that they might be constituted in royal freedom and that by true penance and a holy life they might conquer the reign of sin in themselves (cf. Romans, vi, 2). Further, He has shared this power so that serving Christ in their fellow men they might by humility and patience lead their brethren to that King for whom to serve is to reign. But the Lord wishes to spread His kingdom also by means of the laity, namely, a kingdom of truth and life, a kingdom of holiness and grace, a kingdom of justice, love and peace. In this kingdom creation itself will be delivered from its slavery to corruption into the freedom of the glory of the sense of God (cf. Romans, viii, 21). Clearly then a great promise and a great trust is committed to the disciples: "All things are yours, and you are Christ's, and Christ is God's" (I Corinthians, iii, 23).

The faithful, therefore, must learn the deepest meaning and the value of all creation, as well as its role in the harmonious praise of God. They must assist each other to live holier lives even in their daily occupations. In this way the world may be permeated by the spirit of Christ and it may more effectively fulfill its purpose in justice, charity and peace. The laity have the principal role in the over-all fulfillment of this duty. Therefore by their competence in secular training and by their activity, elevated from within by the grace of Christ, let them vigorously contribute their effort, so that created goods may be perfected by human labor, technical skill and civic culture for the benefit of all men according to the design of the Creator and the Light of his word. May the goods of this world be more equitably disributed among all men, and may they in their own way be conducive to universal progress in human and Christian freedom. In this manner, through the members of the church, will Christ progressively illumine the whole of human society with His saving light.

Moreover, let the laity also by their combined efforts remedy the customs and conditions of the world, if they are an inducement to sin, so that they all may be conformed to the norms of justice and may favor the practice of virtue rather than hinder it. By so doing they will imbue culture and human activity with genuine moral values; they will better prepare the field of the world for the seed of the Word of God; and at the same time they will open wider the doors of the Church by which the message of peace may enter the world.

Because of the very economy of salvation the faithful should learn how to distinguish carefully between those rights and duties which are theirs as members of the Church, and those which they have as members of human society. Let them strive to reconcile the two, remembering that in every temporal affair they must be guided by a Christian conscience, since even in secular business there is no human activity which can be withdrawn from God's domination. In our own time, however, it is most urgent that this distinction and also this harmony should shine forth more clearly than ever in the lives of the faithful, so that the mission of the Church may correspond more fully to the special conditions of the world today. For it must be admitted that the temporal sphere is governed by its own principles, since it is rightly concerned with the interests of this world. But that ominous doctrine which attempts to build a society with no regard whatever for religion, and which attacks and destroys the religious liberty of its citizens, is rightly to be rejected.

37. The laity have the right, as do all Christians, to receive in abundance from their pastors the spiritual goods of the Church, especially the assistance of the word of God and of the Sacraments. They should openly reveal to them their needs and desires with that freedom and confidence which is fitting for children of God and brothers in Christ. They are, by reason of the knowledge, competence or outstanding ability which they may enjoy, permitted and sometimes even obliged to express their opinion on those things which concern the good of the Church. When occasions arise let this be done through the organs erected by the Church for this purpose. Let it always be done in truth, in courage and in prudence, with reverence and charity toward those who by reason of their sacred office represent the person of Christ.

The laity should, as all Christians, promptly accept in Christian obedience and decisions of their pastors, since they are representatives of Christ as well as teachers and rulers in the Church. Let them follow the example of Christ, who by His obedience even unto death, opened to all men the blessed way of the liberty of the children of God. Nor should they omit to pray for those placed over them, for they keep watch as having to render an account of their souls, so that they may do this with joy and not with grief (cf. Heb. 13:17).

Let pastors recognize and promote the dignity as well as the responsibility of the laity in the Church. Let them willingly employ their prudent advice. Let them confidently assign duties to them in the service of the Church, allowing them freedom and room for action. Further, let pastors encourage lay people so that they may undertake tasks on their own initiative. Attentively in Christ, let them consider with fatherly love the projects, suggestions and desires proposed by the laity. However, let pastors respectfully acknowledge that just freedom which belongs to everyone in this earthly city.

A great many wonderful things are to be hoped for from this familiar dialogue between the laity and their pastors: in the laity a strengthened sense of personal responsibility; a renewed enthusiasm; a more ready application of their talents to the projects of their pastors. The latter, on the other hand, aided by the experience of the laity, can more clearly and more incisively come to decisions regarding both spiritual and temporal matters. In this way, the whole Church, strengthened by each one of its members, may more effectively fulfill its mission for the life of the world.

38. Each individual layman must stand before the world as a witness to the resurrection and life of the Lord Jesus and a symbol of the living God. All the laity as a community and each one according to his ability must nourish the world with the fruits of the Spirit (cf. Gal. 5:22). They must diffuse in the world that spirit which raises up the poor, the meek, the peace makers—those whom the Lord in the Gospel proclaimed blessed (cf. Mt. 5:3–9). In a word, "as the soul is in the body, so let this spirit be in the Christian world."

CHAPTER V
The Universal Vocation to Holiness in the Church

39. The Church whose mystery is being set forth by this sacred synod, is believed to be indefectibly holy. Indeed Christ, the Son of God, who with the Father and the Spirit is praised as "uniquely holy," loved the Church as His bride, delivering Himself up for her. He did this that He might sanctify her (cf. Eph. 5, 25–26). He united her to Himself as His own body and brought it to perfection by the gift of the Holy Spirit for God's glory. Therefore in the Church, everyone whether belonging to the hierarchy, or being cared for by it, is called to holiness, according to the saying of the Apostle: "For this is the will of God, your sanctification" (1 Thess. 4, 3; Eph. 1, 4). However, this holiness of the Church is unceasingly manifested, and must be manifested, in the fruits of grace which the Spirit produces in the faithful; it is expressed in many ways in individuals, who in their walk of life, tend toward the perfection of charity, thus causing the edification of others; in a very special way this (holiness) appears in the practice of the counsels, customarily called "evangelical." This practice of the counsels, under the impulsion of the

Holy Spirit, undertaken by many Christians, either privately or in a Church-approved condition or state of life, gives and must give in the world an outstanding witness and example of this same holiness.

40. The Lord Jesus, the divine Teacher and Model of all perfection, preached holiness of life to each and every one of His disciples of every condition. He Himself stands as the author and consummator of this holiness of life: "You therefore are perfect, even as your heavenly Father is perfect" (Mt. 5, 48). Indeed He sent the Holy Spirit upon all men that He might move them inwardly to love God with their whole heart and their whole soul, with all their mind and all their strength (ct. Mc. 12, 30) and that they might love each other as Christ loves them (ct. Jo. 13, 34; 15, 12). The followers of Christ are called by God, not because of their works, but according to His own purpose and grace. They are justified in the Lord Jesus, because in the baptism of faith they truly become sons of God and sharers in the divine nature. In this way they are really made holy. Then too, by God's gift, they must hold on to and complete in their lives this holiness they have received. They are warned by the Apostle to live "as becomes saints" (Eph. 5, 3), and to put on "as God's chosen ones, holy and beloved, a heart of mercy, kindness, humility, meekness, patience" (Col. 3, 12), and to possess the fruit of the Spirit in holiness (ct. Gal. 5, 22; Rom. 6, 22). Since truly we all offend in many things (ct. Jac. 3, 2) we all need God's mercies continually and we all must daily pray: "Forgive us our debts" (Mt. 6, 12).

Thus it is evident to everyone, that all the faithful of Christ of whatever rank or status, are called to the fulness of the Christian life and to the perfection of charity; by this holiness as such a more human manner of living is promoted in this earthly society. In order that the faithful may reach this perfection, they must use their strength accordingly as they have received it, as a gift from Christ. They must follow in His footsteps and conform themselves to His image seeking the will of the Father in all things. They must devote themselves with all their being to the glory of God and the service of their neighbor. In this way, the holiness of the People of God will grow into an abundant harvest of good, as is admirably shown by the life of so many saints in Church history.

41. In the various classes and differing duties of life, one and the same holiness is cultivated by all, who are moved by the Spirit of God, and who obey the voice of the Father and worship God the Father in spirit and in truth. These people follow the poor Christ, the humble and cross-bearing Christ in order to be worthy of being sharers in His glory. Every person must walk unhesitatingly according to his own personal gifts and duties in the path of living faith, which arouses hope and works through charity.

In the first place, the shepherds of Christ's flock ought to holily and eagerly, humbly and courageously carry out their ministry, in imitation of the eternal high Priest, the Shepherd and Guardian of our souls. They ought to fulfill this duty in such a way that it will be the principal means of their sanctification. Those chosen for the fulness of the priesthood are granted the ability of exercising the perfect duty of pastoral charity by the grace of the sacrament of Orders. This perfect duty of pastoral charity is exercised in every form of episcopal care and service, be it prayer, sacrifice or preaching. By this same sacramental grace, they are given the courage necessary to lay down their lives for their sheep, not to mention the ability of promoting greater holiness in the Church by their daily example—a pattern to their flock (I Pet. 5, 3). Priests, who resemble bishops to a certain degree in their participation of the sacrament of Orders, form the spiritual crown of the bishops. They participate in the grace of their office and they should grow daily in their love of God and their neighbor by the exercise of their office through Christ, the eternal and unique Mediator. They should preserve the bond of priestly communion, and they should abound in every spiritual good and thus present to all men a living witness to God. All this they should do in emulation of those priests who often, down through the course of the centuries, left an outstanding example of the holiness of humble and hidden service. Their praise lives on in the Church of God. By their very office of praying and offering sacrifices for their own people and the entire people of God, they should rise to greater holiness. Keeping in mind what they are doing and imitating what they are handling, these priests, in their apostolic labors, rather than being ensnared by perils and hardships, should rather rise to greater holiness through these perils and hardships. They should ever nourish and strengthen their action from an abundance of contemplation, doing all this for the comfort of the entire Church of God. All priests, and especially those who are called "diocesan priests," due to the special title of their ordination, should keep continually before their minds the fact that their faithful loyalty toward and their generous cooperation with their bishop is of the greatest value in their growth in holiness.

Ministers of lesser rank are also sharers in the mission and grace of the Supreme Priest. In the first place among these ministers are deacons, in as much as they are dispensers of Christ's mysteries and servants of the Church, should keep themselves free from every vice and stand before men as personifications of goodness and friends of God (cf. I Tim. 3, 8–10 and 12–13). Clerics, who are called by the Lord and are set aside as His portion in order to prepare themselves for the various ministerial offices under the watchful eye of pastors, are bound to bring their hearts and minds into accord with this special election (which is theirs). They will accomplish this by their constance in prayer, by their burning love and by their unremitting recollection of whatever is true, just and of good repute. They will accomplish all this for the glory and honor of God. Besides these already named, there are also lay-folk, chosen of God and called by the bishop. These layfolk spend themselves completely in apostolic labors, working the Lord's field with much success.

Furthermore, married couples and Christian parents should follow their own proper path (to holiness) by faithful love. They should sustain one another in grace throughout the entire length of their lives. They should embue their offspring, lovingly welcomed as God's gift, with Christian doctrine and the evangelical virtues. In this manner, they offer all men the example of unwearying and generous love; in this way they build up the brotherhood of charity; in so doing, they stand as the witnesses and cooperators in the fruitfulness of Holy Mother Church; by such lives, they are a sign and a participation in that very love, with which Christ loved His Bride and for which He delivered Himself up for her. A like example, but one given in a different way, is that offered by widows and single people, who are able to make great contributions toward holiness and apostolic endeavor in the Church. Finally, those who engage in labor—and frequently it is of a heavy nature—should better themselves by their human labors. They should be of aid to their fellow citizens. They should raise all of society, and even creation itself, to a better mode of existence. Indeed, they should imitate by their lively charity, in their joyous hope and by their voluntary sharing of each others' burdens, the very Christ who plied His hands with carpenter's tools and Who in union with His Father, is continually working for the salvation of all men. In this, then, their daily work, they should climb to the heights of holiness and apostolic activity.

May all those who are weighed down with poverty, infirmity and sickness, as well as those who must bear various hardships or who suffer persecution for justice's sake—may they all know they are united with the suffering Christ in a special way for the salvation of the world. The Lord called them blessed in His Gospel and they are those whom "the God of all graces, who has called us unto His eternal glory in Christ Jesus, will Himself, after we have suffered a little while, perfect, strengthen and establish" (1 Pet. 5:10).

Finally all Christ's faithful, whatever be the conditions, duties and circumstances of their lives—and indeed through all these, will daily increase in holiness, if they receive all things with faith from the hand of their heavenly Father and if they cooperate with the divine will. In this temporal service, they will manifest to all men the love with which God loved the world.

42. "God is love, and he who abides in love, abides in God, and God in Him" (1 Jn. 4:16). But, God pours out his love into our hearts through the Holy Spirit, Who has been given to us (cf. Rom. 5:5); thus the first and most necessary gift is love, by which we love God above all things and our neighbor because of God. Indeed, in order that love, as good seed may grow and bring forth fruit in the soul, each one of the faithful must willingly hear the Word of God and accept His Will, and

must complete what God has begun by their own actions with the help of God's grace. These actions consist in the use of the sacraments and in a special way the Eucharist, frequent participation in the sacred action of the liturgy, application of oneself to prayer, self-abnegation, lively fraternal service and the constant exercise of all the virtues. For charity, as the bond of perfection and the fullness of the law, rules over all the means of attaining holiness and gives life to these same means. It is charity which guides us to our final end. It is the love of God and the love of one's neighbor which points out the true disciple of Christ.

Since Jesus, the Son of God, manifested His charity by laying down his life for us, so too no one has greater love than he who lays down his life for Christ and His brothers (cf. 1 Jn. 3:16; Jn. 15:13). From the earliest times, then, some Christians have been called upon—and some will always be called upon—to give the supreme testimony of this love to all men, but especially to persecutors. The Church, then, considers martyrdom as an exceptional gift and as the fullest proof of love. By martyrdom a disciple is transformed into an image of his Master by freely accepting death for the salvation of the world—as well as his conformity to Christ in the shedding of his blood. Though few are presented such an opportunity, nevertheless all must be prepared to confess Christ before men. They must be prepared to make this profession of faith even in the midst of persecutions, which will never be lacking to the Church, in following the way of the cross.

Likewise, the holiness of the Church is fostered in a special way by the observance of the counsels proposed in the Gospel by Our Lord to His disciples. An eminent position among these is held by virginity or the celibate state (cf. 1 Cor. 7:32-34). This is a precious gift of divine grace given by the Father to certain souls (Mt. 19:11; 1 Cor. 7:7), whereby they may devote themselves to God alone the more easily, due to an undivided heart. This perfect continency, out of desire for the kingdom of heaven, has always been held in particular honor in the Church. The reason for this was and is that perfect continency for the love of God is an incentive to charity, and is certainly a particular source of spiritual fecundity in the world.

The Church continually keeps before it the warning of the Apostle which moved the faithful to charity, exhorting them to experience personally what Christ Jesus had known within Himself. This was the same Christ Jesus, who "emptied Himself, taking the nature of a slave . . . becoming obedient to death" (Phil. 2:7-8), and because of us "being rich, he became poor" (2 Cor. 8:9). Because the disciples must always offer an imitation of and a testimony to the charity and humility of Christ, Mother Church rejoices at finding within her bosom men and women who very closely follow their Saviour who debased Himself to our comprehension. There are some who, in their freedom as sons of God, renounce their own wills and take upon themselves the state of poverty. Still further, some become subject of their own accord to another man, in the matter of perfection for love of God. This is beyond the measure of the commandments, but is done in order to become more fully like the obedient Christ.

Therefore, all the faithful of Christ are invited to strive for the holiness and perfection of their own proper state. Indeed they have an obligation to so strive. Let all then have care that they guide aright their own deepest sentiments of soul. Let neither the use of the things of this world nor attachment to riches, which is against the spirit of evangelical poverty, hinder them in their quest for perfect love. Let them heed the admonition of the Apostle to those who use this world; let them not come to terms with this world; for this world, as we see it, is passing away (cf. 1 Cor. 7:31 ff).

CHAPTER VI
Religious

43. The evangelical counsels of chastity dedicated to God, poverty and obedience are based upon the words and examples of the Lord. They were further commended by the Apostles and Fathers of the Church, as well as by the learned doctors and pastors of souls. The counsels are a divine gift, which the Church received from its Lord and which it will always observe with the help of His grace. Church authority has the duty, under the inspiration of the Holy Spirit, of interpreting these evangelical counsels, of regulating their practice and finally to build on them stable forms of living. Thus it has come about, that, as if on a tree which has grown in the field of the Lord, various forms of solitary and community life, as well as various religious families have branched out in a marvelous and multiple way from this divinely given seed. Such a multiple and miraculous growth augments both the progress of the members of these various religious families themselves and the welfare of the entire body of Christ. These religious families give their members the support of a more firm stability in their way of life and a proven doctrine of acquiring perfection. They further offer their members the support of fraternal association in the militia of Christ and of liberty strengthened by obedience. Thus these religious are able to tranquilly fulfill and faithfully observe their religious profession and so, spiritually rejoicing, make progress on the road of charity.

From the point of view of the divine and hierarchical structure of the Church, the religious state of life is not an intermediate state between the clerical and lay states. But, rather, the faithful of Christ are called by God from both these states of life so that they might enjoy this particular gift in the life of the Church and thus, each in his own way, may be of some advantage of the salvific mission of the Church.

44. The faithful of Christ bind themselves to the three aforesaid counsels either by vows, or by other sacred bonds which are like vows

in their purpose. By such a bond a person is totally dedicated to God, loved beyond all things. In this way, that person is ordained to the honor and service of God under a new and special title. Indeed through Baptism a person dies to sin and is consecrated to God. However, in order that he may be capable of deriving more abundant fruit from this baptismal grace, he intends, by the profession of the evangelical counsels in the Church, to free himself from those obstacles which might draw him away from the fervor of charity and the perfection of divine worship. By his profession of the evangelical counsels, then, he is more intimately consecrated to divine service. This consecration will be the more perfect in as much as the indissoluble bond of the union of Christ and His bride, the Church, is represented by firm and more stable bonds.

The evangelical counsels which lead to charity join their followers to the Church and its mystery in a special way. Since this is so, the spiritual life of these people should then be devoted to the welfare of the whole Church. From this arises their duty of working to implant and strengthen the Kingdom of Christ in souls and to extend that Kingdom to every clime. This duty is to be undertaken to the extent of their capacities and in keeping with the proper type of their own vocation. This can be realized through prayer or active works of the apostolate. It is for this reason that the Church preserves and fosters the special character of her various religious institutes.

The profession of the evangelical counsels, then, appear as a sign which can and ought to attract all the members of the Church to an effective and prompt fulfillment of the duties of their Christian vocation. The people of God have no lasting city here below, but look forward to one that is to come. Since this is so, the religious state, whose purpose is to free its members from earthly cares, more fully manifests to all believers the presence of heavenly goods already possessed here below. Furthermore, it not only witnesses to the fact of a new and eternal life acquired by the redemption of Christ, but it foretells the future resurrection and the glory of the heavenly kingdom. Christ proposed to His disciples this form of life which He, as the Son of God, accepted in entering this world to do the will of the Father. This same state of life is accurately exemplified and perpetually made present in the Church. The religious state clearly manifests that the Kingdom of God and its needs, in a very special way, are raised above all earthly considerations. Finally it clearly shows all men both the unsurpassed breadth of the strength of Christ the King and the infinite power of the Holy Spirit marvelously working in the Church.

Thus, the state which is constituted by the profession of the evangelical counsels, though it is not the hierarchical structure of the Church, nevertheless undeniably belongs to its life and holiness.

45. It is the duty of the ecclesiastical hierarchy to regulate the practice of the evangelical counsels by law, since it is the duty of the same hierarchy to care for the People of God and to offer them abundant

possibilities of spiritual growth. The importance of the profession of the
evangelical counsels is seen in the fact that it fosters the perfection of
love of God and love of neighbor in an outstanding manner and that
this profession is strengthened by vows. Furthermore, the hierarchy,
following with docility the prompting of the Holy Spirit, accepts the
rules presented by outstanding men and women and authentically approves these rules after further necessary adjustments. It also aids by
its vigilant and safeguarding authority those institutes variously established for the building up of Christ's Body in order that these same
institutes may grow and flourish according to the spirit of the founders.
Any institute of perfection and its individual members may be removed
from the jurisdiction of the local Ordinaries by the Supreme Pontiff
and subjected to himself alone. This is done in virtue of his primacy
over the entire Church in order to more fully provide for the necessities
of the entire flock of the Lord and in consideration of the common
good. In like manner, these institutes may be freed from or committed
to the charge of the proper patriarchical authority. The members of
these institutes, in fulfilling their obligation to the Church due to their
particular form of life, ought to show reverence and obedience to
bishops according to the sacred canons. The bishops are owed this
respect because of their pastoral authority in their own churches and
because of the need of unity and harmony in the apostolate.

The Church not only raises the religious profession to the dignity of
a canonical state by her approval, but even manifests that this profession is a state consecrated to God by the liturgical setting of that profession. The Church itself, by the authority given to it by God, accepts the
vows of the newly professed. It begs aid and grace from God for them
by its public prayer. It commends them to God, imparts a spiritual
blessing on them and accompanies their self-offering by the Eucharistic
sacrifice.

46. Religious should carefully keep before their minds the fact that
the Church presents Christ to believers and non-believers alike in a
striking manner daily through them. The Church thus portrays Christ
in contemplation on the mountain, in His proclamation of the kingdom of God to the multitudes, in His healing of the sick and maimed,
in His work of converting sinners to a better life, in His solicitude for
youth and His goodness to all men, always obedient to the will of the
Father who sent Him.

All men should take note that the profession of the evangelical
counsels, though entailing the renunciation of certain values which
are to be undoubtedly esteemed, does not detract from a genuine
development of the human person, but rather by its very nature is most
beneficial to that development. Indeed the counsels, voluntarily undertaken according to each one's personal vocation, contribute a great deal
to the purification of heart and spiritual liberty. They continually stir
up the fervor of charity. But especially they are able to more fully mold

the Christian man to that type of virginal and detached life which Christ the Lord chose for Himself and which His Mother embraced. This is clearly proven by the example of so many holy founders. Let no one think that religious have become strangers to their fellowmen or useless citizens of this earthly city by their consecration. For even though it sometimes happens that religious do not directly mingle with their contemporaries, yet in a more profound sense these same religious are united with them in the heart of Christ and spiritually cooperate with them. In this way the building up of the earthly city may have its foundation in the Lord and may tend toward Him, lest perhaps those who build this city shall have labored in vain.

Finally, this Sacred Synod encourages and praises the men and women, Brothers and Sisters, who in monasteries, or in schools and hospitals, or in the missions, adorn the Bride of Christ by their unswerving and humble faithfulness in their chosen consecration.

47. Let each of the faithful, therefore, carefully see to it that he perseveres and ever grow in whatever vocation God has given him. Let him do this for the increased holiness of the Church, for the greater glory of the one and undivided Trinity, which in and through Christ is the font and the source of all holiness.

CHAPTER VII
The Eschatological Nature of the Pilgrim Church and Its Union with the Church in Heaven

48. The Church, to which we are all called in Christ Jesus, and in which we acquire sanctity through the grace of God, will attain its full perfection only in the glory of heaven, when there will come the time of the restoration of all things (Acts 3, 21). At that time the human race as well as the entire world, which is intimately related to man and attains to its end through him, will be perfectly re-established in Christ (Eph. 1, 10; Col. 1, 20; II Pet. 3, 10–13).

Christ, having been lifted up from the earth has drawn all to Himself (Jn. 12, 32). Rising from the dead (Rom. 6, 9) He sent His lifegiving Spirit upon His disciples and through Him has established His Body which is the Church as the universal sacrament of salvation. Sitting at the right hand of the Father, He is continually active in the world that He might lead men to the Church and through it join them to Himself and that He might make them partakers of His glorious life by nourishing them with His own Body and Blood. Therefore the promised restoration which we are awaiting has already begun in Christ, is carried forward in the mission of the Holy Spirit, and through Him continues in the Church in which we learn the meaning of our terrestrial life through our faith, while we perform with hope in the future the work committed to us in this world by the Father, and thus work out our salvation (Phil. 2, 12).

Already the final age of the world has come upon us (I Cor. 10, 11), and the renovation of the world is irrevocably decreed and is already anticipated in some kind of a real way; for the Church already on this earth is signed with sanctity which is real although imperfect. However, until there shall be new heavens and a new earth in which justice dwells, the pilgrim Church in her sacraments and institutions, which pertain to this present time has the appearance of this world which is passing, and she herself dwells among creatures who groan and travail in pain until now and await the revelation of the sons of God (Rom. 8, 22 and 19).

Joined with Christ in the Church and signed with the Holy Spirit "who is the pledge of our inheritance" (Eph. 1, 14), truly we are called and we are sons of God (I Jo. 3, 1), but we have not yet appeared with Christ in glory (Col. 3, 4), in which we shall be like to God since we shall see Him as He is. (I Jo. 3, 2). And therefore while we are in the body, we are exiled from the Lord (II Cor. 5, 6), and having the first-fruits of the Spirit we groan within ourselves (Rom. 8, 23) and we desire to be with Christ (Phil. 1, 23). By that same charity however, we are urged to live more for Him Who died for us and rose again (2 Cor. 5, 15). We strive therefore to please God in all things (2 Cor. 5, 9), and we put on the armor of God, that we may be able to stand against the wiles of the devil and resist in the evil day (Eph. 6, 11–13). Since. however, we know not the day nor the hour, on Our Lord's advice we must be constantly vigilant so that, having finished the course of our earthly life, we may merit to enter into the marriage feast with Him (Mt. 25, 1–13) and be numbered among the blessed (Mt. 25, 31–46) and that we may not be ordered to go into eternal fire (Mt. 25, 41) like the wicked and slothful servant (Mt. 25, 26), into the exterior darkness where "there will be the weeping and the gnashing of teeth" (Mt. 22, 13 and 25, 30). For before we reign with Christ in glory, all of us will be made manifest "before the tribunal of Christ, so that each one may receive what he has won through the body, according to his works, whether good or evil" (2 Cor. 5, 10) and at the end of the world "they who have done good shall come forth unto resurrection of life; but those who have done evil unto resurrection of judgment" (Jo. 5, 29; 25, 46). Reckoning therefore that "the sufferings of the present time are not worthy to be compared with the glory to come that will be revealed in us" (Rom. 8, 18; 2 Tim. 2, 11–12), strong in faith we look for the "blessed hope and the glorious coming of our great God and Savior, Jesus Christ" (Tit. 2, 13), "Who will refashion the body of our lowliness, conforming it to the body of His glory" (Phil. 3, 21) and Who will come "to be glorified in His saints and to be marveled at in all those who have believed" (2 Thess. 1, 10).

49. Until the Lord shall come in His majesty, and all the angels with Him (Mt. 25, 31) and death being destroyed, all things are subject to Him (I Cor. 15, 26–27), some of His disciples are exiles on earth,

some having died are purified, and others are in glory beholding "clearly God Himself triune and one, as He is"; but all in various ways and degrees are in communion in the same charity of God and neighbor, and all sing the same hymn of glory to our God. For all who are in Christ, having His Spirit, form one Church and cleave together in Him (Eph. 4, 16). Therefore the union of the wayfarers with the brethren who have gone to sleep in the peace of Christ is not in the least weakened or interrupted, but on the contrary, according to the perpetual faith of the Church, is strengthened by a communication of spiritual goods. For by reason of the fact that those in heaven are more closely united with Christ, they establish the whole Church or more firmly in holiness, lend nobility to the worship which the Church offers to God here on earth, and in many ways contribute to its greater edification (I Cor. 12, 12–27). For after they have been received into their heavenly home and are present to the Lord (II Cor. 5, 8), through Him and with Him and in Him they do not cease to intercede with the Father for us, showing forth the merits which they won on earth through the one Mediator between God and man (1 Tim. 2, 5), serving God in all things and filling up in their flesh those things which are lacking of the sufferings of Christ for His body which is the Church (Col. 1, 24). Thus by their brotherly interest our weakness is greatly strengthened.

50. Fully conscious of this communion of the whole Mystical Body of Jesus Christ, the pilgrim Church from the very first ages of the Christian religion has cultivated with great piety the memory of the dead, and "because it is a holy and wholesome thought to pray for the dead that they may be loosed from their sins" (2 Mach. 12, 46), also offers suffrages for them. The Church has always believed that the Apostles and Christ's martyrs who had given the supreme witness of faith and charity by the shedding of their blood, are closely joined with us in Christ, and she has always venerated them with special devotion, together with the Blessed Virgin Mary and the holy angels. The Church has piously implored the aid of their intercession. To these were soon added also those who had more closely imitated Christ's virginity and poverty, and finally others whom the outstanding practice of the Christian virtues and the divine charisms recommended to the pious devotion and imitation of the faithful.

When we look at the lives of those who have faithfully followed Christ, we are inspired with a new reason for seeking the City that is to come (Heb. 13, 14; 11, 10) and at the same time we are shown a most safe path by which among the vicissitudes of this world, in keeping with the state in life and condition proper to each of us, we will be able to arrive at perfect union with Christ, that is, perfect holiness. In the lives of those who, sharing in our humanity are however more perfectly transformed into the image of Christ, God vividly manifests His presence and His face to men. He speaks to us in them, and gives us a sign of His Kingdom, to which we are strongly drawn, having so great a cloud of witnesses over us (Heb. 12, 1) and such a witness to the truth of the Gospel.

Nor is it by the title of example only that we cherish the memory of those in heaven, but still more in order that the union of the whole Church may be strengthened in the Spirit by the practice of fraternal charity (Eph. 4, 1–6). For just as Christian communion among wayfarers brings us closer to Christ, so our companionship with the saints joins us to Christ, from whom as from its fountain and head issues every grace and the very life of the people of God. It is supremely fitting therefore, that we love those friends and coheirs of Jesus Christ, who are also our brothers and extraordinary benefactors, that we render due thanks to God for them and "suppliantly invoke them and have recourse to their prayers, their power and help in obtaining benefits from God through His Son, Jesus Christ, Who is our Redeemer and Savior." For every genuine testimony of love shown by us to those in heaven, by its very nature tends toward and terminates in Christ Who is the "crown of all saints," and through Him, in God Who is wonderful in His Saints and is magnified in them.

Our union with the Church in heaven is put into effect in its noblest manner especially in the sacred liturgy, wherein the power of the Holy Spirit acts upon us through sacramental signs. Then, with combined rejoicing, we celebrate together the praise of the divine majesty; then all those from every tribe and tongue and people and nation (Apoc. 5, 9) who have been redeemed by the blood of Christ and gathered together into one Church, with one song of praise magnify the one and triune God. Celebrating the Eucharistic sacrifices therefore, we are most closely united to the Church in heaven in communion with and venerating the memory first of all of the glorious ever-Virgin Mary, of Blessed Joseph and the blessed Apostles and martyrs and of all the saints.

51. This sacred Council accepts with great devotion this venerable faith of our ancestors regarding this vital fellowship with our brethren who are in heavenly glory or who having died are still being purified; and it proposes again the decrees of the Second Council of Nicea, the Council of Florence and the Council of Trent. And at the same time, in conformity with our own pastoral interests, we urge all concerned, if any abuses, excesses or defects have crept in here or there, to do what is in their power to remove or correct that, and to restore all things to a fuller praise of Christ and of God. Let them therefore teach the faithful that the authentic cult of the saints consists not so much in the multiplying of external acts, but rather in the greater intensity of our love, whereby, for our own greater good and that of the whole Church, we seek from the saints "example in their way of life, fellowship and their communion, and aid by their intercession." On the other hand, let them teach the faithful that our communion with those in heaven, provided that it is understood in the fuller light of faith according to

its genuine nature, in no way weakens, but conversely, more thoroughly enriches the latreutic worship we give to God the Father, through Christ, in the Spirit.

For all of us, who are sons of God and constitute one family in Christ (Heb. 3, 6), as long as we remain in communion with one another in mutual charity and in one praise of the most holy Trinity, are corresponding with the intimate vocation of the Church and partaking in foretaste the liturgy of consummate glory. For when Christ shall appear and the glorious resurrection of the dead will take place, the glory of God will light up the heavenly City and the Lamb will be the lamp thereof (Apoc. 21, 24). Then the whole Church of the saints in the supreme happiness of charity will adore God and "the Lamb who was slain" (Apoc. 5, 12), proclaiming with one voice: "To Him who sits upon the throne, and to the Lamb blessing, and honor, and glory, and dominion forever and ever" (Apoc. 5, 13–14).

CHAPTER VIII
The Blessed Virgin Mary, Mother of God, in the Mystery of Christ and the Church

52. Wishing in His supreme goodness and wisdom to effect the redemption of the world, "when the fullness of time came, God sent His Son, born of a woman, . . . that we might receive the adoption of sons" (Gal. 4, 4).

"He for us men, and for our salvation, came down from heaven, and was incarnate by the Holy Spirit from the Virgin Mary." This divine mystery of salvation is revealed to us and continued in the Church, which the Lord established as His body. Joined to Christ the Head and in the unity of fellowship with all His saints, the faithful must in the first place reverence the memory "of the glorious ever Virgin Mary, Mother of our God and Lord Jesus Christ" (Gal. 4, 4–5).

53. The Virgin Mary, who at the message of the angel received the Word of God in her heart and in her body and gave Life to the world, is acknowledged and honored as being truly the Mother of God and Mother of the Redeemer. Redeemed by reason of the merits of her Son and united to Him by a close and indissoluble tie, she is endowed with the high office and dignity of being the Mother of the Son of God, by which account she is also the beloved daughter of the Father and the temple of the Holy Spirit. Because of this gift of sublime grace she far surpasses all creatures, both in heaven and on earth. At the same time, however, because she belongs to the offspring of Adam, she is one with all those who are to be saved. She is "the mother of the members of Christ . . . having cooperated by charity that faithful might be born in the Church, who are members of that Head." Wherefore she is hailed as a preeminent and singular member of the Church, and as its type and excellent exemplar in faith and charity. The Catholic Church,

taught by the Holy Spirit, honors her with filial affection and piety as a most beloved mother.

54. Wherefore this Holy Synod, in expounding the doctrine on the Church, in which the divine Redeemer works salvation, intends to describe with diligence both the role of the Blessed Virgin in the mystery of the Incarnate Word and the Mystical Body, and the duties of redeemed mankind toward the Mother of God, who is mother of Christ and mother of men, particularly of the faithful. It does not, however, have it in mind to give a complete doctrine on Mary, nor does it wish to decide those questions which the work of theologians has not yet fully clarified. Those opinions therefore may be lawfully retained which are propounded in Catholic schools concerning her, who occupies a place in the Church which is the highest after Christ and yet very close to us.

55. The Sacred Scriptures of both the Old and the New Testament, as well as ancient Tradition show the role of the Mother of the Savior in the economy of salvation in an ever clearer light and draw attention to it. The books of the Old Testament describe the history of salvation, by which the coming of Christ into the world was slowly prepared. These earliest documents, as they are read in the Church and are understood in the light of a further and full revelation, bring the figure of the woman, Mother of the Redeemer, into a gradually clearer light. When it is looked at in this way, she is already prophetically foreshadowed in the promise of victory over the serpent which was given to our first parents after their fall into sin (cf. Gen. 3, 15). Likewise she is the Virgin who shall conceive and bear a son, whose name will be called Emmanuel (cf. Is. 8, 14; Mich. 5, 2-3; Mt. 1, 22-23). She stands out among the poor and humble of the Lord, who confidently hope for and receive salvation from Him. With her, the exalted Daughter of Sion, and after a long expectation of the promise, the times are fulfilled and the new economy established, when the Son of God took a human nature from her, that He might in the mysteries of His flesh free man from sin.

56. The Father of Mercies willed that the incarnation should be preceded by the acceptance of her who was predestined to be the mother of His Son, so that just as a woman contributed to death, so also a woman should contribute to life. This is true in outstanding fashion of the mother of Jesus, who gave to the world Him Who is Life itself and who renews all things, and who was enriched by God with the gifts which befit such a role. It is no wonder therefore that the usage prevailed among the Fathers whereby they called the Mother of God entirely holy and free from all stain of sin, as though fashioned by the Holy Spirit and formed as a new creature. Adorned from the first instant of her conception with the radiance of an entirely unique holiness,

the Virgin of Nazareth is greeted, on God's command, by an angel messenger as "full of grace" (Lk. 1, 28), and to the heavenly messenger she replies: "Behold the handmaid of the Lord, be it done unto me according to thy word" (Lk. 1, 38). Thus Mary, a daughter of Adam, consenting to the divine Word, became the mother of Jesus, the one and only Mediator. Embracing God's salvific will with a full heart and impeded by no sin, she devoted herself totally as a handmaid of the Lord to the person and work of her Son, under Him and with Him, by the grace of almighty God, serving the mystery of redemption. Rightly therefore the holy Fathers see her as used by God not merely in a passive way, but as freely cooperating in the work of human salvation through faith and obedience. For, as St. Irenaeus says, she "being obedient, became the cause of salvation for herself and for the whole human race." Hence not a few of the early Fathers gladly assert in their preaching: "The knot of Eve's disobedience was untied by Mary's obedience; what the virgin Eve bound through her unbelief, Mary loosened by her faith." Comparing Mary with Eve, they call her "the Mother of the living," and still more often they say: "death through Eve, life through Mary."

57. This union of the Mother with the Son in the work of salvation is made manifest from the time of Christ's virginal conception up to His death. It is shown first of all when Mary, arising in haste to go to visit Elizabeth, is greeted by her as blessed because of her belief in the promise of salvation and the precursor leaped with joy in the womb of his mother (cf. Lk. 1, 41–45). This union is manifest also at the birth of Our Lord, Who did not diminish His mother's virginal integrity but sanctified it, when the Mother of God joyfully showed her firstborn Son to the shepherds and Magi. When she presented Him to the Lord in the temple, making the offering of the poor, she heard Simeon foretelling at the same time that her Son would be a sign of contradiction and that a sword would pierce the mother's soul, that out of many hearts thoughts might be revealed (cf. Lk. 2, 34–35). When the Child Jesus was lost and they had sought Him sorrowing, His parents found Him in the temple, taken up with the things that were His Father's business; and they did not understand the word of their Son. His Mother indeed kept these things to be pondered over in her heart (cf. Lk. 2, 41–51).

58. In the public life of Jesus, Mary makes significant appearances. This is so even at the very beginning, when at the marriage feast of Cana, moved with pity, she brought about by her intercession the beginning of miracles of Jesus the Messiah (cf. Jn. 2, 1–11). In the course of her Son's preaching she received the words whereby, in extolling a kingdom beyond the calculations and bonds of flesh and blood, He declared blessed (cf. Mk. 3, 35; Lk. 11, 27–28) those who heard and kept the word of God, as she was faithfully doing (cf. Lk. 2, 19, 51). After this manner, the Blessed Virgin advanced in her pilgrimage of

faith, and faithfully persevered in her union with her Son unto the
cross, where she stood, in keeping with the divine plan (cf. Jn. 19, 25),
grieving exceedingly with her only begotten Son, uniting herself with a
maternal heart with His sacrifice, and lovingly consenting to the im-
molation of this Victim which she herself had brought forth. Finally,
she was given by the same Christ Jesus dying on the cross as a mother
to His disciple, with these words: "Woman, behold thy son" (Jn. 19,
26–27).

59. But since it has pleased God not to manifest solemnly the mystery
of the salvation of the human race before He would pour forth the
Spirit promised by Christ, we see the Apostles before the day of
Pentecost "persevering with one mind in prayer with the women and
Mary the Mother of Jesus, and with His brethren" (Acts 1, 14), and
Mary by her prayers imploring the gift of the Spirit, Who had already
overshadowed her in the Annunciation. Finally, the Immaculate Virgin,
preserved free from all guilt of original sin, on the completion of her
earthly sojourn, was taken by the Lord as Queen of the Universe, that
she might be the more fully conformed to her Son, the Lord of lords
and the conqueror of sin and death.

60. There is but one Mediator, as we know from the words of the
Apostle, "for there is one God and one mediator of God and men, the
man Christ Jesus, who gave himself a redemption for all" (1 Tim. 2,
5–6). The maternal duty of Mary toward men in no wise obscures or
diminishes this unique mediation of Christ, but rather shows His
power. For all the salvific influence of the Blessed Virgin on men
originates, not from some inner necessity, but from the divine pleasure.
It flows forth from the superabundance of the merits of Christ, rests on
His mediation, depends entirely on it, and draws all its power from it.
In no way does it impede, but rather does it foster the immediate
union of the faithful with Christ.

61. Predestined from eternity by that decree of divine providence
which determined the incarnation of the Word to be the Mother of
God, the Blessed Virgin was on this earth the virgin Mother of the
Redeemer, and above all others and in a singular way the generous
associate and humble handmaid of the Lord. She conceived, brought
forth, and nourished Christ, she presented Him to the Father in the
temple, and was united with Him by compassion as He died on the
cross. In this singular way she cooperated by her obedience, faith, hope
and burning charity in the work of the Savior in giving back supernatural life to souls. Wherefore she is our mother in the order of grace.

62. This maternity of Mary in the order of grace began with the
consent which she gave in faith at the Annunciation and which she
sustained without wavering beneath the cross, and lasts until the

eternal fulfillment of all the elect. Taken up to heaven she did not lay aside this salvific duty, but by her constant intercession continued to bring us the gifts of eternal salvation. By her maternal charity, she cares for the brethren of her Son, who still journey on earth surrounded by dangers and difficulties, until they are led into the happiness of their true home. Therefore the Blessed Virgin is invoked by the Church under the titles of Advocate, Auxiliatrix, Adjutrix, and Mediatrix. This, however, is to be so understood that it neither takes away from nor adds anything to the dignity and efficaciousness of Christ the one Mediator.

For no creature could ever be counted as equal with the Incarnate Word and Redeemer. Just as the priesthood of Christ is shared in various ways both by the ministers and by the faithful, and as the one goodness of God is really communicated in different ways to His creatures, so also the unique mediation of the Redeemer does not exclude but rather gives rise to a manifold cooperation which is but a sharing in this one source.

The Church does not hesitate to profess this subordinate role of Mary. It knows it through unfailing experience of it and commends it to the hearts of the faithful, so that encouraged by this maternal help they may the more intimately adhere to the Mediator and Redeemer.

63. By reason of the gift and role of divine maternity by which she is united with her Son, the Redeemer, and with His singular graces and functions, the Blessed Virgin is also intimately united with the Church. As St. Ambrose taught, the Mother of God is a type of the Church in the order of faith, charity and perfect union with Christ. For in the mystery of the Church, which is itself rightly called mother and virgin, the Blessed Virgin stands out in eminent and singular fashion as exemplar both of virgin and mother. By her belief and obedience, not knowing man but overshadowed by the Holy Spirit, as the new Eve she brought forth on earth the very Son of the Father, showing an undefiled faith, not in the word of the ancient serpent, but in that of God's messenger. The Son whom she brought forth is He Whom God placed as the first-born among many brethren (cf. Rom. 3, 29), namely the faithful, in whose birth and education she cooperates with a maternal love.

64. The Church indeed, contemplating her hidden sanctity, imitating her charity and faithfully fulfilling the Father's will, by receiving the word of God in faith, becomes herself a mother. By her preaching she brings forth to a new and immortal life the sons who are born to her in Baptism, conceived of the Holy Spirit and born of God. She herself is a virgin, who keeps the Faith given to her by her Spouse whole and entire. Imitating the mother of her Lord, and by the power of the Holy Spirit, she keeps with virginal purity an entire faith, a firm hope and a sincere charity.

65. But while in the most holy Virgin the Church has already reached that perfection whereby she exists without spot or wrinkle, the followers of Christ still strive to increase in holiness by conquering sin (cf. Eph. 5, 27). And so they turn their eyes to Mary who shines forth to the whole community of the elect as the model of virtues. Piously meditating on her and contemplating her in the light of the Word made man, the Church with reverence enters more intimately into the great mystery of the Incarnation and becomes more and more like her Spouse. Since she has entered intimately into the history of salvation, Mary, who unifies and re-echoes in a certain way the greatest teachings of the faith in herself, when she is being preached and venerated calls the faithful to her Son and His sacrifice, and to love of the Father. Seeking after the glory of Christ, the Church becomes more like her exalted type, and continually progresses in faith, hope and charity, seeking and doing the will of God in all things. Hence the Church in her apostolic work also justly looks to her, who, conceived of the Holy Spirit, brought forth Christ, Who was born of the Virgin that through the Church He may be born and may increase in the hearts of the faithful also. The Virgin in her own life lived an example of that maternal love by which it behooves that all should be animated who cooperate in the apostolic mission of the Church for the regeneration of men.

66. Placed, by the grace of God, as God's Mother, next to her Son, and exalted above all angels and men, Mary intervened in the mysteries of Christ and is justly honored by a special cult in the Church. Clearly from earliest times the Blessed Virgin is honored under the title of Mother of God, under whose protection the faithful took refuge in all their dangers and necessities. Hence after the Synod of Ephesus the cult of the people of God toward Mary wonderfully increased in veneration and love, in invocation and imitation, according to her own prophetic words: "All generations shall call be blessed, because He that is mighty hath done great things to me" (Lk. 1, 48). This cult, as it always existed, although it is altogether singular, differs essentially from the cult of adoration which is offered to the Incarnate Word, as well to the Father and the Holy Spirit, and it is most favorable to it. The various forms of piety toward the Mother of God, which the Church within the limits of sound and orthodox doctrine, according to the conditions of time and place and the nature and ingenuity of the faithful, has approved, bring it about that while the Mother is honored, the Son, through whom all things have their being (cf. Col. 1, 15–16) and in whom it has pleased the Father that all fullness should dwell (cf. Col. 1, 19), is rightly known, loved and glorified, and that all His commands are observed.

67. This Holy Synod deliberately teaches this Catholic doctrine, and at the same time admonishes all the sons of the Church that the cult, especially the liturgical cult, of the Blessed Virgin be generously fostered

and the practices and exercises of piety recommended by the magisterium of the Church toward her in the course of centuries be made of great moment, and those decrees, which have been given in the early days regarding the cult of images of Christ, the Blessed Virgin and the saints, be religiously observed.

But it exhorts theologians and preachers of the Divine Word to abstain zealously both from all false exaggerations as well as from a too great narrowness of mind in considering the singular dignity of the Mother of God. Following the study of Sacred Scripture, the Holy Fathers, the doctors and liturgy of the Church, and under the guidance of the Church's magisterium, let them rightly illustrate the duties and privileges of the Blessed Virgin which always look to Christ, the source of all truth, sanctity and piety. Let them assiduously keep away from whatever, either by word or deed, could lead separated brethren or any other into error regarding the true doctrine of the Church. Let the faithful remember, moreover, that true devotion consist neither in sterile or transitory affection, nor in a certain vain credulity, but proceeds from true faith, by which we are led to know the excellence of the Mother of God and we are moved to a filial love toward our mother and to the imitation of her virtues.

68. In the interim, the Mother of Jesus in the glory which she possesses body and soul in heaven is the image and beginning of the Church as it is to be perfected in the world to come. Likewise she shines forth on earth, until the day of the Lord shall come (cf. II Pet. 3, 10), a sign of sure hope and solace to the wandering people of God.

69. It gives great joy and comfort to this Holy and General Synod that even among the separated brethren there are some who give due honor to the Mother of our Lord and Savior, especially among the Orientals, who with devout mind and fervent impulse give honor to the Mother of God, ever virgin. The entire body of the faithful pours forth instant supplications to the Mother of God and Mother of men that she, who aided the beginnings of the Church by her prayers, may now, exalted as she is above all the angels and saints, intercede before her Son in the fellowship of all the saints, until all families of people, whether they are honored with the title of Christian or whether they still do not know the Savior, may be happily gathered together in peace and harmony into one People of God, for the glory of the Most Holy and Undivided Trinity.

Statements Regarding Chapter III of the Constitution

READ BY THE SECRETARY GENERAL IN THE COUNCIL
ON NOVEMBER 16, 1964.*

✠

It has been asked: what is the theological note of the doctrine set forth in the schema *On the Church* and subject to vote? The Theological Commission has given the following response:

It is clear that the text of a Council must always be interpreted ac-

---

* These statements were declared by the Secretary General, on the Council floor, to form part of the "Acts" of the Council. They were appended to the Latin and Italian versions of the Constitution which the Vatican newspaper, *L'Osservatore Romano,* published in its editions of November 25 and December 13, 1964, but, significantly, they were *not* included in the official pamphlet containing the final text of the constitution voted by the Fathers. The page references refer to the booklet or pamphlet in which they appeared, distributed to the bishops and experts on Nov. 13, 1964. The meaning will necessarily be somewhat obscure, to the average reader, without the official Latin documents before him, but the general purport seems clear enough. The passages commented on can be found without too much difficulty by referring to the text of the constitution (Appendix p. 297).

cording to the general rules known to all. Since that is the case, the Theological Commission refers to its declaration of March 6, 1964, the text of which we here transcribe:

Taking into consideration the usages of a Council and the pastoral purpose of the present council, this sacred synod defines to be held by the Church only those matters of faith or morals which it clearly declares itself to be defining.

Other matters which the sacred synod proposes must be received and embraced by each and all of the faithful as the doctrine of the supreme magisterium of the Church according to the mind of the sacred synod. The mind of the Council is made known either from the subject matter or from the wording of the Council's statements, according to theological rules of interpretation.

(By Superior Authority a prior note of explanation about the *modi* on chapter three of the schema *On the Church* is communicated to the Fathers. The doctrine set out in the third chapter should be explained and understood according to the mind and opinion of the note.)

The (Theological) Commission has decided to preface its treatment of the *modi* with the following general observations:

1. "College" is not understood in a *strict juridical sense,* that is, of a body of equals who entrust their power to their president, but rather of a stable body whose structure and authority must be deduced from Revelation. Therefore, in response to *modus* 12, it is said explicitly of The Twelve (Apostles) that the Lord established them "after the manner of a college or *stable group.* Cf. also modus 53, c. For the same reason the words "order" or "body" are used in several places of the college of bishops. The parallelism between Peter and the rest of the Apostles on the one hand and the Sovereign Pontiff and the bishops on the other, does not imply the transmission of the extraordinary powers of the Apostles to their successors, nor, obviously, *equality* between the head and members of the college, but only a proportionality between the first relation (Peter and the Apostles) and the second (the pope and the bishops). Hence the commission decided to phrase page 63, lines 16–19 not "the same" (*eadem*) reason but "equal" (*pari*) reason. Cf. modus 57.

2. One becomes a member of the college in virtue of eipscopal consecration and hierarchical communion with the head of the college and its members. Cf. page 63, line 33–36.

In the *consecration,* there is given an *ontological participation* of the *sacred* offices (*munerum*)—as is established beyond doubt from tradition and even from the liturgy. But the word "offices" (*munerum*) rather than "powers" (*potestatum*) is used advisedly, because this latter word can be understood of a power *immediately usable* (*ad actum expedita*). But in order to have such an immediately usable power, there must be added a canonical or juridical *determination* by hierarchial authority. This determination of power can consist in the concession of a particular office or in the assignment of particular subjects and is given according to norms approved by the supreme authority. This further norm is required *from the very nature of the case,* because it involves offices which must be exercised *by many holders* who, according to the will of Christ, hierarchically cooperate. It is evident that this "communion" was applied in the life of the Church according to the circumstances of the times before it was codified into law.

For this reason the text says explicitly that there is required *hierarchical* communion with the head and members of the Church. *"Communion"* is a concept which was held in high honor in the ancient Church (as it is even today, especially in the East). But it does not mean a kind of vague *affection,* but an *organic* relationship which demands juridicial form and at the same time is animated by charity. Hence the commission, almost unanimously, decided on the phrase "in *hierarchical* communion." Cf. modus 40 and also what is said about "canonical mission" under n. 24, p. 67, lines 17–24.

The documents of more recent Sovereign Pontiffs about the jurisdiction of bishops are to be understood as dealing with this necessary determination of powers.

3. The college, which cannot exist without its head, is said "to be the *holder of supreme and full power* over the universal Church." This must be admitted so that the full power of the Roman Pontiff will not be placed in contention. The college always and necessarily is understood together with its head *because (the pope) retains intact in the college his office as vicar of Christ and pastor of the universal Church.* In other words, the distinction is not between the Roman Pontiff and the bishops taken collectively, but between the Roman Pontiff by himself and the Roman Pontiff together with the bishops. Since the Sovereign Pontiff is the *head* of the college, he alone can perform certain acts which are not within the competence of the bishops at all: e.g., convoking and directing the college, approving norms for its actions, etc. Cf. modus 81. It is within the judgment of the Sovereign Pontiff, to whom the care of the whole flock of Christ has been given, to determine, according to the needs of the Church as they vary in the course of time, the manner in which it is advisable to discharge this care—whether personally or collegially. The Roman Pontiff proceeds to the ordering, promoting, and approving of a collegial exercise according to his own judgment, with the good of the Church in view.

4. The Sovereign Pontiff, as supreme pastor of the Church, can exercise his power at all times at will—as his office requires. But the college, although it always exists, does not therefore permanently carry on strictly collegial action—as the tradition of the Church shows. In other words, it is not always in full act (*in actu pleno*); indeed it performs

strictly collegial acts only at intervals and only with the consent of its head. The text says: with the *consent* of its *head*," lest this dependence be thought of as though it were on someone *outside* the college: the term "consent" evokes on the contrary *communion* between the head and members, and implies the necessity of an act which is proper to the head. This is explicitly affirmed on p. 64, line 11 ff. and is explained on the same page, lines 29–43. The negative formula "only (with the consent)" (*nonnisi*) embraces all cases, from which it is apparent that norms approved by the supreme authority must always be observed. Cf. modus 84.

In all of these it is apparent that we are dealing with a *joining* of the bishops *with their head*, and never with an action of the bishops *independently* of the pope. In that case, lacking the authority of the head, the bishops cannot act as a college—as is clear from the very notion of "college." This hierarchical communion of all the bishops with the Sovereign Pontiff is certainly a solemn teaching of Tradition.

N. B. Without hierarchical communion, the sacramental-ontological office, which must be distinguished from the canonical-juridical aspect, cannot be exercised. The commission, however, thought it best not to enter into questions of liceity and validity, which are left to the discussions of theologians, in particular insofar as the question deals with the power which is in fact exercised by the separated Eastern brethren. Various opinions exist about the explanation of this authority.

PERICLE FELICI
Tit. Archbishop of Samosata
Secretary General.

Decree on Ecumenism

PROMULGATED NOVEMBER 21, 1964

✠

Introduction

1. The restoration of unity among all Christians is one of the principal concerns of the Second Vatican Council. Christ the Lord founded one Church and one Church only. However, many Christian communions present themselves to men as the true inheritors of Jesus Christ; all indeed profess to be followers of the Lord but differ in mind and go their different ways, as if Christ himself were divided (cf. 1 Cor. 1, 13). Such division openly contradicts the will of Christ, scandalizes the world, and damages the holy cause of preaching the Gospel to every creature.

But the Lord of Ages wisely and patiently follows out the plan of grace on our behalf, sinners that we are. In recent times more than ever before, he has been rousing divided Christians to remorse over their divisions and to a longing for unity. Everywhere large numbers have felt the impulse of this grace, and among our separated brethren also

there increases from day to day the movement, fostered by the grace
of the Holy Spirit, for the restoration of unity among all Christians.
This movement toward unity is called "ecumenical." Those belong to
it who invoke the Triune God and confess Jesus as Lord and Saviour,
doing this not merely as individuals but also as corporate bodies. For
almost everyone regards the body in which he has heard the Gospel
as his Church and indeed, God's Church. All however, though in different ways, long for the one visible Church of God, a Church truly universal and set forth into the world that the world may be converted to
the Gospel and so be saved, to the glory of God.

The sacred council gladly notes all this. It has already declared its
teaching on the Church, and now, moved by a desire for the restoration
of unity among all the followers of Christ, it wishes to set before all
Catholics the ways and means by which they too can respond to this
grace and to this divine call.

CHAPTER I
Catholic Principles on Ecumenism

2. What has revealed the love of God among us is that the Father
has sent into the world his only-begotten Son, so that, being made man,
he might by his redemption give new life to the entire human race and
unify it (cf. 1 Jn. 4, 9; Col. 1, 18–20; Jn. 11, 52). Before offering himself
up as a spotless victim upon the altar, Christ prayed to his Father for
all who believe in him: "That they all may be one; even as thou, Father,
art in me, and I in thee, that they also may be one in us, so that the
world may believe that thou has sent me" (Jn. 17, 21). In his Church
he instituted the wonderful sacrament of the Eucharist by which the
unity of his Church is both signified and made a reality. He gave his
followers a new commandment to love one another (cf. Jn. 13, 34), and
promised the Spirit, their Advocate (cf. Jn. 16, 7), who as Lord and life-
giver should remain with them forever.

After being lifted upon the cross and glorified, the Lord Jesus poured
forth his Spirit as he had promised, and through the Spirit he has called
and gathered together the people of the New Covenant, who are the
Church, into a unity of faith, hope and charity, as the Apostle teaches
us: "There is one body and one Spirit, just as you were called to the
one hope of your calling; one Lord, one faith, one Baptism" (Eph. 4,
4–5). For "all you who have been baptized into Christ have put on
Christ . . . for you are all one in Christ Jesus" (Gal. 3, 27–28). It is the
Holy Spirit, dwelling in those who believe and pervading and ruling
over the Church as a whole, who brings about that wonderful communion of the faithful. He brings them into intimate union with Christ,
so that he is the principle of the Church's unity. The distribution of
graces and offices is his work too (cf. 1 Cor. 12, 4–11), enriching the
Church of Jesus Christ with different functions "in order to equip the
saints for the work of service, so as to build up the body of Christ"
(Eph. 4, 12).

In order to establish this his holy Church everywhere in the world till the end of time, Christ entrusted to the College of the Twelve the task of teaching, ruling and sanctifying (cf. Mt. 28, 18–20, collato Jn. 20, 21–23). Among their number he selected Peter, and after his confession of faith determined that on him he would build his Church. Also to Peter he promised the keys of the kingdom of heaven (cf. Mt. 16, 18, collato Mt. 18, 18), and after his profession of love, entrusted all his sheep to him to be confirmed in faith (cf. Lc. 22, 32) and shepherded in perfect unity (cf. Jn. 21, 15–18). Christ Jesus himself was forever to remain the chief cornerstone (cf. Eph. 2, 20) and shepherd of our souls (cf. 1 Petr. 2, 25; CONC. VATICANUM *I*, Sess. IV (1870), *Constitutio Pastor Aeternus: Collac 7*, 482 a).

Jesus Christ, then, willed that the apostles and their successors—the bishops with Peter's successor at their head—should preach the Gospel faithfully, administer the sacraments, and rule the Church in love. It is thus, under the action of the Holy Spirit, that Christ wills his people to increase, and he perfects his people's fellowship in unity: in their confessing the one faith, celebrating divine worship in common, and keeping the fraternal harmony of the family of God.

The Church, then, is God's only flock; it is like a standard high lifted for the nations to see it (cf. Is. 11, 10–12): for it serves all mankind through the Gospel of peace (cf. Eph. 2, 17–18, collato Mc. 16, 15) as it makes its pilgrim way in hope toward the fatherland above (cf. 1 Petr. 1, 3–9).

This is the sacred mystery of the unity of the Church, in Christ and through Christ, the Holy Spirit energizing its various functions. It is a mystery that finds its highest exemplar and source in the unity of the Persons of the Trinity: the Father and the Son in the Holy Spirit, one God.

3. Even in the beginnings of this one and only Church of God there arose certain rifts (cf. 1 Cor. 11, 18–19; Gal. 1, 6–9; 1 Jn. 2, 18–19), which the Apostle strongly condemned (cf. 1 Cor. 1, 11 sqq; 11, 22). But in subsequent centuries much more serious dissensions made their appearance and quite large communities came to be separated from full communion with the Catholic Church—for which, often enough, men of both sides were to blame. The children who are born into these Communities and who grow up believing in Christ cannot be accused of the sin involved in the separation, and the Catholic Church looks upon them as brothers, who respect and affection. For men who believe in Christ and have been truly baptized are in real communion with the Catholic Church even though this communion is imperfect. The differences that exist in varying degrees between them and the Catholic Church—whether in doctrine and sometimes in discipline, or concerning the structure of the Church—do indeed create many obstacles, sometimes serious ones, to full ecclesiastical communion. The ecumenical move-

ment is striving to overcome these obstacles. But even in spite of them it remains true that all who have been justified by faith in baptism are members of Christ's body (cf. CONC. FLORENTINUM, Sess. VIII (1439), *Dectreum Exultate Deo: Mansi* 31, 1055 A), and have a right to be called Christian, and so are with solid reasons accepted as brothers by the children of the Catholic Church (cf. S. AUGUSTINUS, *In Ps. 32, Enarr. II, 29:* PL 36, 299).

Moreover, some and even most, of the significant elements and endowments which together go to build up and give life to the Church itself, can exist outside the visible boundaries of the Catholic Church: the written word of God; the life of grace; faith, hope and charity, with the other interior gifts of the Holy Spirit, and visible elements too. All of these, which come from Christ and lead back to Christ, belong by right to the one Church of Christ.

The brethren divided from us also use many liturgical actions of the Christian religion. These most certainly can truly engender a life of grace in ways that vary according to the condition of each Church or Community. These liturgical actions must be regarded as capable of giving access to the community of salvation.

It follows that the separated Churches (cf. CONC. LATERANENSE IV (1215) *Constitutio IVa: Mansi* 22, 990; CONC. LUGDENENSE II (1274), *Professio fidei Michaelis Palaeologi: Mansi* 24, 71 F; CONC. FLORENTINUM, Sess. VI (1439), *Definitio Laetentur caeli: Mansi* 31, 1026 E.) and Communities as such, though we believe them to be deficient in some respects, have been by no means deprived of significance and importance in the mystery of salvation. For the Holy Spirit has not refrained from using them as means of salvation which derive their efficacy from the very fullness of grace and truth entrusted to the Church.

Nevertheless, our separated brethren, whether considered as individuals or as Communities and Churches, are not blessed with that unity which Jesus Christ wished to bestow on all those who through him were born again into one body, and with him quickened to newness of life—that unity which the Holy Scriptures and the ancient Tradition of the Church proclaim. For it is only through Christ's Catholic Church, which is "the all-embracing means of salvation," that they can benefit fully from the means of salvation. We believe that our Lord entrusted all the blessings of the New Covenant to the apostolic college alone, of which Peter is the head, in order to establish the one Body of Christ on earth to which all should be fully incorporated who belong in any way to the people of God. This people of God, though still in its members liable to sin, is ever growing in Christ during its pilgrimage on earth, and is guided by God's gentle wisdom, according to his hidden designs, until it shall happily arrive at the fullness of eternal glory in the heavenly Jerusalem.

4. Today, in many parts of the world, under the inspiring grace of the Holy Spirit, many efforts are being made in prayer, word and action

to attain that fulness of unity which Jesus Christ desires. The sacred council exhorts all the Catholic faithful to recognize the signs of the times and to take an active and intelligent part in the work of ecumenism.

The term "ecumenical movement" indicates the initiatives and activities planned and undertaken, according to the various needs of the Church and as opportunities offer, to promote Christian unity. These are: first, every effort to avoid expressions, judgments and actions which do not represent the condition of our separated brethren with truth and fairness and so make mutual relations with them more difficult; then, "dialogue" between competent experts from different Churches and Communities. At these meetings, which are organized in a religious spirit, each explains the teaching of his communion in greater depth and brings out clearly its distinctive features. In such dialogue, everyone gains a truer knowledge and more just appreciation of the teaching and religious life of both communions. In addition, the way is prepared for cooperation between them in the duties for the common good of humanity which are demanded by every Christian conscience; and, wherever this is allowed, there is prayer in common. Finally, all are led to examine their own faithfulness to Christ's will for the Church and accordingly to undertake with vigor the task of renewal and reform.

When such actions are undertaken prudently and patiently by the Catholic faithful, with the attentive guidance of their bishops, they promote justice and truth, concord and collaboration, as well as the spirit of brotherly love and unity. This is the way that, when the obstacles to perfect ecclesiastical communion have been gradually overcome, all Christians will at last, in a common celebration of the Eucharist, be gathered into a single Church in that unity which Christ bestowed on his Church from the beginning. We believe that this unity subsists in the Catholic Church as something she can never lose, and we hope that it will continue to increase until the end of time.

However, it should be evident that, when individuals wish for full Catholic communion, their preparation and reconciliation is an undertaking which of its nature is distinct from ecumenical action. But there is no opposition between the two, since both proceed from the marvelous ways of God.

Catholics, in their ecumenical work, must assuredly be concerned for their separated brethren, praying for them, keeping them informed about the Church, making the first approaches toward them. But their primary duty is to make a careful and honest appraisal of whatever needs to be done or renewed in the Catholic household itself, in order that its life may bear witness more clearly and faithfully to the teachings and institutions which have come to it from Christ through the hands of the Apostles.

For although the Catholic Church has been endowed with all divinely revealed truth and with all means of grace, yet its members fail to live by them with all the fervor that they should, so that the radiance of the

Church's image is less in the eyes of our separated brethren and of the world at large, and the growth of God's kingdom is delayed. All Catholics must therefore aim at Christian perfection (cf. Iac. 1, 4; Rom. 12, 1–2) and, each according to his station, play his part that the Church may daily be more purified and renewed. For the Church must bear in her own body the humility and dying of Jesus (cf. 2 Cor. 4, 10; Phil. 2, 5–8), against the day when Christ will present her to himself in all her glory without spot or wrinkle (cf. Eph. 5, 27).

All in the Church must preserve unity in essentials. But let all, according to the gifts they have received enjoy a proper freedom, in their various forms of spiritual life and discipline, in their different liturgical rites, and even in their theological elaborations of revealed truth. In all things let charity prevail. If they are true to this course of action, they will be giving ever better expression to the authentic catholicity and apostolicity of the Church.

On the other hand, Catholics must gladly acknowledge and esteem the truly Christian endowments from our common heritage which are to be found among our separated brethren. It is right and salutary to recognize the riches of Christ and virtuous works in the lives of others who are bearing witness to Christ, sometimes even to the shedding of their blood. For God is always wonderful in his works and worthy of all praise.

Nor should we forgot that anything wrought by the grace of the Holy Spirit in the hearts of our separated brethren can be a help to our own edification. Whatever is truly Christian is never contrary to what genuinely belongs to the faith; indeed, it can always bring a deeper realization of the mystery of Christ and the Church.

Nevertheless, the divisions among Christians prevent the Church from attaining the fulness of catholicity proper to her, in those of her sons who, though attached to her by baptism, are yet separated from full communion with her. Furthermore, the Church herself finds it more difficult to express in actual life her full catholicity in all her bearings.

This sacred council is gratified to note that the participation by the Catholic faithful in ecumenical work is growing daily. It commends this work to the bishops everywhere in the world to be vigorously stimulated by them and guided with prudence.

CHAPTER II
The Practice of Ecumenism

5. The attainment of union is the concern of the whole Church, faithful and clergy alike. This concern extends to everyone, whatever his talent, whether it be exercised in his daily Christian life or in his theological and historical research. This concern itself reveals already to some extent the bond of brotherhood between all Christians and it helps toward that full and perfect unity which God in his kindness wills.

6. Every renewal of the Church is essentially grounded in an increase of fidelity to her own calling. Undoubtedly this is the basis of the movement toward unity.

Christ summons the Church to continual reformation as she goes her pilgrim way. The Church is always in need of this, insofar as she is an institution of men here on earth. Thus if, in various times and circumstances, there have been deficiencies in moral conduct or in church discipline, or even in the way that church teaching has been formulated—to be carefully distinguished from the deposit of faith itself—these can and should be set right at the opportune moment.

Church renewal has therefore notable ecumenical importance. Already in various spheres of the Church's life, this renewal is taking place. The Biblical and liturgical movements, the preaching of the word of God and catechetics, the apostolate of the laity, new forms of religious life and the spirituality of married life, and the Church's social teaching and activity—all these should be considered as promises and guarantees for the future progress of ecumenism.

7. There can be no ecumenism worthy of the name without a change of heart. For it is from renewal of the inner life of our minds (cf. Eph. 4, 24), from self-denial and an unstinted love that desires of unity take their rise and develop in a mature way. We should therefore pray to the Holy Spirit for the grace to be genuinely self-denying, humble, gentle in the service of others, and to have an attitude of brotherly generosity towards them. St. Paul says: "I, therefore, a prisoner for the Lord, beg you to lead a life worthy of the calling to which you have been called, with all humility and meekness, with patience, forbearing one another in love, eager to maintain the unity of the spirit in the bond of peace" (Eph. 4, 1–3). This exhortation is directed especially to those raised to sacred orders precisely that the work of Christ may be continued. He came among us "not to be served but to serve" (Mt. 20, 28).

The words of St. John hold good about sins against unity: "If we say we have not sinned, we make him a liar, and his word is not in us" (1 Jn. 1, 10). So we humbly beg pardon of God and of our separated brethren, just as we forgive them that trespass against us.

The faithful should remember that the more effort they make to live holier lives according to the Gospel, the better will they further Christian unity and put it into practice. For the closer their union with the Father, the Word, and the Spirit, the more deeply and easily will they be able to grow in mutual brotherly love.

8. This change of heart and holiness of life, along with public and private prayer for the unity of Christians, should be regarded as the soul of the whole ecumenical movement, and merits the name, "spiritual ecumenism."

It is a recognized custom for Catholics to have frequent recourse to that prayer for the unity of the Church which the Saviour himself on the eve of his death so fervently appealed to his Father: "That they may all be one" (Jn. 17, 20).

In certain special circumstances, such as the prescribed prayers "for unity," and during ecumenical gatherings, it is allowable, indeed desirable that Catholics should join in prayer with their separated brethren. Such prayers in common are certainly an effective means of obtaining the grace of unity, and they are a true expression of the ties which still bind Catholics to their separated brethren. "For where two or three are gathered together in my name, there am I in the midst of them" (Mt. 18, 20).

Yet worship in common (communicatio in sacris) is not to be considered as a means to be used indiscriminately for the restoration of Christian unity. There are two main principles governing the practice of such common worship: first, the bearing witness to the unity of the Church, and second, the sharing in the means of grace. Witness to the unity of the Church very generally forbids common worship to Christians, but the grace to be had from it sometimes commends this practice. The course to be adopted, with due regard to all the circumstances of time, place, and persons, is to be decided by local episcopal authority, unless otherwise provided for by the Bishops' Conference according to its statutes, or by the Holy See.

9. We must get to know the outlook of our separated brethren. To achieve this purpose, study is of necessity required, and this must be pursued with a sense of realism and good will. Catholics, who already have a proper grounding, need to acquire a more adequate understanding of the respective doctrines of our separated brethren, their history, their spiritual and liturgical life, their religious psychology and general background. Most valuable for this purpose are meetings of the two sides—especially for discussion of theological problems—where each can treat with the other on an equal footing—provided that these who take part in them are truly competent and have the approval of the authorities. From such dialogue will emerge still more clearly what the situation of the Catholic Church really is. In this way too the outlook of our separated brethren will be better understood, and our own belief more aptly explained.

10. Sacred theology and other branches of knowledge, especially of an historical nature, must be taught with due regard for the ecumenical point of view, so that they may correspond more exactly with the facts.

It is most important that future pastors and priests should have mastered a theology that has been carefully worked out in this way and not polemically, especially with regard to those aspects which concern the relations of separated brethren with the Catholic Church.

This importance is the greater because the instruction and spiritual formation of the faithful and of religious depends so largely on the formation which their priests have received.

Moreover, Catholics engaged in missionary work in the same territories as other Christians ought to know, particularly in these times,
the problems and the benefits in their apostolate which derive from the
ecumenical movement.

11. The way in which the Catholic faith is expressed should never
become an obstacle to dialogue with our brethren. It is, of course,
essential that the doctrine should be clearly presented in its entirety.
Nothing is so foreign to the spirit of ecumenism as a false irenicism, in
which the purity of Catholic doctrine suffers loss and its assured
genuine meaning is clouded.

At the same time, the Catholic faith must be explained more profoundly and precisely, in such a way and in such terms as our separated
brethren can also really understand.

In ecumenical dialogue, when Catholic theologians join with separated brethren in common study of the divine mysteries, they should,
while standing fast by the teaching of the Church, pursue the work with
love for the truth, with charity, and with humility. When comparing
doctrines with one another, they should remember that in Catholic
doctrine there exists a "hierarchy" of truths, since they vary in their
relation to the fundamental Christian faith. Thus the way will be
opened whereby this kind of "fraternal rivalry" will incite all to have a
clearer awareness and a deeper realization of the unfathomable riches of
Christ (cf. Eph. 3, 8).

12. Before the whole world let all Christians confess their faith in
God, one and three in the incarnate Son of God, our Redeemer and
Lord. United in their efforts, and with mutual respect, let them bear
witness to our common hope which does not play us false. In these days
when cooperation in social matters is so widespread, all men without
exception are called to work together, with much greater reason all
those who believe in God, but most of all, all Christians in that they
bear the name of Christ. Cooperation among Christians vividly expresses
the relationship which in fact already unites them, and it sets in clearer
relief the features of Christ the Servant. Such cooperation, which has
already begun in many countries, should be developed more and more,
particularly in regions where a social and technical evolution is taking
place. It should contribute to a just evaluation of the dignity of the
human person, to the establishment of the blessings of peace, the application of Gospel principles to social life, and the advancement of
the arts and sciences in a truly Christian spirit. Cooperation among
Christians should also employ every possible means to relieve the
afflictions of our times such as famine and natural disasters, illiteracy
and poverty, lack of housing and the unequal distribution of wealth.
All believers in Christ can, through such cooperation, be led to acquire
a better knowledge and appreciation of one another, and so is made
smooth the road which leads to the unity of Christians.

CHAPTER III

*Churches and Ecclesial Communities Separated from
the Roman Apostolic See.*

13. We now turn our attention to the two chief types of division as they affect the seamless robe of Christ.

The first divisions occurred in the East, when the dogmatic formulae of Ephesus and Chalcedon were challenged, and later when ecclesiastical communion between the Eastern Patriarchates and the Roman See was dissolved.

Other divisions arose more than four centuries later in the West, stemming from the events which are usually referred to as "The Reformation." As a result, many Communions, national or confessional, were separated from the Roman See. Among those in which Catholic traditions and institutions in part continue to exist, the Angelican Communion occupies a special place.

These various divisions differ greatly from one another not only by reason of their origins, place and time, but still more in the serious matters of belief and church order. Therefore, without minimizing the differences between the various Christian bodies, and without over-looking the bonds between them which exist in spite of these differences, the council proposes the following considerations for prudent ecumenical action.

I. THE SPECIAL POSITION OF THE EASTERN CHURCHES

14. For many centuries the Church of the East and that of the West each followed their separate ways though linked in a brotherly union of faith and sacramental life; the Roman See by common consent acted as guide when disagreements arose between them over matters of faith or discipline. Among other matters of moment, it is a pleasure for this council to remind everyone that there exist in the East many particular or local Churches, among which the Patriarchal Churches hold first place, and many of which trace their origins back to the apostles themselves. Hence a matter of primary concern and care among the Easterns, in their local churches, has been, and still is, to preserve the family ties of common faith and charity which ought to exist between sister Churches.

Similarly it must not be forgotten that from the beginning the Churches of the East have had a treasury from which the Western Church has drawn extensively—in liturgical practice, spiritual tradition, and law. Nor must we undervalue the fact that it was the ecumenical councils held in the East that defined the basic dogmas of the Christian faith, on the Trinity, on the Word of God, who took flesh of the Virgin Mary. To preserve this faith these Churches have suffered and still suffer much.

However, the inheritance handed down by the apostles was received with differences of form and manner, so that from the earliest times of the Church it was explained variously in different places, owing to diversities of genius and conditions of life. All this, quite apart from external causes, prepared the way for divisions arising also from a lack of charity and mutual understanding.

For this reason the council urges all, but especially those who intend to devote themselves to the restoration of full communion between the Churches of the East and the Catholic Church, to give due consideration to this special feature of the origin and growth of the Eastern Churches, and to the character of the relations which obtained between them and the Roman See before separation. They must take full acount of all these factors and, where this is done, it will greatly contribute to the dialogue in view.

15. Everyone knows with what great love the Christians of the East celebrate the sacred liturgy, especially the eucharistic mystery, source of the Church's life and pledge of future glory, in which the faithful, united with their bishop, have access to God the Father through the Son, the Word made flesh, suffering, and glorified, and so, in the outpouring of the Holy Spirit, they enter into communion with the most holy Trinity, being made "sharers of the divine nature" (2 Petr. 1, 4). Hence, through the celebration of the Holy Eucharist in each of these churches, the Church of God is built up and grows in stature (cf. S. IOANNES CHRYSOSTOMOS, In Ioannem Homelia XLVI, PG 59, 260–262.) and through concelebration, their communion with one another is made manifest.

In their liturgical worship, the Christians of the East pay high tribute, in beautiful hymns of praise, to Mary ever Virgin, whom the ecumenical Synod of Ephesus solemnly proclaimed to be the holy Mother of God, so that Christ might be acknowledged as being truly Son of God and Son of Man, according to the Scriptures. Many also are the saints whose praise they sing, among them the Fathers of the universal Church.

These Churches, although separated from us, yet possess true sacraments and above all, by apostolic succession, the priesthood and the Eucharist, whereby they are linked with us in closest intimacy. Therefore some worship in common (communicatio in sacris), given suitable circumstances and the approval of Church authority, is not merely possible but to be encouraged.

Moreover, in the East are to be found the riches of those spiritual traditions which are given expression especially in monastic life. From the glorious times of the holy Fathers, monastic spirituality flourished in the East, then later flowed over into the Western world, and there provided the source from which Latin monastic life took its rise and has drawn fresh vigor ever since. Catholics there are earnestly recommended to avail themselves of the spiritual riches of the Eastern Fathers which lift up the whole man to the contemplation of the divine.

The rich liturgical and spiritual heritage of the Eastern Churches should be known, venerated, preserved and cherished by all. They must recognize that this is of supreme importance for the faithful preservation of the fullness of Christian tradition, and for bringing about reconciliation between Eastern and Western Christians.

16. From the earliest times the Eastern Churches followed their own forms of ecclesiastical law and custom, which were sanctioned by the approval of the Fathers of the Church, of synods, and even of ecumenical councils. Far from being an obstacle to the Church's unity, such diversity of customs and observances only adds to her comeliness, and is of great help in carrying out her mission, as has already been stated. To remove, then, all shadow of doubt, this holy synod solemnly declares that the Churches of the East, while remembering the necessary unity of the whole Church, have the power and duty to govern themselves according to the disciplines proper to them, since these are better suited to the character of their faithful, and more for the good of their souls. The perfect observance of this principle which, for all its periodical neglect, is sanctioned by longstanding tradition, is one of the essential prerequisites for any restoration of unity.

17. What has just been said about the variety that can exist in the Church must also be taken to apply to the differences in theological expression of doctrine. In the study of revelation East and West have followed different methods, and have developed differently their understanding and confession of God's truth. It is hardly surprising, then, if from time to time one tradition has come nearer to a full appreciation of some aspects of a mystery of revelation than the other, or has expressed it to better advantage. In such cases, these various theological expressions are to be considered often as mutually complementary rather than conflicting. Where the authentic theological traditions of the Eastern Church are concerned, we must recognize the admirable way in which they have their roots in Holy Scripture, and how they are nurtured and given expression in the life of the liturgy. They derive their strength too from the living tradition of the apostles and from the works of the Fathers and spiritual writers of the Eastern Churches. Thus they promote the right ordering of Christian life and, indeed, pave the way to a full vision of Christian truth.

All this heritage of spirituality and liturgy, of discipline and theology, in its various traditions, this holy synod declares to belong to the full Catholic and apostolic character of the Church. We thank God that many Eastern children of the Catholic Church, who preserve this heritage, and wish to express it more faithfully and completely in their lives, are already living in full communion with their brethren who follow the tradition of the West.

18. After taking all these factors into consideration, this sacred council solemnly repeats the declaration of previous councils and Roman Pontiffs, that for the restoration or the maintenance of unity and communion it is necessary "to impose no burden beyond what is essential" (Acts 15, 28). It is the council's urgent desire that, in the various organizations and living activities of the Church, every effort should be made toward the gradual realization of this unity, especially by prayer, and by fraternal dialogue on points of doctrine and the more pressing pastoral problems of our time. Similarly, the council commends to the pastors and faithful of the Catholic Church to develop closer relations with those who are no longer living in the East but are far from home, so that friendly collaboration with them may increase, in the spirit of love, to the exclusion of all feeling of rivalry or strife. If this cause is wholeheartedly promoted, the council hopes that the barrier dividing the Church between East and West will be removed, and that at last there may be but the one dwelling, firmly established on Christ Jesus, the cornerstone, who will make both one (cf. CONC. florentinum, Sess. VI (1439), Definitio Laetentur caeli: Mansi 31 1026 E).

II. SEPARATED CHURCHES AND ECCLESIAL COMMUNITIES IN THE WEST

19. In the great upheaval which began in the West toward the end of the Middle Ages, and in later times too, Churches and ecclesial Communities came to be separated from the Apostolic See of Rome. Yet they have retained a particularly close affinity with the Catholic Church as a result of the long centuries in which all Christendom lived together in ecclesiastical communion.

However, these Churches and ecclesial Communities have different convictions in matters of doctrine and the spiritual life. Since they vary considerably not only with us, but also among themselves, the task of describing them at all adequately is extremely difficult; and we have no intention of making such an attempt here.

Although the ecumenical movement and the desire for peace with the Catholic Church have not yet taken hold everywhere, it is our hope that ecumenical feeling and mutual esteem may gradually increase among all men.

It must however be admitted that in these Churches and ecclesial Communities there exist important differences from the Catholic Church, not only of an historical, sociological, psychological and cultural character, but especially in the interpretation of revealed truth. To make easier the ecumenical dialogue in spite of these differences, we

wish to set down some considerations which can, and indeed should
serve as a basis and encouragement for such dialogue.

20. Our thoughts turn first to those Christians who make open confession of Jesus Christ as God and Lord and as the one mediator between God and men, to the glory of the one God, Father, Son and Holy
Spirit. We are aware indeed that there exist considerable divergences
from the doctrine of the Catholic Church concerning Christ Himself, the
Word of God made flesh, the work of redemption, and consequently,
concerning the mystery and ministry of the Church, and the role of
Mary in the plan of salvation. But we rejoice to see that our separated
brethren look to Christ as the source and center of Church unity. Their
longing for union with Christ inspires them to seek an ever closer
unity, and also to bear witness to their faith among the peoples of the
earth.

21. A love and reverence of Holy Scripture which might be described
as devotion, leads our brethren to a constant meditative study of the
sacred text. For the Gospel "is the power of God for salvation to every
one who has faith, to the Jew first and then to the Greek" (Rom. 1, 16).
While invoking the Holy Spirit, they seek in these very Scriptures
God as it were speaking to them in Christ, whom the prophets foretold,
who is the Word of God made flesh for us. They contemplate in the
Scriptures the life of Christ and what the Divine Master taught and
did for our salvation, especially the mysteries of His death and
resurrection.
But while the Christians who are separated from us hold strongly
to the divine authority of the Sacred Books, they differ from ours—
some in one way, some in another—regarding the relationship between
Scripture and the Church. For, according to Catholic belief, the authentic teaching of the Church has a special place in the interpretation
and preaching of the written word of God.
But Sacred Scriptures provide for the work of dialogue an instrument
of the highest value in the mighty hand of God for the attainment of
that unity which the Saviour holds out to all.

22. Whenever the Sacrament of Baptism is duly administered as Our
Lord instituted it, and is received with the right dispositions, a person
is truly incorporated into the crucified and glorified Christ, and reborn
to a sharing of the divine life, as the Apostle says: "You were buried
together with Him in baptism, and in Him also rose again—through
faith in the working of God, who raised Him from the dead" (Col. 2, 12)
(cf. Rom. 6, 4).
Thus baptism establishes a sacramental bond of unity which links all
who have been reborn by it. But of itself baptism is only a beginning,
an inauguration wholly directed toward the fullness of life in Christ.
Baptism, therefore, envisages a complete profession of faith, complete

incorporation in the system of salvation such as Christ willed it to be, and finally completeness of unity which eucharistic communion gives.

Though the ecclesial Communities which are separated from us lack the fullness of unity with us which should flow from baptism, and though we believe they have not retained the proper reality of the eucharistic mystery in its fullness, especially because of the absence of the sacrament of Orders, nevertheless when they commemorate His death and resurrection in the Lord's Supper, they profess that it signifies life in communion with Christ and look forward to His coming in glory. For these reasons, the subjects which should be subjects of dialogue are those of the Lord's Supper and the other sacraments, of worship, and of the Church's ministry.

23. The daily Christian lives of these brethren are nourished by their faith in Christ. They are strengthened by the grace of baptism and by hearing the word of God. This shows itself in their private prayer, their meditation on the Bible, in their Christian family life, and in the worship of a community gathered together to praise God. Moreover, their form of worship not seldom displays notable features of the liturgy which they shared with us of old.

Their faith in Christ bears fruit in praise and thanksgiving for the good things received from the hands of God. Among them, too, is a strong sense of justice and a true charity toward others. This active faith has been responsible for many organizations for the relief of spiritual and material distress, the furtherance of the education of youth, the improvement of the social conditions of life, and the promotion of peace throughout the world.

While it is true that many Christians understand the moral teaching of the Gospel differently from Catholics, and do not accept the same solutions to the more difficult problems of modern society, nevertheless they share our desire to stand by the words of Christ as the source of Christian virtue, and to obey the command of the Apostle: "And whatever you do, in word or in work, do all in the name of the Lord Jesus Christ, giving thanks to God the Father through Him" (Col. 3, 17). For that reason an ecumenical dialogue might start with discussion of the application of the Gospel to moral conduct.

24. Now that we have briefly set out the conditions for ecumenical action and the principles by which it is to be directed, we look with confidence to the future. This sacred council exhorts the faithful to avoid superficial and imprudent zeal, for these could only hinder real progress toward unity. Their ecumenical action must be fully and sincerely Catholic, that is to say, faithful to the truth which we have received from the apostles and Fathers of the Church, in harmony with the faith which the Catholic Church has always professed, and at the same time directed toward that fullness to which Our Lord wills His Body to grow in the course of time.

It is the urgent wish of this holy council that the measures undertaken by the sons of the Catholic Church should in practice develop in step with those of our separated brethren. No obstacle must be placed to the ways of divine Providence or any limit set to the future inspirations of the Holy Spirit. The council moreover professes its awareness that human powers and capacities cannot achieve this holy objective—the reconciling of all Christians in the unity of the one and only Church of Christ. It is because of this that the council rests all its hope on the prayer of Christ for the Church, on our Father's love for us, and on the power of the Holy Spirit. "And hope does not disappoint, because God's love has been poured into our hearts through the Holy Spirit, who has been given to us" (Rom. 5, 5).

Declaration on the Jews: Two Versions

✠

32. (*On the inheritance common to Christians and Jews.*) The Church of Christ gladly acknowledges that the beginnings of its faith and election, in accordance with God's mystery of salvation, are to be found already among the Patriarchs and Prophets. Indeed, all Christians believe that, as sons of Abraham by faith (cf. Gal. 3, 7), they are included in this Patriarch's vocation and that the salvation of the Church is mystically prefigured in the exodus of the chosen people from the land of bondage. Nor can the Church as a new creation in Christ (cf. Eph. 2, 15) and as the people of the New Covenant ever forget that it is a continuation of that people with whom God in his ineffable mercy once designed to enter into the Old Covenant and to whom he chose to entrust the revelation contained in the Books of the Old Testament.

Moreover, the Church does not forget that from this Jewish people

* *New York Herald Tribune,* Sept. 30, 1964. The document was originally an Appendix or Annex to the schema on Ecumenism, hence the numbering of the paragraphs.

were born Christ, according to the flesh, the mother of Christ, the Virgin Mary, as well as the Apostles, the foundation and the pillars of the Church.

Further, the Church was always mindful and will never overlook Apostle Paul's words relating to the Jews, "whose is the adoption, and the glory, and the covenants and the giving of the law, and the service, and the promises" (Rom. 9, 4).

Since such is the inheritance accepted by Christians from the Jews, this Holy Council is resolved expressly to further and to recommend reciprocal understanding and appreciation, to be obtained by theological study and fraternal discussion and, beyond that, in as much as it severely disapproves of any wrong inflicted upon men wheresoever, it equally deplores and condemns hatred and maltreatment of Jews.

It is also worth remembering that the union of the Jewish people with the Church is a part of the Christian hope. Accordingly, and following the teaching of Apostle Paul (cf. Rom. 11, 25), the Church expects in unshakable faith and with ardent desire the entrance of that people into the fullness of the people of God established by Christ.

Everyone should be careful, therefore, not to expose the Jewish people as a rejected nation, be it in Catechetical tuition, in preaching of God's Word or in worldly conversation, nor should anything else be said or done which may alienate the minds of men from the Jews. Equally, all should be on their guard not to impute to the Jews of our time that which was perpetrated in the Passion of Christ.

33. (*All men have God as Father.*) The Lord Jesus has clearly confirmed that God is the Father of all men, as this was already stated in the Writings of the Old Testament and is suggested by reason itself. But we surely cannot appeal or pray to God as the Father of all, if we deny brotherly behavior to some men who are all created in the image of God. The attitude of man towards God as Father and the attitude of man towards man as brother are so closely connected that any negation of human brotherhood carries with it or leads to the negation of God himself with whom there is no respect of persons (cf. 2 Par. 19, 7; Rom. 2, 11; Eph. 6, 9; Col. 3, 25; 1 Petr. 1, 17). The first commandment is in fact so interwoven with the second that we cannot be acquitted from our debts unless we ourselves wholeheartedly acquit our debtors. Indeed, it was said already in the Old Law: "Have we not all one Father? Hath not one God created us? Why do we deal treacherously every man against his brother?" (Mal. 2, 10); the same is even more clearly reaffirmed in the New Law: "He that loveth not his brother whom he hath seen, how can he love God whom he hath not seen? And this commandment have we from him that he who loveth God love his brother also." (1 Jo. 4, 20–21.)

Impelled by such love for our brethren, let us consider with great diligence views and doctrines which, though in many points different from ours, in so many others, however, carry the ray of that truth which gives light to every man born into this world. Thus we embrace also, and first of all, the Moslems who worship one personal and recompensing God and who in religious feeling as well as through many channels of human culture came closer to us.

34. (*Any kind of discrimination is to be condemned.*) In consequence, any theory or practice which leads to discrimination between man and man or between nation and nation, insofar as human dignity and the rights flowing therefrom are concerned, is devoid of foundation.

It is imperative, therefore, that all men of good will and Christians in particular abstain from any discrimination or vexation of human beings on grounds of their race, color, social status or religion. As to the Christians, the Holy Council solemnly entreats them "to behave seemly among gentiles" (1 Petr. 2, 12) and if possible and insofar as it depends on them, to maintain peace with all men (cf. Rom. 12, 18); it enjoins them, moreover, to love not only the neighbor, but even the enemies, should they think to have them, that they should be in truth the sons of the Father who is in heaven and who makes his sun rise over all (cf. Mt. 5, 44–45).

II. REVISED DRAFT DECLARATION ON THE CHURCH'S RELATIONSHIP TOWARD NON-CHRISTIAN RELIGIONS, APPROVED IN A FIRST VOTE ON NOVEMBER 20, 1964*

In this age of ours when mankind is being drawn closer together, day by day, and the ties between peoples here and there are made stronger, the Church weighs earnestly her relationship toward non-Christian religions.

One is the community of all peoples, one their origin, for God made the entire human race live on all the face of the earth (cf. Acts 17, 26). One, too, is their ultimate end, God: His providence, His goodness—of which creation is the witness—His saving design extend toward all men (cf. Wisd. 8, Acts 14, 17; Rom. 2, 6–7, 1 Tim. 2, 4). And in the end all the elect will be united in that Holy City whose light is the glory of God, that City where the nations will walk in His radiance (cf. Apoc. 21, 23 f).

Men expect from the various religions answers to the unsolved riddles of the human condition, riddles that move the hearts of men today as they did in olden times: What is man? What is the meaning, what is the purpose of our lives? What is the moral good, what sin? Which is the road to true happiness? What are death, judgment, and retribution after death? What, finally, is that ultimate, inexpressible mystery which encompasses our existence, which is the fountain as well as the destiny of our being?

Ever since primordial days, numerous peoples have had a certain

* *The Catholic Herald*, London, Dec. 4, 1964.

perception of that hidden Power which hovers over the course of things and over the events that make up the lives of men: some have even come to know of a Supreme Being and Father.

Religions, however, that are entwined with an advanced culture have been able to use, in their struggle for an answer to man's great questions, more refined concepts and a more developed language.

In Hinduism, for instance, men try to fathom the divine mystery, expressing it through an inexhaustible abundance of myths and through keen efforts of a philosophical kind; they seek freedom from the anguish of our human condition through ascetical methods, profound meditation, and a flight to God, full of love and trust.

Again, Buddhism realises the radical inadequacy of this changeable world; it teaches a way by which men, with minds devout and confident, seek to liberate themselves, through a self-denial and inner cleansing, from the fleetingness of things, and to attain a state of lasting quiet. Other religions, everywhere on earth, counter the restlessness of the human heart, each in its own manner, by proposing ways, that is to say, doctrines, rules of life, and sacred rites.

The Catholic Church scorns nothing in these religions that is true and holy. For ceaselessly she proclaims Christ, "the Way, the Truth, and the Life" (Jn. 14, 6), in whom God reconciled all things to Himself (cf. 2 Cor. 15, 19). Having learned of various dispositions toward salvation (cf. Irenaeus, *Adv. Haer.* IV, 28, 2; PG 7, 1062), she regards with sincere reverence those ways of action and of life, those precepts and teachings which, differ though they do from the ones she sets forth, reflect nonetheless a ray of that Truth which enlightens all men!

The Church, therefore, admonishes her sons that they converse and collaborate with the followers of other religions in order to preserve, indeed, advance those spiritual and moral goods as well as those sociocultural values that have a home among men of other religious traditions.

The Church is filled with esteem for Moslems: they adore the one God who lives, exists in Himself, and wields all power; they adore the Creator of heaven and earth who has spoken to men; they strive to obey wholeheartedly even His incomprehensible decrees, just as Abraham did, to whose faith they like to link their own.

Though Moslems do not acknowledge Jesus as God, they revere Him as a Prophet. They also honour Mary, His Virgin-Mother; at times, they even call on her with devotion. Again, they await the day of judgment when God will reward all those who have risen.

Furthermore, as they worship God through prayer, almsgiving, and fasting, so they seek to make the moral life—be it that of the individual or that of the family and society—conform to His Will.

In the course of centuries, however, not a few quarrels and hostilities have arisen between Christians and Moslems. Hence this sacred synod urges all not only to forget the past but also to work honestly for mutual understanding and to further as well as guard together social justice, all moral goods, especially peace and freedom so that the whole of mankind may benefit from their endeavour.

As this sacred synod searches into the mystery of the Church, it remembers the bond that ties the people of the New Covenant to Abraham's stock.

With a grateful heart, the Church of Christ acknowledges that, according to God's saving design, the beginnings of her faith and her election were already among the patriarchs, Moses, and the prophets. She professes that all who believe in Christ—Abraham's sons according to faith—were included in the same patriarch's call, likewise that her salvation is typically foreshadowed by the chosen people's exodus from the land of bondage.

The Church, therefore, cannot forget that she received the revelation of the Old Testament from the people with whom God in His ineffable mercy concluded the former Covenant. Nor can she forget that she feeds upon the root of that cultivated olive tree into which the wild shoots of the Gentiles have been grafted (cf. Rom. 11, 17–24). Indeed, the Church believes that by His Cross Christ our Peace reconciled the Jews and Gentiles, making both one (cf. Eph. 2, 14, 16).

The Church keeps ever in mind the words of the Apostle about his kinsmen: "Theirs is the sonship, the glory, the covenants, the giving of the law, the worship, and the promises. Theirs are the patriarchs, and of them is the Christ according to the flesh," the Son of Mary the Virgin (Rom. 9, 4–5).

No less does she recall that the Apostles, the Church's mainstay and pillars, as well as most of the early disciples who proclaimed Christ's Gospel to the world, sprang from the Jewish people.

Even though a large part of the Jews did not accept the Gospel, they remain most dear to God for the sake of the patriarchs. This is the witness of the Apostle as is the utterance that God's gifts and call are irrevocable (cf. Rom. 11, 28 f). In company with the prophets and the same Apostle, the Church awaits that day, known to God alone, on which all peoples will address the Lord in a single voice and "serve Him shoulder to shoulder" (Soph. 3, 9; cf. Is. 66, 23; Ps. 65, 4; Rom. 11, 11–32).

Since the spiritual patrimony common to Christians and Jews is of such magnitude, this Sacred Synod wants to support and recommend their mutual knowledge and respect, a knowledge and respect that are the fruit, above all, of biblical and theological studies as well as of fraternal dialogues.

Moreover, this synod, in her rejection of injustice of whatever kind and wherever inflicted upon men, remains mindful of that common patrimony and so deplores, indeed, condemns hatred and persecutions of Jews, whether they arose in former or in our own days.

May all, then, see to it that in their catechetical work or in their preaching of the word of God they do not teach anything that could give rise to hatred or contempt of Jews in the hearts of Christians.

May they never present the Jewish people as one rejected, cursed, or guilty of deicide. All that happened to Christ in His passion cannot be attributed to the whole people then alive, much less to that of today.

Besides, the Church has always held and holds now that Christ underwent His passion and death freely, because of the sins of all men and out of infinite love. It is, therefore, the burden of Christian preaching to proclaim the Cross of Christ as the sign of God's all-embracing love and as the fountain from which every grace flows.

We cannot truly address God the Father of all, if we refuse to treat some men or other in a brotherly way, even though they are created in His image. Man's attitude toward God the Father and his attitude toward his human brethren are so intimately linked, one to the other, that Scripture is able to say: "He who does not love does not know God" (1 Jn. 4, 8; cf. 1, Jn. 2, 9–1 Lk. 10, 25–37).

Thus any theory or practice that, so far as their human dignity is concerned, discriminates between man and man or people and people, creating a different set of rights for each of them—any such theory or practice is shown to be without foundation.

All men, therefore, but especially Christians must refrain from discrimination against, or harassment of, others because of their race, colour, creed or walk of life. But this is not enough. Treading the footsteps of the holy Apostles Peter and Paul, this Sacred Synod ardently implores the faithful that they rather "maintain good conduct among the Gentiles" (1 Pet. 2, 12) and live, if possible, that is, so far as it depends on them, in peace with all men (cf. Rom. 12, 18), so that they may really be sons of the Father who is in heaven (cf. Mt. 5, 44).

Decree on Eastern Rite Churches

PROMULGATED NOVEMBER 21, 1964

✠

1. The Catholic Church holds in high esteem the institutions, liturgical rites, ecclesiastical traditions and the established standards of the Christian life of the Eastern Churches, for in them, distinguished as they are for their venerable antiquity, there remains conspicuous the tradition that has been handed down from the Apostles through the Fathers and that forms part of the divinely revealed and undivided heritage of the universal Chuch. This Sacred Ecumenical Council, therefore, in its care for the Eastern Churches which bear living witness to this tradition, in order that they may flourish and with new apostolic vigor execute the task entrusted to them, has determined to lay down a number of principles, in addition to those which refer to the universal Church; all else is remitted to the care of the Eastern synods and of the Holy See.

2. The Holy Catholic Church, which is the Mystical Body of Christ, is made up of the faithful who are organically united in the Holy

Spirit by the same faith, the same sacraments and the same government and who, combining together into various groups which are held together by a hierarchy, form separate Churches or Rites. Between these there exists an admirable bond of union, such that the variety within the Church in no way harms its unity; rather it manifests it, for it is the mind of the Catholic Church that each individual Church or Rite should retain its traditions whole and entire and likewise that it should adapt its way of life to the different needs of time and place.

3. These individual Churches, whether of the East or the West, although they differ somewhat among themselves in rite (to use the current phrase), that is, in liturgy, ecclesiastical discipline, and spiritual heritage, are, neverthless, each as much as the others, entrusted to the pastoral government of the Roman Pontiff, the divinely appointed successor of St. Peter in supreme government over the universal Church. They are consequently of equal dignity, so that none of them is superior to the others as regards rite and they enjoy the same rights and are under the same obligations, also in respect of preaching the Gospel to the whole world (cf. Mark 16, 15) under the guidance of the Roman Pontiff.

4. Means should be taken therefore in every part of the world for the protection and advancement of all the individual Churches and, to this end, there should be established parishes and a special hierarchy where the spiritual good of the faithful demands it. The Ordinaries of the different individual Churches with jurisdiction in one and the same territory should, by taking common counsel in regular meetings, strive to promote unity of action and with common endeavor to sustain common tasks, so as better to further the good of religion and to safeguard more effectively the ordered way of life of the clergy.

All clerics and those aspiring to sacred orders should be instructed in the rites and especially in the principles that must be applied in interritual questions. The laity, too, should be taught as part of its catechetical education about rites and their rules.

Finally, each and every Catholic, as also the baptized of every non-Catholic church or denomination who enters into the fulness of the Catholic communion, must retain his own rite wherever he is, must cherish it and observe it, without prejudice to the right in special cases of persons, communities or areas, of recourse to the Apostolic See, which, as the supreme judge of interchurch relations, will, acting itself or through other authorities, meet the needs of the occasion in an ecumenical spirit, by the issuance of opportune directives, decrees or rescripts.

5. History, tradition and abundant ecclesiastical institutions bear outstanding witness to the great merit owing to the Eastern Churches by

the universal Church. The Sacred Council, therefore, not only accords to this ecclesiastical and spiritual heritage the high regard which is its due and rightful praise, but also unhesitatingly looks on it as the heritage of the universal Church. For this reason it solemnly declares that the Churches of the East, as much as those of the West, have a full right and are in duty bound to rule themselves, each in accordance with its own established disciplines, since all these are praiseworthy from their venerable antiquity, more harmonious with the character of their faithful and more suited to the promotion of the good of souls.

6. All Eastern Rite members should know and be convinced that they can and should always preserve their legitimate liturgical rite and their established way of life, and that these may not be altered except to obtain for themselves an organic improvement. All these, then, must be observed by the Easterners themselves. Besides, they should attain to an ever greater knowledge and a more exact use of them, and, if in their regard they have fallen short owing to contingencies of times and persons, they should take steps to return to their ancestral traditions.

Those who, by reason of their office or apostolic ministries, are in frequent communication with the Eastern Churches or their faithful should be instructed according as their office demands in the knowledge and veneration of the rites, discipline, doctrine, history and character of the Easterners. To enhance the efficacy of their apostolate, congregations and associations of Latin Rite working in Eastern countries or among Eastern faithful are earnestly counseled to found houses or even provinces of Eastern rite, as far as this can be done.

7. The patriarchate, as an institution, has existed in the Church from the earliest times and was recognized by the first ecumenical councils.

By the name Eastern patriarch, is meant the bishop to whom belongs jurisdiction over all bishops, not excepting metropolitans, clergy and people of his own territory or rite, in accordance with canon law and without prejudice to the primacy of the Roman Pontiff.

Wherever an Ordinary of any rite is appointed outside the territorial bounds of the patriarchate, he remains attached to hierarchy of the patriarchate of that rite, in accordance with canon law.

8. Though some of the patriarchates of the Eastern Churches are of earlier and some of later date, nonetheless all are equal in respect of patriarchal dignity, without however prejudice to the legitimately established precedence of honor.

9. By the most ancient tradition of the Church the patriarchs of the Eastern Churches are to be accorded exceptional respect, seeing that each is set over his patriarchate as father and head.

This Sacred Council, therefore, determines that their rights and privileges should be re-established in accordance with the ancient tradition of each of the Churches and the decrees of the ecumenical councils.

The rights and privileges in question are those that obtained in the time of union getween East and West; they should, however, be adapted somewhat to modern conditions.

The patriarchs with their synods are the highest authority for all business of the patriarchate, including the right of establishing new eparchies and of nominating bishops of their rite within the territorial bounds of the patriarchate, without prejudice to the inalienable right of the Roman Pontiff to intervene in individual cases.

10. What has been said of patriarchs is valid also, in harmony with the canon law, in respect to major archbishops, who are over the whole of some individual church or rite.

11. Seeing that the patriarchal office in the Eastern Church is a traditional form of government, the Sacred Ecumenical Council ardently desires that new patriarchates should be erected where there is need to be established either by an ecumenical council or by the Roman Pontiff.

12. The Sacred Ecumenical Council confirms and approves the ancient discipline of the sacraments existing in the Oriental Churches, as also the ritual practices connected with their celebration and administration and ardently desires that this should be re-established if there be need.

13. The established practice in respect of the minister of Confirmation that has obtained from most early times among the Easterners should be fully restored. Therefore, priests validly confer this sacrament, using chrism blessed by a patriarch or a bishop.

14. All Eastern Rite priests, either in conjunction with Baptism or separately from it, can confer this sacrament validly on all the faithful of any rite including the Latin; licitly, however, only if the regulations both of the common and the particular, local law are observed. Priests, also, of Latin Rite, in accordance with the faculties they enjoy in respect of the administration of this sacrament, validly administer it also to the faithful of Eastern Churches; licitly if the regulations both of the common and of the particular law are observed.

15. The faithful are bound to take part on Sundays and feast days in the Divine Liturgy or, according to the regulations or custom of their own rite, in the celebration of the Divine Office. That the faithful may

be able more easily to fulfil their obligation, it is laid down that the period of time within which the precept should be observed extends from the Vespers of the vigil to the end of the Sunday or the feast day. The faithful are earnestly exhorted to receive Holy Communion on these days, and indeed more frequently—yes, even daily.

16. Owing to the fact that the faithful of the different individual churches dwell intermingled with each other in the same area or territory, the faculties for hearing confessions duly and without restriction given to priests of any rite by their own Ordinaries extend to the whole territory of him who grants them and also to the places and faithful of any other rite in the same territory, unless the Ordinary of the place has expressly excluded this for places of his rite

17. In order that the ancient established practice in the Eastern Churches may flourish again, this sacred council ardently desires that the office of the permanent diaconate should, where it has fallen into disuse, be restored. The legislative authorities of each individual church should decide about the subdiaconate and the minor orders and the rights and obligations that attach to them.

18. To obviate invalid marriages when Eastern Catholics marry baptized Eastern non-Catholics and in order to promote fidelity in and the sanctity of marriage, as well as peace within the family, the sacred council determines that the canonical "form" for the celebration of these marriages is of obligation only for liceity; for their validity the presence of a sacred minister is sufficient, provided that what is by law to be observed is observed.

19. It belongs only to an ecumenical council or to the Apostolic See to determine, transfer or suppress feast days common to all the Eastern Churches. On the other hand, to determine, transfer or suppress the feast days of any of the individual churches is within the competence not only of the Apostolic See but also of the patriarchal or archiepiscopal synod, due regard being had to the whole area and the other individual churches.

20. Until such time as all Christians are agreed on a fixed day for the celebration of Easter, with a view meantime to promoting unity among the Christians of the same area or nation, it is left to the patriarchs or supreme authorities of a place to came to an agreement by the unanimous consent and combined counsel of those affected to celebrate the feast of Easter on the same day.

21. Individual faithful dwelling outside the area or territory of their own rite may follow completely the established custom of the

place where they live as regards the law of the sacred seasons. In families of mixed rite it is permissible to observe this law according to one
and the same rite.

22. Eastern clerics and Religious should celebrate in accordance with
the prescriptions and traditions of their own established custom the
Divine Office, which from ancient times has been held in high honor in
all Eastern Churches. The faithful too should follow the example of
their forebears and assist devoutly as occasion allows at the Divine Office.

23. It belongs to the patriarch with his synod, or to the supreme
authority of each church with the council of the Ordinaries, to regulate
the use of languages in the sacred liturgical functions and, after reference to the Apostolic See, of approving translations into the vernacular
of texts.

24. The Eastern Churches in communion with the Apostolic See of
Rome have a special duty of promoting the unity of all Christians,
especially Eastern Christians, in accordance with the principles of the
decree, "About Ecumenism," of this sacred council, by prayer in the
first place, and by the example of their lives, by religious fidelity to the
ancient Eastern traditions, by a greater knowledge of each other, by
collaboration and a brotherly regard for objects and feelings.

25. If any separated Eastern Christian should, under the guidance
of the grace of the Holy Spirit, join himself to the unity of Catholics,
no more should be required of him than what a bare profession of the
Catholic faith demands. Eastern clerics, seeing that a valid priesthood is
preserved among them, should be permitted to exercise the Orders they
possess on joining the unity of the Catholic Church, in accordance with
the regulations established by the competent authority.

26. Such "communicatio in sacris" as harms the unity of the Church
or involves formal acceptance of error or the danger of aberration in the
faith, of scandal and indifferentism, is forbidden by divine law. On the
other hand, pastoral experience shows clearly that, as regards our Eastern brethren, there should be taken into consideration the different
cases of individuals, where neither the unity of the Church is hurt nor
are there verified the dangers that must be avoided, but where the
needs of the salvation of souls and their spiritual good are impelling
motives. For that reason the Catholic Church has always adopted and
now adopts rather a mild policy, offering to all the means of salvation
and an example of charity among Christians, through participation in
the sacraments and in other sacred functions and things. With this in
mind, "lest because of the harshness of our judgment we be an obstacle
to those seeking salvation" and in order more and more to promote

union with the Eastern Churches separated from us, the sacred council lays down the following policy.

27. Without prejudice to the principles noted earlier, Eastern Christians who are in fact separated in good faith from the Catholic Church, if they ask of their own accord and have the right dispositions, may be admitted to the sacraments of Penance, the Eucharist and the Unction of the Sick. Further, Catholics may ask for these same sacraments from those non-Catholic ministers whose churches possess valid sacraments, as often as necessity or a genuine spiritual benefit recommends such a course and access to a Catholic priest is physically or morally impossible.

28. Further, without prejudice to the truth of those same principles, common participation by Catholics with their Eastern separated brethren in sacred functions, things and places is allowed for a good reason.

29. This conciliatory policy with regard to *communicatio in sacris* (participation in things sacred) with the brethren of the separated Eastern Churches is put into the care and control of the local Ordinaries, in order that, by combined counsel among themselves and, if need be, after consultation also with the Ordinaries of the separated churches, they may by timely and effective regulations and directives direct the intercourse of Christians.

30. The sacred Council feels great joy in the fruitful zealous collaboration of the Eastern and the Western Catholic Churches and at the same time declares: All these directives of law are laid down in view of the present situation till such time as the Catholic Church and the separated Eastern Churches come together into complete unity.

Meanwhile, however, all Christians, Eastern as well as Western, are earnestly asked to pray to God fervently and assiduously, nay, indeed daily, that, with the aid of the most holy Mother of God, all may become one. Let them pray also that the strength and the consolation of the Holy Spirit may descend copiously upon all those many Christians of whatsoever church they be who endure suffering and deprivations for their unwavering avowal of the name of Christ.

"Love one another with fraternal charity, anticipating one another with honor" (Rom. 12, 10).

Closing Address of Pope Paul VI

NOVEMBER 21, 1964

✠

After two months of intense brotherly effort, we render thanks to God for the happy celebration of this Second Vatican Ecumenical Council, of which we conclude today the third session with this solemn and sacred assembly. Truly indeed, we must offer God the expression of our grateful and rejoicing souls for having granted us the great fortune of being present and, what is more, the fortune of ourselves giving consistency, meaning and fullness to this historic and providential event as humble and happy protagonists. Truly we may regard as spoken for us today the words of the Gospel: "Blessed are the eyes that see what you see and the ears that hear what you hear" (Matt. 13, 16).

Here is present before us, in the persons of its shepherds followed by their respective flocks, the Holy Church of God, called together by Him through our voice. Here is the Catholic hierarchy on whom it is incumbent to form and guide the holy People of God, gathered together in one place, in one sentiment, with one prayer, one faith, one charity on their lips and in their hearts.

We shall never tire of admiring, nor shall we ever forget this incomparable assembly entirely intent on proclaiming the glory of the Father, the Son and the Holy Spirit, concerned only with re-evoking the blessed words of Revelation and penetrating into their true and deep sense.

This is an assembly of men free like none other from self-interest and engaged in giving witness to divine truths; men as we are, weak and fallible, but convinced of being able to pronounce truths that admit neither contradiction nor termination; men who are sons of our own times and our own earth, yet above time and above earth in order to take upon our shoulders the burdens of our brothers and to lead them to spiritual salvation. This we do with a love greater than these same hearts that house it, with a strained effort that might seem foolhardy, but is full of serene trust in its search for the meaning of human life and history to give it value, greatness, beauty, union in Christ, only in Christ Our Lord!

Brethren, the fact that you are here is stupendous. It is stupendous for those who behold us from the outside. Never shall we behold a scene more impressive, more pious, more dramatic or more solemn.

Our happiness increases as, in this final moment of the Council session we are about to close, we recall the things that have been discussed, the things finally approved. The doctrine on the Church has been described and studied, and thus the doctrinal task of the First Vatican Ecumenical Council has been completed. The mystery of the Church was explored, and the divine plan of its fundamental constitution was outlined.

Once again we thank God for this happy result and we allow our souls to be filled with legitimate bliss. From now on we can enjoy greater understanding of divine thought relative to the Mystical Body of Christ, and from this we can draw clear and safer rules for the life of the Church, greater energy for her incessant effort to lead men to salvation, further hope for the progress of the reign of Christ in the world. Let us bless the Lord.

Too much would need to be said on the work accomplished. Deserving of special mention are the reverent and exacting studies to make this doctrine conform perfectly with Biblical truth and the genuine tradition of the Church; the efforts made to discover the innermost significance and substantial truth of the constitutional law of the Church herself, to determine what is immobile and certain therein and what is a derivation by a process of natural and authoritative evolution from basic principles. The purpose of this has been to provide a fair treatment of every part, every function and every aim of the Mystical Body. It remains true that the most difficult and most memorable part of these spiritual efforts revolved around the doctrine on the episcopate. And on this point alone we should like to dwell briefly.

We shall say only that we are satisfied that this doctrine has been enacted with sufficient breadth of study and discussion and with similar clarity of conclusion. It was a duty to do this, being a completion of the First Vatican Ecumenical Council. It was the time to do it because of the advance of theological studies in modern times; because of the spread of the Church throughout the world; because of the problems encountered by ecclesiastical government in the daily life of the Church, and because of the expectations of many bishops who were anxiously awaiting a clarification of the Church's doctrine pertaining to them. That was also the way to handle the question. Thus we do not hesitate— bearing in mind the explanations furnished both on the interpretation to be given the terms used, as well as the theological qualification which this Council intends to give to the doctrine discussed—we do not hesitate, with the help of God, to promulgate the present Constitution on the Church.

It would seem to us that the best commentary is that through this promulgation nothing in traditional doctrine is really changed. What Christ wants, we also want. That which was, remains. What the Church has taught for centuries, we likewise teach. The only difference is that what was simply lived previously is now declared expressly; what was uncertain has been clarified; what was meditated on, discussed and in part disagreed with now reaches a serene formulation.

Truly we can say that Divine Providence has prepared a shining hour for us; yesterday slowly maturing, today resplendent, tomorrow surely rich in teachings, to stimulate and improve the life of the Church.

We also say we are happy this constitution renders honor also to the People of God. Nothing can give us greater pleasure than to see proclaimed the dignity of all our brothers and sons who make up the holy People of God, to whose vocation, to whose sanctification, to whose salvation and guidance the hierarchical ministry is oriented.

How happy we are also to see the constitution proclaim the dignity of our brothers in the episcopate, honor their role in the Church and recognize their powers. We cannot thank God sufficiently for having granted us the privilege of honoring the sacred character of your ministry and the fullness of your priesthood, beloved and venerated brothers, to acknowledge the loyalty that binds you to each other and to us.

We have observed with edification how the principal, unique and universal mission entrusted to Peter by Christ and transmitted to his successors, the Roman Pontiffs, whose authority we today hold, unworthy as we are, is fully and repeatedly recognized and venerated in this solemn document which we have just promulgated.

We cannot fail to be pleased by this, not for the prestige deriving from it to our person, since we are fearful rather than eager for such a mission, but for the honor rendered to the word of Christ, for the consistency manifested with the teaching and the tradition of the Church, for the guarantee assured for the unity of the Church itself and the harmonious and secure effectiveness assured to her government. It was of highest importance that this recognition of the prerogatives of the office of the sovereign pontiff should be stated explicitly at this time when the question of episcopal authority in the Church was to be dealt with in order that this authority would not be in contrast with the power of the pope but should stand out in full harmony with the vicar of Christ as head of the apostolic college.

And it is this intimate and essential relation that makes a unified assembly of the episcopate, that finds the successor of Peter not different and extraneous, but rather its center and head. This in turn makes us anxious to laud your prerogatives with ours, to rejoice in their exultation, to vindicate their excellence, so as to integrate them with our own. Thus acknowledging the episcopal mission in its fullness, we feel the communion of faith, of charity, of coresponsibility, of collaboration increasing around us.

We do not fear that our authority will be lessened nor hampered while we acknowledge and extol yours; but rather we feel stronger because of the tie that draws us together; we feel more able to guide the universal Church with the knowledge that each of us is working toward the same end; we feel more trustful in the help of Christ because we are and want to be all gathered together more closely in His name.

It is not easy to say what practical consequences these doctrinal clarifications may have, but it is not difficult to foresee that they will be fruitful in spiritual insights and canonical ordinances.

The Ecumenical Council will have its definite conclusion with the fourth session. But the application of its decrees will involve a network of post-conciliar commissions in which the collaboration of the bishops will be indispensable; as likewise the occurrence of questions of general interest to the modern world will make us even more disposed than we now are, venerable brothers, to call some of you, designated, at the proper time, together and consult you at determined times, in order to have around us the comfort of your presence, the help of your experience, the support of your counsel, the assistance of your authority.

This will be useful also because the reorganization of the Roman Curia, which is now undergoing careful study, will be able to profit from the experienced help of diocesan bishops, thus integrating its organization, already so efficient in faithful service, with bishops from various countries bringing the help of their wisdom and charity. This plurality of studies and discussions may entail some practical difficulties. Collective action is more complicated than individual action, but if it better serves the monarchical and hierarchical character of the Church, and comforts our labor with your cooperation, we shall be able to overcome with prudence and charity the obstacles inherent in a more complex organization of ecclesiastical government.

We like to think that the doctrine of the mystery of the Church, illustrated and proclaimed by this Council will, from this moment, find a positive echo in the minds of Catholics. Especially it will let the faithful see the real face of the Bride of Christ more fully delineated and revealed; it will let them see the beauty of their mother and teacher;

the simplicity and the majesty of the lines of such a venerable institution; it will let them admire a prodigy of historical fidelity, of stupendous sociology, of outstanding legislation, a forward-moving realm in which divine and human elements blend in order to reflect on believing humanity the outlines of the Incarnation and the Redemption—the whole Christ our Savior, to use the expression of St. Augustine.

May this spectacle bring intoxicating joy especially to those whose only and constant profession is the search for Christian perfection. We mean the Religious, who are the exemplary members of the Church, its generous supporters, its dearest sons.

And may joy and consolation come also to those our brothers and sons who live in places where sufficient and dignified religious liberty is still denied to them or is so restricted that we have to number them in the ranks of the Church of silence and tears. Let them rejoice in the doctrinal splendor that illuminates Holy Church, to which their suffering and fidelity offers stupendous witness, thereby deserving for themselves the greater glory—that of Christ, victim for the salvation of the world.

We also hope that the same doctrine of the Church will be benevolently and favorably considered by the Christian brothers who are still separate from us. We wish that this doctrine, completed by the declarations contained in the schema on Ecumenism, likewise approved by this Council, might have in their souls the power of a loving leaven for the revision of thoughts and attitudes which may draw them closer to our communion, and finally, God willing, may merge them in it. To us this same doctrine gives the surprising joy of observing how the Church, by precisely tracing its own outlines, does not restrict, but widens the boundaries of its charity and does not check the movement of its multiform progress, inviting catholicity.

May we be allowed at this point to express, on this occasion also, our reverent greeting to the observers who are here representing Christian churches or confessions separate from us, our thanks for their welcome assistance at the conciliar meetings, and our warmest wishes for their Christian prosperity.

And finally we should like for the doctrine of the Church to radiate some attractive light on the profane world in which it lives and by which it is surrounded. It must appear like a sign raised among the peoples (Is. 5, 26) to offer orientation to all on their way toward truth and life. In fact, as anyone can see, while the elaboration of this doctrine observes the theological rigor that justifies and magnifies it, it never forgets mankind which assembles in the Church and which constitutes the historical and social environment in which its mission is exercised.

The Church is for the world. The Church does not desire any other earthly power for itself than that which enables it to serve and to love. By perfecting its thought and its structure, the Church does not aim at estranging itself from the experience which is proper to the men of its time, but it aims rather at understanding them better, at sharing better in their sufferings and their good aspirations, at better sustaining the effort of modern man towards his prosperity, his liberty, his peace. But this recurrent theme will have its development at the end of the Council when the schema on religious liberty, which will crown the work of the Council, and which, only because of lack of time at the end of this session could not be ended, and the one on relations between the Church and the world, which has already been deliberated on at the present session, will be finally and completely treated at the next session.

And now, in conclusion, another thought strikes us. Our thought, venerable brothers, cannot but rise with sentiments of sincere and filial gratitude to the Holy Virgin. Also, to her whom we like to regard as the protectress of the present Council, the witness of our toil, our most kindly adviser, because it is to her, as a heavenly patron, together with St. Joseph, that the work of our ecumenical assembly was entrusted by Pope John XXIII right from the start.

Moved by these same sentiments, last year we offered to the Most Blessed Mary a solemn act of common homage, by gathering in the Liberian basilica (Ed. Note—St. Mary Major), round the image venerated with the glorious title of *Salus Populi Romani* (Salvation of the Roman people).

This year, the homage of our Council appears much more precious and significant. By the promulgation of today's constitution, which has as its crown and summit a whole chapter dedicated to Our Lady, we can rightly affirm that the present session ends as an incomparable hymn of praise in honor of Mary.

It is the first time, in fact—and saying it fills our souls with profound emotion—that an Ecumenical Council presents such a vast synthesis of the Catholic doctrine regarding the place which the Blessed Mary occupies in the mystery of Christ and of the Church.

This corresponds to the aim which this Council set itself of manifesting the countenance of the Holy Church, to which Mary is closely linked, and of which, as it has been authoritatively affirmed, she is *portio maxima, portio optima, portio praecipua, portia electissima* (greatest, finest, principal, most elect part) (Rupert, in Apc. I, VII, c 12, P.L. 169, 10434).

Truly, the realty of the Church is not exhausted in its hierarchical structure, in its liturgy, in its sacraments, in its juridical ordinances. The intimate, the primary source of its sanctifying effectiveness is to be sought in its mystic union with Christ; a union which we cannot conceive as separate from her who is the Mother of the Word Incarnate and whom Jesus Christ Himself wanted closely united to Himself for our salvation. Thus the loving contemplation of the marvels worked by God in His Holy Mother must find its proper perspective in the vision of the Church. And knowledge of the true Catholic doctrine on Mary will always be a key to the exact understanding of the mystery of Christ and of the Church.

Meditation on these close relationships between Mary and the Church, so clearly established in today's conciliar constitution, makes us feel that this is the most solemn and appropriate moment to fulfill a wish which, after we mentioned it at the end of the preceding session, very many Council Fathers made their own, pressing for an explicit declaration at this Council of the motherly role of the Virgin among the Christian people. To achieve this aim, we have felt it opportune to consecrate in this very public session, a title which was suggested in honor of the Virgin from various parts of the Catholic world and which is particularly dear to us because it sums up in an admirable synthesis the privileged position recognized by the Council for the Virgin in the Holy Church.

Therefore, for the glory of the Virgin Mary and for our own consolation, we proclaim the Most Blessed Mary Mother of the Church, that is to say of all the people of God, of the faithful as well as of the pastors, who call her the most loving Mother. And we wish that the Mother of God should be still more honored and invoked by the entire Christian people by this most sweet title.

This is a title, venerable brothers, not new to Christian piety; it is precisely this title, in preference to all others, that the faithful and the Church address Mary. It truly is part of the genuine substance of devotion to Mary, finding its justification in the very dignity of the Mother of the Word Incarnate.

Just as, in fact, the divine maternity is the basis for her special relationship with Christ, and for her presence in the economy of salvation brought about by Jesus Christ, thus it also constitutes the principal basis for the relations between Mary and the Church, since she is the mother of Him, Who, right from the time of His Incarnation in her virginal bosom, joined to Himself as head His Mystical Body which is the Church. Mary, then as mother of Christ, is mother also of all the faithful and of all the pastors.

It is therefore with a soul full of trust and filial love that we raise our glance to her, despite our unworthiness and weakness. She, who has given us in Jesus the fountainhead of grace, will not fail to succor the Church, now flourishing through the abundance of the gifts of the Holy Ghost and setting herself with new zeal to the fulfillment of its mission of salvation.

And our trust is even more lively and fully corroborated if we consider the very close links between this heavenly mother of ours and mankind. Although adorned by God with the riches of admirable prerogatives to make her a worthy mother of the Word Incarnate, she is nevertheless very close to us. Daughter of Adam, like ourselves, and therefore our sister through ties of nature, she is, however, the creature who was preserved from original sin in view of the merits of the Savior, and who possesses besides the privileges obtained the personal virtue of a total and exemplary faith, thus deserving the evangelical praise *beata quae credidisti* (blessed art thou who believed). In her earthly life, she realized the perfect image of the disciple of Christ, reflected every virtue, and incarnated the evangelical beatitudes proclaimed by Christ. Therefore, in her the entire Church, in its incomparable variety of life and of work, attains the most authentic form of the perfect imitation of Christ.

We trust then, that with the promulgation of the Constitution on the Church, sealed by the proclamation of Mary as Mother of the Church, that is to say of all the faithful and all the pastors, the Christian people may, with greater ardor, turn to the Holy Virgin and render to her the honor and devotion due to her.

As for ourselves, just as at the invitation of Pope John XXIII we entered the Council hall, along with "Mary, the Mother of Jesus," so at the close of the third session we leave this temple with the most holy and sweet name of Mary, Mother of the Church.

As a sign of gratitude for her loving assistance, lavished on us during this last conciliar period, let each of you, venerable brothers, pledge himself to hold high among the Christian people the name and the honor of Mary, indicating in her the model of faith and of the full response to any call from God, the model of the full assimilation of the teaching of Christ and of His charity, so that all the faithful, united in the name of the common mother, may feel themselves ever more firmly rooted in the Faith and in union with Jesus Christ, and at the same time fervent in charity towards the brothers, promoting love for the poor, dedication to justice and defense of peace. As the great St. Ambrose exhorted: *sit in singulis Mariae anima ut magnificet Dominum; sit in singulis spiritus Mariae et exultet in Deo* (Let the soul of Mary be in each one, that it may magnify the Lord; let the spirit of Mary be in each one, that it may rejoice in the Lord). (St. Ambrose, *Exp. in Luc.* II, 26, 15, 1642.)

Above all, we desire that it should be made clear that Mary, the humble handmaid of the Lord, exists only in relation to God and to Christ, our sole Mediator and Redeemer. And likewise, may the true nature and the aims of the Marian veneration in the Church be illustrated, particularly where there are many separated brothers, so that those who are not part of the Catholic community may understand that devotion to Mary, far from being an end in itself, is instead a means essentially ordained to orient souls to Christ and thus unite them with the Father in the love of the Holy Ghost.

While we turn in ardent prayer to the Virgin, that she may bless the Ecumenical Council and the entire Church, hastening the hour of union of all Christians, our glance opens on the endless horizons of the whole world, the object of the most lively care of the Ecumenical Council, and which our venerated predecessor, Pius XII of venerated memory, not without inspiration from on high, solemnly consecrated to the Immaculate Heart of Mary. Today, we consider it particularly opportune to recall this act of consecration.

Bearing this in mind, we have decided to send a special mission to

Fatima in the near future in order to carry the Golden Rose to the sanctuary of Fatima, more dear than ever not only to the people of the noble Portuguese nation—always, but particularly today, dear to us—but also known and venerated by the faithful throughout the entire Catholic world. In this manner we intend to entrust to the care of this heavenly mother the entire human family, with its problems and anxieties, with its legitimate aspirations and ardent hopes.

O, Virgin Mary, Mother of the Church, to you we recommend the entire Church and our Ecumenical Council.

You, *auxilium Episcoporum,* aid of bishops, protect and assist the bishops in their apostolic mission, and all those priests, Religious and laymen who help them in their arduous work.

You who were presented by your Son Himself, at the moment of His redeeming death, as mother to His best-loved disciple, remember the Christian people who entrust themselves to you.

Remember all your sons; support their prayers to God, preserve their faith, strengthen their hope, increase their charity.

Remember those who are in tribulation, in need, in danger and particularly those who suffer persecution and who are in prison because of their faith. For these, O Virgin, obtain fortitude and hasten the desired day of just freedom.

Look with benign eyes on our separate brothers and condescend to unite us, you who brought forth Christ as a bridge of unity between God and men.

O, temple of light without shadow and without blemish, intercede with your only Son, mediator of our reconciliation with the Father (cf. Rom. 5, 11) that He may have mercy on our shortcomings and may dispel any difference between us, giving us the joy of loving.

To your Immaculate Heart, O Mary, we finally recommend the entire human race. Lead it to the knowledge of the sole and true Savior, Jesus Christ; protect it from the scourges provoked by sin, give to the entire world peace in truth, in justice, in liberty and in love.

And let the entire Church, by celebrating this great ecumenical assembly, raise to the God of mercy the majestic hymn of praise and thanksgiving, the hymn of joy and of exultation, because the Lord has worked great things through you, O clement, O loving, O sweet Virgin Mary.

Index

✠